DATE OF RETURN

UNLESS RECALLED BY

KU-288-988

Securing Japan

Other books by Richard J. Samuels

Machiavelli's Children:
Leaders and Their Legacies in Italy and Japan

"Rich Nation, Strong Army":
National Security and the Technological Transformation of Japan

The Business of the Japanese State:
Energy Markets in Comparative and Historical Perspective

The Politics of Regional Policy in Japan

Securing Japan

Tokyo's Grand Strategy
and the Future of East Asia

Richard J. Samuels

Cornell University Press

Ithaca and London

A volume in the series
CORNELL STUDIES IN SECURITY AFFAIRS
edited by Robert J. Art, Robert Jervis, and Stephen M. Walt

Copyright © 2007 by Cornell University

All rights reserved. Except for brief quotations in a review, this book, or parts thereof, must not be reproduced in any form without permission in writing from the publisher. For information, address Cornell University Press, Sage House, 512 East State Street, Ithaca, New York 14850.

First published 2007 by Cornell University Press
Printed in the United States of America

Library of Congress Cataloging-in-Publication Data

Samuels, Richard J.
  Securing Japan : Tokyo's grand strategy and the future of East Asia / Richard J. Samuels.
    p. cm. — (Cornell studies in security affairs)
  Includes bibliographical references and index.
  ISBN 978-0-8014-4612-2 (cloth : alk. paper)
  1. National security—Japan. 2. Japan—Military policy. 3. Japan—Foreign relations—1945– 4. East Asia—Foreign relations. I. Title. II. Series.

  UA845.S328 2007
  355'.033052—dc22   2007010999

Cornell University Press strives to use environmentally responsible suppliers and materials to the fullest extent possible in the publishing of its books. Such materials include vegetable-based, low-VOC inks and acid-free papers that are recycled, totally chlorine-free, or partly composed of nonwood fibers. For further information, visit our website at www.cornellpress.cornell.edu.

Cloth printing   10 9 8 7 6 5 4 3 2 1

UNIVERSITY
OF SHEFFIELD
LIBRARY

for Roger, with thanks

Contents

Acknowledgments

Each year, a number of midcareer Japanese government officials and businesspersons sent by their ministries and firms to improve their English and make connections come to study here at MIT. Some are unsure how to intervene in seminar discussions and remain quiet, but most enhance these discussions considerably with their contributions. One foreign ministry official particularly stands out in my memory. About a decade ago, in the mid-1990s, she interrupted my opening day introductory lecture to a class on Japanese security policy and insisted that I stop referring to a "Japanese military." Japan, after all, had only a "Self-Defense Force." This was not the first time I had been confronted by such self-deception, but it was the first time it had been offered up in my own classroom. What a wonderful teaching opportunity! I set aside my lecture notes and focused the diplomat's attention on what Japan's $45 billion defense budget actually was buying. Then I focused the attention of the non-Japanese in the class on how frightfully defensive Japanese officials could be about such matters. What seemed to some as Japanese quibbling over trifles was actually the warp and woof of Japan's security debate. Thanks to the diplomat's intervention, we all learned something important about Japanese security. Just as important, though, was a parallel intervention four years later in the opening session of the same course, when another Japanese student, a retired Maritime Self-Defense Force flag officer, proudly introduced himself to the class as an "admiral of the Japanese navy." Again, I had to set aside the lecture notes, but this time the unplanned lesson focused on how much had changed in four years!

And indeed, while much had changed, the willingness of Japanese government officials, journalists, politicians, and intellectuals to chat has not. I am grateful to each of more than three dozen government officials affiliated with the Japanese Ministry of Defense—at its headquarters in Ichigaya, at the National Defense Academy, and at the National Institute for Defense Studies—and to the many uniformed officers who took the time to answer my questions. While I have complied with their wishes not to identify them by name, I do regret that I cannot thank them publicly. I can, however, thank several academic colleagues who were reliable guides and arbiters of information: Soeya Yoshihide, Sadō Akihiro, Nishikawa Shinichi, Tanaka Akihiko, Kawakatsu Chikako, Watanabe Tsuneo, Michishita Narushige, and Tadokoro Masayuki were especially generous with their time and insights. Likewise several journalists, among whom Katō Yōichi and Honda Masaru of the *Asahi Shimbun*, Ina Hisayoshi of the *Nihon Keizai Shimbun*, Takahata Akio of the *Mainichi Shimbun*, and Hayashi Michio of the *Yomiuri Shimbun* were particularly helpful. So were the librarians at the library of the National Institute for Defense Studies and Shimizu Isao, Japan's leading cartoon archivist. I also thank more than one dozen LDP and DPJ Diet politicians (including four cabinet ministers) who granted me interviews and consented to be identified.

Back at MIT, Laurie Scheffler was an unerring assistant of incalculable (and indefatigable) energy and wisdom. There is no way to adequately thank her for looking after this project (and me)—first from long distance, later right next door. It could not have been easy, and her considerable pluck and resourcefulness does not go unappreciated. Llewelyn Hughes, Pat Boyd, and Reo Matsuzaki were energetic research assistants for whom no request was too large or small. Their knowledge of Japanese politics and public policy is extraordinary, and they were my colleagues from the day they arrived on campus. Thanks, too, to Yumi Shimabukuro and Nathan Cisneros, who arrived at MIT a couple of years later—just in time to help police the manuscript.

In this business, as I tell my graduate students, it is always helpful to have really smart friends. I am especially grateful to two friends of long-standing, Mike Mochizuki of George Washington University and Eric Heginbotham of the RAND Corporation, for their willingness to wrestle with (often undigested) draft chapters. Their thoughtful and unyielding critiques meant a lot to me as I worked on the manuscript. Ken Pyle, T. J. Pempel, and Bob Art helped enormously in the final stages.

Thanks, too, to Allan Song, who first suggested this project, and to the Smith Richardson Foundation, which funded my year in Japan. My host institution, the Keizai Kōhō Center of Keidanren, could not have been more hospitable. I am grateful to its director, Hayashi Tadashi, and to all of his staff for providing such a comfortable and supportive setting. Thanks are also due to Nakamura Yoshio and Aburaki Kiyoaki of Keidanren for helping make such congenial arrangements. The Istituto Pedro Arrupe in Palermo was a particularly hospitable place to isolate myself while producing

a rough first draft. After remarking on this extraordinary gift of time and soli-
tude to one of my Jesuit hosts, I was lectured on the benefits of monasticism.
I could not disagree. But Palermo itself was hardly monastic. After spending all day in unprecedented silence, my wife Debbie and I could meet in
the *piazze* to enjoy their many charms—food, chaos, new friends. I took a
lot of good-natured ribbing from Japanese and American friends who had
trouble imagining that I could possibly get any work done in Sicily, where
the food, wine, and people are so famously congenial. But I cannot recall
ever working with more focus—or enjoying it more. I can only hope the
book has benefited from this combination of hard work and wide-eyed dis-
covery. Debbie and I are still working off the collateral damage.

Finally, I dedicate this book to its extraordinary editor, Roger Haydon.
Like each of his authors, I stand in awe of his good judgment and great talent. Roger is surely used to being thanked in prefaces, but he needs to know
that he has always deserved much more.

Japanese names are presented in the conventional style—family names
first. Parts of this book have appeared in the *Journal of Japanese Studies* and
the *Washington Quarterly*.

Securing Japan

Introduction

Understanding Japan's Grand Strategy

Many Japanese analysts do not believe Japan now has a coherent grand strategy, and more than a few insist that it never had one. One of Japan's most distinguished diplomats declares that Japanese foreign policy has long been marked by "a conspicuous absence of strategic thinking."[1] A former ambassador maintains that apart from an "exceptional decade" between 1895 and 1905, Japanese strategy has been "naïve" and, in the postwar period, "sterile."[2] These eminent practitioners are hardly alone. A distinguished historian dedicates an entire chapter of his influential book to the irrationality of the prewar military.[3] Another scholar argues that one of the great misfortunes of Japanese history has been the extent to which idealism has dominated realism.[4] Compare that view to Gen. Tōjō Hideki's famous argument for war, which he made to Prince Konoye Fumimaro in 1941: "Sometimes a man has to jump, with his eyes closed, from the veranda of Kiyomizu Temple."[5]

Much Japanese assessment of postwar strategy is not much more positive. In 1981, an outspoken general, Takeda Gorō, was forced to resign from the Ground Self-Defense Force (GSDF) after complaining publicly that Japan's security policy was based on uninformed political debate and lobbying rather than careful strategic analysis.[6] Most observers agree that Japan has been unable to play a great power game because the ratio of noise to knowledge is too high; and Japan is left "groping" (*mosaku*) for strategy.[7] For some, postwar Japanese strategy is incoherent for the same reason prewar strategy was—Japan is chasing too many hares at once. A foreign policy that is simultaneously UN-centered, Asia-oriented, autonomous, and consistent with the goals of the bilateral alliance with the United States ends up as porridge.[8]

[1]

But the most common explanation for Japan's strategic deficit is its partnership with the United States. U.S. security guarantees, critics say, have left Japan with only a limited sense of external threat. Japan had little reason during the cold war to build a military or to develop its own strategies to deter aggression or to affect the outcome of conflict, so the nation could avoid strategic thinking and remain in its "cocoon."[9] Sakuma Makoto, former chair of Japan's Joint Staff Council, believes that Japan can no longer afford to live in a "closed space" (*heisa kukan*).[10] Even one of the prime minister's own commissions makes this claim: "Reliance on the United States to uphold Japan's security and the international order became an ingrained habit during the Cold War, diminishing both Japan's sense of responsibility regarding its international role and its ability to make decisions for itself."[11] Rather than grand strategy, then, Japan had mere "*karaoke* diplomacy"— background music and lyrics are determined by the United States, and all that Japanese diplomats have to decide is what to wear and how to sing the songs.[12] As late as 2006, one of Japan's leading dailies declared Japan had a "strategy allergy" (*senryaku arerugii*) and launched a yearlong series "in search" of one for Japan (*shin senryaku o motomete*).[13]

This is a lazy way to explain grand strategy—Japanese strategists deserve more credit. Not surprisingly, they get that credit from Korean and Chinese analysts, who see a Japanese diplomacy that is once again being configured for regional domination. Japan's neighbors are convinced that Japanese militarism, supported by an invigorated nationalist right wing, lurks just beneath the surface.[14] Most North American and European analysts do not go so far. Although no one ignores the extent to which Japanese strategy has been reactive, most grudgingly credit Japanese strategists with dexterity, if not vision.[15] The consensus is that postwar Japanese planners made a strategic choice to consistently punch below their weight in international politics. The United States would provide deterrence, and Japan did not need, nor would it seek, to act like a great power. It was eminently rational for Japan to acquire just enough "basic defense capabilities" to repel aggressors—but no more than that.[16] In 1975, the Japanese government adopted the Basic Defense Force Concept (Kiban Bōeiryoku Kōsō), what one analyst has called "postwar Japan's only comprehensive and sophisticated national security strategy."[17] It had five key assumptions, each realist: the global security environment would remain stable; the Self-Defense Forces (SDF) could perform essential defense functions; Japan had adequate intelligence and surveillance capabilities to cope with limited aggression; the SDF could be rapidly reinforced if the need arose; and the worst thing Japan could do would be to establish an independent military capability that would upset the regional balance of power. On this account, Japanese strategists were quite sophisticated. They considered the Soviet Union's intent as well as its capability, and concluded that since no threat was imminent Japan need not reach beyond its grasp.[18] Indeed, one of the early analysts concluded that "Japanese leaders had a well thought out defense policy, based on their own strategic views, several years before the United States government formulated its Far Eastern security policy."[19] A more contemporary analysis concludes that it is not the passivity of karaoke but the defensive nature of the martial art aikido that best characterizes Japanese security policy.[20]

During the 1980s and 1990s, other analysts—I was one of them—were impressed by Japan's "comprehensive security" strategy, which creatively combined economic and technological capabilities with a low-cost military posture.[21] Japan subordinated military to economic security, deliberately practicing mercantile realism to generate prosperity and provide security at the same time.[22] As long as the United States was a credible partner, Japan was smart—indeed, strategic—in building a military that could deter but not punish. It was also acting strategically in amassing wealth to accumulate prestige and buy friends.[23]

We should not be surprised. Pragmatic strategic thinking is not unique to postwar Japan. Even if Japan's first modernizers were dealt a weak hand, and even if they were not able to steer Japan directly toward peace and prosperity, they understood power politics from the very beginning. What could be more realist than the observation of one of Japan's leading intellectuals, Fukuzawa Yukichi, in the early 1880s: "The English export opium, a poisonous drug, to China. The Chinese lose money, injure their health, and year by year their national strength is sapped.... This depends solely on the fact that one country is stronger and one weaker."[24]

His junior contemporary, Yamagata Aritomo, would become Japan's preeminent military strategist for the first half century of Japan's industrialization. Observing in 1890 that "the heritages and resources of the East are like so many pieces of meat about to be devoured by tigers," Yamagata drew a "line of sovereignty" around the archipelago and a "line of interest" around the region. Japan now had its first modern strategic plan—one that served it well, even though it left considerable room for doctrinal differences. Yamagata's plan guided Japan toward a maritime alliance with Great Britain and into cooperative arrangements with most of the other great powers.[25]

There is no mystery to the ends-means rationality of this or any grand strategy. In practice, a coherent grand strategy requires that national objectives not be mutually exclusive, and that the means to achieve them—soft power, diplomacy, military force—be consistent with national capabilities. If they are met, these requirements ensure viability on the international stage, a necessary but not sufficient ingredient for success. A viable grand strategy also demands effective management of domestic politics. If power is not consolidated at home, it cannot be used effectively abroad. So, like much else in the bare-knuckled, chaotic world of international politics, grand strategy is easier to discuss than to construct. Every country talks about it—and each country has made horrible mistakes trying to execute it. To be sure, grand strategies serve as mirrors of national identity and communal longing; they are best built on a platform of ideas about a nation's place in history and its people's aspirations for the future. Inspiration, as I have suggested in a different context, is cheaper and more efficient than bullying or buying.[26] Still, grand strategies cannot be merely rhetorical devices. They must mobilize political, economic, and military resources to ensure a nation's vital interests as well.[27]

In Japan, as elsewhere, the combination of political, economic, and military means shifts with world affairs *and* with domestic politics. Peter Katzenstein probably overstates the importance of the latter by insisting that "Japan's security policy will continue to be shaped by the domestic *rather than* the international balance of power."[28] And Kenneth Pyle probably exaggerates the ease with which domestic politics fell in line behind shifts toward new world orders: "Repeatedly, through the course of 150 years of its modern history, each time the structure of the international system underwent fundamental change, Japan adopted its foreign policies to that changed order and restructured its internal organization to take advantage of it."[29]

Neither Pyle nor Katzenstein is entirely wrong, and both acknowledge that domestic and international politics play off each other in Japanese history. Both appreciate how domestic political processes can mediate international pressures on policymakers—and vice versa. But as there is no telling a priori which would drive the construction of Japanese grand strategy, there is no compelling reason to privilege one or the other.

This has never been more evident than it is today. With the end of the cold war, the Soviet Union disappeared and with it the most serious threat to Japanese security. Indeed, by any conventional measure of military capabilities, the USSR was a far graver threat to Japan than China is today: its Far Eastern fleet and its air and ground units in the region were better equipped and better trained than China's People's Liberation Army (PLA). Yet the Japanese government did not begin its sustained program of military modernization—a subject of this book—until after the USSR was gone. Something else was at work.

A large part of that "something else" was the emergence of four "new" threats: (1) a rising China, (2) a miscreant regime in North Korea, (3) the possibility of abandonment by the United States, and (4) the relative decline of the Japanese economy. Japan responded to each—and to lesser ones, such as the weakening nonproliferation regime—with strategic agility. It responded to China first by embracing it economically and then by pushing back against a newly envisioned "China threat." Its response to Pyongyang has been to alternate between warm and cold diplomatic initiatives.

[4]

It has responded to the possibility of abandonment by the United States by "hugging it close"—thereby enhancing the danger of entanglement.[30] And it has responded to the specter of economic decline by readjusting familiar technonational ideas to the complex dynamics of a globalizing world economy. *Each* of these threats has been used to justify the modernization of Japan's military. Japanese strategists have determined that China and North Korea need to be confronted, the United States needs to be reassured, and Japan's industrial vitality—not least of all its defense industrial base—needs to be reinvigorated.

A second factor in Japan's force modernization lies in the security dilemma that grips Northeast Asia today.[31] Japan, China, and North Korea have legitimate security concerns. Pyongyang's is existential—the regime fears for its survival in a world in which the lone remaining superpower, with "globo-cop" pretensions, has identified it as a cancer. China borders on more states than any other and perceives (no doubt correctly) that the United States and Japan want to contain its rise. Japan is concerned about losing its protector (and enabler), the United States, as the latter becomes distracted by its "war on terror." The response to these concerns has been predictably excessive—each state is overinsuring against perceived risk. North Korea acquires nuclear weapons, China compensates for a decade of relative military decline by funding a rapid force modernization, and, to U.S. cheers, Japan overinsures by acquiring missile defense and eyes force-projection capabilities. Japan's military posture has not been this robust since before the Pacific War. And as each country acts to increase its own security, of course it makes the others less secure.

This textbook security dilemma suggests a third, critically important, part of this "something else." Each regional power has made tough choices *within constraints*. Each threat, each response, each political calculation has been filtered through domestic institutions and (presumably) through domestic debates. The ones in Tokyo have been the most transparent. A new security discourse—one with identifiable historical predicates—has taken shape in the context of a new national leadership. Those who believe Japan should be more "normal" are only one of four groups participating in the contemporary security discourse in Japan. These "normal nation-alists" believe that national strength is the key to national prestige, their core security value. Others argue that strength should serve the goal of greater autonomy from the United States. Contrary to both these groups are two groups that insist that prosperity ought to be the nation's core security value. These ideas—held both by liberals and by leftists—were marginalized as "normal nation-alists"—revisionists led by Koizumi Junichirō and Abe Shinzō—consolidated their power during the early 2000s. They combined the new external threats—fabricating none, but amplifying all—with the old ambitions of their forebears, the "antimainstream" conservatives.

[5]

Once in power, these revisionists seized the opportunity to reform the domestic institutions of national security and to marginalize their political opponents. There is precedent here; there is context; and there is strategy. All are subjects of this book.

World politics may be awash in misperceptions and in mistakes, but rarely is it the simple product of shifts either in external balances of power or in domestic debate. The argument about whether Japan has—much less whether it *can* have—a grand strategy therefore has a *Rashomon*-like feel to it. Nothing was, or is, automatic; nothing was, or is, derived directly from the structure of world order or from domestic political debate. As I shall explore in some detail, Japan has evolved a "strategic culture" and a national identity in which vulnerability (*fuan*) has long been a central feature. But the history of Japanese security policy is not one of extended irrationality; it is one of lengthy periods of active, often highly divisive, debate punctuated by broad consensuses sealed by regimes that have consolidated power at home.

On three separate occasions, secure at home, Japan's leaders have constructed a deeply coherent and widely embraced national security strategy. I suspect they are in the process of doing so again today. Each national strategy has had to deal with similar choices: Should Japan be closer to Asia or to the West? Would Japan be safer if it were big or if it were small? Is wealth a prerequisite for strength, or is it the result of strength? And each consensus has come out differently. The first was the nineteenth-century consensus on constructing a "rich nation and strong army." The second was the early twentieth century consensus on imperial Japanese hegemony in Asia. The third was the cold war consensus on Japan as a cheap-riding trading state. In between these historic moments of consensus—as today—there were extended battles over two values at the heart of Japan's (indeed, of any nation's) national objectives: autonomy and prestige.

Japan consistently has been pragmatic on the world stage despite being mired in persistent ideological debates at home. However emotional, these debates never strayed too far from a pragmatic respect for power and an ability to adapt to shifts in the strategic geography.[32] Japanese strategists certainly made mistakes, sometimes catastrophic ones. But they kept their eyes on the twin prizes of autonomy and prestige, and the values of strength and of wealth embedded therein, finely calculating how each would feed national power. Having learned realpolitik at the feet of Bismarck himself, Japan's leaders understood that theirs is a self-help world in which states could count on only limited assistance from others.[33] In this sense, Japan's postwar dependence on U.S. security guarantees—and the "pacifist norms" that appeared to drive policy choice—were anomalies. But every practitioner, from Prime Minister Yoshida Shigeru, who first embraced that dependence and crafted what became the doctrine of "defensive defense,"

[6]

to former prime minister Nakasone Yasuhiro, an early postwar advocate of "autonomous defense," appreciated the need for change. Yoshida expected the cheap ride to end decades ago and declared in his 1963 memoirs that "Japan, an independent nation that has reached the highest level in its economy, technology, and education, will always be in a state of weakness if it continues to depend upon another nation for its self-defense."[34] After becoming director general of the Defense Agency in 1970, Nakasone tilted in the opposite direction, declaring the alliance with the United States a "semipermanent necessity" (*haneikyūteki ni hitsuyō*), noting hopefully that "the substance [of autonomous defense] would change depending on the times."[35]

There is nothing new in these shifts and ambiguities. There has been no more pragmatic or more rational state than Japan: few have been more agile, and none has been more "normal." Japan successfully managed its dependence on the United States throughout the cold war, and continues to do so with considerable skill today. Japan has long been doing what all states do to reduce risk and maximize gain in an uncertain world—it has hedged. Japanese strategists know as well as any others that international politics takes place among rocks and hard places—in an anarchic world filled with risks and constraints that demand strategic thinking and make hedging the mother's milk of all "normal nations." Prince Klemens von Metternich, the nineteenth-century Austrian grand strategist, is a historical archetype of strategic hedging with particular relevance for postwar Japan: after Austria's disastrous defeat in 1809, Metternich allied with the dominant French but never broke relations with the British or Russians. Metternich "hedged [his] risks by the careful involvement of the largest possible number of allies...and would repair by cunning, patience, and manipulation what had been lost by total commitment."[36]

Normal nations, like normal firms, overinsure their security because alliances, like contracts, can easily be broken.[37] Many realist theories of international relations—on deterrence, on arms racing, on alliances—start from assumptions about the nature of anarchy and the consequent fact that no state can be certain of its safety. But the fact of anarchy can generate two opposite kinds of responses to risk: states may hedge and exercise caution, or preempt and exercise daring. Even hedging can be more or less assertive. States facing an unpleasant choice between abandonment and entrapment can try to dodge that choice by avoiding aggressive behavior or by hedging judiciously. Hedging can also be more enthusiastic, as when states enhance their military, diplomatic, and economic options simultaneously.[38] Liberals agree with realists that anarchy in the international system induces uncertainty about the intentions of other states but contend that international institutions can mitigate the risks stemming from all this uncertainty.[39] We know, then, that anarchy induces states to worry about an unpredictable

[7]

future, that states respond differently to the same risk, and that institutions can ameliorate risk taking. But as yet we have no general theory of this important and ubiquitous aspect of grand strategy. Our received theoretical guidance about the conditions under which states will hedge—with what instruments and with how much recklessness—remains nearly as contradictory as the history of international relations. Timothy Crawford helps us sort through this with the reminder that "most states have a mixed bag of preferences. They play defense and offense at the same time, seeking to preserve the status quo in some situations and upend it in others."[40]

Indeed, this is why Japan's simultaneous wielding of its mercantile sword and military shield has been quite "normal." Since the seventeenth century, Japan has systematically aligned itself with what it perceived to be the world's dominant power: the Netherlands, Great Britain, Germany, and the United States.[41] But, as we shall see, Tokyo's historical penchant for bandwagoning has never been unqualified. Japan has also relied consistently on hedging in its conduct, and it has been a hedging that has differentiated consistently between economic and military risks. Even within the postwar security regime, Japan's elevation of economic security has led it to engage with some states in ways that diverge from (and possibly undermine) U.S. interests. Japanese strategists have been deeply committed to managing economic risks that are given less prominence by other states (and by some theorists), often because they are comfortable in policy areas that their counterparts consider inappropriate for state intervention—such as technology and industrial policy. It hedges against U.S. and European protectionism by promoting regional economic integration in Asia.

But Japan is not yet ready to let go of the United States, and, indeed, it may never wish to do so. Certainly it is not in U.S. interests to force Japan's hand. But while Japan seems to be allowing itself to become more reliant than ever on the United States for military security, this dependence is balanced by new economic opportunities and greater military capability. Viewed this way, hedging—in the form of a declaration that Japan will play a "global" security role—is not only a way for Japan to reduce risk but is also a way to create options. When the debates currently under way are resolved, I suspect that Japan will not only have provided itself with more security options but it will have done so on its own terms. It will have ceased pretending to ignore the realist dictum of "self-help" and will have used the alliance to enhance its own autonomy.[42] Indeed, Tokyo has already rejected its earlier, tentative justifications of making "international contributions" (*kokusai kōken*) in favor of acting boldly in the "national interest."[43]

This book is designed to provide a historical understanding of the fundamental rationality of Japanese security policy and the constraints within which it has been exercised. It is also designed to explore the options Japanese strategists are creating for themselves today. Japanese strategists have diligently and deliberately sliced away much of the "pacifist loaf" that Yoshida Shigeru baked in the postwar period. Amid considerable public debate about contours and objectives, a fourth consensus is now brewing, one that, if successful, should enable Japan to exist securely without being either too dependent on the United States or too vulnerable to China. If it succeeds, this "Goldilocks consensus" (a grand strategy that is not too hard but not too soft, not too Asian and not too Western) will strike a balance between national strength and national autonomy to create new security options for Japan.

PART I

HISTORICAL CONTEXT

[1]

Japan's Grand Strategies
Connecting the Ideological Dots

Foreign affairs are always and everywhere domestic affairs as well. Japan has been no exception. By enforcing isolation for 250 years, the Tokugawa rulers were required to regulate, and often repress, scientists, Christians, and merchants at home. When regulation failed and the world forced itself upon the shogunate, fundamental differences about how to respond to the Western powers—whether to try to achieve national autonomy or acquiesce to foreign domination—stimulated the 1868 coup d'état that ended the regime. Likewise, five years later, when pragmatic oligarchs blocked Saigō Takamori's impetuous plans to invade Korea, the result was civil war and consolidation of the Meiji state. Later Meiji leaders repeatedly used foreign adventure to legitimate their rule, proving Japan could be as "normal" as any other state. And it was. Catch-up industrialization combined with catch-up imperialism, and Japan achieved something close to parity with Western powers.

At first Japan took small bites, later big gulps. But its pervasive sense of vulnerability in world affairs was always reflected in domestic politics, not least after Japan's devastating defeat in the Pacific War. For a half century, contested views of the cold war, expectations for the alliance with the United States, and beliefs about the legitimacy of the Japanese military formed the central divide in Japanese politics. Securing Japan has always been the central axis of Japanese political life, and it remains so today.

In this chapter I examine the ebb and flow of debates over Japan's international posture and their importance for domestic politics. I demonstrate how international constraints and domestic politics have interacted repeatedly—across a range of domestic and world orders—to filter and frame security policy choices. Alternating periods of dispute and consensus have engaged the entire national intellect, mobilizing at different times and

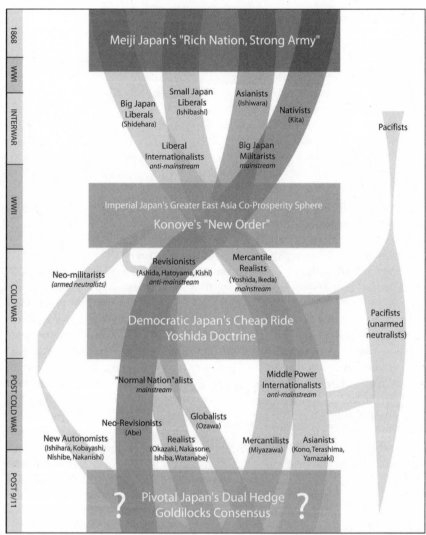

Figure 1. Connecting the ideological dots.

in different measures liberals, nativists, Asianists, internationalists, militarists, nationalists, mercantilists, globalists, realists, and revisionists. These players have had shifting connections, many extending across the formation of the several new world orders to which Japan has had to adjust.[1]

Here we seek to connect these "ideological dots"—or at least to sketch them in historical context—to understand both the enduring values that have informed the choices of Japanese leaders and to map contemporary Japanese grand strategy in its fullest context.

The pattern is straightforward. Vigorous—indeed, sometimes debilitating—debate over Japanese security has been punctuated by three moments of consensus since 1868. And a fourth is now under construction. A widespread belief in "catching up and surpassing" the West helped elites forge the Meiji era consensus: borrow foreign institutions, learn Western rules, master Western practice. This "rich nation, strong army" model was a great success, but by the end of World War I, when it was clear that the West viewed Japanese ambitions with suspicion, the consensus had become tattered. After a period of domestic violence and intimidation, a new consensus was forged on a less conciliatory response to world affairs. Prince Konoye's Greater East Asia Co-Prosperity Sphere attracted support from across Japan's ideological spectrum. Now Japan would be a great power, the leader of Asia. The disaster that resulted is well known, and from its ashes—again, after considerable debate and creative reinvention—Prime Minister Yoshida Shigeru forged a pragmatic path to cheap security. But it was not free. It cost Japan its autonomy, a cost increasingly seen as more than Japan should pay. In recent years, the Yoshida Doctrine that joined Japan at the U.S. hip has been questioned—both by those who support the alliance and by those who oppose it. A fourth consensus has yet to reveal itself, though its contending political and intellectual constituents are clearly identifiable.

THE MEIJI CONSENSUS: "RICH NATION, STRONG ARMY"

Japan, like most rising powers, had a trying debut on the world stage.[2] Its geostrategic environment was constantly in flux. Japanese strategists chafed at how the nation was constrained by unequal treaties. They were uncomfortable with the condescension of Western powers and were determined to achieve equality in world councils. But it was not abstract ideology that animated them. These were realists who fully understood power and who closely calculated its international balance.[3] They viewed Russian ambitions in the Far East with suspicion and reluctantly bided their time before extracting advantages from decrepit Chinese and Korean monarchies. Important decisions were deferred until Japan was sure of its own strength.

After all, there were—and would continue to be—a great many options. As *Taiyō* magazine asked on its cover in 1913: "Do we advance to the South or to the North?"[4]

Strategists spent the first decades of Japan's industrial modernization sorting this all out before arriving at a Meiji consensus. They would not allow Korea to fall into the hands of a hostile power, Russia's access to the Pacific would be contained, contiguous territories such as Okinawa in the south and the Kuriles in the north would be incorporated, and technology would be acquired to build a military industry and modernize the nation simultaneously. Autonomy was privileged in a pragmatic strategic vision that subordinated prestige, if only slightly. As Akira Iriye argues: "National independence, treaty revision, and modern transformation were all aspects of the same agenda, that of emulating the powerful and advanced Western nations."[5]

The army's patience was rewarded when the Meiji state began to feed its continental ambitions. Two wars—the first with China in 1895, the second against Russia in 1905—were fought under the banner of Yamagata Aritomo's 1890 grand strategic doctrine that etched a "line of sovereignty" (*shukensen*) around the Japanese homeland and a "line of interest" (*riekisen*) extending into neighboring areas such as Korea and Manchuria.[6] In 1907 Yamagata elaborated his blueprint for empire. His Basic Plan for National Defense identified Russia, the United States, and France as potential enemies. The latter two threats were less pressing, best left for the Imperial Navy, which still needed time to grow. Russia was the clear and present danger, and the Imperial Army of twenty-five standing divisions would confront it.[7]

Japanese leaders proved repeatedly that they could confidently step onto the international stage to alter the status quo and earn the indulgence (if not the respect) of the great powers in doing so. In 1876 Japan subjected Korea to its influence by "opening" it with impunity. Japan defeated Qing China in 1895 to gain significant concessions, and shortly thereafter, in 1900, Japan contributed twenty thousand troops—nearly double the contingent of any other nation—to a multinational force that crushed the Boxer Rebellion. Japan was rewarded in 1902 with an alliance with Great Britain, the world's greatest maritime power, and soon thereafter defeated their common threat, Russia, in modern warfare.

By the time this first wave of adventure had subsided, Japan had increased to include southern Sakhalin, southern Manchuria, Taiwan, and Korea. To some in Western capitals it seemed that Japan had begun overreaching, and Japanese military gains were rolled back. Treaties at Shimonoseki in 1895 and Portsmouth in 1905 were object lessons about international politics: Japanese strategists thought they had coordinated their national ambitions with the great powers, but the West did not agree with Gen. Tanaka Giichi that Japanese claims on the continent were "heaven-given."[8]

[16]

On the eve of World War I, domestic politics were unsettled, but Japan was already a rising industrial powerhouse that believed dominance of the continent would dampen domestic unrest. Yamagata and Tanaka, his deputy, welcomed war in Europe as an opportunity to develop an "autonomous" military program. They would "ally" with China and push Westerners out of Asia.[9] Some civilians agreed; other no less ambitious proponents of Japan's continental interests insisted that greater benefit would come from cooperation with the allied powers. Foreign Minister Katō Takaaki, a future prime minister (and Yamagata's chief antagonist), played a balance-of-power game that aimed to keep Russia out of Manchuria by maintaining relations with Britain. That meant declaring war on Germany. There was no consensus, even within the military. The Imperial Navy distanced itself from the army's objectives. Ultimately, the Japanese government sided with the Allies, helped expel the Germans from Asia, and rubbed its hands in anticipation of the gains that would be showered on it.

And some were. Because the war had been fought far away, its economic, technological, and trade benefits were harvested at low cost and high benefit. It left Japan richer and stronger than ever. Japanese forces were awarded rights in Shandong Province, and Japan became a creditor nation for the first time. What in the recent past—indeed in living memory—had been an isolated chain of islands on the very rim of Asia was now an empire with outsized designs on the continent.[10] Japan sat at Versailles as one of the Big Five victors.

The indulgence of the Western powers, however, and the patience of Japan's militarists were both already wearing thin. The Twenty-One Demands that Katō Takaaki issued in 1915 to a weakened China—over the objections of most Japanese liberals—had the unintended effects of stirring Chinese nationalism and Western suspicions of Japan simultaneously.[11] These suspicions were hardly allayed when, in 1918, Japan dispatched far more troops to Siberia to contain the Red Army than the Western powers had been led to expect. The Siberian Intervention only deepened domestic divisions over one of the most enduring questions of Japanese geopolitics: Would Japan give priority to its Western diplomacy or to its Asian ambitions?[12]

The Meiji Consensus on regional consolidation and industrial catching up had become frayed by the early 1900s, and it would be some time before Japan settled its domestic debates about foreign policy choices and national security. Although parts of the original consensus—particularly those concerning industrial development and technology—would be the foundation for policy choices for generations, the military was riven by competition between the navy and army for resources and among internationalists, nationalists, and Asianists on how to position Japan for maximum power and prestige. Business leaders, wanting to make sure that commercial as well as military interests would be protected, funded political parties to make their

voices heard. But trade was not first on the military's mind. Almost immediately after defeating Russia, Yamagata and his clique came to believe that
the Anglo-Japanese alliance had outlived its usefulness and thought that
Japan and Russia could "share" Manchuria and Mongolia. There were also
debates about the wisdom of finding common cause with China against
the "white races." Other battles raged over how soon the United States and
Japan would struggle for regional supremacy.[13] In short, the Meiji Consensus was unraveling and democracy was messy—especially in a country that
had neither a tradition of populism nor the institutions of mass politics.
The debate was especially frustrating for autocrats such as Yamagata who
thought that their control of the prerogatives of the emperor would give them
carte blanche in military affairs.[14]

THE KONOYE CONSENSUS: THE "NEW ORDER IN EAST ASIA"

Yamagata's military control of the political and administrative classes
was achieved only after epochal domestic struggle. The ideological divisions that shaped the interwar discourse—and, ultimately, Japanese security policy—put into opposition those who believed that Japan was a nation
in spiritual decay and those who wished Japan to modernize. The former
included, but was not limited to, reactionary nativists, and they were joined
by Asianists who embraced modernization but rejected Westernization.
They wanted to broaden Japanese influence without returning to what they
saw as an anachronistic, if not idealized, imperial rule. The modernizers
also included liberals, who imagined a stable world-trading system guaranteed by economic interdependence, as well as more radical progressives,
who believed that Japan, to protect its gains, had to reduce the influence of
excessively conciliatory party politicians and their zaibatsu supporters.[15]

Thus the battle was joined. Nativists (*nihonshugisha*), like Kita Ikki and
Ōkawa Shūmei, were animated by an urgent mission to cleanse the "national
essence" (*kokusui*) and rectify Japan's "national spirit" (*yamato damashii*).
They helped educate Asianists, some of whom, like Okakura Tenshin, were
intellectuals, others, like Col. Ishiwara Kanji, cynical realists. Both groups
believed that Asia was one and that Japan should assume its rightful place
as leader, unifier, and liberator. Westerners had to be expelled from Japan's
natural sphere of influence.[16] Opposing this mainstream were two groups of
cosmopolites. The first were the "Big Japan liberals" like Shidehara Kijūrō,
whose great power ambitions for Japan were fixed on national expansion
but by means of the purse rather than the sword. The second were the
"Small Japan liberals," like Ishibashi Tanzan, who preferred that Japan assume a lower profile in foreign affairs. This struggle was literally one of life
and death among rational actors who had varying levels of passion for the

[18]

ideals they deployed and the causes they espoused. Many changed sides as the Konoye consensus took shape.

The Mainstream

The nativists were a force beyond their numbers, largely because they inspired their adversaries as well as the public at large. Some came out of the Nichiren tradition, a messianic Japanese Buddhism that identified Japan's national life with global regeneration. Others were Shinto based, focused on the imperial family as the very quintessence of Japan. Both groups touched a deep chord in those who feared that industrial modernization was robbing Japan of its moral direction. Japan was greater and purer than the rampant egoism that was debasing contemporary social life. Feeling threatened by foreign powers that encroached on the nation and region, they believed in the inevitability of war—and in the inevitability of Japanese victory. As with talk of Anglo-Saxon racial superiority in the United States, talk of race war and of protecting the Japanese race had become politically correct.[17]

There was at best a thin line between nativists and Asianists, and they comfortably converged on a common nationalism.[18] Meiji leaders, preferring a more pragmatic foreign policy, had kept nineteenth century Asianists at arm's length—understanding pan-Asianism as a threat to their young regime. The oligarchs' insistence that Japan's rights on the continent needed no further justification beyond the Monroe Doctrine was wearing thin by the turn of the century. In 1906, Tōgō Minoru wrote that Japan should establish overseas colonies in order to "develop its power, expand its race, and become predominant over the world."[19] Japanese ideologues imagined a community of shared identities—an essentialist, hierarchical community, headed by Japan, that would "offer a tempting rationale for Japan's regional leadership."[20]

Asianism had leftist variants as well, but it was the rightists, embracing Japan's imperial mission and deploying nativist rhetoric, whose secret societies grew like Topsy during the interwar period—especially after the Treaty for the Limitation and Reduction of Naval Armament (London Naval Treaty) in 1930.[21] According to police records, the ideals of these groups varied. Some believed fervently in the imperial household as the foundation of family, nation, and empire. Others threatened the imperial family by demanding a second restoration to cleanse Japan of its moral filth. Japanese subjects were advised to acquaint themselves with the "ancient Japanese spirit," and many were tested on that knowledge at the point of a sword. Some groups were openly revolutionary, devoted to cleansing Japan of foreign ideas through the assassination of liberal leaders. Most were closely monitored, even though many had supporters within the state. The Home Ministry recorded fewer than ten such groups in 1922, but that number rose to forty in 1930 and doubled again in each of the next three years.[22]

[19]

Now the nationalist Right mobilized to identify traitors (internationalists) who had sold out Japan to Anglo-American imperialism and betrayed the throne. Those who had strayed must be eliminated, and, in a paroxysm of nationalist violence, many were. Prince Saionji Kinmochi, a leading internationalist and aristocrat, had earlier dismissed nativism as a fraud, declaring that behind its insistence on "an 'aggressive fighting spirit'... are lies and greed."[23] He barely escaped assassination in the February 1936 coup d'état; his voice, like those of other cosmopolites, had long since been silenced by nationalist violence.

Many of Japan's leading Asianists were in the military. Indeed, the benefits to Japan of a racially justified regional hegemony was one thing that the Imperial Army and Navy could agree on. The oligarch Yamagata Aritomo had been warning of a coming race war, a clash of civilizations, for years. Admiral Katō Hiroharu (Kanji), the antitreaty naval leader, spoke disparagingly of Western materialism and admiringly of "Japan's great mission to purify world thought."[24] Interwar nativism now merged with Asianism, creating a nationalist force at the disposal of balance-of-power realists. Only alliance between China and Japan, nations that shared "color and culture," could stave off Western domination of Asia.[25] China would accede to Japanese leadership out of a sense of racial solidarity, much as Korea already had. There were, after all, "master peoples" (*shujin minzoku*), "friendly peoples" (*yūjin minzoku*), and "guest peoples" (*kigū minzoku*).[26] Each had (and knew) its place. China required guidance and a way out from its "present tyrannous leadership" toward happiness and prosperity.[27] It was *Japan* that would become Asia's new Middle Kingdom, its sovereignty built on the ruins of a feeble, decadent China. Asianists espoused a doctrine of "same race, same culture" (*dōshu dōbun*) but also of "same race, different status." "Asia for the Asians" meant a region under Japanese control: "We, the Yamato people... should always stay above other peoples of other countries and maintain a level of dignity and superiority as the leader figure."[28] Colonel Ishiwara Kanji, the sometime-renegade strategist, famously called for the expulsion of the white race from continental Asia. Even the far more decorous Yamagata, godfather of the imperial military and pragmatic architect of Japan's "cautious expansion in the framework of cooperation with the Western powers," warned Japan in 1914 that the white race would reunify and resume its offensive in Asia again China and Japan.[29] As Mark Peattie observes, "Racial harmony was to become a weapon in the arsenal of the Final War."[30]

But race was only a sideshow. The main event was control of the continent's resources in order to resist Western military and economic pressure. Who could trust the West? What value was there in their treaties? What, beyond power, did they really understand? Ishiwara's skepticism was especially transparent. In 1932 he wrote that he hoped the Chinese would join Japan in preparing for the coming conflict—but if not, they would be compelled to cooperate. Manchuria was the first step on the way to the final war with the West:

> When the military preparations are completed, we do not need to go to great lengths to find a motive or occasion; all we need to do is pick the time and then proclaim to the world our absorption of Manchuria the way we proclaimed the annexation of Korea.[31]

The lesson of World War I for Ishiwara was that the next war would be total, and so Japan would need a sufficient base for autarky. That base had to come from hegemony in Asia. In this sense, Asianism was a moral justification for a realist grand strategy, not a cause of Japanese expansion.[32] A cultural theory had been hijacked for strategic purposes.

Asianism had broad appeal, especially after the Western powers rejected the joint Chinese-Japanese proposal for a racial equality clause in the Treaty of Versailles. Prince Saionji, a sophisticated internationalist, was Japan's senior representative at the peace conference. He believed that regional stability was more important that continental expansion, but he and his delegation (a remarkable collection of talent including Yoshida Shigeru, Prince Konoye Fumimaro, and Matsuoka Yōsuke) also believed it was important to establish norms of equality in the new international order. Japanese businessmen had often been humiliated abroad, and Japanese citizens, whose children were forced to attend segregated schools even in San Francisco, had lost the right to own land in the United States. In one of a continuing series of unpleasant lessons in American civics, Woodrow Wilson simply overruled a majority vote that accepted the "racial equality clause."[33] Japanese public opinion was outraged. Japan joined the League of Nations with serious reservations, even though it was one of only four permanent members of the League's Council.

The Antimainstream

Prime Minster Hara Kei and the business community put a positive spin on Versailles, celebrating it as the first recognition of Japan's proper place in the world.[34] Although some idealistic liberals wondered how Japan could possess colonies while opposing colonialism, most were thoroughly pragmatic. It would be good if Japan were powerful, and few questioned its natural right to dominate Asia. But colonies were expensive and distracting, and they continued to resist supporting a militarized foreign policy. Japanese hegemony and security could be achieved and maintained more inexpensively through trade and investment. A rich nation did not have to maintain too strong an army. The operative metaphor for their view, most famously associated with Akamatsu Kaname, was a benign regional division of labor presided over by Japan. Japan would be the "lead goose" in a convoy of nations flying directly on the path of industrial development and prosperity. Most economic internationalists were, in fact, nationalists with an international agenda rather than liberals in any textbook sense. They concurred that Japan should become a trading state rather than a colonial power and, therefore, that military spending should be restrained.[35] But this national vision—which would be crushed by militarism but would flower as "mercantile realism" on the other side of the coming Pacific War— was itself contested. There were those who imagined Japan was big, and those who imagined Japan small.

The Small Japan liberals (*shōnihonshugisha*), who would inspire much of postwar Japanese foreign policy, took their cues from a 1906 debate in Great Britain between members of the Liberal and Conservative parties about the nature of empire. In the spring of 1913, Miura Tetsutarō, a true economic liberal who believed that the basis for national welfare was individual liberty, penned a series of editorials in the economic weekly *Tōyō Keizai*, in which he argued that Japan could not afford to replicate Britain's imperial reach.[36] He accepted that Japanese security was enhanced by control of the Korean Peninsula but systematically attacked arguments for further expansion. Colonies would neither absorb Japan's excess population nor enhance trade. In fact, Miura argued, colonial expansion had perverse effects, slowing and distorting growth on the one hand and stimulating anti-Japanese nationalism on the other. Japan's expansion should be rolled back.

In 1924 Miura stepped aside and made Ishibashi Tanzan editor in chief of *Tōyō Keizai*. Ishibashi had already established himself as the leading theorist of Small Japanism.[37] He had argued against joining the Allies in World War I, lest Japan be emboldened to seize Manchuria and China. His analysis demonstrated there was no economic advantage to be gained; indeed, success would place Japan in direct conflict with the Western powers and inflame Chinese nationalism. Japan would be cut off from the Western sources of technology that would make it truly strong. He vigorously opposed the Twenty-One Demands issued in 1915, as politically and economically ill-advised. Advocating a maritime strategy, he insisted that Japan relinquish all claims on the continent after 1918. Free trade—in competing blocs, if necessary—and strong international organizations such as the League of Nations were better guarantees of Japanese security. By 1921 Ishibashi was convinced that Japan was no longer vulnerable to Russian or Anglo-American threats, that it was preeminent in East Asia, and that "Japan was creating its own vulnerability by sowing hatred and suspicion through acts of aggression."[38] In July 1921, on the eve of the Washington Naval Conference, Ishibashi published a series of editorials under the title

"The Fantasy of Great Japanism," in which he proposed abandoning all of Japan's colonies in order to reduce economic burdens and enhance Japan's moral standing.

But Small Japanism was not fundamentally a moral argument. Its pragmatic liberalism was based on economic self-interest. Trade outside the empire was greater than trade within and was the source of Japan's technology, so why invite war with countries Japan could be trading with?[39] The U.S. and European markets held far more potential for enriching Japan than did continental markets. It was not worth jeopardizing Japan's vital interests for the sake of regional domination, aggressors expose themselves to danger in the form of balancing by other powers, and autarky was a losing proposition. After all, it was capital and technology, not territory, that made a nation truly strong. Ishibashi took on all comers, including nativists, national socialists in the "progressive" bureaucracy, the military, and Big Japan liberals, alike.[40]

Big Japan liberals dominated both major conservative parties, the Minseitō and the Seiyūkai, and because they held power for most of the period from the end of World War I until the Manchurian Incident in 1931, they had a great advantage over the Small Japanists. They agreed that Japan should pursue trade and investment rather than military aggression, but they parted ways with the Small Japanists on two issues. First, the Big Japanists benefited from alliances with Japan's economic bureaucrats, and thus they were more comfortable with state intervention in the economy. Second, they accepted the idea that Japan was Asia's natural leader.[41] To them there was nothing illiberal about defending Japan's rights on the continent. They were "nationalist actors in the internationalist theater."[42] Small Japanists believed that a sovereign China was good for Japan; Big Japanists were openly imperialist. They insisted Japan had special interests in China. After all, hadn't Japan won Manchuria by beating back the Russians? Why should they recognize Chinese claims? Their support for international organizations was premised on the idea that through them Japan would gain its rightful place in Asia. Thus, they consciously opposed formal annexation and the militarists who sought to crush Chinese nationalism. Cooperating with the other great powers through arms limitation agreements and in international forums, they supported an "economic diplomacy" (*keizai gaikō*) that would deliver Japan its rights on the continent as well as its autonomy and security.

Their first great test after Versailles was the Washington Naval Conference in 1921–22 at which a new international military balance would be negotiated. The ambassador to the United States, Shidehara Kijūrō, led the Japanese delegation, and his "Shidehara diplomacy" came to be most closely associated with Japan's first, abortive, attempt at an economics-oriented foreign policy.[43] Japan agreed to return parts of Shandong that it had seized from Germany, and Japan's naval strength was frozen in a subordinate position, but Britain, France, Japan, and the United States pledged mutual respect for one another's Asian possessions and mandates and agreed to peaceful resolution of any disputes. Japan was confident it could achieve privileged entry through the "open door" in China. For the United States, the naval limitation agreement stabilized the status quo and contained Japan.[44] This was anathema to the Japanese militarists, of course, and domestic politics would never be the same. But Shidehara and his colleagues believed that no amount of arms racing could push Japan ahead of the combined power of the United States and Great Britain. In their view, the treaty marked a new age for Japanese diplomacy.

The future soon seemed less rosy. Shidehara's moderate, cooperative diplomacy (in his first term as foreign minister in 1925–26, Shidehara negotiated nearly a dozen bilateral trade agreements with countries in Asia, Europe, and Latin America) was undermined at every turn by a wounded but politically powerful military, by economic recession, and by rising Chinese nationalism.[45] It was also undermined by exclusionary immigration laws, antimiscegenation statutes, and racial segregation in the United States. The liberals' admiration for American values had been betrayed before, at Versailles, and by the mid-1920s no one could claim that the United States was a champion of justice and equality. Nitobe Inazō, one of Japan's leading internationalists and a pioneer of American studies who had married an American, famously refused to return to the United States until the laws were revised.[46] U.S. immigration policy was the main topic at the first meeting of the Rockefeller-funded and internationalist-leaning Institute for Pacific Relations in 1925, but Japanese delegates could not put a dent in the policy, in part because many of the other delegations were themselves colonies of imperial powers. Both the radical Right and the radical Left gained considerable political traction from Western racism—and liberal internationalists, who had no mass support, began abandoning their idealism and tilting in a nationalist direction.[47] Ironically, nativists in the United States had fortified the position of nativists in Japan.

In one of history's many odd coincidences, the federal law banning Japanese immigration went into effect on 1 July 1924, the very day Foreign Minister Shidehara delivered his inaugural address to the Diet emphasizing global cooperation and patience with regard to China. At the Washington conference, the Chinese delegation had demanded tariff autonomy, a matter tabled for later action, but before talks could get under way in 1925 the nationwide antiforeign May 30th Movement gripped China. Now Foreign Minister Shidehara saw a chance to turn these events to Japan's advantage. He skillfully diffused the crisis by refusing to send Japanese troops to quell disturbances, and facilitated a strike settlement between Chinese workers and Japanese factory owners. Shidehara broke ranks with the other powers and with promilitary politicians by agreeing with Chinese warlords on a return of tariff autonomy to placate Chinese nationalists. He supported China's claim and then capitalized on the resulting goodwill to establish a bilateral, graduated tariff system so that Japanese exporters would not be disadvantaged. Shidehara's hard-nosed economic diplomacy presaged the mercantile realism that would characterize Japanese policy after 1945.[48]

First, however, there was war. The China tariff agreement proved Japan could act in its perceived interests, but it hardly solved Japan's problems, many of which were now domestic. Shidehara knew it, and to protect what remained of his power he stiffened his posture. In mid-1931 he declared: "Some of the rights we enjoy in Manchuria are inextricably linked to our nation's existence, and no matter how generous a policy we take towards China, these rights can never be given up."[49] It was too late. The year before, 1930, Japan had signed the London Naval Treaty, requiring further cuts in Japan's naval strength to a level the government had already declared inadequate to assure Japanese security. The nationalists and the military were infuriated, and nothing Shidehara could say or do would placate them.[50] What benefits had Japan gained from economic diplomacy? What had cooperation with the selfish Western powers achieved? With Small Japan liberalism discredited and Big Japan liberalism stripped of its moderation, there was no space left for economic diplomacy. Confrontation would replace engagement with the West, and military power would no longer be subordinated to economic power. Maruyama Masao makes Japan's transition to authoritarianism seem simple: "All that the rightists had to do in order to awaken those people who had lapsed into dreams of 'individualistic pleasure' and 'socialistic utopias' and to bring them back to their patriotic senses was to ring an alarm bell."[51] It was hardly so straightforward. First the military had to seize the prerogatives of the emperor. It did so in the epochal Manchurian Incident of September 1931. Led by Ishiwara Kanji, a group of junior officers took action to force the government's hand. They blew up a section of railway track in Mukden and, blaming Chinese nationalists, used the attack as a pretext to take over southern Manchuria. As Yale Maxon vividly describes it: "Field-grade officers, with a segment of the general staff, had initiated a chain of events which the War Minister endorsed and for which he obtained retroactive approval from the civil government on the basis of a *fait accompli*."[52] They also received tacit approval from the emperor and benefited from the inability or unwillingness of liberals to mount much protest. They and their allies in the bureaucracy simply ignored the instructions of Prime Minister Wakatsuki Reijirō, who feared the negative impact of their actions on Japan's international standing. Even the Ministry of Foreign Affairs had come under the sway of the so-called progressive (*kakushin*) bureaucrats who opposed conciliatory diplomacy.

Now there was no stopping the military and its allies. They seized control of Japan's foreign policy and suborned a half decade of domestic terrorism, which Hugh Byas has aptly termed "government by assassination."[53] In February 1932, former finance minister Inoue Junnosuke was murdered by a member of the nativist Blood Oath Corps. As Mark Metzler writes, "The worlds of cosmopolitan finance and nationalist resentment had collided."[54] The same group murdered Japan's most senior business leader, Baron Dan Takuma, four weeks later, just a day after he hosted a dinner for the Lytton Commission, which was in Japan to investigate the Manchurian Incident. On May 15, a small group of naval cadets and army officers murdered Prime Minister Inukai Tsuyoshi, just one week after he declared that Japan would not send additional soldiers to China. At this point, all normal functioning of party government was abandoned. The army, "intoxicated with its own prestige (*gun no isshin*)," had seized effective control. It achieved a political autonomy that "ran like a fatal thread" through the 1930s and 1940s.[55]

The Consensus

Under relentless pressure from militarists who were adamantly unwilling to compromise with the Western powers in China and intimidated by domestic terror, liberal internationalists weakened. In February 1932 Nitobe Inazō declared militarism more dangerous than Communism; after rightist groups denounced him as "traitorous," he hired armed guards. He appeared soon thereafter before a military group and retracted his statement. Nitobe returned to the United States, sent by the foreign ministry to present the "correct Japanese perspective" and to "clarify the Japanese position."[56] Japan's leading internationalist was now the leading apologist for Japanese diplomacy. Small Japanists also came around. Within months of the Manchurian Incident, Ishibashi Tanzan changed the editorial policy of *Tōyō Keizai*. In January 1932 its editorial registered concern about China's inability to maintain order in Manchuria. Ishibashi still opposed the creation of a puppet state and the army's vision of a planned economy, but he conceded that Japan deserved special trade and investment rights.[57]

By the spring of 1932 it was clear that a new consensus was taking shape. Liberalism had proved less than compelling, and the same pragmatism that had led most liberal internationalists to oppose coercive solutions now turned toward support for the military.[58] By the end of the decade, the various tributaries in Japan's national discourse were flowing into a single mighty river. Liberals and leftists who had once dismissed the ranting of nativists and Asianists "now indulged in the same emotional worship of the nation."[59]

The leader of this new consensus was not a soldier and was never a liberal. Prince Konoye Fumimaro was the only politician in the 1930s related by blood to the imperial family. The charismatic Konoye had long been in the public eye. In December 1918, less than a month after the Armistice was signed, he asserted the necessity of Japanese expansion on the continent and vowed to repudiate Anglo-American privilege. At Versailles (he had whee-dled membership in the delegation) he had observed how Japan's concerns for racial equality had been shunted aside, and minced no words as to how the treaty was rigged to legitimate Western domination. The young Konoye rejected the status quo as a construction by "haves" determined to dominate the "have-nots" of Asia, and vigorously encouraged Asia to resist free trade as an ideology of the rich.[60] He argued that "Japan should join the League, but it should insist on the exclusion of economic imperialism and discriminatory treatment between white and yellow races. It is not only militarism which harms social justice."[61] The prince was certain that a race war was in the off-ing and, like many rightists, criticized Western racism without questioning the Japanese version. Konoye remained in the public eye for more than two decades, appealing to pan-Asian idealism while remaining a shrewd realist, convinced that in international affairs only power mattered.[62]

Konoye built his own power—and the architecture for his Greater East Asia Co-Prosperity Sphere—by recruiting the best and brightest in the bu-reaucracy, military, and academia. In November 1933 he created the Shōwa Kenkyūkai (Shōwa Research Association) to serve as his personal think tank and shadow cabinet. One of its leading designers was Rōyama Masamichi, a Tokyo University professor who had been a prominent liberal interna-tionalist but "who came to embrace the wartime mobilization program of the Japanese state."[63] Rōyama became an intellectual leader of the Konoye consensus, believing that the "selfish" Western powers would simply have to accommodate to Japan's "natural" and "constructive" leadership of Asia. Even Ishibashi Tanzan became an affiliate. The Shōwa Kenkyūkai imme-diately began spinning out justifications for Japanese domination of Asia, including modernist economic institutions such as an East Asian Coopera-tive Economic Organization (Tōa Keizai Kyōdōtai) and (later) Philosophical Principles for a New Japan (Shin Nippon no Shisō Genri).[64] By the time Konoye became prime minister in July 1937, his think tank addressed the entire range of domestic and foreign policy issues, including a corporatist domestic economic structure that was modeled on Fascist Italy.[65] Konoye not only attracted intellectuals from across the spectrum, many of whom stepped directly into government when he took office, but he also main-tained excellent relations with leading factions of the army.

This was no small achievement, since the military itself was deeply split on how to make Japan secure. The army's Imperial Way faction (Kōdōha) argued for preemptive war against the Soviet Union. Its Control faction (Tōseiha) preferred a more cautious defense buildup, assigning priority to economic organization and industrial mobilization. In June 1936, the army's general staff issued a memorandum laying out the General Principles of National Defense Policy, the first being "to establish our status as protector and leader of East Asia. To do this we must have the power to expunge the pressure of the white races in East Asia."[66] The war in China, which Japan initiated in earnest in 1937, was merely a prelude to a new world war. While the army was focused on confronting Russia in Manchuria and pacifying nationalists in China, the navy cast its eyes southward.[67] After the abrogation of the naval treaties, the Imperial Navy issued its own strategy in 1935 designed to control the sea-lanes of the South China Sea and to establish itself as the stabilizing force in the western Pacific.[68] There was little coordination across the services and no coordinated military strategy. Military planners simply expected that the Western powers, and particularly the United States, would continue to accept Japanese expansion and "understand (Japan's) intentions."[69]

This may have been wishful thinking, and Japanese strategists certainly misperceived the dynamics of world politics, but Japan's intentions were no mystery. They represented "a vigorous defense of Japan's right to define her own interests."[70] This defense was articulated repeatedly by Prince Konoye, by his study groups, and by "progressive" bureaucrats.[71] Dissent had been extinguished along with civilian control of the military.[72] In November 1938 Konoye announced the New Order in East Asia (Tōa Shin Chitsujo): "Our Empire wholly trusts the powers to adapt themselves to this new situation in East Asia by accurately recognizing the real intention of our Empire."[73] Part nostalgic agrarianism, part pan-Asian sloganeering, and fully anti-Western, Konoye's leadership harmonized the many disparate voices from decades of debate. Under his banner, Japan fashioned its own grand design to "secure international justice, perfect joint defense against communism, and create a new culture.... The establishment of a new order in East Asia ... is the exalted responsibility with which our generation is trusted."[74] Japan would serve as the "nucleus" of a new civilization.[75] In August 1940, once it seemed clear that Japan could seize the low-hanging fruit of Southeast Asia, the predominantly continental New Order was supplanted by the even grander fiction of the Greater East Asia Co-Prosperity Sphere.[76]

The incongruent threads of Japan's strategic discourse—internationalism, liberalism, Asianism, mythic nativism—had converged in a common belief in the integrity of the Japanese nation and were bound together within the unquestioned authority of the Japanese state. In the Konoye consensus, nationalism and internationalism were not mutually exclusive, something that was true long before and ever since. At the core of the Konoye consensus was a belief in the use of force and a belief in the inherent justice of the national mission. Once the mission failed—and for at least the next half century—the very idea of the state's use of force would be off the table. It was a dark and terrible lesson, but the ghost of Yamagata Aritomo would continue for generations to cast a shadow over the Japanese military, its prestige extinguished along with much of Japan's national autonomy.

[28]

The Yoshida Doctrine: Democratic Japan's Cheap Ride

It was a long road back to national autonomy and international prestige, a road that was ultimately paved by the creativity and pragmatism of Japan's postwar leaders. The tightly woven Konoye consensus was shredded by war, but by no means were all of the threads of Japan's interwar security discourse lost. Indeed, after several tumultuous decades of reinvention, debate, and repositioning, they were rewoven into a new, more lustrous fabric. In what came to be known as the Yoshida Doctrine, a nonmilitary "invisible hand" borrowed energetically from interwar liberal internationalism to guide a nonaggressive, low-cost postwar Japanese security policy for a half century.[77] As in the 1920s, there was a "mainstream" and an "antimainstream," but now the internationalists had the upper hand.

The Antimainstream

The consensus was enhanced by the fact that one group, nativists and neomilitarists, who hoped to reestablish Japan as a great power, was effectively sidelined by the U.S. Occupation and by popular revulsion.[78] Still, for a time these ultranationalists made their presence felt. So long as their parties were banned and imperial military officers were purged, they met in groups of "classmates' associations." Then, after the newly sovereign Japanese government depurged the officer corps in 1951, their political associations sprung up across Japan. They were all over the ideological map as well. The so-called National Party was inspired by Ishiwara Kanji, who remarkably had not been executed as a war criminal. It advocated agrarian national socialism under imperial rule and even sprinkled in a bit of democratic sloganeering, arguing that only full Japanese rearmament could enable full cooperation with the United Nations. After emerging from Sugamo Prison, where he spent three years as an unindicted Class A war criminal, Sasakawa Ryōichi transformed his National Essence Mass Party into the National League of Working People before settling down to work with establishment politicians to build one of the world's largest philanthropic empires.[79] The Eastern Association of Nagano Seigō, another wartime propagandist, was renamed the People's Rights Comrades Association, and openly set out to reconstruct a fascist order. Others, like the Hattori Organization (Hattori kikan), which fashioned itself a sort of secret general staff, remained clandestine. Some dispersed into rural cells.

Indeed, the wartime split between the "moderate" Control faction and the "extremist" Imperial Way faction was reproduced in veteran organizations.[80] Most, though, wound their way toward the center as a matter of sheer opportunism and welcomed John Foster Dulles in December 1951 with the banner: "Welcome Dulles! Promote rearmament!"[81] The most extreme among these

[29]

ultranationalists were marginalized, but some found common cause with a revisionist group of establishment conservatives, many of whom had also been purged. Together they "weathered the Occupation storm."[82] Indeed, once the United States made it clear in the early 1950s that rearmament was desirable after all, most official plans to rebuild the Japanese military were authored by former officers, like Hattori, who served informally as advisors to the Occupation, to conservative politicians, and to industrialists who wanted to get back into the defense business.[83]

The revisionist politicians, who later formed the antimainstream group within the Liberal Democratic Party (LDP), built a powerful alliance with industrialists. Together they maintained constant pressure on Yoshida and his liberal internationalists. Led in the immediate postwar years by Ashida Hitoshi, Shigemitsu Mamoru, Hatoyama Ichirō, and, later, by Kishi Nobusuke—three of whom served as prime minister—many had been economic bureaucrats in Manchuria or career politicians during the prewar years as members of the Seiyūkai Party. Occupation purges forced a large portion of the group from public life, and so members had to reinvent themselves as democrats. Imbued with traditional nationalist (though not ultranationalist) sentiments, they held to an organic vision of Japan as a unique "national polity" (*kokutai*), distinguished primarily by its imperial institution and neo-Confucian values, which emphasize unity and sacrifice for the national order. They coupled a muscular notion of national identity with realpolitik beliefs emphasizing the nation's duty to ensure its own security. As ex–foreign minister (and paroled Class A war criminal) Shigemitsu Mamoru put it in 1953: "The people have to retain their self-respect by defending the fatherland through their own efforts."[84] Kishi Nobusuke, himself an unindicted Class A war criminal and future prime minister, proclaimed in 1954: "It is not the policy of an independent nation to have troops of a foreign country based on its soil."[85] Accordingly, they favored a combination of rearmament and conventional alliances. To achieve these ends, they called for revision of the constitution's antiwar Article 9, argued that Japan should rebuild its military capabilities, and sought a reciprocal security commitment with the United States as a step toward their holy grail of "autonomous defense."

These revisionists seemed diametrically opposed to the pacifist Japanese Left, which, in the postwar period, had for the first time become a legitimate political force.[86] This group brought together intellectuals, labor activists, and leftist politicians, who insisted Japan become a "peace nation" (*heiwa kokka*) and categorically opposed the use of force in international affairs. Initially put forward by a group of progressive intellectuals known as the Heiwa Mondai Danwakai (Peace Issues Discussion Group), the "peace nation" idea comprised both an abstract commitment to peace as a supreme value and a pragmatic conviction that it was Japan's unique mission to demonstrate how world peace could be achieved, a mission

[30]

that fell to Japan as a consequence of its wartime suffering and "natural" pacifist tendencies.[87]

Left-wing socialists led by Suzuki Mosaburō, who had opposed the war and suffered under militarism, were the initial champions of pacifism. Early enthusiasts of Article 9, they were committed pacifists and adherents of its strictest interpretation—one that would not permit the use of force even in self-defense. Shaped by their experiences and the ideas of the Heiwa Mondai Danwakai, the Suzuki faction institutionalized their ideas in the Socialist Party's "principles of peace," which called for neutralism and opposed rearmament. By the early 1950s, the Japan Socialist Party had pledged support for Article 9 and opposition to rearmament and to the United States–Japan Security Treaty, a doctrine it called "unarmed neutrality" (*hibusō chūritsu*). Pacifists did not trust Japan with a full military capability, preferring to rely on international public opinion, diplomacy, and passive resistance to counter security threats. They expanded their grassroots networks during the 1950s and became a considerable force by the end of the decade, when they occupied one-third of the seats in the Diet. It was their considerable power that kept the conservative camp united in a single party—and therefore that formed the central left-right divide in cold war domestic politics.

The Mainstream

Left versus Right may have been emblazoned on the marquee of postwar Japanese politics, but the most interesting and important politics played out within the conservative camp. The revisionists met their match in—indeed, were overmatched by—the pragmatic conservative politicians led immediately after 1945 by Yoshida Shigeru and later by his disciples such as Ikeda Hayato, Satō Eisaku, Ōhira Masayoshi, and Miyazawa Kiichi.[88] Yoshida built this group of liberal internationalists, heirs of the Small Japanism of the interwar period, through his long tenure as prime minister during and immediately after the U.S. Occupation. He surrounded himself with likeminded politicians, many of whom had served with him in the foreign ministry.[89] Like the revisionists, many liberal internationalists were devoted to the emperor and dedicated to seeing Japan reemerge among the ranks of great nations. They also came to appreciate that the United States was simultaneously "Japan's most dangerous enemy and most desirable ally."[90] However, echoing the split between Big Japanists and Small Japanists, these two groups of conservatives differed on questions of foreign policy and national development.

The liberal internationalists held the view that economic success and technological autonomy were the prerequisites of national security, and that an alliance with the world's ascendant power was the best means to buy time until the former could be achieved. They rejected military spending in favor of a broader plan for state-led development of the private sector. Burdened by the costs of reconstruction and cut off from promising regional markets by the emerging cold war, theirs was a near single-minded emphasis on the civilian economy. They accepted the unequal alliance with the United States and used it as a shield behind which they could regenerate prosperity. Japan would be a merchant state, not a samurai one.[91] Regaining its national wealth through maritime trade, Japan would make the world its market, not its battlefield.[92] Only after prosperity had returned would Yoshida and his group consider further investment in military preparedness.[93] They were, above all, pragmatic.

The preferences of the two groups of conservatives—revisionists and pragmatists—diverged in two important respects: First, they disagreed about the *causes* of national wealth and power. And second, although the term had not yet entered the national discourse, they disagreed about whether Japan should be a "normal" nation, one with military capabilities commensurate with its economic strength. Specifically, the pragmatists correctly read that the United States was eager to use Japan as an "unsinkable aircraft carrier" and judged that they could hedge the risks of a U.S. alliance with a focus on commercial economic development. They were mercantile realists who understood that the superpowers would reward their allies. Japan could enjoy a cheap ride on U.S. security guarantees, receiving not only security but access to U.S. markets and technology as well. The only dangers to Japanese prosperity and security were abandonment by the United States or entanglement in U.S. wars. Because these pragmatists dominated the cabinets under which all three pillars of Japan's postwar security apparatus were established—Article 9 of the Japanese Constitution, the Self-Defense Forces, and the U.S.-Japan Security Treaty—they are widely known as "mainstream conservatives" (*hoshu honryū*). As we shall see in chapter 2, these same mainstream conservatives also adopted such pacifist codicils as the three "nonnuclear principles," the "arms export ban," and the "1 percent of GDP" limit on defense spending. For decades the mainstream defended each position from attacks by revisionists within the Liberal Democratic Party, known as "antimainstream conservatives" (*hanhoshu honryū*), until the latter came to power in the early 2000s.

These two groups fought three protracted battles over national security on the road toward the Yoshida consensus.[94] The first concerned the constitution itself, which revisionists insisted was "imposed" by the United States and ill-suited to Japan. They found Article 9 especially repugnant and pressed for its revision. Pragmatists favored retention because Article 9 proved useful in two ways. First, it allowed pragmatists to deflect U.S. pressure for the acquisition of military capabilities they judged unnecessary or inimical to Japan's strategic interests. Second, they found Article 9 an effective means of resisting U.S. demands for Japanese participation in international military operations. The constitutional ban on the exercise of collective self-defense was a useful way to avoid entanglements in U.S. cold war strategy.[95] To pragmatists who turned back two formal efforts by Kishi to revise the constitution, Article 9 was an indispensable instrument for protecting Japanese interests within the U.S.-Japan alliance.[96]

The second struggle concerned whether Japan should use defense production as the engine of postwar economic reconstruction.[97] Neither Article 9, which prohibits Japan from maintaining "war potential" and renounces Japan's "right of belligerency," nor anything else in the 1947 constitution precludes the production or export of arms. Indeed, prospects for both looked particularly bright by 1948–50, when the United States reversed its Asian security policy (and the intent of Article 9, which it authored) and established Japan as its military and industrial bastion in the Far East. "Special procurement" (*tokuju*) by U.S. forces during the Korean War and other forms of economic aid to Japan were the price the United States paid for Japanese bases. Nearly 70 percent of Japanese exports during the 1950–52 period were U.S. military "special procurements," which contributed significantly to the rehabilitation of the Japanese economy. The Japanese machinery industry was poised to shift to full-scale munitions production once the United States granted Japan permission to resume arms and aircraft manufacture in March 1952. Weapons sales of seven *million* yen in 1952 grew to fifteen *billion* yen in 1954.[98]

Industrial and finance capital did not agree on the wisdom of this strategy. The former, representing the heavy industrial firms of the old zaibatsu, such as Mitsubishi, used former high-ranking military officers to generate ambitious rearmament plans and optimistic projections for the arms industry as the engine of postwar redevelopment.[99] "Defense production" was supported by the Ministry of International Trade and Industry (MITI) as well, which sought to restore it to a central place in Japan's technology strategy. Hatoyama, Kishi, and the other revisionists were lined up to assist in the budget battle. But the bankers and the Ministry of Finance (MOF) were not convinced. They sided with Yoshida, arguing that arms production would divert resources from sectors with greater (and more stable) prospects for growth. Former zaibatsu bankers refused financing to firms with plans to become more than 20–30 percent dependent on defense products.[100] MOF bureaucrats, recalling wartime pressures from militarists, feared a return to deficit budgeting.

The debate came to a head during preparation of the 1954 budget.[101] The MOF and Yoshida firmly opposed MITI efforts to support the arms industry; the MOF was abetted by MITI officials who doubted the efficacy of such support and who favored the electric power industry, which they considered more strategic. MITI and Kishi had to settle for limited regulatory power through the Arms Manufacturing Law (Buki tō Seizō Hō) passed by the Diet in July 1953. Unlike other industrial policy of the period, this law signaled capital markets that arms production would *not* be targeted for special assistance. Defense contractors exited from the armaments industry in large numbers, in some cases not to return for thirty or forty years.

The third battle, over the institutions of security policymaking, recognized the deep divisions between revisionists allied with former military officers and internationalists with their broader bureaucratic base. The former had lobbied vigorously for a self-defense forces law that would include responsibilities for domestic order and for a national security council that would limit the power of the civilian bureaucracy. Former prime minister Ashida and his conservative Kaishintō Party worked with other revisionists to press for a council of civilians—preferably with heavy representation of former Imperial Army officers—that could dominate both the bureaucrats and more moderate conservatives who might constrain the development of an independent military.[102] Yoshida would have none of this. He made sure that the ex-officio members of the National Security Council (Kokubō Kaigi) were limited to cabinet ministers and that former flag officers were explicitly barred from posts in the new Defense Agency. Japan had no national security council until two years after the Defense Agency and Self-Defense Forces were established in 1954. Later, as prime minister, Kishi tried a different tack—he sought to upgrade and reorganize the Defense Agency. But this initiative also failed, as the uproar over the Security Treaty in 1960 made defense policy nearly untouchable. His successor, Ikeda Hayato, a mainstream Yoshida pragmatist, made sure that the issue did not return to the Diet.

The Consensus

Like the 1930s, the 1950s was a period of strange bedfellows. Former Shidehara allies, like Yoshida, tilted away from Big Japan liberalism, for example, but the iconic Small Japanist, Ishibashi Tanzan, became an ally of Hatoyama and Kishi and supported rearmament and defense-led industrialization.[103] Of greater importance was the way in which the revisionists and the pragmatists vied to find common cause with the pacifists. The former, mostly great power nationalists, found common ground in nationalism with the pacifists. Together they trumpeted U.S. base issues as matters of national sovereignty, which they agreed had never really been returned to Japan.[104] The continued presence of U.S. forces in Japan and, in particular, their extraterritorial privilege was an affront to Japanese prestige and a constraint on Japanese autonomy. Each also expressed concern that the U.S. presence invited entanglement and that Japan could become a "battlefield." Both the pacifists and the revisionists demanded an "independent diplomacy" (*jishu gaikō*).[105] Yoshida and his pragmatic allies, though, trumped their intraparty rivals, by giving the pacifist Left something they valued

[34]

even more—constitutional guarantees that Japan would not again become a great military power. The more that Hatoyama, Kishi, Shigemitsu, and their colleagues demanded an autonomous military (*jieigun*) and an "autonomous defense" (*jishu bōei*), the closer the pacifists were drawn to Yoshida's moderation.

Indeed, Yoshida steered Japan brilliantly between Article 9 and the U.S. alliance, "squeezing it between" (*hasamiuchi*) pacifism and traditional nationalism.[106] He kept constitutional revision off the agenda and the Socialists out of power. After he left the scene, and the revisionists mishandled the tumultuous Security Treaty Revision Crisis (*Ampo tōsō*) in 1960, his pragmatic mainstream returned and prospered by crafting "comprehensive security" as Japan's central doctrine. Yoshida's mainstream successors expelled the ultranationalists, pacified the revisionists, and watched as the pacifists revised their own position.[107] The Left learned to live with the alliance and the Right with Article 9. Security policy would now aim to enhance autonomy but would center on trade and international cooperation. A new consensus would be achieved around a Japan that would be a "non-nuclear, lightly armed, economic superpower."[108]

One measure of the strength of the new consensus was the acceptance of its central tenets by leading revisionists such as Nakasone Yasuhiro. Nakasone had first come to public attention as a brash young politician waving the outlawed rising sun flag during the Occupation and calling for the removal of U.S. bases. Nakasone had been an early champion of autonomous defense, a cause with which he was associated throughout his career. In 1971, after becoming director general of the Japan Defense Agency, Nakasone issued a long-term defense plan (*Nakasone kōsō*) based on "five principles of autonomous defense." But as he drew closer to power, his principles expanded to include such moderate (and nonrevisionist) positions as opposition to nuclear weapons, civilian control of the military, and unqualified support for the alliance. Indeed, by the time he became prime minister in 1982, Nakasone's call for "autonomous defense" was premised above all else on a tighter coupling with the United States, a position that not a few Japanese commentators have called "discrepant" (*sōi*).[109] The realist Nakasone, like many revisionists, had migrated to a widened center. The autonomy he advocated would not pull Japan away from the United States but would render Japan, in his terms, a "conventional nation" (*zairaigata kokka*)—a full generation before the term was popularized as "normal nation" (*futsū no kuni*) by Ozawa Ichirō. Across the aisle, but in parallel, the Socialists agreed to share power with Ozawa's clique in 1994, renouncing four decades of insistence on the unconstitutionality of the Self-Defense Forces and opposition to the Japan-U.S. alliance.

Kosaka Masataka was the first to pronounce the success of the Yoshida Doctrine (*Yoshida ronsō*) in 1963.[110] The label is less important than the fact that its core ideas came to be embraced across the board as Japan's consensus view of its national security identity. The Yoshida mainstream opportunistically embraced the pacifist Left in order to keep the antimainstream at bay, and the antimainstream eventually came around to accept the central tenets of the doctrine. By the 1960s, "pro-Americanism, Asianism, anti-communism, and commercialism coexisted in happy harmony" for both groups of conservatives.[111] Acceptance of the idea that a trading state had to maintain a minimum level of power to protect its commercial interests was not far behind. Japan would have a defense capability, but it would be a "peace nation" (*heiwa kokka*). It would not threaten its neighbors, and its role in the U.S. alliance would remain sharply circumscribed. It would pursue economic cooperation in the region and become what Kishi Nobusuke, the iconic revisionist, called "top dog in Asia" (*Ajia meishu*).[112] The alliance was the dominant fact of Japanese strategic life, and the "top dog" would be on a U.S. leash, but Japan would use its support of U.S. foreign policy to pick up an increasing portion of the world economy.

Like the successful doctrine of the Meiji oligarchs and the unsuccessful doctrine of Konoye, the Yoshida consensus was built on a profoundly realist understanding of international affairs made operable by the consolidation of domestic power. Strategists saw that the cold war made Japan as important to the United States as the United States was to Japan, and that the nominally weak partner could also become rich and strong. The Yoshida Doctrine borrowed considerably from the past. Its mercantile realism was focused on generating wealth and technological independence per the "rich nation, strong army" doctrine, but it eschewed the military component. It would safeguard Japan through commerce, and it would be as hard-nosed in defense of Japan's commercial interests as Shidehara had been in Peking in 1925—but without the imperialist trappings.[113] Like the *Tōyō Keizai* editorialists in 1915 who saw no profit in Japanese possession of China, the Yoshida mainstream understood that aggression would stimulate balancing behavior and would close markets. They saw clearly the benefits of cheap riding.[114] But the Yoshida mainstream not only connected back to the liberal internationalists, they also echoed one of Japan's most distinguished naval strategists. Katō Tomosaburō, the navy minister who agreed to the Washington Naval Treaty restrictions, had foreseen their "comprehensive security" with remarkable clarity: "No matter how well prepared we may be militarily, this will be of little use unless we develop our civilian industrial power, promote our trade, and develop our natural resources fully."[115]

Their vision of the world was clear-eyed, but their main challenge was domestic. Yoshida and his successors balanced the nationalisms of the Left and of the Right by invoking their most valued issues—the alliance and the constitution—opportunistically. The revisionists, demilitarized heirs of Konoye, were kept at bay, while the pacifists had their say but never shared power.[116] Once they consolidated power, pragmatic Japanese strategists enjoyed a long period of success. For the first sixty years of the postwar period, Japan kept a low international profile. Japan was a "middle power" that could have its cake and eat it too.

Japan came to great power diplomacy through the merchants' entrance, but the Yoshida Doctrine was not built for the post–cold war world. It provided some prestige but little autonomy, and this imbalance began to drive a new debate over Japan's national raison d'être. At first this debate replayed the old rivalry between revisionism and pacifism. But they were soon overtaken by new positions, as realists split from neoconservatives and the Small Japanists seemed to have lost their way altogether. A new generation was emerging that turned Admiral Katō's admonition on its head: no matter how rich Japan becomes, they argued, it will have no influence or prestige without independent military power. The mainstream and antimainstream traded places, and by the early 2000s the revisionists had a full grip on power, and both the pragmatists and the pacifists were marginalized. If a new consensus had not yet taken shape, a new discourse certainly had. The Yoshida consensus seemed to be changing. After first exploring the institutions of the Yoshida consensus, I will examine its transformation and then examine the new security policy discourse. Japan, I believe, is headed toward a new consensus that will give the nation the autonomy and muscularity that have been missing for so long.

[2]

Baking the Pacifist Loaf

Japanese security policy has traveled a consistent path since the nineteenth century. Periods of extensive debate have been followed by periods of broad consensus, but only when a coherent grand strategy dovetailed with effective political management. Alone, neither brilliant strategy nor effective political control was ever sufficient to support a broad national strategic consensus. Unexpected shifts in world order have been critical for change, but creative leadership was always required to institutionalize those changes. The Meiji Consensus was enabled when oligarchic power holders deployed a brilliant developmental strategy. The Konoye consensus marked the triumph of authoritarian politics combined with a coherent imperial strategy. Yoshida Shigeru operated under enormous constraints, yet he skilfully guided Japan toward scaled-back ideas about its military posture and scaled-up ideas about its economic potential. Each debate and every consensus centered on how to maximize wealth and strength in order to enhance the nation's core values of autonomy and prestige.

The Yoshida Doctrine required the efforts of two generations of mainstream conservative politicians with political skill as well as a viable strategic model before it could become Japan's national security doctrine. At home, it required the management of nationalists on both the Right and the Left. The former—fellow conservatives—were embraced within the same ruling party, and the latter—the leftist opposition—received periodic guarantees that Article 9 would be preserved. Both were kept at arm's length from Yoshida and his successors as they deepened their alliance with bureaucrats and a downsized Japan. A recently imperial power was now restyled as a small island trading nation; militarism was eschewed in favor of mercantilism. It helped enormously that these strategists could invoke the spirit of Article 9, both to deflect U.S. demands and to mobilize popular support. By layering pacifist interpretations of the constitution with self-imposed constraints on the expansion of the military, they made pacifist ideals central to the institutional base of Japanese security policy. The baking of this "pacifist loaf" and the institutions that the process engendered are the subjects of this chapter. I begin with the single greatest constraint on both foreign policy and domestic politics during the cold war: the U.S.-Japan alliance.

The Alliance and Its Discontents

For the United States, the alliance with Japan was always an instrument of "dual containment." U.S. planners designed an unequal treaty because they had three concerns about Japan. The first was that it might remilitarize after the Occupation and launch a revanchist attack. The second was that it might remain unstable and require excessive U.S. attention. The third was that it might make a separate peace with the Communist powers and give them access to its considerable industrial potential. Timothy Temerson makes U.S. ambitions quite clear: "In entering into a security alliance with Japan in September 1951, the United States sought both to defend against Soviet/communist aggression and to control the future course of Japanese rearmament, foreign policy, and domestic politics."[1] The challenge for U.S. policy was to make Japan rich and stable and peaceable. As George Kennan wrote in October 1948, the Occupation needed to "make it seem profitable to the Japanese to behave themselves," and by the spring of 1949 the U.S. State Department was actively engaged in plans for an entangling alliance.[2] Shiraishi Takashi best characterizes the strategy: "to place a light hand on Japan's carotid artery, which, if the need arose, could increase its pressure and cause Japan to faint."[3]

Prime Minister Yoshida, operating from a position of weakness (much like Konrad Adenauer in West Germany), understood that the United States did not trust Japan. He encouraged the United States to keep its bases in Japan as a way to accelerate the return of sovereignty, and even granted U.S. forces considerable extraterritorial privilege to sweeten the deal.[4] Iokibe Makoto gets right to the heart of the arrangement by calling it "a swap of material for manpower" in which "Japan acquires security while the U.S. acquires control."[5] Actually, Japan acquired a great deal more, not the least of which was nearly unlimited access to U.S. markets and technology— precisely what Yoshida's mercantilist grand strategy focused on. This was far from a boilerplate contract between partners preparing for war. From the beginning, its asymmetric reciprocity involved a complex exchange of goods, services, and guarantees. In the U.S-Japan alliance, the United States could control the pace and character of Japanese rearmament. At least it could try. When the United States wanted more from Japan, Japan could resist with impunity. As one senior LDP politician has suggested, Japan used Article 9 as a "hedge" against U.S. pressure.[6] Reflecting on the deal in his memoirs, Yoshida stops short of declaring his strategy a victory of weakness over strength, but he does allow that "those who believe the U.S.-Japan Security Treaty is designed for war-fighting are mistaken."[7]

Indeed, Yoshida's position was not all that weak. Certainly his vision was not at all clouded. Yoshida bet correctly that Japan would be of signal geostrategic importance to the United States. If the United States commanded the air and sea around Japan, Japan would not need to maintain a large standing force. Tokyo could get by—safely and cheaply—by minimally satisfying Washington.[8] He was right, but only *just*. First, of course, the United States had to decide that this was what it wanted. In retrospect it was a remarkably close call. In 1948 State Department Policy Planning Director George Kennan held that the United States and the Soviet Union should reach an agreement about spheres of influence in Northeast Asia. He believed that with such an agreement, and the stabilization of "internal conditions" in Japan, U.S. troops could return home. He was more concerned about popular dissatisfaction with the U.S. presence than with any advantages the USSR might gain from U.S. withdrawal.[9] Kennan lost this fight when, in June 1949, the U.S. National Security Council concluded that the United States could not risk losing a productive Japan to Soviet domination. U.S. policy would require Japan as the geostrategic key to an America-friendly Asia, in which northern Pacific trade routes and transit through the East China, South China, and Japan seas would all be preserved.[10] Japan need not do more than use hand-me-down weapons (*osagari heiki*) to maintain domestic tranquillity and allow the United States use of the archipelago as an "unsinkable aircraft carrier."[11] The greater danger for Yoshida and his disciples was entanglement rather than abandonment, for Japan was more likely to become a "proxy target" of a common enemy than a U.S. orphan, so they assiduously deflected all U.S. overtures to create a collective security regime in Asia. Nor would they allow the formation of expeditionary forces within the SDF.[12]

Achieving this balance was no small accomplishment. Yoshida and his allies needed to box out fellow conservatives and industrialists who wished to rebuild the Japanese military; they had to repress escalating U.S. demands for Japanese contributions to the common defense; and they had to quiet leftists who disapproved of the alliance to begin with. Making the cheap ride a fundamental aspect of Japan's grand strategy was just the ticket. By the early 1950s, the United States was already conspiring with former imperial officers to reconstitute a 350,000-man army, a 4.6 million-ton navy, and a 7,000-airplane air force—a plan Yoshida rejected.[13] At home, the industrialists were placated by the idea that cheap riding would free up other forms of wealth generation, and the Left was disarmed by the conservatives' embrace of Article 9. They came to appreciate Yoshida's wisdom: a Japan that could not project force abroad would make a more attractive trading partner. The best the United States could get was a promise that "Japan will increasingly assume responsibility for its own defense."[14] Talk, too, was cheap.

No one now disputes that Japan enjoyed a cheap ride or that this was a matter of grand strategy. Although the absolute level of Japanese defense spending is far from insignificant, and Japan's host-nation support is the highest of any U.S. ally, Japanese defense spending was never terribly high as a percentage of national economic activity. Indeed, it plummeted from a postwar high of 1.78 percent of GDP in 1955 to less than 1 percent of GDP by 1967, where it was frozen by cabinet order.[15] Even as U.S. military assistance to Japan was cut sharply in the late 1950s, the Japan Defense Agency (JDA) was not bulked up. Its share of Japan's general account budget, as high as 13 percent in 1953, fell below 10 percent in 1960, below 8 percent in 1966, and below 7 percent in 1972. It stabilized at about 6 percent in 1977, where it remained through 2007, by which time the JDA was elevated to ministry status (Ministry of Defense, MOD).[16] The U.S. Defense Department appreciates Japan's high level of support but insists that Japan has done less than other U.S. allies. In a rare public criticism, its 1998 "Report on Allied Contributions to the Common Defense" argued that

> Japan's share of contributions [to the common defense] remains substantially below its share of ability to contribute....[In view of] the complex legacy of WWII, [Japan's] responsibility sharing has focused more on assuming a substantial share of U.S. stationing costs and less on other aspects, such as active participation in shared regional and global military roles and missions.[17]

If the U.S. military were to leave Japan—and Okinawa in particular—the SDF, and the military budget, would have to be enlarged.[18] During the cold war, as former JDA director general Ishiba Shigeru explains, Japan recognized that it would be in Washington's interest to protect Japan, so Tokyo simply "lay down on the job" and left its security policy to the United States.[19]

It is important to recognize that "laying down on the job" was part of the U.S. calculus as well and that the cheap ride was not free. Washington was as determined that Japan's military power should develop within the context of the bilateral relationship as Tokyo was determined that its military should be limited. As a result, the greatest costs of the alliance came in the form of reduced national autonomy, one measure of which was the uneven distribution of the costs of Japan's give-and-take arrangement with the United States. Some localities, such as Okinawa and Kanagawa, have done most of the giving—in the form of environmental degradation

UNIVERSITY OF SHEFFIELD LIBRARY

and increased crime—while the nation as a whole has derived most of the benefit, in the form of national security.[20] Because the alliance has never been tested in war, those who provide the bases have not always appreciated the risks taken by those who provide the troops; and because the LDP has successfully bought off the opposition, those who provide the troops have not always appreciated the costs borne by those who provide the bases.[21] Even though U.S. forces in Japan dropped sharply from 260,000 in 1952 to 46,000 in 1960 (excluding Okinawa, which was not part of Japan at the time), national sovereignty was never returned to everyone's satisfaction. Indeed, as Shiraishi Takashi suggests, a basic premise of the U.S.-Japan alliance was that Japan would be a "semisovereign nation (*hanshuken kokka*)."[22] Japan was—and remained—tethered to a U.S. leash.

Thus, it was ironic, but not surprising, that both the Left and the Right at first found themselves opposing not each other but Yoshida and his grand strategy. The Left—both the Japan Communist Party (JCP) and the Japan Socialist Party (JSP)—took every opportunity to criticize the "unequal treaty" that Yoshida and Dulles had wrought.[23] The JCP magazine, *Zenei* (Vanguard), declared: "We 80 million Japanese do not want to become slaves of a foreign country....Our national pride has been completely trampled upon."[24] The Right, for its part, never forgot that the alliance was crafted during an occupation that never really ended. Kishi Nobusuke, Yoshida's nemesis within the conservative camp, declared in 1954 that independent nations do not allow foreign troops to be based on their soil.[25] Another antimainstream conservative and future prime minister who would become a close friend of the United States, Nakasone Yasuhiro, was equally determined to reduce the footprint of U.S. forces in Japan.[26] They and other antimainstream allies insisted on planning for the day when U.S. forces would withdraw. Their Japan would pursue an autonomous defense program with a large military, and (sotto voce) it would pursue an "independent diplomacy" (*jishu gaikō*).[27] Because they, and not Yoshida, controlled the formation of the LDP in 1955, the original platform of the party actually stated:

> In order to protect the liberty of our citizens, the independence of our nation and the peace of the world, we will ready—under a collective security system—a self-defense military capability commensurate with our national power and conditions that will prepare the country for the withdrawal of foreign forces stationed here.[28]

It is a matter of no small historical interest that the United States won over these conservatives, and that it did so while the Yoshida Doctrine was being institutionalized.[29]

Winning over the antimainstream conservatives required U.S. promises of greater autonomy, reduced base presence, and more.[30] In 1960, at

Kishi's urging, the United States agreed to renegotiate the Security Treaty and eliminated some inequities, including American rights to intervene in domestic unrest. But the United States wanted to have it both ways. Throughout the 1950s and 1960s it pressed Japan to do more, encouraging the SDF and its political allies to believe that a full partnership might be in the offing; concerned that Japan might abandon the alliance, however, it never delivered. In 1960, the U.S. National Security Council spoke of the need to treat Japan as a "full and major ally."[31] Only then could it "develop and maintain armed forces capable of assuming increasing responsibility for the defense of the Japan area and, thereby, together with U.S. forces, of coping with and deterring communist aggression."[32] But, when the U.S. Defense Department and the Joint Chiefs of Staff called the State Department's bluff and demanded a more expansive Japanese military, U.S. policy was limited "to assur[ing] that Japan continues to exercise its international role in concert with free world interests." The United States would "not stimulate an active [Japanese] military."[33] The Defense Agency received only a fraction of the $50 million a year in U.S. military assistance it had budgeted for its second build-up plan (1961–64).[34] In 1963, Nakayama Sadao, chief of naval operations for the Maritime Self-Defense Force (MSDF), spoke plaintively of his frustrations: "We will stand shoulder to shoulder with the United States, but it won't work if we get pistols and they get rifles."[35]

By this time, though, Kishi's antimainstream conservatives had broken their swords on the revision of the Treaty of Mutual Cooperation and Security between the United States and Japan (Mutual Security Treaty). Now, and for most of the next three decades, the Japanese government would be firmly under the control of Yoshida's successors, mercantile realists who were determined not to increase defense spending and to resist any larger regional role. These pragmatic moderates—members of the Kōchikai led by Ikeda Hayato and of the Keiseikai led by Satō Eisaku (and, later, Tanaka Kakuei, the only leading Yoshida disciple who was not a former bureaucrat)—would have great success mollifying Left and Right and establishing a broad national consensus on security doctrine.[36] In 1966–67, when President Lyndon Johnson lobbied Japan to increase its contribution to the common defense, Prime Minister Satō uttered the phrase "autonomous defense" to placate the Right, but agreed only that Japan would increase economic assistance as its contribution to regional stability. He committed Japan to join the United States in defense of Taiwan and Korea, but only to get Okinawa returned to Japanese sovereignty.[37] And in his most publicized act—one aimed at the Left and for which he would later win the Nobel Peace Prize—Prime Minister Satō declared "three nonnuclear principles." Japan henceforth would not produce, possess, or permit the introduction of nuclear weapons.[38]

Satō had tied Okinawa reversion to pacifism, even if superficially, and had tied both to autonomy.[39] Now even some leading revisionists were coming around to embrace the Yoshida logic. When the United States increased pressure on Japan in the 1970s, it was met with the promise by Prime Minister Fukuda Takeo (a disciple of Kishi) that Japan would not seek a military role in Asia and would contribute to regional security by economic and diplomatic means only.[40] Until 1983, when Nakasone declared "the security of the West is indivisible" at the Williamsburg summit, Japanese prime ministers came to summit meetings of the G-5 (which also included France, West Germany, the United States, and the United Kingdom) unprepared to contribute to the conversation on global security. Increasingly, Japan's Self-Defense Forces were seen as little more than a national guard, an adjunct to a real military that wore the Stars and Stripes.[41] Even this was a stretch, given that there were no formal exchanges on joint military operations until the 1980s and no formal alliance guidelines until a decade later.[42] Indeed, in the mid-1970s Japanese and U.S. uniformed officers began consultations on joint planning for the defense of Japan, but they did so without the full knowledge of Japan's political leadership. Only after JDA director general Sakata Michita learned about it were steps taken to create the Japan-U.S. Consultative Committee, from which formal guidelines eventually were issued.[43] As one U.S. defense planner has wryly observed: "During the Cold War, there was no clear certainty, or even reasonable assurance, that the United States could employ bases in Japan in a direct conflict with the Soviet Union."[44] But no one was fooled: this was less an alliance of cooperative security and more one of dependent security.

After all, U.S. control of Japanese defense policy—from the Japanese perspective, dependence on the United States for national security—was exactly what leaders of both countries had originally bargained for. For Washington, this control was more valuable than any Japanese military contribution. Indeed, the leash would come in handy in unforeseen ways. During their opening to China in the early 1970s, diplomacy that "reset the world's diplomatic and economic chessboard," Henry Kissinger and Richard Nixon each reassured Chou En-Lai and Mao Tse-Tung that the United States would not allow Japan to become a "runaway horse."[45] In June 1984, Assistant Secretary of Defense Richard Armitage explained to Congress that the United States remained cognizant of the fact that Japan's neighbors "do not... want to see Japan play a major military role in the region."[46] So, the leash would remain attached despite U.S. exhortations that Japan do more strategically, and those who called attention to it would be ushered out the door.[47] For Tokyo, this dependence was also very handy. Although Yoshida had used the term "alliance" (*dōmei*) in 1963 to describe the U.S.-Japan relationship, that term was openly rejected by the early 1980s by Prime Minister Suzuki Zenkō.[48] Yoshida's successors preferred to sustain the cheap ride, avoid getting entangled in U.S. wars, and generate unprecedented wealth. Japan would not abandon the United States, the United States would not abandon Japan, and mainstream conservatives would enjoy nearly four decades of uninterrupted power. They would use this power to institutionalize a national security strategy filled with self-imposed restraints on the military. They would bake a hearty "pacifist loaf," one that even antimainstream competitors and pacifist opponents would find savory.

TYING ONE'S HANDS

The primary formal restraint on Japanese remilitarization has always been Article 9 of the "U.S.-imposed" constitution, the text of which was modeled on the ill-conceived Pact of Paris (Kellogg-Briand Pact) of 1928. It seems straightforward:

> Aspiring sincerely to an international peace based on justice and order, the Japanese people forever renounce war as a sovereign right of the nation and the threat or use of force as a means of settling international disputes.
>
> In order to accomplish the aim of the preceding paragraph, land, sea and air forces, as well as other war potential, will never be maintained. The right of belligerency of the state will not be recognized.[49]

But like the Bill of Rights of the U.S. Constitution, these two paragraphs have been at the center of Japan's most hotly contested legal disputes. As in the American case, disagreement begins with differences about original intent. Was Article 9 designed to eliminate the military itself, or was it aimed only at preventing aggression? Aggressive war and the armaments for that purpose were renounced, but did Japan retain the right to possess and exercise force necessary to preserve its sovereign existence? If so, "war potential" could be maintained for both self-defense and collective self-defense. The article's presumed author, Shidehara Kijūrō, the prewar liberal internationalist who returned after the Pacific War to assist the U.S. Occupation, argued that Article 9 mandated a doctrine of *nonviolence*. Participation in *any* war, aggressive or defensive, and the maintenance of any type of military capabilities were prohibited. Japan would have to entrust its security to international society.[50]

Of course, that is not how the conservative Japanese government or its U.S. alliance partner came to see things, especially after 1954 when the Self-Defense Forces were established. But were the Self-Defense Forces even constitutional? Japanese courts have the explicit right of judicial review, but they often avoid the issue.[51] A supreme court opinion issued in 1973 was exceptionally clear as to why:

> Whether or not the SDF corresponds to the so-called "war potential" prohibited by Article IX of the Constitution is not a matter to be examined by

the judicial branch.... [The judiciary] does not bear political responsibility to the people... [and] these are not matters into which the Court should inquire.[52]

As a result, the interpretation of Article 9 has been driven by executive action. During the long years of mainstream LDP dominance, the de facto power to interpret Article 9 lay in the hands of cabinet politicians who delegated much of the interpretive work to bureaucrats in the Cabinet Legislation Bureau (CLB). The baseline was their 1952 definition of "war potential" (*senryoku*). Prime Minister Yoshida ordered the CLB to craft an interpretation that would allow some military capabilities and the use of such capabilities to repel direct attack. The "use of force" banned in the second paragraph was related only to the purposes of the first paragraph, which did not explicitly proscribe self-defense. In its first formal interpretation, the CLB declared:

> [War potential (*senryoku*)] refers to a force with the equipment and organiza-
> tion capable of conducting modern warfare.... Determining what constitutes
> war potential requires a concrete judgment taking into account the temporal
> and spatial environment of the country in question.... It is neither unconsti-
> tutional to maintain capabilities that fall short of war potential nor to utilize
> these capabilities to defend the nation from direct invasion.[53]

War potential was definable only in relation to other states' capabilities and international conditions. It was, in effect, a sliding scale.

Since one person's sliding scale is another's slippery slope, it was no surprise that this "modern warfare" standard provoked continuing disagreement. Even the legality of defending itself was a major shift in that, in June 1946, Prime Minister Yoshida had declared in the Diet that Japan had effectively (if not formally) renounced even self-defense. After all, he declared, "the Manchurian and Greater East Asian wars were justified as 'self-defense.' The suspicion harbored toward our country is that Japan is fond of war, and that it will rearm and threaten world peace."[54] This line was useful in 1950, after the outbreak of the Korean War, when Yoshida's government created the heavily armed 75,000–man National Police Reserves (NPR) and denied that it would be responsible for external security. Article 9 could also function as Yoshida's shield to protect against U.S. demands for rearmament and as a wedge to split domestic opponents. For a time, as the cold war progressed and as U.S. demands intensified, Yoshida took full advantage of his new flexibility. By 1954, though, categorical denial of Japan's right to self-defense had run its course. Yoshida now had to work with CLB bureaucrats to utilize the ambiguities of "modern warfare" to establish the SDF. The constitution need not be revised.

Yoshida's immediate successors, all revisionists between 1955 and 1960, established an even more flexible interpretation. Now the "war potential"

[46]

forbidden by Article 9 was any military capability in excess of the "minimum necessary level" required to protect Japan from direct attacks. The new interpretation specified the conditions under which Japan could exercise self-defense: when it is facing an imminent and illegitimate act of aggression; when there is no other means of countering this act; and when the use of force in self-defense is limited to the minimum necessary level (*jiei no tame ni hitsuyō na jitsuryoku*). Although self-defense was narrowly understood as defense of national territory, it allowed for the preemptive use of force and even for the possession of a nuclear deterrent.[55] In the spring of 1957 Prime Minister Kishi testified in the Diet that Japan had no intention of acquiring nuclear weapons but that it would not be unconstitutional if it did so.

The definition of "minimum necessary force" has never been settled. Political disputes over "necessary limits" (*hitsuyō na gendo*) gave way to arguments over the "necessary proper sphere" (*hitsuyō sōtō na hani*) and then "necessary minimum limit" (*hitsuyō saishō gendo*). Hairs have been split over whether "armed force" (*buryoku*) is different from the "war potential" (*senryoku*) that is clearly banned. Japan can defend itself, but by what means? At first, jet fighters were excluded; later, they were accepted, but not with aerial refueling capabilities. Then, aerial refueling was judged acceptable. Japan insists that it cannot maintain aircraft carriers, but it is acquiring assault ships with hardened decks that can accommodate helicopters and, presumably, VTOL (vertical takeoff and landing) jets. It banned the military use of space, but the MOD maintains a surveillance satellite system for intelligence gathering, and the LDP plans more.[56] Kishi's insistence in 1957 that "there are many varieties of nuclear arms" has been reaffirmed repeatedly, despite the 1967 adoption of Japan's "three nonnuclear principles."[57] And now we know that in 1969 a Ministry of Foreign Affairs (MOFA) report suggested that Japan "should take care to always maintain the economic and technological potential to manufacture a nuclear device, and not be restrained by others."[58]

Still, the Japanese government did strive to adopt a less threatening formal posture even if it did not constrain its security planners. In 1968, the CLB reaffirmed that the SDF can act only "when there is a sudden unprovoked attack on Japan and there are no other means available to protect the lives and safety of the people."[59] Thus was born one of the central tenets of the Yoshida Doctrine, the concept of "defensive defense," which prohibits armed attack as a means of self-defense.[60] Defensive defense—often compared to the way porcupines (nonaggressive but well-armed beasts) defend themselves—has served at least three functions. The first two are obvious: it has been used to reassure Japanese citizens that its government would not embark on foreign adventures and its neighbors that Japan no longer posed a military threat. But it also has provided the defense industry and its allies with a critically important guideline for the acquisition of military systems: so long as it can be construed as defensive, it is in play.

[47]

A tougher problem has resulted from the CLB's 1954 interpretation that collective self-defense is unconstitutional. Japanese officials take pains to distinguish "collective self-defense" (*shūdanteki jiei*) and "collective security" (*shūdanteki anzenhoshō*). The distinction rests on two points: whether the use of force is involved and whether the mission involves the security of an ally (and thus, indirectly, the defense of Japan) or the security of countries without alliances with Japan. Collective self-defense is narrowly defined as the *use of force* to defend an *ally* that has come under attack. The focus here is on bilateral military cooperation, which is banned under the extant interpretation of Article 9. Collective security, by contrast, refers to cooperation with international organizations and other countries to enhance the security of nonallied countries that may or may not involve the use of force. Taken from the United Nations Charter, this concept refers to multilateral cooperation that may include diplomatic, economic, and military action. The government interpretation of Article 9 allows Japan to engage in the diplomatic and economic aspects of collective security but forbids the use of force even in this multilateral situation. At present, Japan could not participate in a UN army (if one were formed) that required the use of force to accomplish its mission.[61]

But there have been many inconsistencies—and much backtracking. In 1951, the vice-minister of foreign affairs told Occupation authorities that Japan could support U.S. troops if they were attacked on Okinawa, which was then not even Japanese territory. But after the 1954 interpretation and until the 1980s, the government interpreted the ban so narrowly that the SDF would not have been allowed to assist a U.S. warship that came under attack while defending Japan. In May 1981, the CLB issued a formal (albeit tortured) interpretation recognizing that Japan has the right of collective self-defense under international law but is forbidden to exercise it under Article 9:

> It is recognized under international law that a state has the right of collective self-defense, which is the right to use actual force to stop an armed attack on a foreign country with which it has close relations, even when the state itself is not under direct attack. It is therefore self-evident that since it is a sovereign state, Japan has the right of collective self-defense under international law. The Japanese government nevertheless takes the view that the exercise of the right of self-defense as authorized under Article Nine of the Constitution is confined to the minimum necessary level for the defense of the country. The government believes that the exercise of the right of collective self-defense exceeds that limit and is not, therefore, permissible under the Constitution.[62]

After 1954, Japan had a military that could acquire every variety of sophisticated weapons, but it assiduously avoided treating it as one. So long as conflicts were "fires on the opposite bank" that Japan would not have to extinguish, the Yoshida Doctrine went a long way toward what Sam Jameson has aptly described as a "draft exemption" for Japan.[63] Political leaders and bureaucrats engineered a military vehicle loaded with options, but the brakes (*hadome*) were more handy than the accelerator.

Yamagata's Ghost

The ghost of Yamagata Aritomo has cast a long shadow over postwar Japan. One of the legacies of World War II was the culpability of Japan's generals for the domestic repression, foreign aggression, and resulting national disaster that so disfigured Japan.[64] Whether this led to "a ubiquitous pacifist culture," the dominance of an "antimilitarist ethos," or to a "military allergy" is much disputed, but clearly the balance of public opinion valued protection *from* overprotection *by* their military.[65] After 1954 Japan had a military, but, as its name suggests, the SDF was not yet accepted as a legitimate instrument of state power. Conservative analysts, such as Okazaki Hisahiko, wondered aloud: "Will the Japanese defend their democracy and freedom?"[66] But attack by hostile powers was the last thing on the public's mind, and Japanese politicians had to be sensitive to public demands for guarantees. How would civilian control of the military be achieved? Who would guarantee there would be no relapse? One way would be to restrain defense and security policy through rigorous legal barriers.[67] But, as we have seen, the courts wanted no part of the matter. Another would be to involve politicians and bureaucrats, a formidable executive team so long as the Yoshida mainstream was in power. Their alliance, a distinctive integration of party government and professional civil service, established and legitimated the institutions of Japanese national security without alienating the pacifist Left.[68] Two bureaucratic institutions were fortified by this alliance, especially after the Security Treaty Revision Crisis of 1960, when many of the politicians ran for cover.

The first was the Cabinet Legislation Bureau, the bureaucratic organ closest to Japan's elected political leadership.[69] The fingerprints of its talented career officials are found everywhere in Japanese governance, not least on defense policy. Theirs has been a disproportionate, if not always decisive, voice in interpreting Article 9 and in establishing the constitutionality of and limitations on the SDF. For more than four decades the CLB has been deeply involved in the interpretation of collective defense: whether visits by cabinet ministers to the Yasukuni Shrine (where fallen soldiers—and convicted war criminals—are enshrined) violate the constitution; whether Japanese troops can be sent abroad; what constitutes the use of force, inter alia. There is no major security policy issue on which the CLB has not ruled.

[49]

Some analysts refer to the CLB as the prime minister's "in-house lawyer" and as a "check" on Diet legislation. Others, like Nishihara Masashi, the former president of Japan's National Defense Academy, worry that the CLB has been used by politicians to (over)compensate for prewar excesses of the military:

> Postwar political leaders, both in and out of power, strongly concerned about the lack of civilian control over prewar and wartime military decisions, have made extra efforts to bind defense and security issues through rigorous legalistic approaches.[70]

Either way, no administrative agency of the Japanese state has enjoyed higher prestige or greater independence than the CLB.[71] Although the CLB is formally an advisory organ within the prime minister's secretariat and its director general does not vote in cabinet meetings, he is always included on the list (and in the group photograph) when a new cabinet is formed.[72] Indeed, the CLB director general is the highest paid bureaucrat in the Japanese government.[73] The considerable authority of its forerunner, the wartime Legislation Bureau (LB), led the Supreme Commander of the Allied Powers (SCAP) to abolish it and purge eleven of its top officials. But Prime Minister Yoshida reestablished the bureau immediately after Japanese sovereignty was restored in 1952.[74] Over time the renamed CLB acquired formal supervisory responsibilities over other ministries and agencies. It is, as Nishikawa has described it, "a government agency within a government agency."[75]

Perhaps its distinguishing characteristic is that there is no such thing as a career (*puropaa*) CLB official. Unlike every other administrative unit in the Japanese government, the CLB has no entrance exam and no "incoming class" of college graduates. Instead, each of its two dozen senior officials arrives on the job as a tested legal specialist with some fifteen to twenty years of experience in the line ministry or agency from which he is seconded. All ministries are eager to be represented within the CLB, but some of the sending ministries are better represented than others, and some are not represented at all. Only the Ministry of Finance and the Ministry of Justice have been guaranteed three slots each in the CLB. Others—the foreign ministry; health and welfare; agriculture, trade and industry; and local affairs—have routinely received two each. The CLB director general, who has nine times been a graduate of the Faculty of Law of Tokyo University, and three times a graduate of its counterpart at Kyoto University, has always come from one of these ministries.[76] Significantly, no official from the Ministry of Defense has ever been assigned to the CLB. Since the term of secondment is a minimum of five years, few of these elite officials return to their original ministry. They often serve two or more terms and then cycle out into lucrative and powerful second careers. In this way, the CLB acts as a sort of *amakudari* way station for elite bureaucrats.[77] Several retired directors general have become presidents of public corporations. Others have chaired large nonprofit organizations, and—to underscore the status of the CLB—three others have been named to the supreme court bench.

The CLB occupies a special place in Japanese civil-military relations. It is the higher of *two* levels of bureaucratic supervision of the uniformed officers, and it is perceived to be more powerful than the ministries that formally colonize the defense bureaucracy and seen by many as more powerful than the politicians who formally monitor it. By reviewing all proposed policy and issuing "unified government interpretations" (*tōitsu kenkai*), the CLB effectively insulates bureaucrats, lawmakers, and jurists alike (*keni o urazukeru mono*). Thus, the CLB's approval is solicited by officials on all matters—from regulations to legislation to speeches. This requires extensive interagency coordination. Government officials confess that they are many times more anxious visiting the CLB to defend draft legislation than they are visiting the Ministry of Finance to defend budget requests.[78] But a CLB interpretation comes in handy when officials are confronted with demands for change: it enables them to dismiss competing policy ideas as "unacceptable to the CLB."[79]

It is easy to appreciate, then, how deference to the CLB's "unified government interpretation" would be used by mainstream politicians to deflect pressures from the United States and from antimainstream competitors. Because prior interpretations are enshrined as—and legitimated by—precedent, effectively they *are* Japanese law and can become a powerful brake on policy change. In fact, between 1947 and 2001, only five acts of government have been declared unconstitutional, and *four* of them had not been reviewed by the CLB because they had been submitted as individual Diet members' bills (*giin rippō*) rather than by ministries as government bills.[80] One former director general defended the idea that the CLB should stand before—and perhaps even above—the courts:

> We often have heard such criticisms as: "Wouldn't it be desirable to leave constitutional issues to the supreme court?" ... But we have to make certain there is no violation of the constitution each time the cabinet implements policy or exercises authority. ... If everything were left for the supreme court to adjudicate after the fact, there would be a great deal of confusion. It is absolutely necessary to eliminate as many problems as possible in advance.[81]

Another put it even more bluntly: "Should we prevent chaos beforehand, or should we settle problems in courts after the chaos arises? The former is lower in social costs."[82]

The CLB enjoyed its alliance with the Yoshida mainstream for nearly half a century and was a key instrument in policy formation. At times, politicians pretended to defer to the bureaucracy on matters of constitutional interpretation; at other times, they directed the CLB interpretation. The best example of the latter was the CLB's interpretation of Article 9 in 1952. Takatsuji Masaki, the director general of the CLB who wrote it, acknowledges in his memoirs that the CLB could not resist "strong pressure" (*tsuyoku shuchō shita koto de aru*) from Prime Minister Yoshida and concludes that "it is undeniable that the interpretation of Article 9 developed alongside political shifts."[83]

The second, far better known, part of the bureaucracy used to control the postwar military was the Japan Defense Agency, which did not become a ministry until January 2007, after the revisionists consolidated control. It was particularly important to Yoshida and his bureaucratic allies that the Defense Agency not have full ministry status. Its director general would be a member of the cabinet, but his agency would be tucked inside the Prime Minister's Office. Convinced, however, that this alone would not suffice to preserve civilian control, Yoshida directed CLB director general Hayashi Shūzō to create "internal bureaus" (*naikyoku*) when drafting the Japan Defense Agency Law in 1954 and to make sure they were supervised by officials without military experience.[84] Hayashi's legislation required that the civilian minister of state be supported by senior civilian assistants (*sanjikan*); neither former imperial military officers nor retired SDF officers would be eligible to serve in these posts. But it was not easy for Hayashi and Yoshida to keep out former military officers, "men with a past" (*iwaku tsuki*). There were many demands to clarify the meaning of "civilian." Advocates—mostly Yoshida's revisionist rivals—demanded to know whether former imperial army officers or retired SDF officers were not now civilians. The JDA's first director general, Kimura Tokutarō, tried to blame their exclusion on the Occupation authorities, but it was clear to all that this was Yoshida's handiwork.[85] Yoshida prevailed. Despite considerable lobbying by friends in high places, former imperial military officials—such as Hattori Takushirō, the former chief of operations for the Imperial Army's General Staff, and retired admiral Nomura Kichisaburō—were never allowed to serve in the JDA.[86]

In this way, Yoshida and his bureaucratic allies built a distinctive system that went well beyond simple civilian control. To keep the uniforms at arm's length, many civilian assistants would be seconded from other ministries. The practice of "reserved seating" (*shiteiseki*) atop the JDA made the agency less attractive to the most ambitious young civil servants.[87] Someone from the Ministry of Finance was routinely dispatched to supervise the JDA Budget Office; a secondee from the foreign ministry would sit atop its Policy Office; and someone from MITI routinely controlled the JDA's Equipment Bureau. Other senior officials were routinely parachuted in from other ministries, including the National Police Agency, the Ministry of Transport, and the Ministry of Posts and Telecommunications. To its critics, this was a "privileged bureaucrat system" (*bunkan yūi shisutemu*). To others, it was simply a "motley crew" (*yoriai shotai*).[88] Either way, it was not until well into the 1980s that the JDA began to "grow its own" top bureaucrats, and it was big news in 1988 when Nishihiro Seiki was named the JDA's first career official to become administrative vice-minister. By design, until recently, most senior officials came to their JDA posts without experience in defense policy. Politicians used the internal bureaus much as they used the CLB—to protect against political opposition from the Left, which feared renewed militarism, and from the Right, which sought a more robust defense posture for Japan.

This politician- and bureaucrat-heavy command structure had operational consequences. Article 8 of the Self-Defense Forces Law gives the prime minister ultimate authority to issue orders to move troops. His orders would have to go through the JDA director general, who in turn would issue orders to the commanders of each service branch, who then would make sure that commanders in the field (merely "advisors" to the director general, per the same law) "see to it that [his] orders are carried out."[89] The 1970 Defense White Paper, the first ever, stressed that SDF troops were *civilians* who must perform their duties as civil servants.[90] Complicating matters further, the prime minister was not permitted to legally authorize the movement of troops without the approval of the Diet and consultation with the National Security Council, comprising ex-officio a half dozen cabinet ministers. There was no provision for field commanders to act in the event of an emergency, and efforts to establish such legal provisions were repeatedly quashed.

Not surprisingly, this led to secret planning by military officers, which in turn led to serial crises of civilian control. In June 1963, while Koizumi Junya (the future prime minister's father) was JDA director general, a senior group of military officers in the Joint Staff Council (including flag officers) created eight study teams to simulate a crisis on the Korean Peninsula. They produced a five-volume, fifteen-hundred-page simulation informally called the "Three Arrows Study" (Mitsuya Kenkyū) in which U.S. bases in Japan would receive rear area support—supplies of ammunition, fuel, and food—from the SDF. They also allowed for the possibility of conscription, suppression of subversive elements in the Japanese Korean community, and the introduction of U.S. nuclear weapons into Japan, none of which was sanctioned by law.[91] The Socialist politician who discovered this "plot," Okada Haruo, denounced the uniformed officers as "reckless" and as "seeking militarist control of Japan." The press was exercised by what it portrayed as the JDA's intervention in politics. Prime Minister Satō was moved to apologize that the public had been "seriously misled" (*hijōni gokai wo ukeru*), and promised to reform military education so that it would take into account democratic values. When the Diet issued its final report on the incident in May 1965, it concluded that the JDA had exceeded its legal authority but congratulated the government for upholding the principle of civilian control. The importance of military planning for homeland security drowned beneath a tsunami of indignation and fear mongering.

This was not the last time that emergency planning would become a lightning rod for concern about civilian control. In 1978, just when Prime Minister Fukuda had submitted emergency legislation (*yūji hōsei*) to the Diet, Air Self-Defense Force general Kurisu Hirōmi, chair of the Joint Staff Council, took it upon himself to support the legislation. Insisting that it was foolish to expect pilots to wait for politicians to issue orders if they were already under attack in midair, he explained to a journalist that due to "deficiencies" in the SDF Law, "there is really no choice but to take supralegal action (*chōhōkiteki ni*)...in an emergency if Japan is suddenly invaded."[92] This set off another firestorm of protest, including claims that Fukuda had embarked on a return to authoritarianism. JDA director general Kanemaru Shin, a political adversary of Fukuda's, dismissed Kurisu, insisting that a frontline commander's decision to take extralegal action is "contrary to the constitution, the SDF Law, and civilian control."[93] Days later, Kanemaru told the SDF that he understood their frustration and promised to work for the enactment of emergency guidelines. But he reminded them they were all public servants, subject to the law. The Kurisu affair brought the need for emergency legislation to the fore—after all, who could imagine a field commander waiting for Diet approval before returning fire? Still, the shadow of Yamagata's ghost was long enough to delay legislation for another twenty-five years.

A subsequent crisis of civilian control was touched off in 1981, after General Takeda Gorō, chairman of the Joint Staff Council, declared in a magazine interview that "defensive defense was insufficiently robust to be a national security doctrine and that roles and missions should take precedence over arbitrary budget caps." Diet budget deliberations were suspended until Prime Minister Suzuki Zenkō and JDA director general Ōmura apologized and dismissed the general. The Sturm und Drang generated by the "Three Arrows," Kurisu, and Takeda crises tested civilian control and, in the event, deepened the institutional foundation of the Yoshida Doctrine.[94]

Meanwhile, mainstream conservatives also used more prosaic methods to institutionalize the "pacifist" foundations of the Yoshida Doctrine. In June 1956, two years after the formation of the SDF, the National Defense Council (Kokubō Kaigi) was established as the most senior interagency advisory group on national security. Its establishment had been delayed by an ongoing battle between mainstream and antimainstream conservatives. The latter had sought to use this council to increase the prime minister's power, and tried unsuccessfully to pack it with former imperial military officers. Mainstream conservatives blocked all such appointments, weakened the council by limiting its members to ex-officio cabinet ministers, and denied it a professional staff.[95] The main function of the council was to discuss and approve defense build-up plans, but it met only six times in the 1960s, and it routinely sided with the finance ministry to deny the JDA the budget increases it was seeking.[96] The council was nominally "upgraded" in 1986, but, still denied resources and staff and administered largely by officials from MITI and MOF, it merely served as a venue for interagency consultation.[97]

Control of the JDA budget was not a problem for the mainstream conservatives. After the Kishi meltdown in 1960, they were firmly in the saddle. Ikeda Hayato was prime minister and Ōhira Masayoshi was chief cabinet secretary in late 1960 (both were former MOF officials) when the second defense build-up program was cut back, and the rules of the road were set for the next forty years. For much of this period, the administrative vice-minister of the JDA had been an MOF official who previously had been responsible for the defense budget at the finance ministry. Japanese defense budgets were based on fiscal rather than military calculations. JDA and MITI pleas for new equipment were often indulged so as to support domestic defense manufacturers, but it was MOF that controlled the bottom line—a bottom line kept exceptionally low.

The only thing that the JDA overpaid for was defense equipment. Waving the tricolor technonational banner of autonomy, nurturance, and diffusion, the Japanese defense industry lobbied successfully to keep a significant portion of defense production inside Japan.[98] They made their case on economic security grounds—Japan needed to maintain a healthy defense industrial base to promote technological advancement and high-value-added jobs. Because the SDF was small, procurement was limited, and because domestic production was preferred, unit costs were very high. They were made even higher when, in 1967, in a move coordinated with the "non-nuclear principles" to overdetermine an uneventful return of Okinawa to Japanese sovereignty, Prime Minister Satō announced that Japan would not export weapons. The ban formally proscribed arms sales to "Communist bloc" countries, countries to which arms sales were prohibited by the United Nations, and to countries involved in or likely to become involved in international conflicts. This action further reduced the possibility of volume production and raised domestic costs, and over time it came to be interpreted as a comprehensive proscription.

Many in the JDA did try for more. With each new cycle of five-year defense planning, the JDA would mobilize its allies in the LDP's antimainstream defense community (*bōei zoku*) and in industry, through the Keidanren's Defense Production Committee. But the result was always less than military analysts insisted was necessary. The larger problem may have been structural. The JDA was designed to be a "shopping ministry" (*okaimono kanchō*) whose policy plans would be subordinated to MOF budget constraints rather than responsive to threats.[99] JDA director general Akagi Munenori announced in 1960 that the Japanese defense budget would double within six years, but his plan was rejected. In the late 1960s, MOF would even fight the JDA on its military logic—and win.[100] Advocates tried everything. Some pressed for a navy-centered acquisition strategy. Since Japan was a trading nation, it needed a strong navy. Japan would work with the United States to protect sea-lanes—and Japanese shipyards would be kept busy.[101] Others lobbied for the Ground Self-Defense Force. There were even times when strong advocates for a defense buildup rose to senior levels within the JDA, as in the case of Okazaki Hisahiko, a secondee from the foreign ministry in the 1970s. Okazaki broke ranks with his colleagues and argued that Japan did not live in a security vacuum. There were "grim threats" facing Japan, which the draft National Defense Program Outline would have to take more fully into account. But he could not get his colleagues to budge; formal recognition of the new security environment would be too expensive.[102] By the late 1970s, it was acceptable to use the defense budget to modernize Japan's technology base, but only secondarily to enhance its military capabilities. The joke among bureaucrats and politicians was that the only thing the JDA was defending against was budget cuts by the Ministry of Finance. In 1976, dovish Prime Minister Miki Takeo announced that Japanese defense spending would be limited to no more than 1 percent of GDP.

The crowning achievement of Yoshida's successors was their institutionalization of "comprehensive security" (*sōgō anzen hoshō*) as the intellectual basis for Japan's national security doctrine.[103] In the complex security environment of the 1970s—one in which an unprecedented oil crisis was followed by a "second cold war" in which the balance of military power in Northeast Asia had tipped in the Soviet's favor—Japanese defense planners came under considerable pressure from the United States to do more. Despite formal acknowledgment of the problem, Japan's leaders were determined to find nonmilitary ways to respond.[104] On becoming prime minister in 1978, Ōhira Masayoshi convened a group of intellectuals to concoct something less transparently duplicitous than his competitor Fukuda Takeo's "multidirectional diplomacy." He wanted guidelines that would elevate economic diplomacy and move Japan closer to the center of world affairs, but without a major defense buildup. An extraordinary concentration of intellectual talent that included Kōsaka Masataka, Inoki Masamichi, Kubo Takuya, and Satō Seizaburō—all of whom understood the hard power threat—delivered a soft power, "comprehensive security" doctrine. They drew on the Meiji idea of "rich nation, strong army" but infused it with liberal internationalism. "Comprehensive security" starts from the idea that economic security is at least as important as military security, and posits that diplomacy ought to accommodate military, economic, and associated resources simultaneously. It emphasizes that security comes in many forms and that policy instruments from different realms, as well as more traditional military instruments, can be used to secure the nation.[105] To be sure, Japan should accept military security as one pillar of the larger, comprehensive approach. But given its low utility for all but self-defense, high costs associated with its use, and (sotto voce) the willingness of the United States to indulge Japanese "cheap riding," discussion of military security could be deemphasized. All that Prime Minister Yoshida had originally conceived for postwar Japan would be brought under a single intellectual banner, its institutions fully legitimated in the crucible of democratic politics.

In the mid-1980s, when Nakasone Yasuhiro was prime minister, he and other antimainstream LDP leaders took one last cut at raising Japanese defense spending and ending the 1 percent ceiling. Their plan for "autonomous defense" included a large supplement for the acquisition of domestically produced weapons systems (*kokusanka*). If the fourth defense build-up plan had gone forward as conceived, Japan's defense budget would have risen dramatically, to close to 2 percent of GDP. But by this time, Japan's cheap ride was formalized at the 1 percent level and its advocates were dug in. Nakasone never did enjoy the presidential powers he openly fancied, and he became hostage to a range of entrenched interests. The best he could achieve was a symbolic breakthrough—a JDA budget that exceeded 1 percent of GDP by .007 percent! The Yoshida Doctrine had become a matter of broad national consensus.

Many who study postwar Japan have been impressed by the extent to which bureaucrats have been granted authority and have wielded power.[106] Nowhere has this bureaucratic authority and power been more warmly embraced than in security policy. The considerable influence of the functionaries of the CLB and in the JDA's internal bureaus has led many to conclude that civilian control of the Japanese military (*bunmin tōsei*) is deformed. To some, politicians abandoned their responsibilities to voters by conferring authority on bureaucrats without defense expertise to supervise uniformed officers. Civilian control was not in this sense "democratic" but rather, bureaucratic control (*bunkan tōsei*).[107] As Hikotani Takako suggests:

> Japan...has never gone through a public debate over how civilians can and should control the military under democratic values. The concept of civilian control is understood either very broadly as a matter of how civilians at large prevent the rise of militarism, or very narrowly as the control of military officers by the civilian officials within the JDA.[108]

Postwar policymakers may have overcompensated for wartime excesses and relied too much on officials who never had to face the electorate. It is also indisputable that Japanese bureaucrats have more independence than civil servants elsewhere. Still, neither the lawyers in the Cabinet Legislation Bureau nor the secondees in the JDA ever strayed far from the preferences of their political supervisors. The CLB, often blamed for dominating security policy, did no more and no less than the prime minister wanted. When Yoshida wanted to establish the SDF without amending the constitution, the CLB obliged. When Kishi wanted the preemptive use of force and nuclear arms declared legal, they were. And when Kishi went too far, the Japanese public—and his mainstream opponents in the LDP—forced his resignation. When Satō Eisaku, Suzuki Zenkō, Kaifu Toshiki, Miyazawa Kiichi, or any other mercantile realist needed cover to avoid U.S. pressure for increased defense spending or to expand Japan's military roles and missions, they could rely on bureaucrats to issue the necessary interpretations. In so doing, these politicians were responding to signals from constituents who, however imperfectly, were voicing their preferences democratically. Thus, it was left for mainstream and antimainstream conservatives to square off about how to provide security and prosperity for postwar Japan. Their choices were always put to an electoral test. Clearly, the voters did not wish Japan to become a military power. The Japanese bureaucracy had considerable power, but it was only one of several players in the drama, and at key moments it followed politicians who were responding to the public. The bureaucrats' power would decline even further, as we shall see, but it is a mistake to assume that it was ever unmatched.

There are many ways to characterize the Yoshida Doctrine. To some, the pacifism enshrined in Article 9 and defended by Japan's postwar leaders is an ironclad "pledge made to the world" that Japan will never again threaten its neighbors.[109] Yet this view understates the cunning and complexity of Yoshida's calculations. For Soeya Yoshihide, the Yoshida Doctrine is classic "middle power" diplomacy.[110] Japan could assume a limited defense posture, not unlike Canada or Australia, and still protect itself by allying with a great power. But neither Canada nor Australia had difficulty supporting U.S. wars or contributing to global peacekeeping, and thus neither faced charges of cheap riding on U.S. security guarantees. In fact, Yoshida and his successors were "mercantile realists" who combined the liberal internationalism of Small Japanism with a calculated realist defense of national interests.[111] They managed some domestic opponents by promising pacifism, others by delivering commercial benefits. Meanwhile, they managed their alliance partner and avoided getting too entangled in its adventures abroad. Military security was not ignored, but neither was it the predominant focus of Japan's grand strategy.

Yoshida Shigeru knew earlier than most that this would finally change. In his memoirs Yoshida remarked:

As Japan's capacity expands, so also must its responsibilities. During the negotiations that preceded the signing of the San Francisco Treaty, I opposed rearmament by Japan and instead stressed the need for my nation to concentrate upon economic development.... Since then, however, the situation in which Japan finds itself, both at home and abroad, has changed completely.... In the matter of defense, we seem to be advancing beyond the stage of depending upon the strength of other countries.[112]

Japan has now caught up to Yoshida—again. It is to his predicted changes, and to the end of his long postwar consensus, that we now turn.

PART II

A WORLD IN FLUX

[3]

The Change to Change

A great deal has changed since the late 1980s, when Japan was known as an economic giant and political pygmy. Japan is still an economic giant, of course, but its willingness to act in world affairs is no longer pygmy-like. Its defense budget, which in fiscal year 2006 was over $41 billion, is one of the five largest in the world, and Japan's Self-Defense Forces have now been dispatched for UN peacekeeping operations to Cambodia, Mozambique, and the Golan Heights, among other places. In the mid-1990s, Tokyo agreed to expand its security role from the homeland to the larger East Asian region. After September 11, 2001, when Japan joined President George W. Bush's "coalition of the willing" by dispatching forces to the Indian Ocean and, later, to Iraq, Tokyo began openly to contemplate a global security role. Major disaster-relief operations emboldened Tokyo to offer SDF assistance in the 2005 tsunami relief effort in Southeast Asia as well as to the southeastern United States in its recovery from Hurricane Katrina in 2005. In 2005, in concert with Germany, India, and Brazil, Japan tried (but failed) to transform the United Nations Security Council. Japan may still be punching below its weight in world affairs, but it has been bulking up.

For the future of great power conflict, all eyes are on Asia. Strategic uncertainty, including a major shift in the balance of power in a region with four great powers, is compounded by the spread of nuclear weapons, growing defense budgets, and weak multilateral security institutions. Moreover, incompatible political systems, long-standing territorial disputes, and growing competition over natural resources all exacerbate instability. Asia, long a dangerous place, is more fluidly so, and Japan is actively trying to figure out how to cope with events—and how to shape them.

To that end, Japanese security policy is changing. Like most historical changes, this one is overdetermined. It has been catalyzed by international events beyond Japan's control, by domestic political struggles, societal change, and institutional reform, and by the "transformation" of the defense establishment of Japan's alliance partner. I start this review beginning with four international catalysts, each of which is connected directly to the first fundamental shift in the global and regional balances of power since 1945. Together, after a hiccup or two of uncertainty, these catalysts stimulated Japanese strategists to imagine the transformation of the domestic institutions of Japanese grand strategy.

THE BIG BANG

The first was the epochal demise of the Soviet Union and the end of the cold war, the closest thing to a "big bang" in international politics in living memory. Robyn Lim places the events of 1989 in their geostrategic and historical context:

> With the end of the Cold War, security in Western Europe [wa]s not only settled, but largely disconnected from the problems of East Asia....For the first time since the East Asian quadrilateral was assembled in 1905, the balance of power in the region is being determined solely by fluctuations among the four powers.[1]

As in all transformational events, much less was apparent while the fires were raging than after the smoke cleared. Indeed, Japan seemed bewildered as the events of 1989–91 unfolded. Tokyo's judgment of what was happening was uncertain, and, as a consequence, its political support for Boris Yeltsin's reforms was late in coming. Indeed, Japanese statesmen arrived at the barricades only after Chancellor Helmut Kohl, President George H. W. Bush, and Prime Minister John Major had already locked arms and pledged solidarity against the counterrevolutionary Communists. Even then, even after it was clear that the global security environment had changed, Tokyo had trouble settling on a strategic direction. All the familiar choices for achieving autonomy, prestige, strength, and wealth presented themselves anew, and, as Park Cheol He notes, "signs of oscillation between the U.S. and Asia became visible."[2] A decade of trade friction with the United States suggested to some that this was a chance to escape from under Washington's thumb. Others justified a new Asianism by linking regional solidarity to the dramatic rise in Japanese investment in Southeast Asia after the 1985 Plaza Accord and to the rise of economic regionalism in Europe and North America. If Southeast Asian leaders such as Malaysia's Mahathir Mohamad were encouraging Japan to join in a new regional solidarity, why should Japan not tilt toward a rising Asia and lead it into prosperity? Why should it continue to hug the United States closely now that the raison d'être for the alliance had slipped away?

Two things were clear: the military balance was shifting rapidly, and "Japanese strategists were not ready."[3] The changes they ultimately made were a matter of "slow unfolding" rather than of decisive discontinuity.[4] On the military side, it took a while for them to appreciate that nothing would ever be the same. When Japan's Basic Defense Policy (Kokubō no Kihon Hōshin) was written in 1957—and for the next half century—Japanese defense policy was Soviet-oriented.[5] Even though the Soviets never really developed the capability to invade the Japanese home islands, Japan's ships, planes, and tanks were configured to repel a Soviet invasion from the north.[6] This "exclusively defensive defense" (*senshu bōei*) was politically inspired. Force levels were determined by the need for a "balanced posture," a vague term that resulted in a fixed number of twelve infantry divisions and eight anti-aircraft units distributed evenly across the archipelago, rather than to optimize resistance to attack.[7]

The drawdown of Russian forces in the Far East was swift and very dramatic. The Maritime Self-Defense Force had reported sighting 141 Soviet naval vessels in the Sea of Japan in 1987, but only nine Russian ships in 1996. No more than 5 percent of Soviet destroyers remained in the Russian Pacific fleet.[8] The central justification for the alliance and for Japanese security policy had to be replaced—and eventually was. After considerable time, debate, and American exhortation, Tokyo began to shift its military focus from Hokkaido and northern Honshu, where it had faced the threat of Soviet invasion, southward, where assets could more easily be deployed against perceived Chinese threats. It reduced the number of Ground Self-Defense Force tanks, improved mobility, and shifted resources into naval and special operations. For the Americans, who lobbied aggressively for these changes every step along the way, it was like pulling teeth.

CATALYTIC CRISES

On the broader strategic front, two major international crises intervened before Tokyo could conclude that it was unwise to set off on an independent regional security strategy. These crises, the first in the Middle East and the second on the Korean Peninsula, did more to transform perceptions than any structural shift in the military balance. If the end of the cold war was the "big bang" that changed the global security architecture, the Gulf War in 1991 and the first North Korean nuclear crisis in 1993–94 were catalysts for a long-sought Japanese awakening to the importance of security.

[65]

It was not pretty watching the Japanese government fail miserably in its first test of the so-called New World Order. At first, it had all seemed so straightforward. Some in the ruling LDP, led by its secretary-general, Ozawa Ichirō, wanted to dispatch Self-Defense Forces to the Middle East as part of the multilateral, UN-sanctioned peacekeeping force being assembled by the United States. Ozawa and his allies understood the extant ban on overseas dispatch, but they insisted that this deployment would be consistent with the preamble of the Japanese Constitution, which acknowledged responsibilities to the international community. They therefore contrived their own interpretation: "collective security" (*shūdanteki anzen hoshō*) could cover participation with other states, and without challenging the ban on "collective self-defense" (*shūdanteki jieiken*).[9]

By the time the Diet opened on 12 October 1990 to debate dispatch of the SDF to the Persian Gulf, however, Prime Minister Kaifu Toshiki (the latest heir to the Yoshida mantle) had grown cautious about this reinterpretation.[10] On that very day Ozawa led a delegation of top LDP officials to meet Prime Minister Kaifu to propose that the SDF be permitted to use arms under UN command. The prime minister reportedly responded by claiming that his hands were tied: "The CLB director general has told me that this is 'constitutionally impossible.'" Not surprisingly, this did not go down well with Ozawa or other senior party officials. They soon left the LDP, after having first sworn a vendetta against bureaucrats in general and against the CLB in particular.[11]

For now, though, the pragmatic mainstream still enjoyed the upper hand. CLB Director General Kudō Atsuo declared in the Diet that because the UN's Kuwait-based peacekeeping force planned for the possibility of violence, its members carried arms and therefore could not be supported by SDF troops. Although Kudō did allow a difference between the "use of force" (*buryoku kōshi*) and the "use of arms" (*buki shiyō*), a difference that later would constitutionally justify participation in peacekeeping *operations* (PKO), it was not enough for Japanese participation in this war.[12] In January 1991 coalition forces acted without Japanese support; the CLB even rebuffed JDA proposals to send transport planes to rescue refugees, on the grounds that the JDA was authorized to fly overseas only for training purposes. The U.S.-led coalition in the Persian Gulf was mobilized with $13 billion raised in a special tax on Japanese citizens but without Japan's physical presence in the theater of operations. Japan's financial support was not even acknowledged by the Kuwaiti government.[13] It was not until hostilities had ceased and the MOFA could declare that sending ships was a matter of "navigational safety" rather than a wartime deployment, that the MSDF swept thirty-four mines from the Persian Gulf.[14] This first-ever overseas deployment of the SDF left the bitter taste of far too little, far too late in everyone's mouth. In March 1991, Ambassador Michael Armacost cabled Washington:

A large gap was revealed between Japan's desire for recognition as a great power and its willingness and ability to assume these risks and responsibilities.... For all its economic prowess, Japan is not in the great power league....Opportunities for dramatic initiatives...were lost to caution...[and] Japan's crisis management system proved totally inadequate.[15]

All Tokyo had to show for having tied itself in knots over participation in the first Gulf War was humiliation: international criticism of its "checkbook diplomacy."[16] Ozawa and his antimainstream allies became more determined than ever to take control from the weak-kneed mainstream and the CLB. Specifically, they vowed to end the "1955 system" that had bogged Japan down just when action was most urgently needed. They knew that "pacifism had become a flimsy shield" and that Japan should no longer expect to get away with international peacekeeping from deep within the rear area.[17]

If the Gulf War tested Tokyo's preparedness to be "normal," the 1993–94 Korean crisis, Northeast Asia's first bona fide security crisis after the end of the cold war, tested its commitment to the alliance with the United States.[18] Once again Japan was not ready. In 1993 the United States discovered a secret North Korean nuclear weapons program. After considerable bluster and brinksmanship on both sides, the Agreed Framework was signed in October 1994 that defused the crisis temporarily. Japan, the Republic of Korea (ROK), and the United States would provide heavy fuel oil and light-water-reactor technology, and in exchange Pyongyang would freeze and ultimately dismantle its nuclear program. This did not happen, and neither did the North Korean regime reform or collapse before the next crisis erupted in 2002. What did come to pass, however, was the realization that Japan was not prepared to act in concert with the United States in the event of a military crisis on the peninsula. Operational plans were limited or nonexistent, and the future of the alliance was suddenly in jeopardy.

North Korea was a big problem, but it also was a big opportunity. Its open hostility served those who sought a stronger alliance and, especially, a stronger Japan. In addition to stimulating the new alliance framework announced in 1996, Pyongyang tested its missiles in Japanese airspace in 1998—leading immediately to approval by the Diet of an intelligence satellite program. In 2001 one of its boats engaged the Japanese Coast Guard in Japan's first postwar military encounter. It was just what Japanese defense planners and conservative politicians had been waiting for. Now they could make their case for new strategic thinking about Northeast Asian security with a credible threat in full view of the nation. As one JDA official remarked to Paul Daniels, a U.S. Army analyst, North Korea provided a "reasonable excuse" for Japan to expand its military.[19]

In retrospect, then, it is clear that both crises were functional in ways that the larger demise of the Soviet Union was not. They catalyzed debate on

fundamental issues about national security and the U.S. alliance. A declassified March 1991 U.S. Embassy cable lists several that were in play as a direct
result of the Gulf War experience: (1) the continued efficacy of the renuncia-
tion of the use of force; (2) the importance of contributing manpower to the
international community in times of crisis; (3) a more equitable division of
roles and missions within the U.S.-Japan alliance; and (4) the desirability
of a more independent foreign policy.[20] The crisis on the peninsula raised
additional issues, such as the need to upgrade Japanese intelligence and,
especially, to enhance interoperability within the alliance. Together, these
incidents drove home to the Japanese public something they and many political leaders had never wished to believe: that the world and, indeed, their
own neighborhood were dangerous places. They were learning, moreover,
that security was not free, and it might not even be cheap any longer.

Certainly the United States was upping the ante, with a good deal of prod-
ding from U.S. alliance managers. In 1994, for the first time in twenty years,
the Japanese government comprehensively reviewed its security posture
and issued a new National Defense Program Outline (NDPO, or *taikō*).
Although it retained the Basic Defense Force Concept, the new NDPO upgraded the alliance in the event of a regional crisis. Thanks to the peacekeeping legislation that had passed in the Diet earlier that year, the new NDPO
also added two new missions to the SDF portfolio: disaster relief and international peacekeeping. At the time, the new NDPO was celebrated as having broadened the scope of Japan's commitments, and certainly this was the
case when new alliance guidelines were issued the following year.[21] Now
Japan would take fuller responsibility for defense of the "areas surrounding
Japan" (*shūhen*), a move that one analyst has called "a significant upgrade of
operability in responding to regional contingencies."[22] But Tokyo insisted
on preserving a degree of strategic ambiguity. MOFA pressed the awkward
line that the term "areas surrounding Japan" was "situational" and not geo-
graphical. Some analysts could now insist that the alliance could enjoy expanded possibilities for joint operations, though most were convinced that
the ambiguity was retained in order to avoid offending Beijing. The greatest
ambiguity remained: Was Japan accepting a U.S.-Japan division of labor in
regional security, or was it avoiding one? Was the Yoshida Doctrine unrav-
elling, or was it entering a new and more sophisticated phase?

RISING CHINA

These questions were being raised just in time for the next major shift
in the regional balance of power—the rise of China. The 1995 NDPO did
not mention China as a threat, but it did touch on nuclear arsenals in
neighboring states, and so justified enhancing forces in the south while

cutting two divisions in Hokkaido. The 2004 *taikō* (now called the National Program Defense Guidelines—NDPG in English) was the first national security document to openly identify a potential threat from the People's Republic of China, noting that the PRC was modernizing its forces and expanding its range at sea. Tokyo's defense specialists are convinced that China intends to establish itself as the world's second superpower and are concerned that domination of Japan will be part of the process.[23] But China's power was shaping up to be far more complex than the Soviet Union's ever was. China turned out to be, after all, determined to be rich as well as strong. On the economic front, the PRC has already established itself as the largest trading partner Japan has ever had. Japan cannot get enough of the Chinese market or of Chinese goods. In 2005, bilateral trade exceeded $225 billion, the seventh record year in a row.[24] Not surprisingly, this has led to a redirection of foreign investment. In the first few years of the 2000s, Japan reduced direct foreign investment to the United States by more than half and increased it to China by more than 300 percent.[25] By 2003, China had become responsible for more than 90 percent of the growth of Japan's exports, and Japanese companies employed more than ten million Chinese.[26] This is, of course, a mixed blessing for Japan. Many insist that the two economies are structurally complementary—Japan excels in R & D upstream and in after-sales service downstream, China provides raw materials, labor, and assembly skills—but others express serious concerns.[27] China is a source of Japanese wealth, but it may be using these relationships in a "rich nation, strong army program of development [with] unique Chinese characteristics [that could lead to] regional hegemony."[28]

Many in Tokyo are concerned that the Chinese market is luring Japanese firms into complacency about China's real intentions. Beijing, they believe, is merely using trade with Japan as way to enrich itself so that it can acquire a fuller arsenal. And even if this is not the case, few senior Japanese leaders are confident there is stable civilian control of the Chinese military.[29] They focus on the divergence of national objectives rather than on the economic complementarities, which they see as temporary. They also focus on the simple geopolitical fact that no vessel can reach Japan from the south without passing through the waters adjacent to Taiwan. If China seizes control of Taiwan, they warn, it seizes control of Japan's sea-lanes as well.[30] This exaggerates Taiwan's geostrategic importance, but Japanese strategists insist that Chinese control of Taiwan would enhance China's coercive power. China and Japan are two of the world's largest energy importers, and they have never been great powers at the same time.[31] There have been repeated Chinese submarine and other incursions into the Japanese Exclusive Economic Zone, where the Chinese navy is suspected of mapping the seabed to deny access to U.S. warships in case of a Taiwan contingency. Security specialists are also concerned that China is acquiring missiles for "sea denial" and that the PLA's buildup seems aimed well beyond any Taiwan contingency. As Beijing has asserted territorial claims and extended itself in the East and South China seas, Japanese security planners have accelerated plans for their own force transformation. As we shall see in chapters 6 and 7, China has supplanted North Korea and has replaced the Soviet Union as the central object of Japanese security planning.

Meanwhile, a 2005 report of the U.S. Congressional Research Service concluded that "China is supplanting Japan as the leader in Asia."[32] China's rise promises to have enormous consequences for U.S. power in the region as well. With close to one hundred thousand troops stationed in Northeast Asia, the United States is still the preeminent military power and remains committed to a strong presence.[33] Nevertheless, decreasing U.S. participation in emerging regional economic institutions and a planned transformation of overseas troop deployments together suggest decreased American influence in the region. Although the United States increasingly depends on Asian finance and on commodity trade, an Asian regional trade and financial system has emerged without U.S. leadership or, in some important cases, even without U.S. participation. It was clear by 2004, when Beijing took the diplomatic lead away from the United States in the six-party talks, that the United States no longer had the ability to disarm North Korea peacefully without Chinese support.

So it was old news when, in August 2005, Japan's leading economic daily proclaimed "an historic shift in the East Asian balance of power is under way."[34] It was clear that the bipolar balance of the long postwar era had long since given way to a brief "unipolar moment," after which U.S. dominance was challenged by China, by the Europeans, and by nonstate actors around the world.[35] Suddenly, the terms of ideological conflict had shifted from arguments about capitalism and authoritarianism to arguments about theocracy and secularism. National arsenals that had bristled with conventional arms and strategic nuclear weapons had to be reconfigured to enhance communications and control; the great powers could no longer count on proxies to fight their wars; and direct deterrence could no longer be their core strategy. For the United States, this meant "force transformation." For Japan, this meant that planners no longer had the luxury of focusing on Soviet conventional warfare, which had always been a low probability event. Now they had to contemplate missile attacks by the Democratic People's Republic of Korea (DPRK), terrorist attacks at home, and Chinese coercion on the high seas—all of them lower intensity but higher probability events. Whereas security once had meant averting great power conflict, now it involved deterring regional conflict and minimizing casualties. Japan is no longer a simple cog in an anti-Soviet deterrent, and it has had to recalculate the prospect that the United States might not stand by its side indefinitely. Now it has to cope with Chinese economic power while defending its territorial claims and contributing to global public goods with more than cash. Japan was expected—and became determined—to contribute positively to the stable functioning of the international security environment. To do this, the SDF had to begin functioning as a modern armed force.[36]

DOMESTIC CHANGE

Japan's strategists know this and are well aware that their military transformation lags far behind the U.S. one. As one U.S. Department of Defense (DoD) official noted publicly in 2005, it still was not even clear if Japan could even *plan* for a military contingency.[37] Japan's China strategy is inchoate at best, with the economic relationship running hot and the political one running cold. The service branches have acquired new capabilities (and, as we shall see, Japan has even elevated its Coast Guard to near "service branch" status), but they have not been integrated under a joint command. Intelligence remains underdeveloped, and for some roles and missions the Japanese military is not yet capable. Still, the Japanese defense establishment is in the midst of significant change, much of which has been enabled by changes in the domestic political environment.

These changes are of three varieties: sociological, ideological, and institutional. None is the direct result of shifts in global or regional balances of power, and each is related to domestic political competition. The most prominent sociological change has been in the status of the Self-Defense Forces. Although Japanese remain more likely than any other people to insist that they would not take up arms even to defend their homeland, and although some question the willingness of even the SDF to engage in war fighting, the forces' status has never been higher.[38] Fifteen years after the end of the Pacific War, Ivan Morris reported that the SDF were barely accepted as "a necessary evil," and in 1973, James Auer reported that the Japanese military was still not a "respected profession."[39] As recently as 1989, analysts insisted that "their countrymen tend to regard [SDF troops] not as forces of national defense in their own right, but as a means to keep the[ir U.S.] protector in good humor."[40] This perception extended to the civilian bureaucrats. Defense officials over fifty years old and retirees reported "JDA bashing," something that their younger colleagues do not.[41] Only limited data on the attitudes of Japanese soldiers are available, but it does seem clear that they are feeling better about their role in society. Soldiers find PKO missions stressful, but they report overwhelmingly that their experience was positive and that Japan should do more peacekeeping.[42]

The "problematic existence" of the postwar military has been addressed actively by the JDA.[43] Certainly their ideals have changed. Whereas Morris wrote in 1960 that military officers "are as unlikely now as they were before the war to ally themselves with liberal, democratic, or egalitarian aspirations," these are the only aspirations in evidence today. When SDF personnel express a desire for higher status in society, their referent is the citizen soldier of "normal" nations rather than the samurai, the imperial servant of the past.[44] To the contrary, Japanese soldiers today seem eager to disassociate themselves from their imperial predecessors and (as one GSDF colonel put it) "to show to the Japanese population, to our neighbors, and to the international community that we *have changed*."[45] Their effort to depict the new Japanese military as "warm and fuzzy" and their embrace of liberal values, such as democracy and civilian control, is evident everywhere, from the recruiting manga produced by the MOD public relations officials to the curriculum of the Defense Academy.[46]

A second sociological change has been generational. The percentage of young people holding a favorable impression of the SDF has never been higher. At the time of the Gulf War in February 1991, less than 57 percent had a favorable impression. In February 2006, just five months before the GSDF troops were withdrawn from Iraq, more than 81 percent held a favorable impression. Those whose impression is unfavorable fell sharply, from 31 percent to just 13 percent in the same period.[47] Recruitment, which is made more difficult by the sharp decline in the population of eligible males, is assisted by the newly positive image of the SDF.[48] A generation gap within the political class also is emerging. In November 2001, 167 conservative young Diet members crossed party lines to create the Young Diet Members' Group to Establish a Security Framework for the New Century (Shin Seiki no Anzen Hoshō Taisei o Kakuritsu Suru Wakate Giin no Kai). Led by Ishiba Shigeru of the LDP and Maehara Seiji of the Democratic Party of Japan (DPJ), the group made up nearly one-quarter of the Diet and nearly half of all members born after 1960. Rather than focus on their elders' traditional issues of defense technology, budgets, and equipment procurement, this group urged Japan to "defend its national interest based upon 'realism'."[49] They insisted that Japan get to work on a grand strategy and even discussed such topics as maritime resources in the East China Sea—including drafting legislation outside normal channels.[50] Internal party organs such as the LDP's Policy Affairs Research Council, which had been instrumental in tying politicians and bureaucrats together on defense policy issues, were being openly supplanted by new forms of interparty policy coordination—led by forty-somethings.

Within the LDP, meanwhile, a separate intergenerational power play was under way that led to a new party—and national security—strategy. After a decade of failed efforts by Ozawa Ichirō and others to wrest power

Figure 2. SDF recruiting is engineered to soften the military's image. Reprinted with permission of the Japan Defense Agency and Kyodo News.

from the LDP mainstream, antimainstream conservatives within the party used shifts in regional and world politics to seize power from within. In 2000, Koizumi Junichirō (whose father had been a defense minister), Abe Shinzō (whose grandfather, Kishi Nobusuke, had been an architect of the Manchurian occupation), and other direct heirs to the antimainstream agenda gained control of the LDP and, thereby, of the Japanese government. They immediately set to work to transform the institutions of national security policymaking. They had the unqualified support of young conservatives with considerable expertise in security affairs, such as Ishiba Shigeru—not to mention the support of the United States.[51] The rise of a new generation of revisionists was surely the most consequential political change in Japan since 1945.

Their first target was to establish firmer political control over the bureaucracy, and they did so by elevating the policy role of the Prime Minister's Office (Kantei).[52] In an unprecedented assault on the prerogatives of elite bureaucrats, in 2001 three major changes were made. The first strengthened the agenda-setting power of the prime minister and increased the institutional resources available exclusively to him. The second reformed the structure of the Cabinet Secretariat; and the third established the Cabinet Office (Naikakufu). Now the prime minister can submit proposals to the cabinet on "basic principles on important policies" without having first to secure broad ministerial support. Because these "basic principles" include a wide array of national security policies and budgetary powers, the Japanese prime minister has never been more presidential. Moreover, the number of special advisers and private secretaries available exclusively to the prime minister has expanded, and the authority of the Cabinet Secretariat to draft policy, as well as to coordinate policies from the line ministries and agencies, has also been enlarged. The secretariat is responsible to the cabinet but also serves as a direct advisory body to the prime minister and is "in charge of final coordination at the highest level."[53] By the end of 2004 fifteen offices within the Cabinet Secretariat bore responsibility for policy development across a wide range of issues. Whereas the number of staff in 1993 had been under two hundred, by 2004 the total was closer to seven hundred. This bulking up of the Cabinet Secretariat altered the balance of power between the ministries and between the government and the LDP's policy organs.[54] So did the creation in January 2001 of the Cabinet Office, which absorbed the former Prime Minister's Office (Sōrifu) and several other units, including the Defense Agency. Now the prime minister had the power to establish ministers for special missions, and they can request materials from the line ministries and report directly to the prime minister.

These reforms have resulted in a significantly more flexible policy apparatus and stronger executive leadership, thereby reducing government response time during crises.[55] They were put in motion before the Koizumi team took office, by Ozawa Ichirō and Hashimoto Ryūtarō, for whom security was only one of many reforms. But the first palpable changes came after September 11, 2001, when Prime Minister Koizumi moved with striking speed to craft Japan's response to U.S. calls for support in the "war on terror."[56] Koizumi established within the Cabinet Secretariat the ad hoc Iraq Response Team (Iraku Mondai Taisaku Honbu), which he chaired. He assigned a small group of JDA and MOFA officials to Assistant Cabinet Secretary Ōmori Keiji to develop a new law to enable SDF deployment. In early April 2002, the group reported that existing UN resolutions would be insufficient to justify SDF deployment under the existing Peacekeeping Operations Law. Koizumi ordered that a new law be drafted. This legislation, invoking UN Resolution 1483 as the legal basis for action, would restrict SDF operations to "noncombat zones" (hisentōchiiki) and avoid any review of existing restrictions on the use of force—or even any mention of Article 9. Despite high levels of public opposition and bureaucratic doubts—and despite the cavalierly tautological way in which Koizumi defined noncombat zones as "the area where the SDF is operating"—the SDF dispatch was swiftly enacted.[57] It is hard to interpret this as anything less than a turning point in postwar Japanese security policy. As the chair of the LDP Policy Committee on Foreign Affairs insists, "the power of the bureaucracy is decreasing and political leadership is increasing."[58]

Not all branches of the bureaucracy were hurt equally by these reforms. The JDA actually benefited. Until the mid-2000s, Japanese security policy had been managed chiefly by the Ministry of Foreign Affairs. But, as James Schoff notes, "the Koizumi years have been a traumatic time for the MOFA."[59] As the role of the Cabinet Office expanded, an increasing number of officials were seconded from the JDA—twice as many in 2005 (more than sixty, including ten military officers) as in 1995.[60] Three deputy cabinet secretary posts were established, one each allotted to foreign affairs, finance, and defense, putting the JDA on an equal footing with MOFA for the first time. Much to the chagrin of Japan's professional diplomats, negotiations with the Pentagon over U.S. "force realignment" in 2006 were led by the JDA and not by MOFA, "as was customary."[61] When he became prime minister in September 2006, Abe Shinzō's first act was to further remodel the Kantei in the image of the White House.[62] Within months he also saw to it that the JDA would become the MOD.

The trimming of bureaucratic prerogative and the rebuilding of bureaucratic powers continued with the second major institutional change, a frontal assault on the power of the Cabinet Legislation Bureau. As we have seen, the CLB had long played a central role in managing the Yoshida Doctrine. The problem, from the perspective of the antimainstream conservatives, was that these officials had worked closely with their political overlords in the LDP mainstream to keep security policy under wraps.[63] In their view, the CLB had usurped the politicians' role in civilian control of the Japanese military. In addition to defining "war potential" (*senryoku*) so narrowly in 1952 that Japanese forces have been hamstrung ever since, the CLB could declare collective self-defense (*shūdanteki bōei*) unconstitutional, both of which infuriated the revisionists. And they had long been apoplectic over the CLB's tortured May 1981 interpretation of Article 9, which recognized Japan's right of collective self-defense but declared its exercise forbidden. When the CLB (again with political approval, of course) dug in its heels during the debate over response to the Gulf War in 1991, making it impossible for the SDF to be dispatched until after the war was over, the newly ascendant revisionists vowed to make changes. And they did.[64]

First, though, their like-minded, sometime ally, Ozawa Ichirō, forced the issue. In August 1999, when he demanded fuller control of the CLB as the price for bringing his Liberal Party into the governing coalition, the CLB director general with whom he had had contretemps on the Diet floor was forced to resign and his successors were barred from answering Diet interpellations on behalf of cabinet ministers.[65] Prime Minister Koizumi brought the CLB—and the rest of the bureaucracy—under further political control. Although the CLB was not eliminated, it was forced to conduct its business on a very short political leash, its noncongenial interpretations left unsolicited.[66] The same CLB that ruled in 1996 that "it is problematic to amend the law to enable the prime minister to control and supervise the ministries and agencies—even during an emergency" now was more fully controlled than ever. It stood aside as the revisionists made the prime minister presidential.[67] In this way, Japanese politicians took a giant step toward reconfiguring civil-military relations.

The CLB was not the revisionists' only target. Koizumi's team also vowed to go after the councillors (*sanjikan*) within the JDA.[68] Director General Ishiba insisted that the (mostly younger) politicians who understood national security issues should assume control of the defense establishment and must no longer rely on the councillors as their proxies. He also elevated the status of the senior military officers in each service branch, making them the equivalent of the councillors. "Prime Minister Koizumi told me," he explained, "that 'politicians need to be able to argue with bureaucrats.' This was a major change. The bureaucrats learned that they can no longer expect ministers who know nothing."[69] Civilian officials predictably developed an "Ishiba strategy" (*Ishiba taisaku*) and "dug in and waited for Ishiba's term to end."[70] But the writing was on the wall, and the civilian bureaucrats had lost considerable ground. In addition to the long-standard posting of junior lawmakers to each ministry as parliamentary vice ministers to educate them about policy issues, the Koizumi team appointed senior politicians as vice ministers to give politicians even further supervisory influence in the policy process. In the JDA, it would be difficult to confuse bureaucratic

Figure 3. Prime Minister Abe reviews the Self-Defense Force honor guard at the ceremony marking the creation of Japan's first Ministry of Defense in January 2007. Reprinted with permission of Kyodo News.

control with civilian control any longer, especially after January 2007 when it became a full-fledged ministry.

The revisionists also brought along a Japanese press that had always reflexively invoked fears of militarism.[71] Even the *Asahi Shimbun* began to publish positive accounts of the SDF, including for the first time interviews with uniformed officers.[72] One *Asahi* senior staff writer went even further, insisting "there is no more likelihood of resurgent militarism in Japan than there is of the reintroduction of slavery in the United States, or of further seizure of Mexican territory."[73] When it was learned in 2004 that the U.S. military and the SDF had produced an annual coordinated joint-outline emergency plan from 1955 to 1975 to unify the military command in an emergency—and that the plans were kept secret from the prime minister—the public could barely stifle a yawn.[74] The very legitimacy of the Japanese military is no longer in question, and concerns about civilian control have receded. Yamagata's ghost had been shoved into the shadows, surely one of the greatest changes since the Pacific War.

A third institutional change—the transformation of the Japan Coast Guard (JCG) into a de facto fourth branch of the Japanese military—may be the most significant and is certainly the least heralded. The Japan Coast Guard

Law (Hoanchō Hō) was revised by the Diet at the same time that the more prominent antiterror legislation authorized the dispatch of ships to Diego Garcia. Unlike the MSDF dispatch to the Indian Ocean, which was limited to the supply of fuel for U.S. and British troops, the Coast Guard Law, as amended, allowed the outright use of force to prevent maritime intrusion and to protect the Japanese homeland. Now the Coast Guard—still legally a "law enforcement agency" within the Ministry of Land, Infrastructure, and Transport and not part of the JDA except in an emergency—is assigned rules of engagement more relaxed than those of the SDF. Local commanders are authorized to use force under the conditions of "justifiable defense" (*seitō bōei*) and during an "emergency" (*kinkyū*). Warning shots, if ignored, can be followed by disabling fire targeted on the offending vessel's propellers in order to disable it.[75] Within one month, in the first Japanese use of force since the end of the Pacific War, Prime Minister Obuchi ordered the Japanese Coast Guard to fire upon a North Korean vessel, which, unmarked and refusing to identify itself, was known as a "mystery ship" (*fushinsen*). The DPRK vessel reportedly scuttled itself in the Chinese Exclusive Economic Zone to avoid capture. Fifteen North Korean crewmembers were killed in the firefight.[76] David Leheny calls revision of the Coast Guard Law "the canary in the coal mine"—a prototype for further expansion of military authority.[77]

Those who guided the development of the Japan Coast Guard (Kaijō Hoanchō) vigorously deny this, insisting instead that the new, improved JCG (the English rendering of the name was changed from Maritime Safety Agency in April 2000) is merely a long overdue modernization, "changing an analog JCG into a digital one."[78] They maintain that while militaries fight one another, coast guards enforce laws and are partners in crime fighting.[79] Still, using the term for "war potential" (*senryoku*), which was declared unconstitutional in Article 9, the JCG White Paper headlines the JCG's "New Fighting Power!" (*arata na senryoku!*) and trumpets repeatedly its expanding security role. It explicitly lists "securing the safety of the sea-lanes" (*kaijō kōtsū no anzen kakuho*) and "maintaining order on the seas" alongside rescue, firefighting, and environmental protection as core missions.[80] In April 2005, Prime Minister Koizumi visited Indian Prime Minister Manmohan Singh in New Delhi, and the two governments announced their Eight-fold Initiative for Strengthening Japan-India Global Partnership, specifying enhanced security cooperation "on a sustained basis" between the nations' navies and coast guards.[81] Insisting that the JCG is not a fourth branch of the SDF, one senior JDA official argues it is Japan's first line of defense, serving as a "litmus paper for MSDF action." He acknowledges that the MSDF and the JCG coordinate more closely than ever before.[82] A senior intelligence officer further acknowledges that the JCG routinely participates in cabinet intelligence briefings.[83]

Certainly, the reinvention of the Japan Coast Guard was politically expedient. Mainstream politicians and political parties (including both the Kōmeitō within the ruling coalition as well as the opposition Japan Communist Party) that would not abide increased defense spending were more than willing to increase maritime safety and international cooperation. Calling it a "tactful approach," one senior JDA official notes: "Prime Minister Koizumi could not increase the defense budget because of the Kōmeitō, so he expanded the roles and missions of the Coast Guard instead."[84]

Senior political leaders can be even more direct. Upper house member Yamamoto Ichita, chair of the LDP Policy Committee on Foreign Affairs, minces no words:

> I am concerned about decreasing defense budgets.... [But] the increase in the Coast Guard Budget is timely and will serve Japan's national interests.... We should increase the MSDF [budget], but this is difficult. Instead, we have to pay more attention to the Coast Guard, where it is easier to increase resources to make Japan's seas safer.[85]

With widespread support, including from defense-related Diet politicians (*bōeizoku giin*), the Coast Guard has developed an impressive fleet with as much as 65 percent of the total tonnage of China's surface fleet.[86] It includes eighty-nine armed patrol ships of over five hundred tons, some fifty-six of which are over one thousand tons. (The Chinese Customs Service, the JCG's closest analogue, acquired its first ship on this scale in 2005.) In 2005, when JDA budgets were cut, the Coast Guard equipment budget was *increased* to an average of fifty billion yen per year for the next seven years, with funds earmarked for modernization, including twenty-one new boats and seven new jets, as well as replacement of older boats and planes.[87] In 2006, when the JDA budget was again cut, the JCG received delivery of two long-range (twelve-thousand-mile) Gulfstream V jets configured like unmanned aerial vehicles for continuous data collection and real time ship identification, as well as two patrol ships with advanced fire-control systems, 20mm and 40mm cannons, and advanced-targeting night vision capabilities, which it dispatched for duty near the disputed Senkaku Islands. These ships have no antisubmarine capabilities and no antiaircraft radar, nor are they armed with missiles. Still, with a top speed of more than thirty knots, a length of ninety-five meters, and weighing nearly two thousand tons, they are about two-thirds the size of *Hatsuyuki*-class destroyers, Japan's most numerous.[88]

The JCG White Paper speaks of "cooperation on the high seas" with Russia, Korea, and China, countries with which there are unresolved—and combustible—territorial disputes.[89] Since 1999 senior leaders of the coast guards of each of these nations have met annually with those from Canada and the United States to discuss marine security, refugee flows, fisheries enforcement, and smuggling. But the Japan Coast Guard has also been deployed far from the Japanese coast—in the South China Sea, along with the MSDF and the naval forces of thirteen countries in the U.S.-led Proliferation Security Initiative, and in Southeast Asia, to participate in multilateral antipiracy exercises. In October 2005 it also participated in the multinational rescue mission after the earthquake in Pakistan, and in May 2006, China, Japan, Russia, Canada, the Republic of Korea, and the United States agreed to conduct an interdiction exercise designed by the JCG, before it was cancelled due to difficulties in Sino-Japanese diplomacy.[90] According to the former JCG director general, "So long as the Japan Coast Guard is in pursuit of a criminal, it can sail out even to the Persian Gulf."[91]

No doubt because the JCG is described as a police force, rather than as a military one, these distant deployments have ruffled few feathers at home or abroad. To assure that a benign view of the JCG persists, the Japanese government has tied it to its foreign aid program. It is now routine for the JCG to assist Southeast Asian states with training and technology to help them police the Strait of Malacca and other areas along the Middle East oil routes.[92] Monthlong conferences on maritime safety attended by coast guard officials from members of the Association of Southeast Asian Nations (ASEAN) are funded through the Japan International Cooperation Agency, Japan's foreign aid agency. Agency funds set aside as "antiterror grant aid" were also used to provide the Indonesian and Philippine coast guards with three fast patrol craft each in 2006.[93] Because these ships were equipped with bulletproof glass, they were classified as "weapons" by the Ministry of Economy, Trade and Industry (METI), but because they were unarmed and were supplied to a coast guard, the Japanese government claimed it was not violating its arms export ban. Acknowledging that this was the first time that the Japanese government had ever used official development assistance to transfer weapons, Chief Cabinet Secretary Abe Shinzō set conditions on their use. The boats (valued at two billion yen) could be deployed only against terrorists or pirates, and any subsequent sale or transfer to a third party would require the permission of the Japanese government. Apparently the Japanese government helped Indonesia (and Malaysia, which purchased similar ships) create their coast guards in order to avoid the overt transfer of arms to foreign militaries, a move one senior JDA official called "very smart."[94] If this is the shape of things to come, Japan has taken another step toward ending its self-imposed ban on the export of arms and providing military aid to neighboring states. The "canary in the coal mine" metaphor again seems apt.

The fourth, impending, institutional change is the most arresting. Revision of the U.S.-imposed constitution—the holy grail of antimilitarism—is once again in play. Indeed, it is closer to realization than at any time in the past sixty years. Picking up on a shift in popular sentiment after the Gulf War—indeed, capitalizing on generational change and unprecedented public acceptance of the SDF—revisionists began to paint Article 9 as an obstacle to "international cooperation." They launched a sustained effort to make the constitution conform to international standards they considered "normal." Revisionists secured several major legislative victories in the 1990s, including the establishment of Diet research commissions that issued final reports in April 2005. They were also joined by influential new allies in the media and academia. Years before the LDP's first draft, the *Yomiuri Shimbun*, Japan's largest daily newspaper, drafted a constitution that would specify the right of collective self-defense. Japanese universities continued to employ academics advocating pacifist positions, but the new generation includes more scholars favoring a change in Article 9 than was the case in the 1950s.[95] By the end of the decade, revisionist support and accomplishments had accumulated. The Self-Defense Forces and Coast Guard were able to engage in a growing list of widely accepted activities once deemed unconstitutional, and the LDP and the Democratic Party of Japan, the major opposition party, were both positioned to support constitutional revision. It looked ever more likely that the constitution would be revised to acknowledge that Japan has a legitimate military and can legally engage in collective defense. Once again, Yoshida Shigeru may have been prophetic. In his memoirs he had defended opposition to revision of Article Nine but allowed that "obviously there exists no reason why revision should not come in the long run [so long as the Japanese people are] watchful and vigilant.... The actual work of revision would only be undertaken when public opinion as a whole has finally come to demand it."[96]

After the end of the cold war—and after serial encounters with North Korea, in particular—Japanese public opinion shifted dramatically. The positive impression of the SDF grew in nearly a straight line from the mid-1970s, according to Cabinet Office polls.[97] The SDF benefited from successful PKO missions to Cambodia and Mozambique, as well as from positive press related to its operations in disaster relief. In fact, the majority of Japanese polled between 1997 and 2003 believed that disaster relief was the top mission for the SDF, a result belying the impression that the Japanese public was embracing a national security mission. After all, the public preferred that SDF capabilities be expanded but was expressing heightened concern about Japan's being drawn into war. The sticking point was cost: the number of Japanese willing to increase the defense budget had risen but remained at barely 10 percent in 2003.[98] Attitudes toward the United States and the alliance were stable and mostly positive, while those toward Russia remained stable and entirely negative. Apart from volatile attitudes toward China and both Koreas, the biggest change in public opinion regarding security issues in the past decade and a half has been

[81]

support for revision of the constitution. Depending on the poll and the question, support for constitutional revision in general first exceeded opposition in the early 1990s (*Yomiuri Shimbun*) or a few years later (*Asahi Shimbun*). By April 2005, those who supported and those who opposed revision of Article 9 were in a statistical dead heat. The Japanese public had come a very long way.[99]

THE ALLIANCE: MOTHER OF ALL CATALYSTS

The United States was cheering these changes, but not from the sidelines. For decades it had pressured Japan to play a more active military role even while it kept Tokyo on a short leash. But Japanese strategists had proclaimed their pacifism, and the asymmetry in the alliance remained acceptable to both sides because their interests were so closely aligned. Christopher Hughes characterizes this with particular clarity:

> The common Soviet threat blurred the distinction between Japan's activities under the security treaty to provide for its own defense and those activities providing support for the United States that could have been construed as providing for the defense of the U.S. and East Asia region....In the post-Cold War period, this strategic bargain threatened to come unstuck as a series of global and regional crises revealed its essential emptiness.[100]

Indeed, after a decade of trade frictions had threatened to destabilize the security relationship, it was the *U.S.* side that relaxed pressure on Japan.[101] President Clinton and Prime Minister Hashimoto reached an agreement in April 1996 that reinforced the alliance and reassured the allies.

But these dynamics changed after 9/11. Defense Secretary Donald Rumsfeld announced plans for U.S. "force transformation" in November 2001, signalling a more flexible global posture. Within two years, it was clear that the formal alliances of the United States could be supplanted by more informal "coalitions of the willing," as in Iraq. The message was not lost on the Japanese. One ASDF general, Marumo Yoshinari, observed that the United States was now "marketizing" its alliances: countries could buy a place by contributing to mutual security.[102] The Japanese Council on Defense Studies concluded that neither treaties nor shared values would suffice to hold partnerships together: "The key to alliances now is risk sharing."[103] Former JDA director general Ishiba acknowledged that everything had changed. The United States ceased to issue demands. Its allies now would have to have an answer ready when the Americans asked: "What are you prepared to do?"[104]

Some Japanese grew as concerned about entanglement as they were about abandonment. The *Asahi Shimbun* concluded that "without its being seen by the public, the cold war U.S.-Japan alliance is being replaced by the unification (*ittaika*) [of U.S. and Japanese forces]."[105] Would the SDF become a fifth branch of the U.S. armed forces?[106] If so, would it be forced to undertake operations beyond the defense of the main islands?[107] After the GDSF was withdrawn from Samawah Province in Iraq, the ASDF was tasked with supporting U.S. troops in Baghdad. A major daily immediately suggested: "Transporting U.S. Troops May Drag the ASDF into America's War."[108] How could Japan avoid entrapment in U.S. wars? The predominant view—expressed by government officials and analysts alike—was that Japan's "near irreversible dependence" on the United States forced security planners to hug the United States more closely than ever and, if necessary, to be prepared to shed blood.[109] The 2004 NDPG adopted the U.S. language of force transformation and stressed "flexibility," mobility," and "adaptability."

This decision has not come cost free. No matter how much the Japanese were prepared to increase their contribution to the alliance, it was never quite enough. Some Japanese believe they have had to play "catch-up" to U.S. demands, whereas the U.S. Department of Defense was convinced that the alliance has been playing "catch-up" to changes in the global security environment.[110] U.S. officials called on Japan to create a more balanced, more equal, more "normal" defense relationship.[111] Their exhortations prompted one U.S. observer to suggest that "the only thing that has risen faster than the level of cooperation between our two nations during the Bush-Koizumi era has been the level of Washington's expectations."[112] Predictably, there were consequences. Japanese scholars and analysts wondered aloud where Japanese national interests are located in the U.S. global agenda.[113] Others pointed to the low (and decreasing) level of public support for U.S. foreign policy. In 2005, a majority of Japanese believed that Japan should cooperate with Washington in world affairs, but more than half also did not trust the United States and an equal number believed that U.S. forces should leave Japan.[114] Indeed, when asked to identify the "number one problem" for the alliance, former JDA director general Ohno Yoshinori replied, "the Occupation-era base structure." He called for a new status of forces agreement (SOFA).[115]

There were other, greater changes afoot. U.S. force transformation, combined with the palpable threat from Pyongyang, provided Japanese revisionists with a long-awaited opportunity to enhance SDF capabilities. The U.S. force transformation made it more acceptable to discuss the need to recognize the right to collective self-defense. Abe Shinzō made this a top priority during his campaign to become prime minister in 2006.[116] Even revision of the Mutual Security Treaty was back on the table. The real challenge was for Japan to learn how to "judiciously utilize the power of the

United States," and its main challenge was to find a way to "manage American hegemony."[117] As one Diet member insisted, "Japan's roles and missions should not be confined to rear-area support."[118] Indeed, many in the Japanese security community welcomed U.S. pressure for this very reason. They were eager to move from the "principle of passive alignment" that guided the Yoshida Doctrine to an "active alliance relationship."[119] U.S. demands factored into Japanese plans for expanded roles and missions as a new division of labor (*yakuwari buntan*) was constructed. Tokuchi Hideshi, an author of the 2004 NDPG, insisted that since the alliance is "indispensable" for security in Asia, Japan's new strategy should acknowledge the need for "shared understandings of the new security environment" and the establishment of "common strategic objectives."[120] After three years of DoD pressure—in the form of a "Defense Policy Review Initiative" that sought a shared assessment of strategy and threats as well as a common assessment of the roles and missions required to meet them—the Japanese government formally signed on to an explicit set of "common strategic objectives" in February 2005.[121]

This overhaul created as many options for Japan as it foreclosed. The press focused on shared bases, but Japanese defense officials avoided endorsing the idea of "joint" commands. Former JDA director general Ishiba Shigeru warned that Japan must "not get caught in America's wake," and explicitly ruled out the possibility that the SDF would ever become part of the U.S. military command. Japan, rather, would become a cooperative, equal partner of the United States because it is in Japan's interests to do so.[122] But adding new missions to the alliance also enhances Japan's ability to act outside the alliance should it choose to do so. Retired MSDF admiral Yamazaki Makoto called for a new maritime defense strategy and insisted that "in addition to strengthening the alliance, Japan has to strengthen its own defense capabilities."[123] One U.S. military analyst noted that integration of forces is less likely than the conversion of a constrained Japanese military into a "labile" one. He argued that Japan has no more attractive strategic option than the U.S. alliance, *"at least not now,"* adding: "By building a record of cooperation, Japan's military capabilities will also grow [thereby providing] more room for independence."[124] The alliance and cooperation are formally reaffirmed at every turn in official documents, but opportunities are seldom lost inside Japan to assert that Tokyo has many security challenges, one of which is the need to "rediscover the ability to make its own decisions."[125]

I have documented a great deal of change. Clearly the tectonic plates of global and Asian security have been shifting. With the Soviet Union gone, the United States was unchallenged, and for a time there was no global balance of power. Now, China is rising. It has displaced the United States as Japan's largest trading partner, and it has begun to acquire if not yet flex coercive muscle. North Korea has become a de facto nuclear power with demonstrated missile capability to reach all of Japan, yet U.S. forces have been reduced and redeployed. Japan is reacting to these uncertainties by embracing the United States closely while developing capabilities of its own to hedge against the risks of a rapidly changing security environment. Japanese policy intellectuals and government officials continue to review their options energetically.[126]

At home, the Japanese military has shifted demonstrably in the direction of liberal democratic values, and both the social status of Japan's troops and their morale have improved. The institutions of Japanese domestic politics have also been transformed in ways that affect security policy. The powers of the prime minister have been centralized in the Kantei at the expense of existing ministries and agencies. This more "presidential" system makes it easier for Japan to act decisively in international affairs. Meanwhile, public support for the Japanese military and for constitutional changes that will provide it more legitimacy have never been stronger. The legal status of U.S. forces in Japan has not changed, however. The original Status of Forces Agreement, signed in 1960, remains in effect. So, therefore, do extraterritorial privileges that rankle Japanese citizens and statesmen. Despite Japan's embrace of its U.S. ally, therefore, local support for U.S. bases sixty years after the end of the war continues to erode. These fundamental changes in international and domestic politics have enabled an evolution in Japanese security strategy and, thereby, in the U.S.-Japan alliance. Let us turn now to a closer examination of the strategic elements of these changes.

[4]

Whither the Yoshida Doctrine?

Even if the 1990s was a "lost decade" in economic terms, it was a period of major transformation for security policy.[1] Senior defense officials may still claim demurely that Japan is in a "rudimentary phase" of determining its grand strategy, but Prime Minister Obuchi Keizō long ago declared that the SDF had passed into a new phase, from an institution being built to one being used.[2] Never since 1945 have the Self-Defense Forces been so capable and so widely accepted—and postwar Japanese diplomats and military planners have never been as openly assertive about the importance of "getting security right."

A reinstitutionalization of Japanese grand strategy is under way in full public view: fifteen new security-related laws were enacted between 1991 and 2003, and a Defense Ministry was created in 2007. Japan's new suite of security-policy institutions reflects a pragmatic effort by politicians and planners to integrate autonomy and prestige for the first time in modern Japanese history. If they succeed, Japan will have its first democratically crafted constitution and a fully legitimate military under civilian control, and it will assume more expansive roles and missions within its alliance with the United States, including the use of force in collective self-defense. Japan will be better positioned to avoid entanglement in U.S. adventures, and better fortified to resist Chinese pressure. Not everything will be brand new, but neither will it be business as usual. The resulting transformation—however incremental—will seem as epochal as what transpired after the Pacific War.

As we saw in chapter 3, there was no single "big bang" forcing this transformation, though the end of the cold war comes close. Instead, the confluence of shifts in global, regional, and domestic balances of power enabled Japanese security strategists to whittle away at the Yoshida Doctrine. Yoshida's grand strategy has not been entirely abandoned—witness the delicate placement of lightly armed SDF troops in Samawah, as far from the violence in Iraq as possible. Still, a sustained mission to support the U.S. Navy in a Middle East crisis and an SDF presence in Iraq during a war never fully blessed by the United Nations suggests how far Japan has come.

STRATEGIC SLICING?

In the early 1990s, German defense minister Volker Rühe openly declared the need for public support if the Bundeswehr was to step up to "new realities, responsibilities, and expectations" in the post–cold war environment.[3] Rühe was determined to coax German public opinion slowly and deliberately from its pacifist shell by deploying an incremental *salami taktik*—one slice at a time. For Germany, this "progressive assertiveness" began with participation in UN peacekeeping in Somalia and Bosnia in medical, supply, and logistical roles. Before long, German forces were used to monitor the Bosnian no-fly zone. The parallels to Japan are obvious.[4]

So are the questions it raises. Did the Japanese follow Rühe's lead and begin slicing with a set strategic vision, or were they merely seizing opportunities as they presented themselves? And if the Japanese were acting strategically, who was their Volker Rühe? Kobayashi Yutaka, an upper house LDP Diet member with an interest in security issues, insists there has been no such Japanese leader. Japan has simply been "going with the flow."[5] But career JDA officials suggest otherwise. One insists that "because the consensus [on the need to do more on security] was so widespread and so deeply rooted, it is hard to think of it as just tactical."[6] Another, who participated in the strategic planning process, agrees and offers an alternative metaphor for "salami slicing." In his view, the series of changes made to Japan's security are like a string of tubers pulled from the earth (*imozuru shiki*). Once one is pulled, all come up from the ground. He reports that soon after the Gulf War and the deployment of Japan's first PKO, Hatakeyama Shigeru, the JDA administrative vice minister, asked each of his bureau chiefs to identify needed reforms. Each contributed a list, with items assigned a priority based on likely public acceptance and political viability. After sorting, these lists were coordinated by the bureaus and distilled into fourteen strategic issues fundamental to future Japanese national security. The first eight themes were assigned to study teams in January 1994:

- Expansion of the UN Security Council
- Draft new Basic Security Law (*Kihon Hō*)
- Response to regional contingencies
- Policies for regional stabilization

[87]

- Weapons management and arms reduction
- Strengthening the technology base
- Review of military base policies
- New functions for armed force in response to contemporary needs

Hatakeyama gave each team six months to generate a report and made it clear that he wanted every part of the JDA involved (*zenchō*). One participant recalls that "it was a lively time, one in which we worked freely with big ideas."[7] This was precisely the point of the exercise: What would it take for Japanese security policy to become "normal"? According to another participant, "the list was designed to challenge the Yoshida approach...[and] to examine how Japan could pull back from the extreme position of postwar Japan."[8] The Hatakeyama remit instructed officials to engage in "free and wide-ranging discussion (*jiyū katsu habahiroku kentō*) to deepen debate within the Defense Agency" on national security issues considered from both "medium- and long-term perspectives" (*chūchōkiteki kanten kara*). It also explicitly called for engaging the efforts of the JDA's next generation of strategists.[9]

The reports were vetted during the summer by office directors, councilors, the vice minister, and the chiefs of staff of the uniformed services. No politicians were involved in the process, but selected political leaders were briefed about the outcome. After considerable "free debate" (*jiyū na giron*) six new themes were added:

- Participation in UN peacekeeping operations
- Strengthening the Japan-U.S. alliance
- Asia-Pacific regional security
- Proliferation of weapons of mass destruction
- SDF Communications, Command, Control, and Intelligence systems (C^3I)
- Nurturing talent to respond to "internationalization"

Participants insist that this bottom-up review was designed to be "informal," but its results have found their way into the public domain and routinely inform Japan's policy debate.[10]

Even if it has not yet been overtly proclaimed by political leaders, Japan has been deliberately assembling (rather than groping to define) a post–cold war grand strategy. Japan's political leaders agreed with professional security bureaucrats about what needed to be changed. Indeed, it is naïve to imagine that grand strategy and opportunism oppose each other. The former clearly can empower the latter. Likewise, it is naïve not to appreciate how opportunism can be justified (and possibly inflated) by international expectations. One can guess that there is no small measure of opportunism at work when the JDA's National Institute for Defense Studies reports that the expansion of Japan's security portfolio "indicates just how strong the demand is in the international community today for defense activities in regions lying beyond the areas surrounding Japan."[11] Japanese politicians often invoke international norms to justify changes they wish made in domestic policy, as David Leheny demonstrates.[12] The notion of "international contribution" was inserted everywhere in the Japanese discourse during the 1990s and was used more than any other justification to legitimate the expansion of Japan's security portfolio.[13] One need not be cynical to appreciate that "international contribution" (*kokusai kōken*) is much more attractive than "U.S. pressure." In this way, opportunity and strategy informed each other and were used with internationalism to transform Japan's post–cold war security posture.

EARLY SLICES

Three important slices were taken long before the end of the cold war and the formation of the Hatakeyama team. All were the result of demands made by the Reagan administration, which was determined to get more from Japan on security than President Carter who had increased Japanese host nation support but shied away from demanding "burden sharing." The first, and most significant, was the 1981 decision that the Japanese Maritime Self-Defense Force would patrol the sea lanes of communication as far as one thousand nautical miles.[14] Announced suddenly by President Reagan and Prime Minister Suzuki at a summit in May 1981, the news generated a fractious Diet debate. The roles and missions of the MSDF had been limited to the so-called *zabuton* (seat cushion) model, that is, simply making sure that the U.S. Seventh Fleet and Marines had a comfortable base from which to operate.[15] Now the MSDF would protect shipping in the Pacific. But it was clear that the Americans actually had other roles and missions in mind. The United States wanted support for its offensive missions and help hunting Soviet submarines. After Foreign Minister Itō Masayoshi declared that such support was not unreasonable for allies—using the word *dōmei*—he was forced to resign, much to the surprise of many on the U.S. side.

Japan may not have been ready to declare itself openly an ally (despite its long-standing Mutual Security Treaty), but after the Diet acquiesced, Washington got what it wanted operationally. Within a year, the JDA nearly doubled procurement of P-3Cs, its maritime patrol aircraft, which were built by Kawasaki Heavy Industries on license from the Lockheed Corporation. Within four years, the number of P-3Cs had increased from forty-five to one hundred, and before long the MSDF had become what seemed to some observers "an integrated arm of the Seventh Fleet."[16] MSDF patrols in the East and South China seas freed up the Seventh Fleet for operations in the Indian Ocean. By the mid-1990s, with the threat from Soviet subs gone, their mission shifted to include patrol of surface ships to stop shipments of illegal workers and surveillance for sea-based missile launches. This change also provided justification for the deployment of minesweepers to the Persian Gulf in 1991 and later for MSDF deployment to Diego Garcia in support of U.S. and British forces operating in Afghanistan after the 9/11 attacks on Washington, D.C., and New York.

The second Reagan-era change happened in 1983, when Prime Minister Nakasone agreed to exclude defense technology exports to the United States from Japan's ban on arms export. By the 1980s it was clear that commercial technologies were driving much U.S. defense procurement. The DoD was buying large volumes of civilian off-the-shelf technologies such as memory chips and fiber-reinforced materials. Japan's rise to global dominance in these and related technologies did not go unnoticed at the Pentagon. In 1984, the U.S. Defense Science Board judged Japanese industry to be at or ahead of U.S. competence in sixteen areas, including optical fibers, artificial intelligence, and x-ray lithography, all of which were deemed critical for the U.S. defense industrial base. Fearing public disapproval, Japanese firms were not eager to sell these technologies to the U.S. military. Thus, the Reagan-Nakasone memorandum of understanding was seen as particularly timely and helpful. Still, between 1983 and 2005, there were only fourteen cases of formal defense technology exports by Japanese firms to the United States.[17] The first case was portable surface-to-air missile (SAM) technology in 1986. Others included technology transfer in naval shipbuilding, propulsion technologies, and, in 1990, radars and co-cured composites for the highly controversial FS-X coproduction project between Mitsubishi Heavy Industries and General Dynamics (later Lockheed). The Japanese also transferred improved P-3C digital flight control technology back to Lockheed in 1992. Given the hoopla surrounding the agreement and the hopes on both sides, fourteen cases in twenty-two years add up to no more than a fragment of the potential. As one JDA official remarked: "We would like to do a lot more."[18]

The third Reagan-era concession also was more symbolic than substantive. In 1985, at the 11th G-7 summit, held in Bonn, President Reagan formally invited allied nations to join his proposed Strategic Defense Initiative (SDI)—the so-called Star Wars system. Under pressure to accommodate the United States during a period of considerable trade friction, and wishing to signal a tough line toward a menacing Soviet Union eager to block SDI, Prime Minister Nakasone eventually agreed. Nakasone clutched at the notion that SDI would be nonnuclear and defensive in nature and that it was ultimately intended to make possible the complete elimination of all nuclear weapons. He also made a show of extracting U.S. promises that SDI was part of a more general multilateral deterrent, that it would lead to nuclear arms reductions, that it would not violate the ABM treaty, and that development and deployment would be undertaken only after consultations among allies and only after negotiation with the USSR.[19] In the event, Japanese companies participated in the Pentagon's WESTPAC project, an early study of missile defense requirements in the western Pacific, and the Japanese government steered clear of most formal activity. Japan's limited participation in SDI has been criticized as "excruciatingly distant" and as "marginal to the overall U.S. program," but it was another early step in the transformation of the Yoshida Doctrine.[20]

SLICING IN EARNEST

The attack on the Yoshida Doctrine began in earnest only after the cold war ended and Japan endured its "greatest trial," the humiliation of failing to respond adequately during the 1991 Gulf War.[21] Over the course of three discrete periods of military modernization, Japanese strategists, having identified a list of necessary changes, moved opportunistically to slice away at antimilitarist restrictions.[22] It was easiest to start with policies that were ideologically most congenial and geographically most distant. The strategy—at least as we can now reconstruct it—was to expand legal and operational capacities for the most overtly peaceful SDF roles and missions, saving for later those which were more publicly military and closest to the homeland.[23] Thus, most accounts begin with Tokyo's determined reaction in 1992 to its fumbled response to the 1991 Gulf War.

Stung by international criticism of the failure to provide troops, and emboldened by public support for the deployment of minesweepers, Japanese revisionists redoubled their efforts to gain legal authority for the dispatch of troops.[24] They attacked pragmatists and pacifists simultaneously and declared war on the CLB. And, for the first time, they began to win. LDP secretary-general Ozawa Ichirō introduced new legislation to allow the SDF to participate in UN peacekeeping operations (the so-called PKO bill). Ozawa was particularly active during the two Diet sessions it took to pass, chairing an LDP ad hoc panel that argued that a reinterpretation of Article 9 was sufficient to allow for SDF participation in multinational forces operating under UN command or sanction. The SDF would thus be permitted to participate in combat roles. Opposition mounted from Prime Minister Miyazawa, other pragmatists in the LDP, and the CLB. When Ozawa finally brokered an agreement on the bill, the SDF's mandate saw only modest expansion.

Passage of the International Peace Cooperation Law (PKO law) in 1992 marked the first revision of the ban on overseas dispatch in nearly forty years. But old constraints were replaced with new ones. A new set of principles required the Japanese government to withdraw its troops at the first sign of hostilities and denied the SDF the right to use force to accomplish a UN mission. This helped gain the support not only of pragmatists in the LDP but of pacifist parties in the Diet. The small centrist parties demanded further concessions, however, including a freeze on peacekeeping force (PKF) participation, which kept the SDF from performing such duties as cease-fire monitoring, weapons collection and disposal, and buffer zone patrols.

It was by no means easy for the SDF to deal with decades of restrictions even after it got the green light to participate in UN missions. Its first mission to Cambodia in 1992 required maps and intelligence provided by the U.S. military. It had no lift capacity to move its six hundred soldiers and four hundred vehicles and had to rely on civilian transports. Worst of all, sending even a single jeep entangled the SDF in arms export regulations. The Japanese military could not even stockpile tires overseas until these regulations were changed.[25] But these missions were so successful that in December 2001 the Diet revised existing law to allow the SDF to be deployed in UN PKF missions. Now the SDF had authority to separate and disarm combatants, collect weapons, and supervise the exchange of prisoners—exactly the sorts of activity it had been denied when the PKO Law passed after the 1991 Gulf War. With this authority "unfrozen," all that was required was an appropriate PKF opportunity. The first such opportunity arrived in early 2005, when the Cabinet Office quietly discussed whether to join the UN PKF being assembled for the Darfur region in Sudan. After considerable deliberation, however, the Cabinet Office decided that "Sudan was too far away and Japan had no national interest at stake there."[26]

With the PKO Law safely passed and the SDF back from successful missions abroad, the Japanese government turned to expanding its roles and missions within the U.S. alliance. The SDF, limited for so long to homeland security by its Basic Defense Force Concept, had made its first "international contribution." The next logical step was to win support for a regional military role. This was made easier by the Mutual Security Treaty, which already stipulated that the alliance covers threats to "international peace and security in the Far East" as well as to the Japanese homeland. The United States, which had long since loosened its leash on Japan, was only too happy to oblige. But Tokyo disappointed Washington during the 1993–94 Korean crisis by balking at the prospect of coordinated military operations. Afterward, the allies engaged in "serious, specific, and substantive" joint analysis, including intelligence exchanges, search and rescue missions, coordinated minesweeping, airspace control, base security, and logistical support.[27]

By the mid-1990s, after years of trade friction that had threatened the security relationship, and after the Korean crisis had revealed serious operational disabilities, both sides were determined to reinforce the alliance. In April

Table 1. The Incremental Transformation of the Yoshida Doctrine

1954–1991	1991	1992	1993	1994	1995	1996	1997	1998	1999	2000	2001	2002	2003	2004	2005	2006	2007
																	Elevation of JDA to ministry
																Central readiness command	
																Precision guided munitions	
															Arms exports		
														Missile defense			
														Emergency measures law			
														Special operations			
													Iraq dispatch				
											Coast Guard law						
											Indian Ocean dispatch						
										Projection of force							
									Maritime interdiction								
									Transport of nationals								
								Surveillance satellite									
							JDA intelligence HQ										
							Constraints relaxed on uniformed officers										
						Acquisition and cross-servicing agreement											
											PKF						
						Areas surrounding Japan											
		PKO															
		International emergency assistance															
	Minesweepers to Persian Gulf																
Defense tech exports to U.S.																	
SDI																	
Sea-lane protection																	
Disaster relief																	
Maintenance of public order																	
Homeland defense																	

1996 in Tokyo, Prime Minister Hashimoto Ryūtarō and President Clinton reaffirmed the importance of the bilateral security alliance. This meeting has been celebrated as the "official end to the 'Japan bashing' era," but it might just as comfortably be called the beginning of an expansion of the alliance to cover regional contingencies.[28] In September 1996, the bilateral Security Consultative Committee (the U.S. secretaries of defense and state and the Japanese minister of foreign affairs and JDA director general—the so-called 2+2) met for the first time, and in September 1997 Japan and the United States adopted new defense cooperation guidelines. A new acquisition and cross-servicing agreement covered bilateral training and logistical support. It was revised in March 2004, allowing the SDF not only to assist U.S. forces during routine training but even to provide ammunition in the event of an armed attack.[29] The 1996 joint-guidelines agreement set up three areas for alliance cooperation: (1) the defense of Japan, (2) regional security, and (3) global cooperation, which provided the framework for all subsequent cooperation, including the dispatch of SDF forces to Iraq.[30]

De Facto Collective Self-Defense

Even if it was not "all of a sudden" or "right before our eyes," the norms of the Yoshida era were changing. In the process, the alliance was being transformed. Ambiguities remained concerning Japan's commitment in specific contingencies, such as in the Taiwan Strait, but now Japan had officially committed the SDF to missions in support of U.S. forces beyond the homeland. This commitment was underscored after Diet passage of the Law Concerning Measures to Ensure the Peace and Security of Japan in Situations in Areas Surrounding Japan (1999).[31] Joint exercises, once sharply limited, became commonplace. Japan had been participating in the U.S. Navy's regional training exercise since 1971, but in 1978 there were only three joint training exercises between the ASDF and the U.S. Air Force. Although the Nakasone government had increased joint training, issues of "collective self-defense" still were raised in the Diet, forcing the JDA to devise elaborate explanations for collaboration with the DoD.[32] In 1985 there had been only thirteen U.S.-Japan joint military exercises. By 2004 there were nearly twice as many, engaging ground as well as naval and air forces for the first time.[33] By 2000, Japanese fighter aircraft were being refueled routinely by U.S. air tankers.[34] This all added up to what one Japanese diplomat acknowledges was "the first attempt by Japan to bear even partial responsibility for the security of the region beyond its border."[35]

The alliance partners were inching their way toward collective self-defense. Even joint basing arrangements came under active review. But long before Japan could get there de jure, which would require either constitutional revision or a new CLB legal ruling, it got there de facto, thanks to the extraordinary political skill of Prime Minister Koizumi Junichirō.

Koizumi had become prime minister in April 2001. In his first press conference, he had called for a CLB study of the government interpretation of collective self-defense. Soon afterward Koizumi announced that there would be no change in the interpretation of Article 9 during his administration, adding that "there is room for cautious and mature deliberation."[36] Well before 9/11, Koizumi had put the bureaucracy and his political opponents on notice that his government was prepared for policy changes without CLB hermeneutics. It therefore was not surprising that Koizumi moved to establish an interministerial task force under his supervision within an hour of the 9/11 attacks and issued six initiatives (*seifu taisho hōshin*) by the following morning, including protection of U.S. forces in Japan and the dispatch of Japanese abroad if necessary. Koizumi got out in front of the cabinet, party, Diet, and CLB by declaring unqualified solidarity with the United States and promising military support. Only after meeting with coalition partners and holding a press conference did he explain the details to the LDP. By presenting a fait accompli to his own party, Koizumi served notice that his antimainstream had become the mainstream. "Lectured" by the CLB about what was and was not permissible in his draft "antiterror legislation," he openly confronted the director general, who never lectured him again.[37]

Nor, it seems, was Koizumi pressured in the familiar way by the United States. After decades of U.S. demands regarding trade and security, analysts ascribed shifts in Japanese public policy to "external pressure" (*gaiatsu*) exerted by the United States.[38] Indeed, some found it impossible to imagine the Japanese government taking bold steps without it. After 9/11, the Japanese media made much of an exhortation attributed to Deputy Secretary of State Richard Armitage, who reportedly asked Japan to "show the flag."[39] But this time, things were different. Although some in Tokyo did ask the United States to make demands, Washington proved more sophisticated. U.S. officials asked the Japanese government to increase protection of U.S. bases, but apart from providing lists of what was needed and of commitments made by other countries, the White House and State Department left it up to Tokyo to decide what responses were possible.[40] They knew the prime minister believed that Japan had failed its first exam a decade earlier in Kuwait, and its midterm exam in Korea in 1993–94, and that this could be a final exam for the alliance. The Cabinet Office compiled a list of suggestions solicited from the JDA, MOFA, MOF, and the service branches, and the result was the pathbreaking dispatch of MSDF ships.[41]

The Antiterror Special Measures Law drafted by Koizumi's task force never mentioned collective self-defense—indeed, CLB officials denied any connection—but it did enable the SDF to engage in "cooperative and supportive activities."[42] Recalcitrant mainstream LDP politicians successfully

Figure 4. A Japanese cartoon depicts Deputy Secretary of State Richard Armitage as a demanding ringmaster ("Show the Flag!" "Boots on the Ground!"), cracking the whip to force Prime Minister Koizumi (the lion labeled "Self-Defense Forces") to jump the fence of Article 9. Reprinted with permission of artist Kumita Ryū and the *Tokyo Shimbun*.

delayed dispatch of Aegis-equipped destroyers to the Indian Ocean, but they could not prevent deployment of Japanese forces far from "areas surrounding Japan."[43] Although CLB director general Tsuno Osamu once had insisted that any reinterpretation would lead to a collapse of Article 9, "like falling dominoes," nothing of the sort happened, and during the development of the Antiterrorism Law, he fell in line behind Prime Minister Koizumi, declaring "there is wide room for interpretation of collective security."[44] As a result of Koizumi's decisiveness, Diet deliberation was swifter than on any security issue in memory. CLB reviews normally take up to three months; this one took two weeks. On 9 November 2001, Japanese naval vessels, with seven hundred sailors aboard, sailed far out into international waters to supply fuel to U.S. and British forces operating in Afghanistan. It was the first foreign dispatch of Japanese forces since 1945, and collective self-defense effectively was a new "fact on the ground." This dispatch had been imagined a decade earlier. Sakuma Makoto, former chair of the Joint Staff Council, recalled that the MSDF had generated a similar plan to support allied troops during the first Gulf War, but that it had been rejected by politicians: "[The plan] was just the same as we are doing in the Indian Ocean today. By and large people's ideas do not change very much."[45] The difference was that now different politicians with different ideas were in charge.

If the 1996 Clinton-Hashimoto summit was Japan's first giant step toward a regional security role, the decision to sail tankers to Diego Garcia was its first step toward collective self-defense and a global security role. Still, questions remained: Was this was a one-time-only policy, possible only after the extraordinary circumstances of September 11, or had antimainstream politicians gained full control of the bureaucracy, the military, and public opinion? While the SDF still stopped short of using force, and the issue of collective self-defense was still being finessed, most evidence points to the latter interpretation. The dispatch of Aegis-equipped ships had been held up in part over legal concerns that their sophisticated intelligence capabilities might be used in the war effort, thereby broaching the proscription on collective self-defense, but the decision was resolved in favor of the dispatch.[46] After the MSDF fueling operation had proceeded uneventfully for about a year, Akiyama Osamu, Uno's successor as CLB director general, opined that "providing support to other countries that have used force against a band of thieves in a tough neighborhood would not pose a constitutional problem."[47] Just in case there were still questions, another year later, in January 2003, Akiyama told the House of Councillors Budget Committee that Japan would not be violating the ban on collective self-defense if a fighter plane based on a U.S. aircraft carrier fueled by MSDF tankers subsequently flew combat missions in Iraq. Japanese ships were, he declared, restricted to areas outside the field of battle.[48] With different politicians in charge, a more compliant bureaucracy was taking different orders.

The next, larger, step was the commitment made by Prime Minister Koizumi to President Bush at the May 2003 Crawford summit. Japan would dispatch the SDF to Iraq. Koizumi had already given this matter considerable attention. In late March 2003, just days after President Bush delivered his final ultimatum to Saddam Hussein, Prime Minister Koizumi created an "Iraq response office" to amend the existing antiterrorism law to allow the provision of support and humanitarian assistance in Iraq, and to begin work on a new law to enable dispatch of the SDF. Within weeks, the government announced policies under five categories: (1) economic assistance; (2) reconstruction assistance; (3) humanitarian assistance; (4) disposal of weapons of mass destruction; (5) landmine removal. In mid-April 2003, when the Japanese government announced plans to send civilian bureaucrats to help the U.S.-led administration in Baghdad, Miyazaki Reiichi, director of the CLB's First Department, explained that even though this administration was run by the U.S. Defense Department, the Japanese government was dispatching civilians and therefore not violating constitutional proscriptions on collective self-defense or the use of force.[49] The dispatch was legal so long as there was no *integration* of the SDF with the use of force—and fueling U.S. fighters to bomb Iraqi cities did not count.

Koizumi and his national security team had engineered a flexible battle plan. If a UN resolution was passed then the SDF could be dispatched under terms of the existing PKO Law. If not, then the government would do what it could under the existing legal framework while drafting new legislation. While Koizumi was in Crawford, UN Resolution 1483, which supported the reconstruction of Iraq, was approved. This was less than Bush sought but all that Koizumi needed. Japan could dispatch forces under UN auspices, effectively defusing opposition within the LDP. Still, his administration went forward with an Iraq reconstruction bill, which passed the Diet with ease in July.[50] In November, Japanese voters returned the LDP to power despite Koizumi's unpopular promise to send forces to Iraq. The Japanese press furrowed its brow over control of the use of weapons, but the issue never came to the fore.[51] Instead, claims were made about the critical importance of supporting the United States—Japan could not afford to risk being abandoned when North Korea was threatening and China was rising. As Prime Minister Koizumi said in the Diet, Japan has "only a single ally, the United States...[and] must not be isolated in international society."[52] Realist claims about Japan's dependence on Middle East oil, a supply that some feared would be denied to nonparticipants in the "coalition of the willing," got equal attention.[53] In January 2004, the GSDF was dispatched to Samawah (pop. 150,000) in southern Iraq, a "non-combat zone" far from the front. Six hundred troops, defended by British and Dutch forces because they were not permitted to use force, set to the tasks of civil engineering, building such public facilities as hospitals, roads, and water treatment facilities. They kept their heads down and, despite occasional shelling of their camp, completed their mission in 2006 without firing a shot or suffering a single casualty. After they were withdrawn, the ASDF was assigned the more dangerous task of ferrying U.S. soldiers and matériel in and out of Baghdad.

The formal decision to "put Japanese boots on the Iraqi ground"—a phrase credited to DoD undersecretary Richard Lawless—was stunning for three main reasons. First, it succeeded despite widespread popular opposition to the war. Opposition never became mobilized as in Britain and the United States, but the Japanese public expressed profound doubts about joining the United States in this venture. Prime Minister Koizumi deflected the criticism by reorienting his November reelection toward the threat from North Korea. Japanese voters were unwilling to toss out an administration that was willing to be tough on Pyongyang. Second, the attack on the pacifist tradition was only partial. Japanese soldiers were part of an occupation force in a Middle Eastern country and did not wear blue helmets, but they did not do all that the DoD initially had hoped. The U.S. side had hoped for more than one thousand soldiers and that the SDF would take responsibility for governing a sector of Iraq, including the defensive use of force if necessary.[54]

Third, Koizumi and his allies demonstrated thorough mastery of the bureaucracy. Deputy Chief Cabinet Secretary Abe took responsibility for reining in the CLB. In June, at a meeting of young Diet members, he declared that "the CLB has been providing misleading explanations on collective defense."[55] Feeling the heat and no doubt hoping to preserve its remaining prerogatives, the CLB weighed in only once during Diet hearings. Responding to a query from Democratic Party representative Haraguchi Kazuhiro, CLB director general Akiyama replied that nothing had changed in the government's interpretation of collective self-defense. The ban was not relevant, he insisted, because the SDF would not be directly engaged in any attack. Instead, he pointed out, the government bill was aimed *primarily* (*shutaiteki*) at helping Iraqi civilians and cooperating with the international community through humanitarian aid and reconstruction: "Consequently, given these purposes and given the content of this legislation, there is nothing related to the right of collective self-defense in this bill."[56] Akiyama opined that the SDF could even transport weapons in Iraq so long as the fighting had ended. They would not, he insisted, be entering combat areas. When pressed, he even chipped away at once bedrock positions with claims such as "there is a difference between the use of weapons under joint international activities and the use of force."[57] Once again, Japan's senior political leaders held the upper hand.

And these leaders were not about to loosen their grip. A panel of experts convened by the Cabinet Office issued a formal report in May 2003 urging the government to take up the right to collective self-defense as a policy matter rather than as a change in constitutional interpretation.[58] Testifying before the upper house Special Committee for Emergency Legislation a few days later, Chief Cabinet Secretary Fukuda Yasuo declared that Japan's use of the right of collective self-defense, banned under current interpretations of the constitution, would have to change. "I don't know which cabinet it will be," Fukuda said, "but I think the time will come when one will look at the situation and make a judgment. I hope that such a time will come soon."[59] Ironically, in making this claim, Fukuda was echoing a long-forgotten observation of Yoshida Shigeru himself. In his 1963 memoirs, Yoshida pointed out that "today's world is an age of collective security. Single nations cannot defend themselves alone."[60]

SLICING CLOSER TO HOME

That day is still not upon us, but a great deal more trimming has occurred in the interim, especially regarding the fundamental legal authority of the government during an emergency. Nor have the capabilities, roles, and missions of the SDF been ignored. The most notable slice, perhaps because it was the longest gestating and most contested, was the June 2003 passage of three "emergency laws" (*yūji hōsei*). These laws provided for the first time a legal framework within which the SDF can respond to an attack by foreign military forces by clearing roads for military vehicles, supervising evacuations, supplying U.S. forces, centralizing authority ordinarily held by local governments, and imposing controls on government information.

This was no small matter. Where most national constitutions confer special powers on their executive branch during emergencies, Japan's is silent. As a result, each time such contingencies have been openly discussed, concerns have been raised about abridging citizens' rights. Would these laws be invoked to silence opposition to government policy? Would the SDF be mobilized to suppress demonstrations? Perhaps they would be used to erode the provisions of Article 9, in particular the interpretation of the ban on collective self-defense. The editorial page of the *Asahi Shimbun* was representative when it reminded readers of the wartime repression and wondered "whether the government would allow prewar mistakes to be repeated, and let the SDF get out of control."[61] Each of these concerns, most of them expressed even before the SDF was created in 1954, combined with the low probability of an armed attack on Japan and LDP mismanagement of the issue to keep emergency legislation off the national agenda.[62] But the Aum Shinrikyō terrorist attack and Kobe earthquake, both in 1995, rekindled popular concerns that the Japanese government lacked legal authority to respond quickly in a crisis. The chain of command, from the national executive to the prefectural offices of police and fire authorities, was unclear. Moreover, the SDF did not even have the authority to capture enemies. After the North Korean missile test in 1998 and the al-Qaida attacks on the United States in 2001, the Japanese public seemed prepared to accept the change and further empower the prime minister. Koizumi was ready and waiting.

In April 2002 the Koizumi cabinet submitted three bills to establish an emergency response system in Japan. Each made liberal use of reports prepared in the late 1970s by commissions established by the Fukuda cabinet. The first bill, the Law Concerning Measures to Ensure National Independence and Security in a Situation of Armed Attack, regulated the government's response to an armed attack or to the imminent threat of such an attack. In the event, the prime minister is required to draw up a contingency plan that must subsequently be approved by both the cabinet and the Diet. The prime minister will thereupon govern through a task force responsible to the cabinet. In an emergency, citizens and local governments are required "to make efforts to cooperate" with the central government. One prime responsibility of the government and the SDF is to make sure that U.S. military facilities are adequately secured and that U.S. forces are adequately supplied.

The second bill, the Law to Amend the Self-Defense Forces Law, allows the SDF to use force to defend itself, to traverse private property, and penalizes firms that do not cooperate with government controls on food and matériel. The third bill, the Law to Amend the Security Council Establishment Law, changed the composition of the National Security Council.[63]

These emergency measures passed the Diet in June 2003 with the support of all three coalition partners as well as the DPJ and Liberal Party. They confer special powers on the national executive that affect relationships both with Japanese citizens and with the U.S. armed forces in Japan. Because they provide a legal justification for wartime cooperation between states, observers suggest that passage of the emergency laws was more important to Prime Minister Koizumi than revision of Article 9. Even former JDA director general Ishiba Shigeru has insisted that getting them passed was the most important initiative during his (very eventful) tenure.[64] They had certainly been desired by the United States for many years. The Armitage-Nye Report of 2000, for example, written before the Bush administration took office, explicitly called on Japan to pass "crisis management legislation."[65] Christopher Hughes summarizes what this means: "This collection of emergency legislation demonstrates that Japan is now contemplating more seriously than at any time in the previous half century the possibility that it needs to ready itself for war fighting."[66]

Although the emergency laws got most attention, the Japanese government kept busy elsewhere. Until 1997, there had been no way for uniformed officers to appeal decisions of the JDA director general, and the relationship between civilian councillors and uniformed officers were often conflictual and "oppressive."[67] Under this distinctive arrangement, designed by Yoshida Shigeru personally, even unanimous decisions of the Joint Staff Council could be stifled by the suits in the JDA; senior political leaders met with uniformed officers very infrequently.[68] In fact, General Staff officers were prohibited by a 1952 National Safety Agency directive from having direct contact with Diet representatives or officials of other government agencies without the presence of a civilian JDA official. The Hashimoto cabinet abolished this directive in 1997 and initiated regular consultations with the chairman of the Joint Staff Council as well as regular briefings by his staff.[69] Soon thereafter, starting in 2003, Director General Ishiba reformed the "councillor system" (*sanjikan seido*) by thinning out the layer of civilian councillors who intermediated contacts between SDF officers and politicians, including the director general. He intended to reform what he ironically referred to as the "SDF Management Agency" (*jieitai kanrichō*) by recognizing officially that the chiefs of each service branch were equivalents in rank to the councillors and so could report directly to the director general.[70] The effort was partially successful. The 2003 JDA White Paper deleted language authorizing the JDA bureaucrats to assist in making security policy, but the system was not abandoned root and branch. The councillors retained "drafting authority" (*kianken*) for military orders.[71]

Other changes enhanced military capabilities. For example, the SDF rules of engagement have been relaxed multiple times since the first PKO deployment. When the freeze on PKF dispatch was lifted in December 2001, the number of situations in which the SDF could use force in its self-defense was increased; the rules of engagement were further relaxed when the GSDF was dispatched to Iraq in 2004.[72] In more than a decade since the enactment of the PKO Law, the SDF has participated in numerous UN operations without major incident and with full public support. None had been free of operational problems, so with each success changes left the SDF less encumbered. Over time, the Cabinet Legislation Bureau "softened" and lifted its ban on the transport of ordnance. The SDF was not only allowed to carry weapons for its own use but could also convey them to the National Police Agency and the Coast Guard.[73] The PKO troops sent to Cambodia (1992) and Mozambique (1993) could carry only pistols and rifles—and, according to Article 24 of the 1992 International Peacekeeping Law, could use them only "within range regarded as necessary for the situation and if there are adequate unavoidable reasons." Those dispatched to Rwanda (1994), the Golan Heights (1996), and East Timor (1999) packed machine guns, which could be used on the order of officers in the field. By December 2001, weapons could be used to protect weapons and equipment as well as personnel.[74] Troops sent to Iraq carried portable antitank missiles. Likewise, in October 2001 the SDF Law was amended to allow use of force in dealing with guerrillas and terrorists.

In 2005, two important changes further empowered field commanders. In July, the Diet approved an amendment of the SDF Law to allow a field commander to launch an interceptor missile after consultation with the prime minister and the director general of the JDA. Before this change, approvals had to be acquired from the National Security Council, the cabinet, and the Diet.[75] In late 2005, the ASDF revised its rules of engagement in anticipation of conflict with the Chinese military in the East China Sea. Previously fire control had been at the discretion of pilots who were reluctant to use force. Now, the CLB approved regional commanders to order pilots to use force after first issuing the prescribed warnings.[76] The Japanese government has come a long way since 1987, when the prime minister had to make the case that minesweeping was not the exercise of force.[77]

Many strategic changes drew minimal attention. During the 1994 Korean nuclear crisis, it became clear that the MSDF and the Coast Guard were not prepared to conduct maritime inspections or noncombat evacuations. Nor, as became apparent after the appearance of a DPRK submarine in 1996, was the Japanese military capable of defending effectively against guerrilla operations. The JDA responded by beginning counterguerrilla training, the first SDF training ever undertaken against a hypothetical enemy other than the Soviet Union.[78] In 1996 the JDA also began studying how to protect Japanese nationals abroad and how to handle large flows of refugees, activities not considered when stricter interpretations of "defensive defense" prevailed. The inability to conduct maritime inspections was also remediated.[79] In March 2001 the MSDF established a seventy-man Special Forces unit (*tokubetsu keibitai*), without much fanfare or explanation, and the newly empowered Coast Guard followed suit in December.[80] In July 2005 the JDA announced plans for a thousand-man regiment within the new GSDF Central Readiness Command that would be prepared for instant overseas deployment.[81] At about the same time, in a thinly veiled message to China about the sovereignty of the disputed Senkaku Islands, U.S. and Japanese forces began joint training in San Diego to defend "remote islands" captured by unnamed enemy forces. This joint training—reported as a "mock invasion by China of Japanese-controlled territory"—was undertaken on a much larger scale near Iwo Jima Island in late 2006.[82] Neither ready deployment nor commando units, not to mention joint assault exercises, were contemplated under the Yoshida Doctrine.

Significant enhancements to Japan's arsenal would once have violated proscriptions on all but defensive defense. The JDA ordered aerial tankers and helicopter-carrying (13,500-ton) destroyers with hardened decks during the first five-year midterm defense build-up plan of the 2000s. Both were justified as necessary for international cooperation, and the GSDF put helicopters on MSDF decks for the first time during the tsunami relief operation in Southeast Asia in 2005. The 2004 budget included funds for Japan's first precision-guided munitions, which involved upgrading of existing missiles. The retrofit was justified by the need "to effectively achieve missions by preventing collateral damage."[83] The 2006 budget included funds for short-range torpedoes and long-range, pilotless aircraft for ballistic missile reconnaissance.

Nor have intelligence capabilities been ignored. In 1997, the JDA established the new Intelligence Headquarters (Jōhō Honbu) within the Joint Staff Command in order to become less dependent on the United States for intelligence. As former chief cabinet secretary Gotōda Masaharu explained at the time, Japan should be more like a rabbit: "Rabbits don't depend on other animals because they have long ears."[84] Gotōda, a strong defender of Article 9, supported an independent intelligence capacity for Japan but expressed concern that Japanese politicians might not be able to control the military. With his support—and promises he extracted that enhanced civilian oversight—the new Central Intelligence Command was designed. Meanwhile, Prime Minister Koizumi, frustrated that "Japan had destroyed its intelligence capabilities," was insisting at a meeting of the National Security Council that Japan beef up human intelligence—what he called a need to have "ninjas."[85]

In August 1998, while the government was still determining how best to enhance its intelligence capabilities, Pyongyang launched a provocative test of its Taepodong rocket. Within a matter of weeks, the Diet had funded an intelligence satellite program that Mitsubishi Electric Corporation had been holding ready for many years. By early 2006, when the LDP announced that it would formally review the longstanding ban on the military use of space, the SDF was already collecting satellite images from its own equipment, and the government had already committed to codevelopment with the United States of a ballistic missile defense that would require space-based sensors and radars and satellite-tracking devices. There was nothing left to study. Although "current coverage" is limited to the archipelago and adjoining waters, plans are in the works for an integrated space-based defense information infrastructure that will enlarge Japan's intelligence footprint to include all of the Persian Gulf, the Arabian Peninsula, East Africa, the Malacca Strait, and Central Asia.[86] In March 2006 the LDP announced its intention to allow the use of space for what it called "nonoffensive defensive purposes," and in September, after North Korea fired another barrage of missiles into the Sea of Japan, the government launched its fourth and final planned intelligence satellite. Now it would cover "any part of the globe once a day."[87]

GOING BALLISTIC

Once again, a significant change in national security doctrine was met with yawns by the Japanese public. By this time the government had already moved ahead with one of the most expensive and complex plans for the military use of space—ballistic missile defense (BMD). Acceptance of BMD measures how remarkably far Japanese security policy had traveled. When JDA officials first selected an air defense system in 1964, they opted for one with no interoperability with U.S. forces.[88] This time, the choice embraced the need to integrate with the U.S. military, even to the point of challenging constitutional interpretation. The Japanese government agreed to undertake joint research with the United States on what was then called "theater missile defense" in 1998, three months after the DPRK missile test through Japanese airspace. Insisting that the entire effort was only research and stopped short of system development, the Japanese government bought three additional years to evaluate its technological options and, more important, to develop a political strategy to sell collaborative missile defense with the United States.

This preparation might have continued indefinitely, but the United States forced Japan's hand. JDA director general Ishiba Shigeru and administrative vice minister Moriya Takemasa, in Washington for consultations in

December 2002, were informed that the United States was going to proceed with BMD just one day before President Bush announced his decision.
Concerned about a widening technological gap, wanting Japanese manufacturers to be part of the deal, and informed by the JDA that missile defense
was technically feasible, they told the U.S. side that Japan was prepared to
participate so long as Japan would be protected.[89] Their "top-down" decision met with resentment from some uniformed officers, who believed that
a system designed for the United States was being imposed on Japan. Some
politicians, even within the LDP, murmured that Ishiba and Moriya's fait accompli was inappropriate.[90] But they had the prime minister's unreserved
support, and the project moved forward. The political leadership was determined to elevate Japan's role in the alliance and enhance its military capability. To do so would obviously entail political and military risks, in part
because the United States was not going to wait.

The biggest problem was not how to get it accepted, for by 2004 Japan's
defense planners were pushing on an open door of public acceptance. The
problem was how to pay for it. The development phase alone would cost
$8–$10 billion over five years, and Japan had agreed to pay one-third.[91]
Ishiba fought to keep funding outside the 1 percent cap on defense spending
but was overruled.[92] Japan's fiscal deficit was already the largest in the industrial world, and however enthusiastic he was about making Japan more
muscular, Prime Minister Koizumi would not budge. He insisted instead on
restructuring Japan's defense force posture, and his defense budget passed
without amendment, still at just under 1 percent of GDP. The first BMD
budget earmarked funds for equipping one Aegis-type destroyer with the
Standard Missile system (SM-3), for the upgraded Patriot ground-to-air
missile (PAC-3), and for upgrading existing air defense systems. Orders for
tanks and for ships and aircraft were sharply reduced. The uniformed services would have to get used to the idea that the political leadership was no
longer content simply to supervise a "shopping ministry." In a remarkable
departure from past practice, the politicians and the JDA were less concerned about the defense industry than about getting a system deployed as
quickly as possible.[93]

Indeed, the second biggest problem was how to ensure a significant work
share for Japanese industry. The good news was that more than 2 percent
of the FY 2004 U.S. defense budget—and fully *12 percent* of the equipment
budget—was earmarked for missile defense. The bad news was that all of
it was to come in the form of foreign military sales. U.S. Defense Secretary Donald Rumsfeld simply refused to consider project shares: U.S. firms
would get *all* of the initial contracts. On learning of these "severe" terms,
an alarmed official from Mitsubishi Heavy Industries lamented that "we
intended to proceed with licensed production. If we buy everything from
the United States, our production will decline to zero and our technology

will also decline."[94] Although Japanese firms were not happy about missing out on some initial system design work, they began signing licensing agreements with U.S. partners within several months. Development of the nose cone would be undertaken by Mitsubishi Heavy Industries, the rocket engines would be designed by Ishikawajima-Harima Heavy Industries, and the infrared seekers would be developed by Fuji Heavy Industries—all on "cost-plus" contracts. The kinetic warhead and the radars would be developed in the United States. After a small bump in the road, U.S. and Japanese defense contractors returned to cooperation as usual.[95]

One of the factors that made this small bump acceptable was the decision to end Japan's long-standing, self-imposed ban on the export of arms. Efforts to repeal this ban were nothing new, of course. The Japanese defense industry began lobbying for access to export markets almost as soon as the ban was imposed in 1967.[96] But the first substantive breakthrough came bundled inside the decision to proceed with codevelopment of BMD in December 2004. Once the program moved into the development phase, Japanese-developed components would have to be transferred to U.S. partners. Moreover, as the influential Araki Commission reported, "if Japan were not able to participate in such international joint development and production, it would be difficult for Japan to support the core technologies indispensable for future security."[97] In a separate announcement made as it was announcing its new National Defense Program Guidelines, the Koizumi government declared that the BMD project would be excluded from nonexport principles. The government also reserved the right to relax restrictions in future cases other than those related to missile defense: "Decisions will be made on the basis of individual examination of each case, in light of Japan's basic philosophy as a peace-loving nation that aims at avoiding the escalation of international conflicts."[98] The significance of this change was lost on no one. The strategic importance of jointly developing BMD had overridden differences among the relevant ministries and had received widespread support from LDP and DPJ politicians.[99] The government had given itself carte blanche to pare away the rest of the arms export ban, piece by piece, whenever it saw fit to do so. The Defense Production Committee of Keidanren, the political voice of the Japanese defense industry, acknowledged this as "a major step forward." But eyeing participation in a growing number of multinational defense programs, it also served notice that it expected the government not to accumulate a backlog of case-by-case decisions.[100]

Nor were military doctrine and hardware the only objects of revision. The Koizumi administration also took on the central element of the Yoshida Doctrine: comprehensive security. Chapter 3 documented how official development assistance (ODA) funds were used by the Coast Guard to fund the transfer of weapons to Southeast Asia in 2006. Earlier, in August

2003, the Diet revised the law governing ODA in order "to ensure Japan's own security and prosperity." It was not the first time that Japan's strategic interests were factored into its ODA calculus, of course, but it was the first time that ODA was openly identified with national security.[101] Now, moreover, Japanese and U.S. ODA budgets would be "coordinated" as part of "alliance transformation."[102] And to make the economic weapon more potent, the government also revised the Foreign Exchange and Control Law in February 2004. Now, also for the first time, it could unilaterally halt remittances to foreign countries, a move that one analyst concluded was "a clear indication that Japan has decided to take coercive measures in diplomacy, [a move that] is perhaps more significant than sending troops to Iraq."[103]

It is clear that "Japan [has] become more active operationally and better prepared legally" to act in its own defense than at any time since the alliance was established.[104] It is also clear that Japan has achieved this incrementally. A series of discrete steps has given Japanese strategists new confidence and increased comfort in assuming additional roles and missions. Some U.S. government officials have called this "maturation," and others have welcomed the "erosion of anti-militarism" and "strategic tinkering."[105] The most decorously indirect expression of the process described in this chapter comes from a report by the MOD's National Institute for Defense Studies, which refers to the "lateral expansion [and] greater depth" of Japan's defense capabilities since the end of the cold war.[106] Whether this has been erosion, tinkering, expansion, or slicing, there has been change aplenty. Whether expressed decorously or in crassly metaphorical terms, these developments have not gone unnoticed. The question is what they all add up to. Has the Yoshida Doctrine been whittled into irrelevance, or does it still set the contours of Japanese grand strategy?

Mike Mochizuki rejects the metaphor of salami slicing and offers an alternative: Japanese strategists have inflated the "inner tube" of defensive defense.[107] In his view, the assault on the Yoshida Doctrine by revisionists has not yet resulted in fundamental doctrinal change. By wrapping SDF deployments in pacifist ideals and by steadfastly refusing to declare Japan capable of collective self-defense, Japan has hewn to the Yoshida line. Tokyo has stretched the idea of defensive defense geographically and has extended its roles and missions to rear areas far from home, but it has not tinkered with basic doctrinal elements. Maintaining the asymmetric alliance with the United States, relying on U.S. forces based in Japan, refusing to adopt offensive rules of engagement, and continuing to cheap ride with limited defense budgets all point toward the extension, rather than the discarding, of Japan's postwar grand strategy. The Yoshida Doctrine is not in tatters, it has been updated.

But Japan's security "inner tube" may be perilously overinflated. The re-institutionalization of Japanese security policy and the legitimization of the military documented in this chapter bring Japan to the precipice of great change. Tokyo is poised to reorient its grand strategy—and, as important, it is *capable* of doing so for the first time in living memory. Japan could decide to opt for a truly symmetrical alliance with the United States. It could elect to use force in a contingency other than a direct attack on Japan. It could decide to end permanent basing of U.S. forces on the archipelago. It could choose to preempt missile threats from the continent. None of these possibilities is any longer unimaginable or fantastic; indeed, each is under intense debate by responsible actors. Although it is impossible to know a priori just what domestic or international political conditions might stimulate such changes, there are enough voices demanding more autonomy and muscularity, less dependence on the United States, and enhanced prestige that it is critical to listen to what they are saying.

[5]

The Discourse

There are few truly new ideas about how nations can protect themselves. Each country is armed with its military, its diplomats, its mix of resources, its ambition, and its wits. The rest is, as ever, derivative. This is why students studying international relations, diplomacy, and national security are still required to read *The Peloponnesian War* by Thucydides, *The Art of War* by Sun Tzu, and Machiavelli's *The Prince*. Ideas about strategy endure because geography, demography, and technology endure as constraints on the ability of leaders to make their people prosperous and safe. But if there are few original ideas about strategy, there are limitless combinations of existing ones. Because the balance among constraints is always in motion, and because the power of neighbors rises and falls, new circumstances always await the application of old ideas. Contexts change, but ideas endure.

So it has been with Japan. If there are few original ideas about Japanese strategy, there has always been debate about choices among conventional ideas. There is nothing Japan's leaders could do to change their location as an archipelago at the edge of a massive continent, but they could debate whether Japan should be a maritime or a continental power. There is little they could do to manufacture natural resources, but they could debate how to acquire (or substitute for) raw materials cheaply and safely. Having embarked on industrialization before their neighbors, they might not wish to narrow the developmental distance, but they could debate whether Japan would be more secure as an Asian power or as a Western one. Once developed, moreover, there was the question of sizing Japan for the current world order. Should Japan be a big country or a small one? Should it seek military autonomy or rely on allies? Is technoeconomic autonomy within its grasp or is it chimerical? Should wealth or strength be Japan's national priority?

These contending preferences have seemed historically consistent. "Asianists" and "nationalists" have long argued with "liberals" and "internationalists." Whether from militarists in the 1920s or from *nihonjinron* intellectuals in the 1980s, "nativism" has always attracted a following. Japanese "liberals" have been debating the merits of economic security for generations. The enemies of liberalism, both on the left and on the right, have been connected across the 1930s to the 1960s.[1] The Asianism of Tokyo governor Ishihara Shintarō, who has advocated using Japanese culture to displace U.S. influence in Asia, connects back to the similarly blunt and accessible views of the Shōwa Kenkyūkai in the 1930s.[2] Direct lines have been drawn from Fukuzawa Yukichi's liberal internationalism in the 1880s to Ozawa Ichirō's a century later.[3] The ideas of liberal internationalists who first argued that Japan would be safest as a small maritime trading nation in the early twentieth century inspired the Yoshida Doctrine that governed Japan's security choices during the cold war. This economics-first national security strategy was modeled on the one that prevailed in the 1920s but was abandoned in the 1930s and 1940s. Liberal internationalism has been an important security option for generations. The same is true of technonationalism, a preference of many from Meiji to the present.[4]

Even if ideas are connected across time, however, changes in world order often skew their applications. For example, nineteenth- and twentieth-century Asianism shares less with twenty-first-century Asianism than the common label suggests.[5] During the Meiji period Asianism often expressed opposition to the state. By the 1920s it had taken on a racialist, antiwhite tone, whereas in the 1960s it was common ground for neutralists on both the left and the right. Today, Asianism is a strategy for balancing against excessive U.S. power. It was likewise with nationalism. In the prewar period, liberal and nativist variants took turns dominating the national security agenda. After the war, anti-American nationalists and anti-Soviet nationalists found common ground in arguing for Japanese leadership of Asia, and today these disparate groups hold common views of how the U.S. alliance deprives Japan of its national sovereignty. In short, Japanese security thinking is rife with variety. In this chapter I explore how this variety reflects (and transforms) long-held preferences, by examining the contemporary security debate in two specific contexts: the history issue and the base issue.

THE LANDSCAPE

In the early twenty-first century there remain strong differences within the chattering classes about how Japan should provide for its security. These differences are not simple matters of Left versus Right. Nor do they strictly reflect party or other institutional affiliations. For example, the ruling Liberal Democratic Party supports the U.S. alliance unconditionally but is divided on how to deal with Asia, whereas the opposition Democratic Party of Japan is unified on regional integration but divided on the alliance.[6] Moreover, the contemporary discourse about Japanese grand strategy provokes strange—and shifting—bedfellows. Heirs to prewar nativism share antipathetic views of the U.S. alliance with heirs of the Old Left. Today's Small Japanists and Big Japanists agree that the alliance matters but disagree fundamentally on how much Japan should pay for its maintenance—and whether part of that cost should include Japan's becoming "normal." The deck is reshuffled on the issue of accommodation with China. Bureaucrats interested in security issues are more likely to be U.S.-oriented and economic bureaucrats to be Asia-oriented. But this rule of thumb is by no means ironclad.[7]

The security policy preferences of contemporary Japanese scholars, commentators, politicians, and bureaucrats can be sorted along two axes. The first is a measure of the value placed on the alliance with the United States. At one extreme is the view that the United States is Japan's most important source of security and must be hugged closely. On this account, the extent of U.S. power and the limits of Japanese capabilities are central, and the strategic importance of the alliance for Japan's security is paramount. U.S. bases in Japan are critical to any coherent national security strategy. At the other extreme is the view that, in a unipolar world, the United States is a particularly dangerous bully that must be kept at great distance, for fear that Japan will become entangled in American adventures. The presence of U.S. bases makes entanglement all the more likely. Located in the middle are those who want Japan to rebalance Asian and U.S. relationships more effectively. They are attracted to the idea of building regional institutions but are not yet prepared to let go of the United States. This first axis, then, is a surrogate measure of the dangers of abandonment and entanglement. Those with a high tolerance for the former are willing to keep a greater distance from the United States than are those with a higher tolerance for the latter.

Those with a high tolerance for entanglement are not all oriented toward the status quo, however. They are divided by the second axis—the willingness to use force in international affairs. Critics of the effort to make Japan "normal" maintain that, stripped to its essence, the idea of a "normal nation" simply means "a nation that can go to war."[8] Whether the valence is militarist or neutral, debate over the legality and efficacy of use of force has been a ubiquitous part of the Japanese discourse for more than half a century, invariably evoking questions of how to understand modern history. After the war, Japanese strategy shifted from the view that force was an instrument of great powers to one that rejected it altogether. Since that time, as we have seen, those who preferred the literal interpretation of Article 9 and those who have endeavored to loosen its constraints have contended for power within the LDP. Support for revision of Article 9, for Japan to assume a more proactive and global defense posture, for the integration of forces with the U.S. military, and for the dispatch of the SDF abroad are all measures of where one stands on this second axis. Because the difference between a great power and a small power is the willingness to use force, moreover, they also define competing Japanese national identities.

Some who support the U.S. alliance are willing to deploy the SDF to "share alliance burdens." They wish Japan to become a great power again and are associated with the idea that Japan should become "normal." In the view of these "normal nation-alists," the statute of limitations for Japan's mid-twentieth century aggression expired long ago; it is time for Japan to step onto the international stage as an equal of the United States. They believe that strength is the way to prestige, their prime value. Opposing them are "middle power internationalists," who believe that Japan must remain a small power with self-imposed limits on its right to belligerency. Japan's contributions to world affairs should remain nonmilitary. They believe that prosperity is the way to prestige. Among those who prefer Japan to keep a greater distance from the United States are "neoautonomists" who would build an independent, full-spectrum Japanese military that could use force, and "pacifists" who eschew the military institution altogether. The former

Use of Force Is OK	
Neoautonomists	**Normal Nation-alists**
Heirs to nativists	Heirs to Big Japanists
Seeking autonomy through strength	Seeking prestige through strength
(Ishihara, Nishibe, Nakanishi, Kobayashi)	(Koizumi, Abe, Ishiba, Ozawa)
Distance from United States	*Hug United States*
Pacifists	**Middle Power Internationalists**
Heirs to unarmed neutralists	Heirs to Small Japanists
Seeking autonomy through prosperity	Seeking prestige through prosperity
(NGOs, Socialist Party, Communist Party)	(Kono, Terashima, Miyazawa)
No Use of Force	

Figure 5. The Discourse. See Nagai (1983) and Mochizuki (1983–84) for prototypes of this array. The fault lines have not changed substantially, but the balance of power has. Shiraishi (2006) is also very relevant.

believe that strength is the way to autonomy, their prime value, whereas the latter, who share that prime value, believe that prosperity is the best way to achieve it. All four groups seek security for Japan, but each closely associates security with a different value: neoautonomists seek security with sovereignty, pacifists security with peace. Normal nation-alists want security with equality; middle power internationalists seek security through prosperity.

REVISIONIST HISTORY

History, as an active instrument of regional diplomacy, has become an outsized presence in Japan's relationships with its neighbors. Indeed, the health of Japan's bilateral relationships, particularly with the Republic of Korea and the People's Republic of China, can be measured by the salience of what Tessa Morris-Suzuki has called "the unresolved problems of historical responsibility."[9] The list of these problems, virtually all of which derive from Japan's imperial expansion in the early to mid-twentieth century, is a long one. It includes but is not limited to: the role of the Japanese emperor in encouraging imperial expansion; the nature and social consequences of the colonization of Taiwan, Korea, and Manchuria; Japanese denials of the Nanjing massacre; the use of sex slaves by the Japanese military; corvée labor in Japanese mines and factories during the war; the disputed legitimacy of the International Military Tribunal for the Far East (Tokyo War Crimes Tribunal); the nuances and frequency of official apologies for Japanese aggression; Japanese textbook revision; and the politicization of the Yasukuni Shrine.[10] Nothing about the conflict between 1931 and 1945 is uncontested, not even now that fewer than 10 percent of living Japanese experienced it. Some Japanese speak of the "Fifteen Year War" (*jūgonen sensō*), others of the "Greater East Asia War" (*dai tōa sensō*), and still others use the "Pacific War" (*taiheiyō sensō*).[11] Was it a war of liberation, of aggression, or of survival? Little has been resolved.

The most prominent physical manifestation of this irresolution is the handsome Yasukuni Shrine compound in central Tokyo.[12] Completed in 1872, the shrine and its priests benefited from the privileged position of Shinto that began during the Meiji period. With each new conquest, the souls of fallen soldiers (and military nurses as well as some colonials) were enshrined as deities (*saijin*) to glorify both the emperor and the Japanese military. Recruits en route to the battlefields of Asia promised one another they would meet again at Yasukuni. Over time, the compound acquired an extraordinary collection of the accoutrements of war. Swords, cannons, artillery, even fighter planes, locomotives, and bloodied battle flags stand on the grounds of the shrine in mute tribute to the fallen. A museum, the Yūshūkan, was built to house this collection and to tell the story of Japan's modern military from a revisionist perspective.[13] Until the end of the war, the shrine and the museum were uncontroversial adjuncts of the Japanese state.

Even after Article 20 of the Japanese Constitution expressly separated church and state (*seikyō bunri*), the Yasukuni Shrine has remained Japan's de facto official war memorial. The Ministry of Health and Welfare supplied biographical information to shrine officials for all war veterans—and even for SDF troops.[14] Virtually every postwar prime minister, regardless of political orientation, visited Yasukuni while in office, including the mainstream Yoshida Shigeru (ten times) and the antimainstream Nakasone Yasuhiro (eleven times).[15] In October 1978, however, the priests at Yasukuni secretly enshrined fourteen Class A war criminals, including General Tōjō Hideki. By honoring rather than just mourning fallen soldiers—and by identifying more than one thousand "martyrs of *Shōwa*" who were in their view "cruelly and unjustly tried as war criminals by a sham-like tribunal of the allied forces"—Yasukuni became a lightning rod for historical memory. Nearly 60 percent of Chinese believe that Yasukuni is a "symbol of militarism," whereas two-thirds of the Japanese see it as "a place to mourn the war dead," which is why official visits by Japanese prime ministers meet with such controversy.[16] Indeed, a great many Japanese are troubled by these visits as well. By November 2005, after Prime Minister Koizumi's fifth official visit, there had been eleven separate Japanese court rulings on the issue, including several that declared the visits illegal. Yasukuni is about far more than the enshrinement of soldiers' souls. It is a barometer of one's view of the colonial experiences of China and Korea and, by implication, of history and politics more generally.

Another barometer is history textbooks. Little has been more incendiary in the relationship between former combatants than how their battles are explained to subsequent generations. Some countries have found it helpful to establish joint textbook commissions; France and Germany even agreed on a common textbook to be used in both countries. Japan and its neighbors have never found such "deep reconciliation."[17] Instead, they have battled endlessly—and without closure—on the basic facts of the past century. In June 2005, a joint study team of Korean and Japanese historians issued their report on interpretations of the past. The group was established after the Republic of Korea protested certification by Japanese authorities of a revisionist textbook prepared by the private Japanese Society for History Textbook Reform (Atarashii Kyōkasho o Tsukurukai). The joint commission could not agree on the fundamentals of a common narrative: the Japanese side insisted that annexation of Korea in 1910 was in accordance with international law, but the Korean side argued it was under threat of force. The historians could not agree on why Korea was invaded—to block Russian expansion or to control the Korean people?—and left the table without any prospect of returning to the effort.[18] Similar initiatives between China and Japan have never proceeded even this far.

THE LONG OCCUPATION

Japanese culpability is not the only unresolved corner of Northeast Asian history. By the early 2000s, a growing number of Japanese, and not just those on the left, had begun to interrogate U.S. and Soviet war guilt. Serious questions began to surface concerning the justice with which the United States prosecuted its war with Japan and the fairness of the postwar settlement. In an op-ed in the *Wall Street Journal* on the sixtieth anniversary of the end of the war, journalist Matsuo Fumio argued that there has been "no true closure with the [United States] over World War II," and asked Americans to consider apologizing for the indiscriminant incineration of civilians in Tokyo, Hiroshima, and Nagasaki.[19] Films, novels, and cartoons have examined the Tokyo War Crimes Tribunal, the firebombing of Tokyo, and Soviet POW camps. In August 2005 the Society of Bereaved Families of Victims of the Tokyo Air Raids filed a class action suit—the first such litigation ever—to demand compensation and an apology.[20] Their complaint is aimed at the Japanese government, but its implications are much wider. The problems associated with "victor's justice" have begun to gain traction.

The network of U.S. military bases in Japan is the most salient physical manifestation of that justice, and it is central to contemporary security politics in Japan. Today, U.S. Forces Japan (USF) have exclusive right to over three hundred square kilometers of land, three quarters of it in Okinawa, Japan's most southern prefecture.[21] The bases are a declaration of U.S. victory and a reminder of Japan's unconditional surrender. It is impossible to ignore their implications. Every Japanese political party, from the Communists to the LDP, has called for a reduction in the "base burden" if not for an outright elimination of the facilities altogether, and even former JDA officials rail against U.S. extraterritorial privilege.[22] Under the headline "Tired of Military Presence," the editorialist Hanai Kiroku wrote in October 2005: "Nationalism is rising in Japan these days. Although it is correctly directed mainly at China and South Korea, America could become a new target of Japanese nationalism if the base relocation issue becomes complicated."[23] It is no surprise that, asked to identify the single most difficult problem for the future of the U.S.-Japan alliance, former JDA director general Ohno Yoshinori immediately declared "the Occupation-era base structure." He insists that a new status of forces agreement needs to be negotiated.[24]

This view has long been widely held in Japan. The base arrangement was first negotiated in 1951, when Japan was still under U.S. occupation. Prime Minister Yoshida offered the U.S. military a Japanese home in exchange

Figure 6. U.S. bases are increasingly seen as a burden in Japan. Reprinted with permission of the *Japan Times* and illustrator Watanabe Ryūji.

for the 1951 peace treaty returning sovereignty. From the outset, however, this arrangement rankled conservatives and progressives alike. In 1960, Prime Minister Kishi arranged for a revision of the treaty to reduce the extraterritorial privileges of U.S. forces. Article 6 of the revised treaty provides "the use of facilities and areas in Japan" by the U.S. armed forces "for the purpose of contributing to the security of Japan and the maintenance of international peace and security in the Far East."[25] The accompanying SOFA stipulates responsibilities for the maintenance of facilities and legal jurisdictions in the event of accidents or crimes by U.S. military personnel (both have occurred with uncomfortable frequency). The National Police Agency investigated nearly three thousand criminal cases involving U.S. military personnel between 1989 and 2004, including fourteen for murder and 323 for group violence.[26] Not surprisingly, many make the headlines, especially after 1995, when three U.S. Marines raped a young Japanese girl in Okinawa.[27]

The pollution issue is also volatile. The U.S. military is seen as Japan's largest polluter.[28] Japanese citizens cannot sue the United States to abate noise pollution, however, because U.S. forces enjoy sovereignty on their bases. Thus they have no recourse but to file lawsuits in Japanese courts to seek redress, an act that is similarly inefficacious.[29] Local officials have even less jurisdiction vis-à-vis base issues than does the central government. Associations of governors and mayors from the fourteen prefectures that host U.S. bases have pressed the case for greater local jurisdiction, particularly regarding search-and-seizure powers and environmental standards.[30] But in practice, diplomats and law enforcement officials—elites from Tokyo— are left to attempt to placate increasingly alienated local citizens.

Their placation is made even more difficult by two factors. First, the central government has expropriated land, often through indirect and nontransparent legal means, for U.S. bases. Because expropriation is not otherwise standard practice, local residents complain that the central government cares more about the U.S. military than about its own citizens. The second problem is the regularity of training accidents and the subsequent invocation of U.S. authority off base, as in the case of the 2004 military helicopter crash on an Okinawan university campus that prompted U.S. officials to bar entry of Japanese investigators.[31] As Sheila Smith notes with considerable understatement: "The marriage between U.S. operational needs and domestic law is often an uncomfortable one."[32] Ina Hisayoshi reflects the widely held (and less restrained) judgment that the conduct of the U.S. military in Japan "resembles that of an occupying force."[33] Although both the treaty and the SOFA have been altered in practice through side agreements that give the Japanese government somewhat greater latitude, neither has ever been formally revised. Nor has the 1996 bilateral agreement to resize U.S. forces in Okinawa ever been implemented.[34] In fact, at no time in the history of the postwar alliance has the base issue not been characterized by extreme displeasure, either of local residents who put up with base pollution and crime, or of alliance managers who spend endless hours finding ways to co-opt opposition and maintain the status quo.[35] The LDP established its first Base Countermeasures Special Committee in 1961 and today continues to debate how Japan ought to cope with the U.S. military in its midst. Like Yasukuni and the history debate that it feeds, U.S. bases are a unique crucible for the making of Japanese discourse about foreign affairs. Let us turn, then, to a closer examination of this discourse.

PACIFISTS

As we have seen, three groups dominated elite discourse during the cold war. The first was pragmatic conservatives, led by Yoshida Shigeru, who became the mainstream within the LDP and governed effectively for most of the cold war. The second was antimainstream revisionists within the LDP, led at first by Hatoyama Ichirō and Kishi Nobusuke, and, later, by Nakasone Yasuhiro. Both groups of conservatives were confronted by antimilitarists on the left who wanted unilateral pacifism. By the end of the cold war, the antimainstream Right had accepted many of the constraints imposed by the pragmatists, while the latter maintained power by pacifying the pacifists, many of whom were "progressive intellectuals" who believed the only threat to Japan was economic.[36] After the cold war, however, the balance of power within the conservative camp shifted dramatically, and no group suffered more than the pacifists. As former JDA director general Ishiba Shigeru has noted sardonically, "the number of those who say fires break out because we have a fire department" has shrunk.[37]

The marginalization of the pacifists can be attributed to three factors. The first is the changing security environment in Northeast Asia. Once the cold war ended, "unarmed neutrality" was an instant anachronism. Without blocs in relation to which Japan should maintain neutrality, only disarmament and the antibase movement were left on the pacifists' agenda. But it soon became apparent that the end of the cold war did not end threats to national security, and disarmament became an increasingly unattractive option. In 1993, just two years after the Soviet Union collapsed, North Korea suddenly withdrew from the Nuclear Non-Proliferation Treaty and was poised to declare itself a nuclear weapons state; these developments shifted the regional balance of power in dangerous and very obvious ways.

Increased regional instability contributed to the second reason for the marginalization of the pacifists—the "awakening" of the Japanese public to issues associated with national security.[38] For the first time in half a century the Japanese public openly discussed a military threat. The percentage of those who believed there could be a war rose, and the percentage of those who believed that pacifism was feasible as a national security doctrine declined.[39] Majorities now accepted the SDF as legitimate and constitutional revision as desirable. Japan was overcoming its "military allergy" (*gun wa aku da*).[40] Wishful thinking about peace was being replaced by realistic discussion of war. What little support still existed for the idea that Japan should be a conscientious objector in world councils declined even further.

The third nail in the pacifists' coffin was the effective "suicide" of the Socialist Party.[41] In June 1994, after the LDP had split and its former members, led by Ozawa Ichirō, had failed in their first attempt to govern, the head of the Socialist Party, Murayama Tomiichi, became prime minister in an extraordinary political deal with the LDP. To do so, Murayama had to disavow fifty years of Socialist Party history. The leader of the pacifist party had to accept the constitutionality of the Self-Defense Forces and the legitimacy of the U.S.-Japan Mutual Security Treaty. Photos of Murayama standing at attention beneath the rising sun flag (which was still unofficial and highly controversial) on the deck of an MSDF destroyer shocked many voters. His administration ran into trouble almost immediately when it responded sluggishly to the January 1995 Kobe earthquake and failed to thwart the Aum Shinrikyō attack in the Tokyo subway two months later.

It got worse. In June, a Socialist-drafted Diet antiwar resolution (*fusen ketsugi*) expressing "deep remorse" for the war and "renewing the determination for peace" was rewritten by the LDP and voted on in the Diet. More representatives (241) abstained than supported it (230); clearly, pacifism's day was passing. Pacifism had one last hurrah on 15 August 1995, the fiftieth anniversary of the end of the Pacific War, when Murayama formally apologized for atrocities committed by Japanese troops. But the prime minister failed to gain Diet support for this declaration, which therefore had to be labeled as his "personal view." Murayama resigned shortly after the next general election in October 1996 when the Socialists were sharply penalized by former supporters who resented the party's abandoning of its stated values. No one was sure what the Socialists now stood for. They had refused to criticize Pyongyang, even after it became clear that DPRK agents had been kidnapping Japanese citizens. The voters let the Socialists know that they were out of touch. Cold war Japan's most viable opposition party, which once held 136 seats in the Diet, was left with fewer than ten by the early 2000s.

Japan's other opposition parties also recognize that pacifism has lost its appeal. Reflecting its religious base, Kōmeitō maintains strong pacifist rhetoric in its manifesto, but it has compromised significantly on security policy in return for entry to the ruling coalition. It supported dispatch of the SDF to the Middle East, acquiesced to LDP plans to elevate the JDA to ministry status, and supports debate on constitutional revision.[42] The DPJ, for its part, continues to emphasize "peace nation" rhetoric while its leadership has grown increasingly hawkish.[43] Even the Japan Communist Party (JCP) offered to "freeze" its call for the abrogation of the Mutual Security Treaty following the 1998 upper house election.[44] Still, it continues to call for the "complete" implementation of Article 9, for a staged process of military reductions, and for disbanding the SDF.[45] The JCP has had only single-digit representation in the Diet since 2003.

Grassroots groups have distanced themselves from the parties and persist in efforts to promote pacifism. Japan's peace activists are less isolationist than before and have broadened their portfolio by adding social justice and sustainable development to nonviolence. Regional solidarity has replaced one-country pacifism. But the peace movement is a shadow of its former self. In 2001, twenty-five thousand people gathered to protest Prime Minister Koizumi's support of the "revengeful war" in Afghanistan by the United States—less than 10 percent of the crowds that gathered in 1960 to protest revision of the Security Treaty or in the 1970s to protest Japanese complicity in the Vietnam War.[46] However disappointing this was to their organizers, the numbers declined further. In 2002, only three gatherings attracted more than ten thousand participants, and Japanese protest of the Iraq invasion in 2003 paled in comparison to that in the world's other democracies. By 2004, antiwar protests focused on the U.S. bases, but the pacifists were more out of step, and more marginalized, than ever. As we shall see, they were even beginning to cede leadership of the antibase movement to the Right.

[119]

If wartime had been a period of "chronic nationalism," and the postwar era had been one of chronic pacifism, the early twenty-first century was becoming a time of chronic debate.[47] Autonomy was central to it. Autonomy had always been a core value in Japan's security discourse, but after the most distinguished and powerful advocates of "autonomous defense" (*jishu bōei*), such as Nakasone Yasuhiro, accommodated to the mainstream center, it became an unfulfilled desire rather than a rallying cry.[48] In the debate over Japan's post-Yoshida direction, however, autonomy has grown new legs. Heirs to the early postwar neomilitarists—advocates of a Gaullist armed neutrality—have challenged establishment conservatives' support for the U.S. alliance.[49] They doubt the U.S. commitment to defend Japan and believe that Japan's subordinate position to the United States is an affront to Japan's national prestige. They demand revision of the constitution and, in some cases, argue a revisionist view of history—one in which the Nanjing massacre did not occur—and criticize Japan for "blindly following" (*tsuizui*) the United States. Their views now occupy a growing if not yet fully legitimate place in Japan's security discourse. In one scholar's formulation, "Wishful thinking about peace by some had been replaced by wishful thinking about the utility of war by others."[50]

Four neoautonomists—politician Ishihara Shintarō, academics Nishibe Susumu and Nakanishi Terumasa, and cartoonist Kobayashi Yoshinori—became media stars. Ishihara, the most senior, is the best known outside of Japan and is the best credentialed of the autonomists. In 1970, as a young Diet representative, he declared on the floor of the Diet that the U.S. nuclear umbrella was unreliable and that Japan needed its own nuclear deterrent. Over the years he often has insisted that Japan become a "defense-centered nation" (*bōei kokka*) and, echoing the antimaterialism of the 1930s, he repeatedly has decried Japan's loss of moral values and lack of national purpose.[51] He was a founding member of a Diet group which called for higher defense spending and constitutional revision, but his views drifted rightward while those of the others headed toward the center. Ishihara has made the United States an object of special scorn. In 1992, he coauthored *The Japan That Can Say "No"*, a broadside attack on the relationship with the United States; he followed up two years later with *The Asia That Can Say "No"*. Elected in 1999 to the bully pulpit of Tokyo governor, Ishihara has continued to generate a stream of books, television appearances, and newspaper columns in which he hammers away at revision of the "U.S.-imposed constitution" and supports autonomous defense. In late 2005 he insisted that

Japan needs to recognize the fundamental weakness of the U.S. military in which it blindly has placed its faith, and must prepare to be able to defend itself independently in a crisis....The United States cannot win a war with China and will not fight one to defend Japan.[52]

One former administrative vice minister of the Japan Defense Agency identified Ishihara as the "extreme of the extreme."[53] But Ishihara is joined by Nishibe, Kobayashi, and Nakanishi, and the idea of autonomy has gained traction with the Japanese public.[54] The days when Japanese nationalists saw the U.S. alliance as a "necessary evil"—to combat the greater threat of Communism—are long gone.[55]

Nishibe, long a controversial figure in Japanese intellectual circles, is every bit as blunt as Ishihara. In 1988 he resigned from Tokyo University, setting off a firestorm of debate about political correctness within the Japanese academy.[56] Like Ishihara, Nishibe is critical of Japan's acceptance of verdicts at the Tokyo War Crimes Tribunal, arguing they should be ignored because they were for and by the victor. Some of his more general critique echoes rightists of the 1930s: "As a Japanese, I feel deeply ashamed that we praise the concept of marketism, an American idea....[If we continue], our system of government and our lives will come crashing down."[57] Nishibe's views are published with remarkable frequency in monthly magazines, and he appears on national television on an almost weekly basis. He is particularly critical of Japanese politicians. He singles out Nakasone, who sought pragmatically to separate the fourteen convicted Class A war criminals from the thousands of others enshrined at Yasukuni Shrine, and Prime Minister Koizumi, whose North Korea policy is, he says, nothing more than "appeasement" of international criminals from a "third-rate country" that, he insists, "invaded" Japan.[58] Nishibe saves his strongest language for Japan's dependence on the United States. He points out the hypocrisy of a national security strategy that depends on the United States for extended nuclear deterrence while eschewing possession of nuclear weapons on moral grounds. He insists that unless Japan plans to become the fifty-first U.S. state, it should assert its independence and go nuclear.[59] The SDF should be made into a proper "national military" (*kokugun*), and not be placed at the disposal of the United States.[60] Indeed, much of his vitriol has been directed at those "pro-U.S." conservatives who would tie Japan closely to Washington. He insists "they are crazy" to believe the United States will side with Japan to confront a rising China.[61] He called the 2003 U.S. invasion of Iraq "a childish attempt to eliminate powers that conflict with U.S. interest," labeling it "state terrorism." George W. Bush and Osama bin Laden, he insisted, are "one and the same."[62] Japan is far too uncritical:

Whether it is the alliance guidelines, the Indian Ocean dispatch with Aegis destroyers, or the deployment of SDF troops to Iraq, it is entirely a matter of cooperation for America's sake. [Japan] makes no effort to build an independent military, a diplomatic strategy, or an autonomous defense.[63]

The popular social critic and professor of international politics at Kyoto University, Nakanishi Terumasa, is similarly troubled by American unilateralism and agrees that Japan must become more capable and more willing to act independently in world affairs.[64] Countries, such as Japan, that specialize only in "economic power" (*keizairyoku*) lose influence, and because Japan has "lost its balance" it must "enter its 'second postwar period' with the national goal of standing on its own feet, keeping firmly rooted in its history and traditions . . . [in order to] revitalize the national spirit."[65] Japan is beset by a "social crisis"—crime, educational decline, the loss of social solidarity—and by a "civilization crisis" that follows from its loss of national identity. To combat the erosion of traditional values, Japan should cast off its "misguided pacifism" of the postwar years, establish a national identity of "uniqueness" (*yuiitsu no kuni de aru nihon*), and become "self-reliant."[66]

Although his social critique evokes 1930s nationalism, Nakanishi offers a more pragmatic prescription for achieving autonomy than other Japanese Gaullists. Splitting with Ishihara and Nishibe, he advocates a Japan that can say "yes" to the partnership with the United States—at least for now. The alliance with Washington is necessary because Japan is not ready to wield power or defend its interests on its own.[67] He is contemptuous of other options for Japanese grand strategy—neither rapprochement with Asian neighbors nor establishing a collective security system is a viable alternative to the alliance.[68] But Nakanishi is convinced that U.S. power is declining globally and that the United States is apt to withdraw suddenly from Asia. To prepare for this day, Japan must establish a "new autonomy (*arata na shutaisei*) based on the awareness that it is our country's destiny to stand up on its own (*nihon ikkoku toshitemo tatsu*)."[69]

His support for the alliance is thus openly instrumental. Nakanishi supported Japanese participation in America's "coalition of the willing" in Afghanistan and, later, in Iraq in the belief it would speed revision of the constitution and hasten the return of Japanese "sovereignty over military affairs as a normal nation."[70] For Nakanishi, North Korea is Japan's most immediate threat, one that also presents an opportunity to achieve sovereignty and bulk up national power.[71] He urges Japan to acquire offensive missiles sufficient for use in preemptive strikes against North Korean missile sites.[72] And, departing from Japanese mainstream conservatives, Nakanishi openly supports acquisition of nuclear weapons should Washington decide to leave Pyongyang's nuclear status "ambiguous."[73] Nakanishi also advocates acquiring nuclear weapons when China's blue-water naval capability becomes a credible threat to Okinawa or the Senkaku Islands.[74]

Kobayashi is the most popular of the four among Japanese youth and has attracted considerable attention from adults as well. He first achieved prominence for his cartoon stories in *Sapio* magazine, a youth-oriented, conservative monthly. These comics, often aimed at revising historical interpretations of the Pacific War and the Japanese empire, have been best sellers for years. He was an author of one of the most controversial textbooks issued under the imprimatur of the Japan Society for History Textbook Reform, which he helped found. Denounced vigorously by Japan's neighbors for its attempt to "advocate imperialism and whitewash history," and by both the Left and the establishment Right for stirring up trouble, the society has had more than modest success in Japan. Its textbooks may not have been widely adopted, but its message has become central to contemporary discourse.[75] Like Nishibe, Kobayashi denounces Japanese intellectuals and politicians who have grown too close to the United States.[76] In the run-up to the 2003 Iraq invasion, they joined forces to attack pro-American politicians as "crippled idiots" (*ahō koshinuke*) and vigorously opposed Japanese support for U.S. "aggression."[77] As one token of his influence, Kobayashi was invited to Ginowan, Okinawa, to speak at an antibase rally on 14 August 2005, one day before the sixtieth anniversary of Japan's surrender.

Echoing the familiar rhetoric of the Left that evokes the heroism of the Okinawan people, Kobayashi spoke from the Right about "the dangers of the Okinawa bases," and attracted more than twelve hundred people—twelve times more than a left-wing rally in the larger Naha City that same day.[78]

Few mainstream academics, bureaucrats, or national politicians openly associate with the neoautonomists, and many disparage them. But some do allow that the neoautonomists could find common cause with more decorous conservatives who advocate the building of a more muscular Japan.[79] Indeed, Nakanishi is a member of Abe Shinzō's brain trust.[80]

Figure 7. Kobayashi expresses disdain for "pro-American conservatives," uncritical lapdogs (*pochi*) whose power is derived merely from bandwagoning with the United States. Reprinted with permission of Gentōsha Publishers.

These more decorous conservatives, of course, are those who want Japan to be a "normal nation." The intellectual scion of this perspective was Ozawa Ichirō who, as we saw in chapter 3, tried and failed to send SDF peacekeepers to participate in the Gulf War in 1991. His effort was not for naught, though, as it led to the first significant debate about Japanese security policy after the end of the cold war and, subsequently, to two decades of policy changes consistent with his preferences. Along the way, "normal nationalism" has been appropriated by the new LDP mainstream. This perspective takes three forms. The first is Ozawa's own, a "globalist" perspective advocating that the Japanese military be strengthened but deployed only under the banner of UN peacekeeping operations.[81] Ozawa, who once had advocated a close embrace of the United States, had accepted international criticism of Japan as a free rider, and agreed that it needed to contribute at a level commensurate with its economic capabilities. In his view, only the United Nations, not the United States, can use force legitimately in the international interest, and Japan needs to limit the exercise of force to legitimate ends. Part of the SDF could be formed as a "UN reserve unit," a change that could be made independently of his preference for revision of Article 9. But Ozawa miscalculated the attractiveness of placing Japanese forces under UN command, argued against collective self-defense in order to keep one of his early splinter parties (Shinshintō) together and, distancing himself from the United States, also distanced himself from Japan's ruling coalition. Ozawa's globalism withered with his declining political fortunes—at least until April 2006, when he won the leadership of the DPJ. He immediately staked out his position contra the revisionists in power and declared that Class A war criminals never should have been enshrined at Yasukuni.[82]

Ruling conservatives agree with Ozawa on the need to revise the constitution, but they part company with him on the importance of the U.S. alliance and collective self-defense.[83] There are two views within this ruling group, views that reflect the widening division within a conservative camp split between straightforward realists and more ideological revisionists. This split first surfaced in 2005 when the *Yomiuri Shimbun*, Japan's largest circulation daily and a conservative institution, began editorializing against visits to the Yasukuni Shrine by public officials and in favor of a clear accounting of Japan's war responsibility. *Yomiuri* president and chief editorial writer Watanabe Tsuneo, an aging veteran of the Pacific War, saw Prime Minister Koizumi's shrine visits as needlessly provocative. He criticised the Yūshūkan Museum for purveying "misleading history," a view shared by LDP Diet representative and vice minister for justice Kōno Tarō, who likewise insists that "the ideology of Yasukuni is wrong. Priests built the Yūshūkan with the wrong idea of history."[84] In January 2006, Kuriyama Takakazu, a former Japanese ambassador to the United States, called on Koizumi to cease visiting Yasukuni because the government's views of history and those of its priests are inconsistent.[85] The realists strongly support a secular memorial for Japan's war dead, a plan whose funding was cut off by Prime Minister Koizumi and Chief Cabinet Secretary Abe in late 2005.[86]

Watanabe also confronts deniers of the Nanjing massacre: "Whether there were 3,000, 30,000, or 300,000 victims, there is no mistake that there was a massacre there."[87] He has called for a Diet history examination committee (*rekishi kenshō iinkai*) to formally sort out war responsibility.[88] Watanabe is no leftist. He is unapologetic about the importance, size, and sophistication of Japan's military: "If a nation is 'normal,' it has a military," one that ought to be referred to as such (*guntai*). Changing the name, he insists, has nothing to do with the "foolish notion" that Japan is switching from peaceful to aggressive.[89] In Watanabe's view, and in the view of such fellow realists as former prime minister Nakasone and former ambassador Okazaki Hisahiko, Japan needs to tilt toward the United States as long as China is rising and North Korea is unpredictable.[90]

Japan's leading realists were unhappy with what they saw as the excessively provocative position of the revisionists on history issues, particularly Yasukuni and textbook reform, and actively disavowed nostalgia for the prewar military. Nor did they see apologies for wartime aggression as a sign of national weakness.[91] Instead, their project has been one in which Japan could highlight its democratic present and provide for a secure future without entangling itself in its authoritarian past. Thus, Nakasone apologized to the Koreans and stopped going to Yasukuni in the 1980s after consulting with the Chinese.[92] Moreover, he has made efforts to detoxify the shrine, appealing for the de-enshrinement of the Class A war criminals. The realists recognize that defending Japan is not the only thing on the U.S. agenda, and insist, therefore, that Japan pay special attention to the relationship. The preferred characterization of the realist perspective is what former JDA director general Ishiba has called "robust pacifism" (*honebuto na heiwashugi*).[93]

But their revisionist coalition partners—Japan's "new conservative mainstream"—have been less apologetic about the past and more willing to pander to those who feel nostalgia for it.[94] In power since the 2000 election of Koizumi Junichirō, this group of revisionists has kept the history pot boiling by visiting the Yasukuni Shrine in their capacity as government officials—visits that Chinese officials insist should be as unimaginable as visits by a German chancellor to Adolf Hitler's grave.[95] They point out that between 1978, when the fourteen Class A war criminals were enshrined, and 1984, Japanese prime ministers visited Yasukuni twenty times without any objection from Beijing. This, they insist, is evidence that Beijing has manufactured the Yasukuni problem for its own political purposes. Koizumi, who held that his own freedom of religion overruled the separation of church and state, ignored court rulings and continued his visits against the strong preference of realists within the party and LDP supporters in industry and the media.[96] His foreign minister, Asō Tarō, even suggested that the emperor visit Yasukuni, something that has not happened since the "martyrs of Shōwa" were enshrined in 1978.[97] Realists can accept official visits to Yasukuni if they are accompanied by apologies and do not glorify war criminals, and they are sensitive to the objections of Japan's neighbors to the political use of the shrine. Revisionists, by contrast, deny that apologies, war crimes, and neighbors' preferences have anything to do with their visits.[98] They insist, moreover, that the religious beliefs of the Japanese are no matter for the Chinese or Koreans. When the Diet issued an apology to Japan's neighbors at the sixtieth anniversary of the end of the Pacific War—one that many on the left could not support because it was diluted—Abe and other Koizumi allies walked out of the chamber because the language was too strong.[99]

Japan's revisionists and realists hold a common view of the importance of the U.S. alliance. In his first policy speech after becoming foreign minister in 2005, Asō declared that the United States should come first, Asia second. They are of one mind on the bases issue as well. Both want better coordinated bilateral command relationships, more joint training, more fully coordinated force planning, and co-basing—all building blocks for a more equal security relationship. They share a concern for civilian control and worry about "military types who want the right of command (*shikiken*)."[100] But they also want the United States to recognize that the bases issue is fundamentally about national sovereignty. In their view, without fuller sovereignty and an end to extraterritorial privileges for the U.S. military, the alliance will always be handicapped. The Committee for Revision of SOFA and the Establishment of a True U.S.-Japan Partnership, chaired by a former vice foreign minister, attracted more than one hundred Diet members from several parties, but predominantly realists and revisionists.[101]

These two groups also share the view that China is a potential threat. Whereas realists focus on China's growing military power, the revisionists leaven the argument with a dash of disdain. In addition to sounding the alarm about the PRC's rapid defense buildup, they also question the extent of civilian control of the Chinese military. They resent Beijing's sustained anti-Japanese rhetoric and patriotic education campaign, as well as what they consider China's lectures on the history issue. Thus, rather than rush to improve relations with Beijing when they became frayed in the 2003–05 period, Koizumi instead turned up the heat by continuing his visits to the Yasukuni Shrine.[102] This split the LDP along familiar lines. There has been a "pro-China faction" since the days of Tanaka Kakuei, the prime minister who followed President Nixon to China, and an "anti-China faction" tracing its ancestry back to Kishi Nobusuke.[103] China policy became a major issue in the competition to succeed Koizumi, in which Abe, Kishi's grandson, prevailed in September 2006.

Although their opponents suspect them of harboring grand ideas about Japanese national identity, both the revisionists and the realists have eschewed identifying Japan as a great power. Perhaps because they are still reeling from Japan's awkward response to the first Gulf War and the 1993 North Korea crisis, they continue to hew to the Yoshida rhetoric of Japan as a peace-loving nation.[104] Rather than thump the drum for increases in defense spending or for independence, they argue vigorously that Japan and the United States should build a more equal security relationship. Toward that end they have made Japanese troops available for training and deployment with U.S. forces in unprecedented ways. Unlike the neoautonomists and the pacifists, all three streams of normal nation-alists are comfortable with the idea that the Japanese military might have to use force as a means of settling international disputes, and all three support constitutional revision. They all believe that incremental improvement of Japan's military security posture is in the nation's long-term interest.

MIDDLE POWER INTERNATIONALISTS

Middle power internationalists are not so sure. They continue to oppose the use of force and question whether muscularity, incremental or otherwise, is really the best path toward national security. Like the normal nation-alists, this group is divided internally by attitudes regarding the U.S. relationship. "Mercantile realists" believe that Japan should continue to eschew military power and remain close to the United States for its security, whereas "middle power Asianists" accept the alliance, in some cases grudgingly, but believe that Japanese policy should strike a better balance between the United States and Japan's neighbors. The former come predominantly from within the LDP, the latter from the opposition DPJ. Both groups are convinced of the salience of economic over military power and prefer that Japanese security policy derive its legitimacy from international institutions rather than through unilateral action.

Kōsaka Masataka, an advisor to both Yoshida Shigeru and Ōhira Masayoshi, first introduced the terms "maritime state" (*kaiyō kokka*) and, later, "mercantile state" (*tsūshō kokka*) to describe the optimal posture for Japan.[105] Kōsaka compared Japan to thirteenth-century Venice and to seventeenth-century Holland, nations that prospered while other states kept the peace, and argued that while they had navies to protect their sea-lanes of communication, they were not excessively aggressive.[106] Soeya Yoshihide has further developed the concept of middle power diplomacy.[107] On his account, it is necessary to convince Korea, China, and the ASEAN countries that Japan has no great power ambitions. Japan must remind its neighbors that it has not acted like a great power since 1945 and, instead, that it has promoted economic growth throughout the region. Like other middle powers—Canada and Germany often are invoked—Japan is and should remain a trading nation whose contributions to international security are under multinational auspices. Middle power internationalists would maintain the alliance with the United States but would also try to construct overlapping regional trade and security regimes. They have championed Japan's "peace cooperation diplomacy" (*heiwa kyōryoku gaikō*); some have even elevated "international contribution" (*kokusai kōken*) over national interest in the national security discourse.[108] Great powers may not hesitate to use force to realize national interests, but Japan must never threaten its neighbors again. It must remain a "civilian power" that creates global public goods in the economic arena, and its aspirations must remain limited.[109] If the United States is the indispensable globo-cop, Japan should position itself as the indispensable globo-merchant, and it would be dangerous to conflate these two roles. This, according to Kyoto University professor Yamamuro Shinichi, requires not "losing self-control": "When Japan thinks of itself as a small country or as a middle power, it conducts its diplomacy with deep care and consideration for its neighbors. But, when it embraces a big power idea [of itself], it fails."[110] Clearly, there are echoes here of earlier debates.

Mercantile realists are the direct heirs of the pragmatic conservatives who brought Japan back to prosperity from wartime devastation, in the process reinventing the Small Japanism of Ishibashi Tanzan and other pioneers of nonexpansive economic liberalism in the early twentieth century. As we have seen, the core of their once-dominant security doctrine was comprehensive security and a cheap ride on the United States. Like the pacifists with whom they tacitly allied, however, Japan's mercantile realists have been outboxed by the revisionists within their own party. One by one, during the ascent of the antimainstream in the early 2000s, powerful mainstream pragmatists such as Nonaka Hiromu, Kōno Yōhei, Miyazawa Kiichi, and Katō Kōichi were shunted aside and their Kōchikai splintered. Some, like Kōno, fought back with vigor, but to no avail.[111] Mercantile realism has not disappeared to quite the same extent as pacifism, but it has ceded the mainstream and control of government.

The second stream of middle power internationalists was the more vigorous by the early 2000s. It involves those who oppose the use of force but would prefer Japan to distance itself from the United States and focus on Asia. If the mercantile realists saw Japan as the "lead goose" flying ahead of a developing Asia, the new Asianists prefer to imagine Japan as another lamb within a larger flock, rather than as a bellwether.[112] Unlike prewar

Asianists, who sought to decouple Japan from the world economy, these are liberal Asianists who seek to build regional institutions to counterbalance U.S. unilateralism and to accommodate the rise of China.[113] This requires an end to Japan's neglect of regional concerns and its excessive orientation toward the preferences of the United States. It also requires more attentiveness on the history issue. Koga Makoto, the former secretary general of the LDP, openly took aim at Abe and other normal nation-alists in 2005 by declaring that building trust with Asian neighbors is more important than reaffirming relations with the United States.[114] He was joined one year later by the New Generation Forum for Cooperation with Asia, formed by first-term Diet members.[115] The business community also has mobilized on this issue. In May 2006 the Japan Association of Corporate Executives (Keizai Dōyūkai) issued proposals to improve Sino-Japanese relations, including sharp criticism of Yasukuni visits by the prime minister and support for a secular memorial to the war dead.

Others have gone further, calling for an "Asian Restoration" and the "reassertion of an 'Asian spirit.'"[116] Distinctly "Asian values," such as discipline, social solidarity, and family, ought to provide the basis for a regional spiritual identity that would trump Western decadence.[117] Yet the idea of a nascent pan-Asianism notwithstanding, most middle power Asianists acknowledge that the region needs—and even wants—a continued U.S. military presence and the stability it provides.[118] The DPJ platform in the September 2005 elections struck just this chord. After acknowledging that the U.S.-Japan alliance is the "lynchpin" of stability in Asia, it added that "blindly following the United States does not contribute to strengthening the alliance. The value of the alliance will increase if we transmit the views of the Japanese and Asian peoples, and urge the United States to exercise self-restraint."[119] Ozawa Ichirō reiterated this point on assuming leadership of the DPJ in April 2006, and two months later he made Beijing the site of his first overseas visit as shadow prime minister.[120]

Some neo-Asianists value the U.S. contribution to regional security less than others. Terashima Jitsurō insists that a strengthened Japan-U.S. alliance has already led to the dissipation of Japanese influence in the Middle East and risks future conflict with China. He insists that Japan be explicit about not intervening in a Taiwan crisis and not supporting the United States if it does.[121] He would not fully decouple Japan from the United States but does argue for a reduced U.S. military footprint and revised SOFA.[122] Japan, after all, must be prepared for a time when U.S. affections will shift from Japan toward a triangular model of equidistance from Japan and China—a model invoked by Ozawa during his June 2006 trip to Beijing. Sounding more like a descendent of prewar pan-Asianists and a kissing cousin of contemporary neoautonomists than like a liberal internationalist, Terashima suggests that "before long the Japanese will have to extricate themselves from the self-satisfied embrace as the only advanced nation of 'honorary Caucasians'" and insists that the United States is a "worn-out superpower" (*tsukareta chōtaikoku*).[123] Japan must abandon its identity as a country "near the United States" (*beikoku shūhenkoku*) and establish "true independence and self-respect" (*shin no jiritsu jison*).[124] He calls for progress toward construction of an East Asian economic community as the only way to stabilize the explosive growth of the region.[125] Asia is not a place to rediscover when things go bad with the United States; it is a regional identity that Japan must vigorously take the lead in constructing.[126]

This view is shared in other, less vituperative, analyses. Shiraishi Takashi reminds us that the reconstruction of East Asia after 1945 was a U.S. project, one guided by Washington's desire to contain Communist expansion and to get Japan back on its feet. U.S. power defined the region's borders, and the U.S. dollar defined much of what went on within its constituent parts. But the once overwhelming United States has reached the "limits to empire," and a region that was shaped under its values is now generating values of its own.[127] A "pan-Asian cultural sphere" is emerging, which, while it may result in a distinctive Asian identity, has been driven by market forces. A burgeoning, well-educated middle class that once made only *things*, increasingly produces, consumes, and shares *culture* as well.[128] Japan, for its part, has been constrained by U.S. power but retains "great freedom of action" in the region (*ōkina kōdō no jiyū*)—freedom built on informal networks of economic relationships that could be expanded.[129]

On his account, there are three separate patterns of Asianism. The first, at the macroeconomic and political levels, is one in which English is the dominant language and the United States is a critical source of technology, security, and consumers. The second is the microeconomic level, which Japan leads through its domination of production systems and industrial policy strategies. The third level, the Sinitic, builds on the widespread Chinese diaspora in the region and the rise of China as a production base. It is clear that three powers are players, and that none necessarily displaces the others.[130] For Tokyo to take advantage of the significant opportunity that exists to exert influence, its diplomacy needs to respond less to U.S. demands and to better anticipate regional needs.[131] It can start, Shiraishi insists, by supporting a regional infrastructure—in energy, trade, intellectual property, and finance.[132] Articulating the strategic preference of his fellow middle power internationalists, Shiraishi insists that in the process of generating these regional public goods, Japan can help manage China's rise without confronting it militarily or on the history issue.

Soeya Yoshihide agrees. He insists that Japan cannot exclude the United States from the region.[133] A middle power Japan allied with the United States is particularly reassuring to Japan's neighbors, each of which is suspicious of the normal nation ideal. On the other hand, rather than fearing the rise of China and treating it as a rival, Japan ought to contribute to the construction of a stable, China-centered regional order.[134] This order would be one in which a middle power Japan could find common cause with other democratic middle powers, such as Australia and the Republic of Korea, neither of which can compete one-on-one with the new China.[135]

As we have seen, there is nothing new under the (rising) sun vis-à-vis the contemporary Japanese debate over grand strategy. Much like their predecessors in the nineteenth and twentieth centuries, Japanese security planners now discuss and make choices about the balance between maritime and continental power, between economic and military instruments, between hard and soft power, among alliance partners, and for or against construction of multilateral security regimes. And like their predecessors, they get lots of advice from a growing spectrum of political groups. What is striking—and what ought to be reassuring to the United States and to Japan's neighbors—is that there is no debate over fundamental values of democracy and freedom. Indeed, all agree that Japan can champion both to its national advantage, and in particular vis-à-vis China.[136]

It remains to be seen how this discourse will evolve. Certainly, the sharp distinctions across these four groups begin to blur once domestic politics and foreign threats intervene to complicate choices. After all, Japanese politicians (and their kitchen cabinets) are no less susceptible to the attractions of logrolling and compromise than U.S. or Italian ones. Perhaps the revisionists who came to power in the early 2000s will consolidate their preferences as national policy and continue to trim away until nothing is left of the Yoshida consensus. But the blurring is already under way, and there seems considerable room for migration across the quadrants. The revisionists have already demonstrated their commitment to the pacifist ideals of the 1947 Constitution, and they do not advocate an autonomous defense buildup, so it is not likely that the Yoshida consensus will be displaced entirely. Some advocates of the normal nation seek greater autonomy, just as autonomists, pacifists, and some middle power internationalists are not yet ready to sever all ties to the United States. While critical of the alliance with the United States and eager to achieve greater sovereignty, few advocate a complete break.

Likewise, no significant party in the Japanese security discourse refuses to accept the legitimacy of the SDF. All agree, moreover, that China, with all its great power ambitions, needs to be integrated peacefully and that a nondemocratic China is inimical to Japanese interests. Thus, it seems at least plausible that the "middle power" road—amended to allow a fuller hedge against Chinese power and U.S. decline—will be an attractive successor to the Yoshida Doctrine. This new consensus is likely to resemble Goldilocks's preferences: Japan's relationships with the United States and China will be neither too hot nor too cold, and its posture in the region will be neither too big nor too small. After examining the diplomatic, economic, and military contexts of these choices, we will return to the nascent Goldilocks consensus in the final chapter of this book.

PART III

THREATS AND RESPONSES

[6]

The New Threat Environment

Threat is the anticipation of harm to a state's population, through the loss of territory, sovereignty, or wealth. Some threats, such as those posed by weapons of mass destruction or by enemy troops at the border, are direct. Other threats are indirect, as rivals exercise their power to raise the costs of preferred policies. Nor, as the Asian financial crisis of 1997 and the attacks on the United States in September 2001 both illustrate, do threats always come from other states. Revolutionary groups, terrorists, and international financial institutions can all pose threats. Because threats come in various shapes and sizes, and because anarchy governs the international order, states worry incessantly about how to enhance their security. They are likely to overensure their security by maximizing their power and, in so doing, stimulate their adversaries to do likewise. This security dilemma is often subtle—to mobilize support, leaders may inflate the capabilities and intentions of rivals. Threat assessment is not a science but a survival art, one that politicians practice at both tactical and strategic levels, always with uncertain success and often with dangerous consequences.

Threats are always filtered through domestic institutions and engage domestic actors, so neither a foreign power's capability nor its intent can ever be objectively assessed.[1] Still, from the end of the Pacific War to the end of the cold war, Japan's preferences have been straightforward. Tokyo elected to cheap ride on U.S. security guarantees and maximize prosperity. It judged the probability of attack by the Soviet Union—"objectively" a far greater threat then than China is today—to be low, and accepted the risk of entanglement in U.S. wars to reap the security benefit of a nuclear umbrella and various technoeconomic gains.

But now both Japan's threat environment and its domestic filters have changed. New threats have combined with the familiar ambitions of new power holders in Tokyo. The result has been a significant improvement in Japan's defense posture. Today, Japan faces minor threats from pirates in the Malacca Strait, who disrupt shipping to and from the world's busiest ports, and major ones from terrorists across the globe, who may find Japanese targets attractive. Japan faces substantive threats from four countries: China, North Korea, the United States, and itself.[2] The threats from North Korea and China are conventional—each is a neighbor with which Japan has unresolved territorial disputes, which can easily mobilize its population in an aggressively anti-Japanese direction, and which is engaged in a rapid military buildup. The relationship with Japan's only ally obviously is very different—the United States is rarely framed as threat. But the United States is engaged in a global transformation of its force structure as well as in a proclaimed "war on terror." Japan needs the United States diplomatically and militarily—but at what cost? Any judgment requires Tokyo to recalibrate its basic question about the alliance: Abandonment or entanglement? Finally, the threat Japan poses to itself is one that has engaged security planners for generations—relative technoeconomic decline. These four threats are not the only ones shaping Japan's contemporary threat environment and are viewed differently in each quadrant of Japan's lively security discourse, but they attract the most attention from defense planners.

RISING CHINA

Although an ascendant China tops virtually everyone's list of threats, it is not clear why a risen China *must* threaten Japan.[3] The two economies now enjoy the largest bilateral trade volume in history and are highly complementary.[4] Japan provides China with technology and capital, while China provides Japan with cheap production and an export platform. Japan's export dependence on China has soared—nearly to U.S. levels—and the share of Japanese imports from the United States has been cut in half since the late 1990s at the same time as the share of imports from China has nearly doubled.[5] Both are energy importers, and so each benefits considerably from global resource development, from stability in the sea-lanes, and from the efficient use of resources. Both have an abiding interest in a vibrant regional economy.[6] By 2003, some 30–40 percent of Japanese production in China was being exported, and China had become responsible for more than 90 percent of the growth of Japan's exports.[7] Ten million Chinese work in Japanese firms, and that number continues to grow as Japan redirects its foreign direct investment (FDI) toward China and away from the United States.[8] One government researcher calls for a Sino-Japanese free trade agreement and insists that "if the comparative advantages of both countries can be realized through trade, China's advancement will not be a threat to Japan but rather a win-win game for both sides."[9] Likewise, the ASEAN+3 regional order integrating the economies of Japan, China, and Korea with those of Southeast Asia is a central feature of Japanese diplomacy.[10] According to a December 2003 *Yomiuri Shimbun* poll, 53 percent of Japanese respondents considered the United States to be the most important country from a political perspective, compared with 30 percent for China. But, when asked who is Japan's most important trade partner, more than half answered China, twice as many as named the United States.[11] As Mike Mochizuki has suggested, Japan sees China as "a potential partner in establishing an attractive global economic balance of power."[12]

Second, there has been considerable evidence that China and Japan can get along politically. Bilateral relations were not unfriendly under the "1972 system," abetted by the United States and enabled by a commonly perceived Soviet threat.[13] Under Deng Xiaoping, who never assumed an anti-Japan posture, China did not make an issue of the Nanjing massacre. China was rewarded in 1979–80, when Japan exempted China from its self-imposed rule not to provide development assistance to arms-exporting or nuclear-armed states.[14] Japanese aid was in no official sense war reparations, but Japanese leaders did see it as a form of atonement, one they hoped would catapult China away from the Cultural Revolution and into modernization.[15] Hu Yaobang and Nakasone Yasuhiro developed a productive relationship in the 1980s, one that promoted a dramatic rise in student exchanges and an end to Yasukuni Shine visits. More recently, the two countries cooperated effectively in the six-party talks concerning North Korean nuclear weapons and in promoting a regional economic integration through the ASEAN+3 prototype. In July 2006, Beijing even voted in the UN Security Council to reprimand North Korea for provocative missile tests in the Sea of Japan. Many Japanese observers see great strategic potential for rapprochement with China.[16]

But rapprochement remains elusive. Economic and cultural ties have deepened, but so have political and military suspicions.[17] China is often painted as a greater threat than the Soviet Union during its heyday, because Japan cannot be as sure of the U.S. commitment as it was during the cold war, China is on a "rich nation, strong army" path, and because doing so is helpful to the normal nation-alists who have long sought to make Japan more muscular and who are now in power. Chinese leaders make no bones about their great power aspirations, and they remember ruefully that Japan has long been the greater power and China the lesser. Chinese history, they note, is not one of colonial expansion, even though until the early nineteenth century China had the means to achieve hegemony in the region. Within the region, moreover, these two great civilizations never coexisted comfortably when both were strong.[18] The Chinese lose no opportunity to remind listeners that it was Japan that invaded China, not the reverse, and proclaim their vigilance vis-à-vis the return of Japanese militarism. Chinese leaders have supported (at least tacitly) the U.S. presence in Northeast Asia as a way to keep the lid on "militaristic elements in Japan"; pointing to visits to Yasukuni, they fear that these elements are now about to have their day.[19] They are wary, moreover, of Japan's sympathy toward Taiwan, which, after the Korean Peninsula, is the most volatile flash point in East Asia. Chinese suspicions have been exacerbated by competition for resources in adjacent seabeds, further raising the stakes and the tensions for both nations. They each face a threat from North Korea—China faces massive refugee flows, while Japan faces nuclear-tipped missiles. These matters add up to more than a few large boulders strewn along the road to rapprochement, and perhaps the largest obstacles are territorial: sovereignty of the Senkaku Islands, located near both Taiwan and Okinawa, and an agreed international border in the East China Sea.[20]

Meanwhile, some in each country find it helpful to maintain a simmering nationalism. Many Japanese had hoped that the history issue would be put to rest by a series of official apologies for Japan's war of aggression and, especially, by Emperor Akihito's October 1992 visit to China, where he acknowledged that Japan had "inflicted great sufferings on the people of China," something he "deeply deplored."[21] But the history issue is as volatile as ever. Many Japanese observers blame this on Beijing's "patriotic education" campaign, which began in 1994. Elementary school students then are young adults today, and they have been exposed to little besides negative news about Japan.[22] In the Chinese media, there is no mention of Japanese development assistance or investment, no recognition of sixty years of Japanese pacifism, and little acknowledgement of formal Japanese apologies for wartime aggression. Few Japanese films are broadcast on Chinese television. Instead, the media actively cover efforts to rewrite Japan's textbooks, deny the Nanjing massacre, and otherwise revise history. The Chinese deny that their schools and media teach a one-sided, "patriotic" version of bilateral history, but Japanese observers are convinced otherwise.[23]

At a minimum, anti-Japanism is a useful tool for China's leaders to deflect domestic criticism of their regime. It is, after all, a fundamental source of their legitimacy.[24] Both the Chinese Communist Party and the People's Liberation Army (PLA) rely on their victory over Japan to undergird their continuing authority. One former GSDF general asks rhetorically: "Does China forever intend to see Japan only as a defendant, forcing it to do penance for being an aggressive criminal invader?"[25] But it is equally clear that Japanese leaders find China a useful bogeyman.[26] Public debate about a "China threat" intensified in the early 2000s, when according to one analysis the discourse became "less restrained and compromising" and accounts of Chinese intentions became increasingly "visceral."[27] In late 2004, just as the defense budget was being compiled, the JDA released data on the number of times SDF fighter jets had responded to PLA incursions. And in 2005, the foreign ministry labeled China a threat for the first time.

Whether it was engineered or spontaneous, bilateral relations took a turn for the worse in 2002 when three decades of relatively placid relations suddenly ended. In May, the Chinese police stepped inside the gates of the Japanese consulate in Shenyang to prevent the entry of a North Korean defector. Japanese pundits and media responded with outrage at this "rape" of Japanese sovereignty; the monthly *Shokun!* revived slogans from the 1930s calling for "punishment of the wayward Chinese," and Tokyo governor Ishihara proclaimed that China had "pissed on" Japan.[28] Prime Minister Koizumi's subsequent Yasukuni visits were followed by anti-Japanese riots in China, first during the Asian football championships in August 2004 and then in April 2005, after a revisionist history textbook had been approved by the Japanese Ministry of Education. Japanese saw Chinese police stand by indifferently as youths pelted their embassy with paint and rocks, and they read posters calling them "Pigs" and "Dogs" and urging China to "Destroy Little Japan" and to "Kill Japanese Because They Killed Our Grandparents."[29]

Japan's sympathy for China, which had begun dissipating after the June 1989 Tiananmen events, evaporated altogether. Whereas more than 80 percent of the Japanese polled in the 1980s viewed China favorably, this number had fallen below 40 percent by 2004.[30] Between September 2004 and June 2005 alone, the number of Japanese reporting a dislike of China rose sharply from 28 percent to over 40 percent. Only 11 percent reported "liking" China.[31] A review of more than five hundred articles in Japanese magazines between 2001 and 2003 revealed three consistent themes: economic relations with China are dangerous, China is not a cooperative neighbor, and China holds dangerous military ambitions.[32] Anti-Chinese comic books, some of which depict a "depraved people obsessed with cannibalism and [a nation] filled with prostitutes," have sold millions of copies in Japan.[33]

Attitudes in China are little different. Younger Chinese hold less friendly attitudes toward Japan than do their parents, and those who came of age after Tiananmen are far more hostile toward Japan than even those who lived through the Japanese occupation.[34] In 2005 only two of the top fifty most-sought employment opportunities in China were with Japanese firms—Sony in twenty-sixth place and Matsushita in forty-sixth.[35] Nearly 90 percent of Chinese polled report that "Japan has not atoned sufficiently for its history."[36] On the sixtieth anniversary of the end of the Pacific War, the *People's Daily* celebrated the "miraculous victory" of the Chinese Communist Party in the "great war of resistance" won by "a weak China over a strong Japan."[37] On the same day, the conservative *Sankei Shimbun* emphasized that "more than thirty million Japanese were victims of the last war," adding that the PRC, a nation that "invaded the Korean Peninsula" and fought wars with Vietnam,

India, and the Soviet Union, has embarked on a "rapid military buildup."[38] By the end of Prime Minister Koizumi's premiership in September 2006, Chinese and Japanese leaders had not met in five years.

Although this set of events is important, most of it is byplay. The larger issues that shape Japan's threat environment are grounded in perceptions of capabilities and intentions. The capabilities of the People's Liberation Army and the People's Liberation Army Navy (PLAN) have grown, even if they are not yet the equivalent of the Soviet Union during the cold war—or of Japan today. Chinese military power had declined significantly during the 1980s, but Beijing's subsequent military modernization—double-digit growth for a decade and a half through 2007–has resulted in deployment of fourth-generation jet fighters, aerial refueling capabilities, an impressive submarine fleet, new destroyers, and even plans for an Airborne Warning and Control System (AWACS) and aircraft carrier. Combined with medium- and long-range missiles and nuclear weapons, this adds up to a growing ability to project considerable force. Other observers point to the exceeding low level from which the PLA began its modernization and the limited number of modern systems that it has deployed. They see merely an increased ability to project limited force. Most analysts agree that the PLA is equipping only a small number of units with very high-end weapons, and that it will be another decade before China can defeat a moderate-sized adversary.[39] Still, even if China will not be able to claim great power status until 2020, its intent and trajectory are clear. As former U.S. deputy secretary of state Richard Armitage noted in 2005: "China has achieved a remarkable strengthening of virtually all the key elements that we traditionally associate with comprehensive national power…and China is achieving real military options in the region."[40]

For some in Japan, China is already a threat. Its missiles and submarines provide coercive capabilities that seriously concern Tokyo.[41] So does its ability to knock out an orbiting satellite, as demonstrated in January 2007. Beijing's plan to deploy a blue-water navy may be 1980s vintage, but it is closer to realization than ever. Japanese concerns begin with Taiwan. In March 2005 China adopted an antisecession law that legalized the use of force to block Taiwan independence. Senior Japanese intelligence experts are certain that China is targeting U.S. bases in Japan, and they note that Tokyo would be within range if Beijing were to redeploy any of the seven hundred missiles now targeted at Taiwan.[42] Others suggest that Chinese naval vessels are installing seabed sensors on the likely routes U.S. warships would take in the event they were deployed to assist Taiwan.[43] PLAN activities in the East China Sea are not limited to oil and gas exploration. PLAN is also doing surveys for submarine navigation, despite demands by the Japanese Coast Guard to desist.[44] Nor has it gone unnoticed that China repeatedly conducts amphibious landing exercises while claiming sovereignty over the Paracel Islands and the Nansha Archipelago.

Figure 8. The SDF is intimidated by a suddenly threatening China. Reprinted with permission of the artist, Kojima Koh, and the *Asahi Shimbun*.

Japanese analysts acknowledge that PLAN subs are noisy and easy to track, but they are concerned that the PLAN has moved aggressively into the East and South China seas—including territory claimed by Japan halfway between Guam and Taiwan—to be able to block U.S. efforts to come to Taiwan's aid.[45] For China, Taiwan is primarily a domestic political issue, but for Japan it is a straightforward security concern. All the seaborne freight entering and leaving southern Japan must pass through waters adjacent to Taiwan. The threat to Japan is complex. At its most indirect, Japanese failure to support the United States in the event of a Taiwan crisis would surely force the alliance to collapse. But the security problem hardly disappears for Japan in the event of a peaceful reunification of Taiwan with the mainland. Control of Taiwan is not required for Beijing to establish a coercive presence in the sea-lanes upon which much of Japan's trade depends, but unification would certainly enhance its position at Japan's expense.[46]

Japanese security specialists insist that Chinese intentions are equally unambiguous in other areas of strategic concern, particularly those related to national boundaries. Some speak of China's "deception diplomacy" and warn that China is simply biding time until its force modernization is complete.[47] Although China has historically lacked "maritime ambition," it now has asserted sovereignty over the Senkaku Islands, and rejects Japanese claims over them as well as over the Okinotori Islands, rocks that Japan has endeavored to interpret as islands under the United Nations Convention on the Law of the Sea in order to extend its own exclusive economic zone (EEZ). Beijing has drawn a border in the East China Sea that extends its claims all the way to the shelf off Okinawa.[48] PLAN submarines and oceanographic vessels have actively sailed the waters of the East and South China seas, as well as in the Sea of Japan, often alarming the Japanese Coast Guard.[49] Probes by the Chinese Air Force set off a record number of scrambles by Japanese fighters in 2004 and again in 2005.[50]

The Senkaku (what the Chinese call the Diaoyutai) case has drawn the most attention. This group of eight uninhabited islands in the East China Sea, east of China, northeast of Taiwan, and southwest of Okinawa, are 410 km from the main islands of the Okinawa chain, but only 330 km from the Chinese coast and 170 km from Taiwan. They came into Japanese possession in 1895, but it is not clear if this was part of the Treaty of Shimonoseki that ended the First Sino-Japanese War.[51] After Japan's defeat in the Pacific War, they were administered by U.S. forces as part of Okinawa, and were returned to Japan with the reversion of Okinawa in 1972. But the Chinese have long disputed Japanese sovereignty, arguing that the Diaoyutai were administered as part of Taiwan until 1945. The dispute was left undisturbed until 1968, when the United Nations suggested there might be oil deposits nearby. At that point, nationalist groups in Taiwan, China, and Japan began to mobilize. In 1978, Deng Xiaoping cut the Gordian knot and called on "the next generation" to resolve the Senkaku dispute, but in 1992 China declared the islands its own. Repeated landings and attempted occupations by nationalist groups from Hong Kong, Okinawa, Japan, Taiwan, and China have kept the Japanese Coast Guard busy with interceptions, arrests, and deportations, and the foreign ministries of all parties busy with démarches.

The existence of energy resources complicated this dispute considerably, because the untapped reserves there straddle borders claimed by Japan and by China based on their sovereignty over the islands. These resources are not considered significant by many energy firms, but no one doubts their political significance. Beijing insists its exploration is being conducted on the Chinese side of the border claimed by Tokyo, but since the reserves straddle the border, Tokyo suspects that China will suck up resources on the Japanese side as well. Invoking the Convention on the Law of the Sea, China insists that its continental shelf stretches to the Okinawa Trough and that this continental shelf is entirely within China's EEZ. The absence of agreement on each country's EEZ—Japan draws a line halfway between the Chinese and Japanese continental shelves, whereas the Chinese claim the standard distance from its own littoral—has invited commercial and military activity from both countries. In 1988 PLAN vessels began maritime surveys inside the area Japan claims for its EEZ. China has signed contracts with foreign oil exploration firms, and Japan awarded rights to Teikoku Oil, a Japanese drilling company. In 2001 Japan and China devised a "notification system" requiring PLAN ships to inform Japan of their entry, which, after all, is not illegal under the Convention on the Law of the Sea.[52] In 2004, however, just after the Asia Cup soccer riots, a nuclear powered *Han*-class Chinese submarine entered without notification, causing the Japanese to demand an apology. Tokyo received an acknowledgement of error from Beijing.[53] Subsequent efforts to negotiate a joint exploration deal continued into 2006, but they came to naught in an environment of increased bilateral mistrust. The incursions fed unsympathetic Japanese perceptions of China. As one retired GSDF general puts it, "A China which calmly declares the property of other nations to be its own is truly a fearsome country."[54] Mincing no words, he declared that China is pursuing a "'rich nation, strong army' program of development (*fukoku kyōhei no seisaku*) according to Chinese principles" aimed at regional domination.[55] Japan has never felt so strong a China threat, and it continues to grow.

INDUSTRIAL AND TECHNOLOGICAL BASE

While the Japanese press makes much of the rise of China as a military threat, it has long been clear to Japanese strategists that China's territorial claims are also (perhaps primarily) economic threats. Few among the political elite believe that the Chinese economic threat is as great as the one from Europe or the United States, but it is often claimed that PRC control of Taiwan would afford it control of Japan's sea-lanes, and PRC control of the Senkaku Islands would deny Japan new energy resources. One Cabinet Office JDA official explains the economic component of Chinese military power: "China's aims are not necessarily aggressive. Their military buildup is designed to keep the oil and energy flowing to facilitate growth. Even so, military confrontation is likely to result, and Japan needs countercoercion capabilities."[56]

It is different, however, for Japanese workers and their communities that are threatened by the displacement of jobs to China. Their managers, moreover, are threatened by the possibility that technology transferred to China will enable Chinese firms to surpass Japanese firms in the generation of new technology. And Japanese government officials are threatened by the prospect that China will seize leadership of the process of East Asian integration. The projected consequences of each of these three threats galvanized into a "China economic threat theory" (*chūgoku keizai kyōiron*) during the 1990s.[57]

The first of these threats, deindustrialization and job displacement, was captured in the popular imagination by the metaphor of "hollowing" (*kūdōka*).[58] "Hollowing" dominated the economic security discourse in the 1990s: jobs would be scooped out by Chinese workers, who would produce the same products more cheaply. Low-cost Chinese competition threatened to destroy Japan's small and medium-sized firms, a threat abetted by Japanese firms that rushed headlong to invest in China.[59] China replaced the United States as Japan's gravest economic threat. Its manufacturers would export deflation, steal Japanese technology, and deindustrialize Japan. All that would be left would be empty factories and empty villages—a Japanese rust belt. By 2001, Japanese think tanks were predicting that "all Japanese products," excluding some chemical goods and information technology production equipment, would be "swamped" by Chinese competitors. Concerns over the hollowing out of the Japanese economy mounted as Japanese companies moved their production bases to China. Some three quarters of those polled in 2001 and 2002 believed that the Chinese economy was already a "threat."[60]

These fears were underscored by macroeconomic data. Japan's manufacturing sector shrank rapidly during the 1990s, and the restructuring of Japanese firms (*risutora*) was a national nightmare come true. Japanese unemployment rose to record levels in the late 1990s, peaking in 2002. Japan's technology trade balance had turned positive for the first time in 1992, as firms supported foreign direct investment with transfers of production technology. Although the United States and the Republic of Korea were always the two top destinations for Japanese technology, China began to catch up quickly. China even surpassed the United States as a destination for Japanese investment in 2004.[61] In the belief that Japanese firms should "strengthen the capacity of secondary manufacturers to assimilate foreign technology to improve the quality of parts produced" and that "market restrictions cannot be placed on technology transferred to China," the Japanese government even produced guidelines to assist firms in transferring their technology to China.[62] By 1997, however, Japanese managers began to express fears of a "boomerang effect," whereby technology transfers would lead to the creation of strong foreign rivals.[63] This fear was exacerbated as the weakest Japanese producers of particular technologies "broke ranks" and transferred them to other Asian countries. Sharp, for example, was excoriated in the Japanese press for being first to leak key DRAM (direct random access memory) computer technology to Korean companies, and Mitsubishi Electric provoked the same treatment for its transfer of LCD (liquid crystal display) technology to Taiwan.[64] As late as 2002, Japanese government officials continued to support the movement of Japanese manufacturing overseas. One METI official, Nakamura Yoshiaki, wrote that "the hollowing out being witnessed in Japan should be regarded as a part of the globalization of Japanese corporations" and should not be obstructed.[65] Few politicians or journalists were so complaisant. The air remained thick with threat.

Compounding this was a threat to Japan's prestige as well as to its long-run economic health. Japan had spent decades positioning itself to lead East Asian economic development. Invoking metaphors of "flying geese" from the 1930s, Japan hoped to inspire a Southeast Asia seeking to reduce dependence on Western capital and markets, and eager to "look East" to promote "Asian values."[66] Japan was poised to seize the initiative when, in 1997, the region plunged into a financial crisis. Tokyo announced plans to create an Asian monetary fund to rescue its neighbors, but retracted the idea under pressure from the United States. From that moment, it seemed to many in the region, Japan was too weak to resist the United States. Soon China, which was already working its way into the World Trade Organization, challenged for de facto regional leadership. Beijing, realizing that the 1989 Tiananmen repression and the 1996 missile tests in the Taiwan Strait were counterproductive, had already shifted toward a "smile strategy." It began to increase regional trade even with Japan, whose exports to China grew from under $30 billion in 1994 to nearly $75 billion a decade later, and whose imports from China grew even faster.[67] China's market was beginning to displace that of the United States as being indispensable to the Asian regional economies. It was far more open to regional trade and direct investment than Japan, a factor that earned Beijing even more influence.

Its diplomatic achievements began to pile up at Japan's expense.[68] China had launched a new "economic security" initiative and began actively promoting regional cooperation. Unlike Japan, which runs a trade surplus with the rest of the region, China runs a deficit, making it a more open and more appealing candidate for regional leadership. Its positive role in the May 2000 Chiang Mai Initiative—a $39 billion collection of bilateral currency swaps during financial crises—helped create the region's first monetary regime. Tokyo could not have accomplished this without Beijing and, in fact, had until then been focusing its economic diplomacy on the United States and Europe.[69] In 2002, China was the first to sign a "comprehensive economic cooperation" accord with ASEAN, setting a 2010 target for a regionwide free trade agreement (FTA) directly challenging Tokyo.[70] All Japan could say in response was that it would "consider" a similar arrangement; its subsequent proposals were largely ignored.[71] In 2003, China signed a treaty of amity and cooperation in Southeast Asia with ASEAN. When the ASEAN+3 was established in 2004, China was every bit the equal of Japan, and it was not clear that Japan had any natural claim on regional leadership. Not only would Tokyo not be writing the rules of the road (à la the United States at Bretton Woods), but now it was going to have to incorporate—or bend to—Chinese preferences as well. Indeed, as a measure of Beijing's self-assured position in the region, when the Chinese ambassador to Japan, Wang Yi, urged Japan to enter into a bilateral free trade agreement (in Kobe, in February 2005), he also scolded Japan on the history issue, blaming it for the deterioration in bilateral relations. According to one press report: "Wang, backed by his confidence in the huge China market, rocked the Koizumi government. He spoke as if to say, 'You'd better not miss the bus.' His FTA advocacy appears to be a sign of China's possible offensive against Japan."[72] China's "offensive" generated a considerable sense of frustration in Japan. Japan and China have different ideas about how to structure the interdependence of the East Asian economies. Their differences start at the top, of course, since each wants to be the leader. Japan, still responding to U.S. pressure, lobbied for an "open architecture" to include the United States and to dilute Chinese influence, but China would have none of it. The most concrete manifestation of the new regional economic architecture was the "ASEAN+3" framework. As T. J. Pempel has observed, the economic achievements of the rest of the region, and especially of China, "reduced the relative influence of Japan's regional economic muscle."[73]

In addition to straightforward commercial challenges is the threat of most direct concern to the Japanese defense industry: the loss of an indigenous defense production and technology base. The Japanese defense industry is very small. In part due to the ban on arms exports, defense production makes up barely one half of 1 percent of total Japanese industrial production. Yet despite limited production of final systems and large-scale weapons platforms, Japanese firms emerged as world leaders in the design and manufacture of materials, components, and subsystems essential for defense systems at home and abroad. Indeed, the most rapid growth in postwar Japan was in sectors closely linked to materials and technologies that enhance the battlefield capabilities of modern weapons: data processing, telecommunications, optoelectronics, and lightweight materials. By making integrated circuits in large volumes for consumer electronics and graphite fiber in large volumes for tennis rackets and golf clubs, Japanese manufacturers were able to accumulate experience and "spin-on" their knowledge to military aerospace. Having responded to the escalating demands of rapidly changing civilian markets for these and other products, they found themselves able to meet military specifications of performance, reliability, and quality, often at low cost.

But Japan's defense manufacturers continue to feel threatened.[74] In part they have themselves to blame. Cost savings from "spin-on" technologies are often negated by a highly inefficient (and often corrupt) procurement system. As a result, the cost of Japanese defense systems is often bloated, which creates fiscal and political pressure to limit subsequent acquisitions.[75] Constraints on defense spending and pressure to end preferential procurement have resulted in increased importation and licensed production of advanced weapons systems. By the mid-2000s, the JDA and Japan's political leaders seemingly had abandoned generations of commitment to "indigenous production" (*kokusanka*). Bureaucrats and business leaders who had cooperated to maximize technological autonomy, its diffusion, and the nurturance of domestic firms—the "three note chord" of Japanese techno-nationalism—seemed to have lost their common voice.[76] Their reports continued to strike the right tone, as in the 2004 National Defense Program Guidelines, which declared that reforms of the weapons acquisition process should proceed with the aim of "establishing a defense production and technology base, especially in core technology areas indispensable for our national security."[77] But in 2004, when the JDA allowed U.S. manufacturers to dominate the first procurements of missile defense equipment, its domestic procurement ratio fell below 90 percent for the first time in nearly a decade.[78] The defense industry, reported "feeling a sense of crisis (*kikikan*)" by one JDA official, acknowledged its concern for the "weakening of the defense production and technology base" and wondered aloud about a "gathering anxiety" among contractors.[79] Whether or not business and government had lost their common voice, the Japanese defense industry has lost a significant part of its already small (148 billion yen) defense technology base.[80] Investment in defense production equipment was 1.5 percent lower in 2000 than in 1995, and the number of engineers in the defense sector had declined by 15 percent.[81] Keidanren has argued that Japan needs a healthy defense industrial base to command better technology from its foreign licensors, adding that once that base is lost, it will require a considerable national effort to reconstitute it.[82]

Given the benefits of dual-use technology, however, this problem seems less critical than the threat of being excluded entirely from the rapidly globalizing defense industry. This threat has two causes, both self-inflicted. The first is related to the reluctance of the domestic defense industry to consolidate. With the exception of two mergers in the space business—the Nissan and IHI missile businesses (2000) and the Toshiba and NEC satellite groups (2001)—and two in shipbuilding—NKK and Hitachi (2002) and IHI and Sumitomo (2002)—the industry is largely unchanged. In the past fifteen years, only five new firms have appeared on the list of JDA contractors. Meanwhile, firms are heading for the exits, and the number of defense contractors has sharply declined. Keidanren's Defense Production Committee had eighty-four members in 1997 and only sixty-six in 2002.[83] The second cause is the increase in multinational programs in which Japan has been unable to participate. While the Japanese defense industry was promoting autonomy, the rest of the world's arms manufacturers were racing ahead with unprecedented consolidations and cross-border collaborations. Japanese firms watched helplessly as high-ticket military systems such as the Joint Strike Fighter were developed with British and other national firms, and as U.S. firms transformed themselves through mergers and acquisitions into profitable high-tech companies.[84] International cooperation became the norm, but Japan was left on the margins with small-lot manufacturing.

North Korea

For historical and ideological reasons, relations between Japan and North Korea are among the most contentious and mutually distrustful of any in the world today.[85] From Pyongyang's perspective, Japan's military alliance with the United States and its history of harsh colonial rule are impediments to normal relations. From Tokyo's perspective, North Korea's brazen abduction of Japanese nationals during the late 1970s and early 1980s, its repressive authoritarianism, and its flagrant militarism make the DPRK a particularly repellent neighbor. In December 2001, the Japanese Coast Guard sank a North Korean spy ship, in the first incident of Japanese hostile fire since the Second World War. The two countries do not have formal diplomatic relations.

The DPRK is poorer than Tottori, Japan's poorest rural prefecture (which has a thirty-seventh of its population), but it is often invoked as Japan's greatest security threat. In the Ministry of Foreign Affairs' Diplomatic Blue Book for 2003, North Korea was listed ahead of terrorism and weapons of mass destruction as the country's greatest diplomatic concern.[86] Meanwhile, the 2003 Defense White Paper issued by the JDA was less diplomatic:

North Korea has sought as a basic national policy to transform itself into a "strong and rising great power" and adopted a "military-first policy" to realize this aim....Despite the serious economic difficulties it faces, North Korea continues to give the military preferential allocation of resources, and is dedicating considerable effort into maintaining and improving its military capabilities and readiness. North Korea possesses weapons of mass destruction, ballistic missiles, and large-scale special operations forces, and the country appears to be maintaining and strengthening its asymmetrical military capabilities. North Korea's suspected development of nuclear weapons impinges on the security of Japan and is also a matter of concern for the entire international community.[87]

Senior Japanese leaders have also invoked the DPRK threat at every turn, often as a surrogate for China. Former JDA director general Ishiba opens his memoirs with an explanation that the DPRK missile "threat can become a reality in an instant."[88] Ishiba hardly mentions China at all, relying instead on horrifying accounts of North Korean capabilities and intentions to make his case for enhancing Japan's defenses.[89]

The DPRK has made it very easy for threat inflators. Rumors of abductions of Japanese citizens by DPRK agents (*rachi mondai*) began to surface in the early 1980s when a North Korean agent was arrested using the name and papers of a missing Japanese citizen.[90] Kim Jong-Il denied the abductions to LDP heavyweight Kanemaru Shin during his visit to Pyongyang in 1990, but admitted that North Korea had abducted thirteen Japanese citizens when Prime Minister Koizumi visited in September 2002. The return of the five surviving abductees only increased Japanese perceptions of threat, in part because their families were held hostage back in North Korea. By the 1990s it had also become clear that Japanese technology had found its way into DPRK military assets.[91] During two rounds of "nuclear diplomacy"— 1993–94 and 2003–06–Pyongyang took such provocative actions as ballistic missile tests and fighter sorties across the maritime border with the Republic of Korea, firing antiship missiles into the Sea of Japan, and harassment of U.S. reconnaissance aircraft.[92] In the second round, after U.S. intelligence revealed that Pyongyang had begun a secret program to generate highly enriched uranium that violated the 1994 Agreed Framework, Pyongyang upped the ante by announcing that it would withdraw from the International Atomic Energy Agency (IAEA). Reversing its former insistence that it had no nuclear weapons ambitions Pyongyang reactivated its Yongbyon nuclear reactor. Now it openly acknowledged a program to stockpile enriched uranium and plutonium, continued testing ballistic missiles, and, in a move that alarmed leaders throughout the world, tested a low-yield nuclear weapon in October 2006.

DPRK saber rattling also rattled public opinion in Japan, tilting it toward support for the LDP and its plans to modernize the Japanese military. In fact, North Korea has been more useful than China in stimulating a pervasive

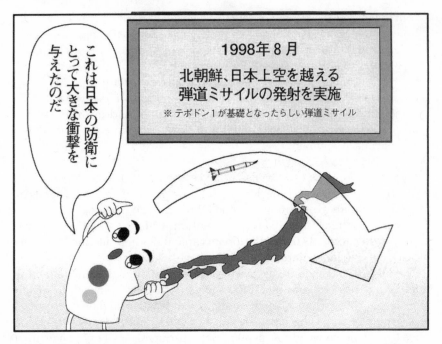

Figure 9. The DPRK threat is invoked in JDA public relations materials as well as in the Diet. Reprinted with permission of the Bōei Kōsaikai Foundation and the artist, Deko-ku-ru.

sense of threat. Unlike China, where the business community acts as a brake on a Japanese hard line, businesses are largely indifferent to relations with North Korea. As a result, the LDP has been free to define the DPRK issue in purely political terms. In May 2003, a group of younger LDP Diet members formed a caucus to revise the Foreign Exchange and Foreign Trade Control Law to make it possible to stop remittances (*sōkin*) to North Korea, estimated at upward of sixty billion yen per year.[93] But the LDP did not need to be goaded into action. The party played the North Korea card to great effect in the November 2003 election campaign. By promising sanctions, the LDP isolated the Socialists and made the DPJ look passive on an issue of clear concern to the electorate. Indeed, the establishment of a Victims' Family Fund Committee (Rachi Higaisha Kazoku Gienkin Iinkai) in October and the appointment of its chairman, Abe Shinzō, as deputy chief cabinet secretary underscored the political salience of the abduction issue. Abe called for a halt to all remittances until the issue is resolved. The LDP was rewarded in the November 2003 elections. Stimulated by support groups for the families of Japanese abductees, some two-thirds of those elected to the lower house in November 2003 supported tougher measures against the DPRK.[94] For the first time since 1945, the Japanese public openly expressed hostility toward another country.

With the broad support of the Japanese electorate, the LDP government was free to fashion its preferred response to North Korea. But Pyongyang's military threat was not all that troubled security planners in Tokyo. They were also concerned that instability in North Korea or a military miscalculation by Pyongyang would invite great power intervention.[95] In a post-9/11 world in which the U.S. government based national security on preventive war, Japan has an interest in restraining the United States. Japan was, as ever, faced with knotty threats that could be untangled only by sorting through its alliance options—and the threats that they posed.

THE U.S. THREAT

The irony of the Japan-U.S. alliance is that the United States poses nearly as great a threat to Japan as any hostile neighbor. U.S. economic might is of overwhelming concern to a Japan that depends on access to its market and technologies. America's military and diplomatic engagements across the globe force Japan to make difficult choices, choices that are far from risk free. If Japan chooses to resist U.S. overtures to join its "coalitions of the willing" in military operations abroad or to deny the United States the use of its bases, it risks abandonment. Without U.S. protection, Japan would have to increase its military spending considerably and would likely become a nuclear power itself. The result would be dangerous for Japan and destabilizing for the entire region. On the other hand, by joining the United States and declaring its security role to be global, Japan risks becoming entangled in wars not of its own choosing. Balancing the risks of abandonment and entanglement is, of course, the central dynamic of any alliance, and it has been central to Japan's calculus for six decades. After the end of the cold war, however, and especially after September 2001, when one alliance manager wrote that the alliance had been "adrift for over a decade," the full costs to Japan of hedging became obvious.[96] One U.S. analyst expresses the concerns of alliance managers on both sides: "The conditions that supported this mutually-suitable arrangement are changing faster than either side is prepared to admit and are chipping away at the foundations of the alliance."[97] Whether through abandonment (the fear of the conservatives who have ruled Japan since the end of the Pacific War) or through entanglement (the fear of the autonomists and pacifists), alliance failure is one of Japan's central security threats.[98]

The prospect of alliance failure is of course reduced by shared interests, which, along with shared values, are the basis for any alliance relationship.

The United States and Japan share a great many vital interests, of which the most significant are:

1. Preserve stability among great and aspiring powers.
2. Preserve the safety of the sea-lanes of communication throughout East and Southeast Asia.
3. Maintain leadership roles in regional and global institutions.
4. Keep the Korean Peninsula peaceful.
5. Maintain peace in the Taiwan Strait.
6. Defend against terrorism.
7. Avoid the proliferation of weapons of mass destruction to unfriendly states and nonstate actors.
8. Ensure the independence of Indochina and Southeast Asia.[99]

Although most Japanese security interests coincide with U.S. ones, shared interests do not translate directly into shared policy. One ASDF officer has observed a "widening gap in threat perception between the United States and Japan."[100] Others worry about estrangement (*kairi*) and speak of different U.S. and Japanese "fields of vision" in dealing with regional problems.[101] There are many areas of divergence, though few threaten to destroy the alliance single-handedly. The Japanese treat repressive regimes such as that in Myanmar with carrots, the United States with sticks. Tokyo also has different perceptions of the threat from North Korea, which for Japan involves direct attack but for the United States is a matter of proliferation.

Perhaps the most obvious area of divergence, though, concerns East Asian economic integration. Japanese trade with Asia as a percentage of its total trade is nearly twice that of the United States, and it is growing. Even allowing that some of this trade is U.S.-bound, the growth of Sino-Japanese interdependence elevates regional integration—not a U.S. priority—on Japan's agenda. Indeed, the United States has repeatedly expressed its displeasure at being sidelined while an East Asian economic community is being built.[102] But the building proceeds. Saadia Pekkanen writes about Japan's "FTA frenzy," which reflects "nothing more and nothing less than an attempt to ensure economic security," an effort that "remains paramount."[103] As we have seen, this effort has engaged Japan in direct competition with the PRC for leadership of the region. But it is also directed at the economic power of the United States and Western Europe, each of which has its own exclusive regional trade bloc.[104]

Similarly, terrorist links to the Middle East have more immediacy for the United States than for Japan. These are precisely the sorts of differences, born in part from different geopolitics and different resource endowments, that contribute to the growing gap in threat perceptions even when interests are shared. The original energy-based divergence in U.S. and Japanese interests was in 1973, when the Japanese government responded to demands from the Organization of Arab Petroleum Exporting Countries (OAPEC) by immediately supporting the creation of a Palestinian state in order to avoid the embargo. A second, well-remembered divergence occurred in 1979–80, when Japan continued its purchases of Iranian oil even after U.S. hostages were taken in Tehran.[105]

The case of Iran in the 2000s is potentially the most consequential, because Japan's commitment to nonproliferation and its alliance with the United States collide head-on with threats to its energy security. Despite gains after the oil shocks of the 1970s, Japan remained more dependent than any other G-8 country on imported oil and was highly dependent on the Middle East in particular. By 2005, Japan's reliance on Middle Eastern oil reached 90.2 percent.[106] Iran alone accounted for 15 percent of Japan's petroleum imports. Japan's relations with Iran—identified by President George W. Bush in 2002 as a member of an "axis of evil"—have been very friendly. In 2001 Japanese firms won preferential negotiating rights for the Azadegan field, believed to contain twenty-six billion barrels of crude reserves.[107] The lead Japanese investor in the project, Inpex, is an exploration and development firm with shareholders that include the Japanese government and some of Japan's most powerful firms, including the Mitsubishi Corporation, Mitsui Oil Exploration, Marubeni, Sumitomo, and JFE Steel. Its presidents have been former METI officials. The Azadegan project required $2 billion in funding, of which the Japanese were to provide $1.5 billion. The Japan Bank for International Cooperation also financed the Iranian side by covering 85 percent of a $1.2 billion syndicated loan.[108]

This deal went ahead despite considerable resistance from Washington, which publicly and privately stated its opposition, including personal appeals from National Security Advisor Condoleezza Rice and Deputy Secretary of State Richard Armitage to Ambassador Katō Ryūzō.[109] When the deal went ahead, a State Department spokesperson told reporters: "Our policy has been, with respect to Iran, to oppose petroleum investment there.... We remain deeply concerned about deals such as this, and disappointed that these things might go forward."[110] U.S. concern intensified after it became clear that Iran was engaged in a secret nuclear enrichment program. In August 2004, Armitage reportedly suggested to MOFA official Takeuchi Yukio that Japan consider switching upstream oil investments from Iran to Iraq and Libya.[111] Undersecretary of State John Bolton promised further pressure on Japan.[112]

But emphasizing its resource scarcity and maintaining that nuclear and energy issues should be negotiated separately, Japan continued to resist U.S. pressure, even after a September 2004 IAEA resolution called on Iran to comply with IAEA regulations.[113] Japanese diplomats insisted energy security was, after all, a matter of vital national interest, something that the

United States should understand.[114] They also emphasized the possibility that China would pick up the pieces of any shattered deal—a consequence that should be of even greater concern to Washington. Other Japanese firms signed deals with Tehran in the face of U.S. sanctions, including a twenty-five billion yen commitment by Itochu to build a new petrochemical complex.[115] Iran even tried to bring Japan onside as an ally during negotiations with the IAEA over access for inspectors to its nuclear program. During his November 2003 visit to Japan, for example, Iranian foreign minister Kamal Kharazi asked Prime Minister Koizumi for his "cooperation at the November [IAEA] meeting, so that it will not be referred to the UN Security Council."[116] Koizumi's response is not on the public record, but he is quoted as accepting that Japan has a role to play in mediating between Iran and the United States: "Japan and America have a very close relationship, so that is why Japan's friendship with Iran is very important."[117]

Japan hedged its economic risk in Iran far more vigorously than it hedged its military risks elsewhere. By mid-2005, Japan began to press Iran to reconsider uranium enrichment.[118] In January 2006, Chief Cabinet Secretary Abe announced that Japan would follow Europe and the United States and support referral of the Iranian nuclear issue to the UN Security Council. And in March, after last-ditch Russian efforts to intervene had collapsed, Koizumi met with Iranian foreign minister Manouchehr Mottaki and called on Iran to suspend uranium enrichment. Japan was pursuing a complex diplomatic strategy, one that diverged from U.S. preferences without abandoning Washington—and without giving up its claim on the Azadegan field. It rejected U.S. requests to abandon that investment but continued to side with Washington at the sharp end of negotiations at the IAEA. By early 2006, long after the rest of the G-8 had given up on avoiding confrontation with Tehran, Japan reluctantly and very tentatively joined the chorus, and began to instruct its firms to find alternative sources of crude oil.[119] Japanese banks agreed to conform to U.S. policy and "voluntarily" refrain from transactions with Iran's largest bank.[120]

This was not the last word. Tokyo carefully avoided challenging the alliance, but it continued to insist that Iran's "alleged" nuclear weapons program and the development of Azadegan were separate issues. Inpex and METI announced plans to go forward with the Azadegan development in late 2005 and again in March 2006.[121] In August, Tehran issued an ultimatum: begin development of Azadegan by mid-September or the deal would go to Russian or Chinese firms.[122] But Tehran relaxed the deadline, and Tokyo still clung to the project, even after the UN Security Council announced plans to apply economic sanctions to Iran if it did not suspend its nuclear program.[123] In late September, the Japanese government announced it would not extend official loans or guarantee debt repayment if the Security Council were to apply sanctions. It still did not say, however, whether it would

[154]

force Japanese firms to cancel the deal. Talks continued.[124] It was, as one industry analyst explained, "an independent project with the rising sun flag on it that Japan could claim in the event of a crisis."[125] METI vice minister Sugiyama Hideji denied that the United States had been pressuring Japan to abandon the project and insisted that Japan had to balance the world's mounting concerns against Japan's energy needs: "We hope that Iran will listen to the international community's concerns, but at the same time it is important to have a stable supply of crude oil from Iran."[126] METI minister Nikai Toshihiro walked a narrow line: "We cannot afford to neglect the need to cooperate with the international community. It is not appropriate for Japan to stand alone. Still, Iran's role in Japan's energy policy is great.... This is a delicate international issue, and I cannot put my cards on the table."[127]

His successor, Amari Akira, was even more blunt. Just days after assuming office as Prime Minister Abe's METI minister, he admitted: "The Japanese government has no bright [new] ideas [to resolve Azadegan]."[128] Japanese security analysts remained insistent that collaboration with the Iranians ought to be pursued as a matter of national interest.[129] Indeed, when asked why Japan did not respond to Iranian president Ahmadinejad's claim that the Holocaust never happened and that Israel should be "wiped off the face of the earth," Vice Minister of Foreign Affairs Shiozaki Yasuhisa dodged the issue by pointing out that "those comments were not directed at Japan."[130] A leading energy analyst argued in Japan's most prestigious foreign policy journal that "Japan must focus on damage control and encourage the United States to change its position on Iran's right to enrich uranium."[131]

It was not until August 2006, and only after the United Nations Security Council issued a direct warning to Tehran to cease all uranium enrichment activities or face sanctions, that Foreign Minister Asō declared unambiguously that for Japan "the nuclear issue has priority" even if the oil project is "taken hostage."[132] In October 2006, after a difficult round of negotiations, the Japanese Ministry of Foreign Affairs announced that nonproliferation concerns were more important than energy security concerns, and Iran announced that the Impex share in Azadegan would be cut from 75 percent to a nominal 10 percent. Still, Japanese interests stayed in the game, keeping the door open for improved relations with Iran.[133] And, for their part, Iranian officials continued to express hope for cooperation. In early 2007, Hojjatollah Ghaminifard, Director of International Affairs for the Iranian National Oil Company, declared that Japanese investors are "always welcome [to] return to Iran" and that bilateral ties would improve."[134] Tokyo may have fallen into line with the rest of the international community, but there remained reason to believe that oil and the Middle East could continue to strain the alliance.

In other geographic and functional areas, too, U.S. and Japanese interests may diverge.[135] If Iran is the most pressing in the near term, how to manage (or respond to) the rise of China is surely the most consequential in the longer term. Of course, both the United States and Japan have a shared interest in the smooth integration of a stable and wealthy China. Realizing that interest has always involved different preferences, however. Whether China gets wealthy with—or at the expense of—U.S. and Japanese firms is a first-order concern. A second-order concern is whether Japanese and U.S. firms will each get their respective share of China's growing pie. They are, after all, in direct competition there.[136] As Saadia Pekkanen has argued:

> It is difficult perhaps for Americans to appreciate just how much—in perception and increasingly in fact—the United States has slipped and China [has] loomed on the Japan trade policy horizon....In the trade policy corridors of Kasumigaseki, China is *the* stuff of the future....While the U.S. is also likely to remain a hotbed of technological innovation...it is already being displaced by China as Japan's most important trade partner.[137]

On the strategic side, until 2005, when Prime Minister Koizumi expressed his hopes for Chinese democratization, Japan avoided all mention of the Communist government in Beijing. In fact, insisting it would be a mistake to isolate China, a pragmatic Japan was quick to resume development assistance after the Tiananmen crackdown in June 1989, and its business leaders returned en masse to China in October. It was also unclear for many years whether the United States and Japan were on the same page regarding the future of Taiwan. Japan's unwillingness to openly support Taiwan during the 1995–96 crisis "exposed glimmers of divergence" from U.S. policy.[138]

In sum, Japan and the United States approach China with very different historical experiences, different geostrategic postures, and different expectations. Some strategists, such as former deputy secretary of state Richard Armitage, believe that China could use these differences to drive a wedge between Japan and the United States.[139] Others imagine a Japanese nightmare in which the United States aligns with a rich, democratic, and powerful China, at the expense of an abandoned Japan, left to cope with its estrangement from both.[140] Either way, divergence—of which the "potential" is "real," according to one U.S. military analyst—can mean abandonment by the United States, one of the greatest threats to Japan.[141]

Tokyo's strategists know that the United States could abandon or entangle Japan as it creates its modus vivendi with a rising China. They know that the relaxation of tension in the Taiwan Strait could also reduce the U.S. incentive to support Japanese territorial and resource claims. But China is not the only threat filtered through the U.S.-Japan alliance. The same is true of the threat to Japan from Pyongyang. As the United States reduces its footprint on the peninsula, Japan would become the sole East Asian home for U.S. forces, in a process transformed into the tripwire that could entangle Japan in an unsought—and previously avoidable—conflict. And Iran, for its part, might be the most immediate crucible for the alliance. Should Japan opt to secure oil supplies and ignore U.S. pleas for solidarity on nonproliferation, it will risk losing U.S. support in its broader quest for security. After all, Japan's economic well-being and technology base are also linked very directly to the alliance. During the cold war, the United States had every incentive to provide Japan its market and know-how in order to maintain it as a prosperous and stable player in the region. It largely ignored Japanese mercantilism and technonationalism. Today, a China open to foreign direct investment—more open than Japan—is poised to supplant Japan economically and technologically, raising yet again the specter of abandonment in Kasumigaseki.

Threats are perceptions, and perceptions vary. Japan's post–cold war discourse on political, military, and economic threats has been wide ranging and very open. China, the DPRK, and abandonment by the United States, as well as the relative decline of its economic power, are all threatening to Tokyo. The first two are painted as existential threats that have been used to justify muscular responses. Some have used the latter two in the same way. The competitiveness of Japanese industry, particularly the defense industry, is a central concern to those who believe that prosperity undergirds national security. Likewise, many believe that the U.S.-Japan alliance plays a critical role in securing Japan. The alliance has been resilient and has served both nations' interests for more than six decades. This, despite a long list of substantive policy differences relating to (a) the Soviet threat (many in Japan thought it was exaggerated by the Americans)[142]; (b) economic policies (decades of resistance to U.S. trade demands and, today, promotion of a regional economic bloc); (c) the efficacy of international treaties (Japan supported the Comprehensive Nuclear Test Ban Treaty, the Kyoto Protocol on Climate Change, the International Landmine Ban Treaty, the Protocol to the Biological Weapons Convention, and the International Criminal Court, all of which the United States opposed); and (d) how best to deal with hostile regimes in North Korea, Myanmar, and the Middle East. Still, the shifting balance of relative power in East Asia could strain the alliance, especially if one or the other partner opts for a smooth adjustment to China's rise or to North Korean nuclearization, while the other resists it. By 2006, the United States had begun warning Japan that its situation in Northeast Asia was deteriorating and urged it to avoid becoming isolated.[143] Japan has responded to these political, military, and economic threats in ways that actually increase the threat of entanglement in the near term yet increase the possibilities for independence in the longer term.

[7]

Meeting (and Making) Threats

Japan clearly lives in a dangerous—or, at least, unstable—neighborhood where military and economic threats abound. The previous chapter documented perceived threats from North Korea, from China, from abandonment by its U.S. ally, and from Japan's own inability to maintain a competitive national economy. Debate about these threats and how to respond to them has never been more lively or more open than it is today.

Are Japan's responses to these threats commensurate with the dangers? After all, what Japan has done may be driven not by threats but by domestic politics or by pressure from its U.S. ally. Or, more likely, it may come from a combination of these, from politicians who use (and may abuse and inflate) threats and pressures to realize their own preferences. And how can we measure success and failure? Before we can come to any reliable conclusions, we first examine Japan's repositioning and its choices—choices that in the unsteady environment of Northeast Asia may seem threatening to Tokyo's neighbors.

Japan's response has proceeded on several fronts simultaneously. Concern about the loss of technoeconomic vitality has led to loosened constraints on participation in international defense programs and to a focus on high-end industrial capabilities. The China threat has been soft-pedalled somewhat to protect Japan's considerable stake in the Chinese economy, but North Korea has been a useful surrogate, allowing military planners to reconfigure Japan's defense posture in a way that deals with both neighbors. Throughout this process the alliance with the United States has been used to sell changes that the ascendant antimainstream leadership long had been seeking. The result has been a new Japanese military, enabled by the United States, that never has been as close as it is now to entanglement in U.S. adventures.

ECONOMIC SECURITY REVISITED

Response to the Threat of Hollowing

During the 1990s, as we have seen, Japanese analysts perceived deindustrialization as a grave economic threat linked to competition from China. Discussion of this threat did not begin to recede until 2004, when Japan began a sustained recovery of its own. At that point, the media shifted sharply from hand-wringing about "hollowing" to celebration of a new era of industrial competitiveness. After a decade in which four-fifths of new capital investment had been made abroad, Japanese firms reversed themselves; now four-fifths of new investment was made at home.[1] This shift required a key transformation—policymakers, researchers, and businessmen had to realize that by moving final assembly to China and other Asian countries, they would free national resources to concentrate on high-value-added, high-tech goods in Japan. Japan could become Asia's exporter of technology and complex machinery, and the rest of Asia would specialize in low-value-added goods and final assembly.[2] Japan would be more secure.

The threat of "hollowing" was declared over, and the "China economic threat theory" was replaced by a more optimistic "China pull theory" (*chūgoku tokujuron*).[3] On this account, the structure of the regional economy had changed from a zero-sum competition between an emerging China and an aging Japan to one in which the rising tide of intraregional trade would lift all boats. By the mid-2000s this transformation was well under way. Intraregional trade, little more than 10 percent of total Japanese trade in 1990, had become nearly one quarter by 2003, roughly on a par with intra-NAFTA volumes.[4] Japan was at the apex of a new industrial "triangle" in which Asia was a single integrated workshop. Vertical supply chains, fragmented by national specialization, seemed to characterize each industry. At the top end, in each case, Japanese firms provided production equipment to Korean and Taiwanese parts manufacturers, and final assembly was done in China and in ASEAN countries. Surveys confirmed this shift. High-value-added activities were now staying at home, and "standard manufacturing" was moving offshore.[5] In short, Japanese firms would benefit from China's growth. They had seized the commanding heights of an integrated Asian production system geared to export to European and U.S. markets, and they positioned themselves for the time when regional consumption would soar as well. But was this the consequence of a visible or an invisible hand at work? Was it a simple matter of macroeconomic adjustment, or was it a strategic move to protect Japanese firms facing an existential threat?

Certainly, the macroeconomic environment of the 1990s conspired against Japanese firms and caught them by surprise. Hollowing was an unwelcome and unprecedented consequence. But the measures put in place to counter this threat, while abetted by improved macroeconomic conditions, were thoroughly strategic. Never converted to the "Washington consensus," Japan's strategists responded to technoeconomic threats by reinventing their three-note chord of autonomy, nurturance, and diffusion, strategic values that long had served Japan well. The strategy that Japanese firms and government seized on was premised on one key point—that Japan's comparative advantage could actually *increase* due to the vertical fragmentation of global production.[6] Consciously transforming a threat into an opportunity, they repositioned Japanese industry by strategically enhancing this fragmentation. Working together in the time-honored fashion of industrial policy's heyday, METI and Japanese firms increased domestic investment and nurtured local capabilities. One after another, firms announced plans to build new capacity at home. There was a more than 40 percent increase in domestic capital investment in 2004 over 2003, virtually all of it directed at high-end sectors such as liquid crystal displays, digital cameras, factory automation, and new steelmaking.[7]

In an explicit response to hollowing, METI began publishing a new manufacturing White Paper (*monozukuri hakusho*) in 2000.[8] In July 2002, the Prime Minister's Office issued a report advocating the use of intellectual property as a tool in the international marketplace.[9] In January 2003, Keidanren unveiled its "Made by Japan" concept, urging an aggressive national policy to respond to deindustrialization and stimulate strategic thinking about technology and security.[10] It dismissed the threat of hollowing so long as Japanese firms could maintain control of high technology. Final assembly abroad was no threat to domestic prosperity, so long as it used Japanese standards, with Japanese designed parts, on Japanese production equipment, built in Japan. Japanese firms should be reconceived as consolidated companies with headquarters in Japan, where technological innovation could be nurtured, and profits from foreign activities—including final assembly—should be earmarked for corporate R & D. In 2003, METI began publishing handbooks to teach firms how to avoid the leakage of technology that might create foreign competitors.[11] In May 2004, METI announced it would "nurture" seven areas in which Japan had state-of-art technologies—including fuel cells, intelligent appliances, and industrial robots—"in anticipation that China will become more competitive."[12] To do so, it resorted to established mechanisms, such as assistance to consortia that would jointly develop technologies for commercialization "so that Japan's technologies will become global standards." It even took the lead in organizing a $3 billion "rising sun chip factory" to recapture Japan's position in semiconductors.[13]

Japanese CEOs openly invoked a U.S. military term to characterize their new approach to technology transfer. They would "black box" technology (*burakku bokkusuka*) to protect it from competitors. President Nakamura Kunio of Matsushita Electrical Company explained that "if we black box our technology and production process from other firms, we will not be defeated by competitors. And it is strategically important that we continuously generate black box technologies that remain within our firm (*jisha nai ni todomete oku koto ga senryakujō jūyō desu*)."[14] President Machida Katsuhiko of Sharp, which had been vilified in the 1990s for transferring turnkey technologies, agreed. Until a technology is fully mature, he now argued, it must be kept at home, adding that "liquid crystal television was born and nurtured in Japan. And because all the developers and the parts and materials manufacturers who supported it are Japanese, we pay special attention to domestic production (*kokunai seisan ni kodawatte imasu*)."[15] By "positioning domestic plants as strategic bases to supply high-technology products worldwide," Japanese firms would increase domestic production and reduce the threats from foreign competition.[16] Canon president Mitarai Fujio, who became chairman of Keidanren in 2006, insisted on the importance of manufacturing "core products" (*seihin no shinzōbu*) domestically to protect national employment.[17] Necessity had become a virtue.

Japanese firms did have locality (indeed, nationality) after all, even in a globalizing economy. As one Japanese reporter put it at the time:

> The manufacture of...products at the Japanese firms' overseas plants, done in search of lower labor costs, has resulted in foreign rivals acquiring their production technologies and know-how. This means that an over-reliance on moving production offshore—a policy that has resulted from intense competition in the domestic market—has driven Japanese manufacturers into a corner.[18]

Morimoto overstates the case, but his "corner" is a familiar place—a *domestic* place, where technology can be shared and nurtured. In this regard, perhaps the most important innovation is the so-called mother factory.[19] Aware that R & D occurs on the shop floor as well as in the laboratory, and threatened by the prospect that innovation in foreign factories will lead to loss of the technological high ground and the control of production, an increasing number of Japanese managers keep at least one production line, with fully integrated R & D functions and "key components," at home. This way, innovation occurs in a site over which they have full control.[20] Japanese technonationalism was alive and well, successfully redeployed for a new age to meet a new security threat.

Response by a Threatened Defense Industry

Defense contractors also responded to globalization and the prospect of increased dependence by resorting to familiar appeals, the central pillar of which was the domestic design and production of weapons systems (*koku-sanka*).[21] They positioned themselves as national champions who would defend autonomy and use it to acquire technology. Their well-rehearsed view had a fallback position: even "international cooperation"—their artful term for licensing foreign know-how—could enhance indigenous technology and strengthen the ability to demand a higher value-added role in subsequent projects. But however familiar these ideas about technology, security, and the national economy may have been, by the 2000s the defense industry was seen by many as "Japan's last protected sector" and that it was threatened with extinction if it did not adjust to the new global economic order.[22]

The greatest threat has been that fiscally constrained procurement officers would find innovative and nimble foreign suppliers irresistible. In fact, by the late 1990s, after a series of domestic procurement scandals, the wisdom of using imports was under close scrutiny.[23] In September 2003 the Japanese government began a formal reassessment of its *kokusan* program. The JDA agreed to invoke the autonomy principle under four conditions: (1) if the system is strategic, (2) if it is secret, (3) if it is special, and (3) if it is necessary to preserve the domestic production base.[24] This cut a broad swath, yet it was clear that the consensus on autonomy as a strategic imperative was not what it once was. For example, the Prime Minister's Council on Security and Defense Capabilities (the 2004 Araki Commission, which issued the pilot report for the new National Defense Program Guidelines) even spoke of the need to "outsource" some arms production and insisted that "the government should reconsider its policy of maintaining indigenous weapons production."[25]

The defense industry responded with characteristic vigor and techno-nationalist bombast. In July 2004, before the new guidelines were released, Keidanren's Defense Production Committee outlined four ways to strengthen Japan's defense industrial base. Among them was reconsideration of the ban on arms exports and of the proscription of the military use of space. It also called for an improved procurement system and for measures to enable more robust cooperation with foreign firms.[26] When the guidelines appeared in December, they explicitly stipulated that the government would "work to establish a defense production and technology base, especially in core technological areas indispensable for our national security (*makoto ni hitsuyō na bōei seisan gijutsu kiban*)."

The Japanese defense industry seized on this phrase and tried to inflate it into a national strategy. They defended the remaining few "national projects" still on the table, such as an unmanned aircraft, the P-3C follow-on patrol aircraft and its engine, and the C-30 transport follow-on—projects that would generate close to 500 billion yen in business and excluded foreign participation. They also emphasized the desirability of nurturance and technology diffusion. A June 2005 JDA study, organized by the Defense

Production Committee of Keidanren, is redolent with technonationalist appeals:

> Japan, as a technology-based nation deploying its technology and produc-
> tive power, will develop, produce, and maintain exceptional equipment by
> retaining a domestic production base and thereby contribute to our nation's
> national security.[27]

Another study, also from Keidanren, calls for heightened "nurturing of advanced technology" and even greater "flexibility" in the application of science and technology across the civil-military divide.[28]

Still, the Japanese defense industry formally acknowledged a "new age"
in defense procurement, and—under pressure from the JDA—it publicly
accepted U.S.-style procurement criteria. Such ideals as "better, faster,
cheaper" were entirely new to the Japanese discourse. Mergers in naval
shipbuilding and space, and the streamlining of the supply chain, also began to change the profile of the defense industry.[29] The new guidelines may
have genuflected in the direction of *kokusanka*, but they also explicitly stated
that Japan would build a "state of the art defense force...with the limited
resources that are available."[30] Despite considerable pressure from the
defense industry and from the U.S. government, the Japanese government
refuses to consider raising the defense budget ceiling until Japan regains its
fiscal health.[31] In the meantime, the industry's response has been to develop
dual-use technology outside the 1 percent limit. The executive director of
the Keidanren Defense Production Committee pointed out that "safety and
security" (*anshin to anzen*) would be central targets of Japan's new Basic Plan
for Science and Technology, and so would stimulate development of surveillance and other dual-use technologies.[32]

Firms also had to respond to dramatic structural changes in the global
defense industry. Japanese defense contractors watched U.S. counterparts
transform themselves through mergers and acquisitions, and stood on the
sidelines as U.S. and European firms shared huge DoD contracts, such as
the $245 billion F-35 Joint Strike Fighter. International cooperation had be-
come the norm, but Japan had tied its own hands, and so was left out. Its
first substantive response to this new order was a relaxation of the arms
export ban. The Japanese defense industrial community, which had lobbied
for this change for many years, welcomed the missile defense package approved in 2004 as a "major step forward." After all, 12 percent of the fiscal
year 2004 equipment budget was associated with missile defense. But they
were in for a surprise. The change allowed for Japanese-U.S. collaboration
in missile defense, but the only orders issued by the JDA were to U.S. firms
in the form of foreign military sales. One Mitsubishi Heavy Industries executive, worried that Japanese firms would be cut out of the systems design

[163]

phase, lamented: "We had intended to proceed with licensed production. If we buy everything from the United States, our production and technology will decline to zero."[33] The defense industry mobilized, and negotiations for licensed production began soon thereafter. By March 2005 the DoD agreed to license PAC-3 missile technology to Mitsubishi Heavy Industries "to enable quick repair"—another artful locution.

The still-threatened defense industry now had full, unqualified participation in the global market directly in its sights. The export ban must be lifted if Japan is to be secure:

> In the course of making progress in raising the level of our defense equipment and technology, by participating in international joint development projects we will be able to acquire the most advanced production equipment. This will strengthen the industrial base of Japan, which is a technologically based nation, and will connect to the nation's economic development.[34]

The fabled case of the F-2 is often invoked in this regard. Procurement of this fighter, formerly known as the FS-X and codeveloped with Lockheed Martin after a bruising bilateral dispute in the 1980s, was discontinued due to technical problems. But Mitsubishi Heavy Industries learned enough about how to design and manufacture co-cured composite wings that it won the contract to do so for the Boeing 787 Dreamliner.[35] Having survived attacks on *kokusanka*, the industry now found itself poised to enter the promised land of international sales. When the government exempted the missile defense project from the ban on arms exports, it stipulated that the same exemption could be extended to other projects. Support had been gathering for some time. In December 2004, as it was relaxing the arms export ban for missile defense, the government also reportedly began to consider participation in the U.S.-led Joint Strike Fighter program (which already included eleven nations).[36] Japanese firms already supply materials for the U.S. Air Force's F-22 jet engines, have received official development assistance funding to supply "demilitarized" patrol craft to the Indonesian and Philippine coast guards, and are poised to sell similar vessels to the Malaysian coast guard. Airplane makers and JDA officials openly contemplate the export of the "civilian" versions of the domestically designed and manufactured next generation patrol (PX) and transport (CX) aircraft.[37] More would follow in the name of securing Japan, but the Japanese defense industry still has a long way to go before it can realize its goal of becoming a global player.

Response to the Threatened Loss of Regional Leadership

The economic nationalism that characterized Japan's response to globalization in both commercial and military sectors was apparent in its larger regional strategy as well. Here, though, Tokyo had less autonomy to respond to threats and precious little cross-border ideological appeal, and so it had far less success. East Asia came to have substantive meaning as an economic region only after the 1985 Plaza Accord stimulated a rapid diversification of Japanese trade and investment. For a while, Japan was alone and had an unprecedented opportunity to shape the region. No longer simply a purchaser of raw materials, the Japanese economy was responsible for the bulk of investment and growth. The expansion of ASEAN trade and the increased sophistication of its economies resulted in large measure from Japanese tutelage and support.[38] But despite a common commitment to market-based economic development, there was no shared political base, and integration slowed. Japan's resistance to importing manufactured goods, its fumbled response to the 1997 financial crisis, its deference to the United States, and not least the rise of China all combined to undermine Japanese leadership of the region.

Not that it did not try. Tokyo launched an "FTA frenzy" of little substantive consequence, despite ASEAN concern that China's rise—and especially its 2001 entry into the WTO—would threaten their exports.[39] Regional economic strategists—their number has increased dramatically within the government and in think tanks—were left to "seek to build an East Asia together with the PRC" in a regional regime that "dispels mistrust through market transactions."[40] This was hardly Japan's preferred position of "lead goose."

Instead, a modus vivendi evolved in which China and Japan competed for regional dominance. Despite several bilateral FTA initiatives—Japan initialed five by 2006—Tokyo has given up the idea of direct competition with Beijing.[41] Rather, competition now takes place within multilateral institutions. The most prominent has been the so-called ASEAN+3 group. Plus 3 summitry began through an invitation extended by ASEAN to the leaders of China, Japan, and South Korea to attend the thirtieth anniversary of the formation of ASEAN in 1997 in Kuala Lumpur. The following year saw an agreement on regular meetings among the heads of state of ASEAN, China, Japan, and South Korea. A joint statement on East Asian cooperation was issued at the Manila summit in 1999, where ministerial-level meetings were added. These now occur annually in foreign affairs (e.g., piracy, AIDS, drugs, illegal immigration), economics (e.g., industrial standards, trade promotion, finance, intellectual property), and other areas. Although substantive policy coordination among ASEAN+3 members is still limited, regularly scheduled talks among the region's senior government officials are hardly insignificant.

Nor is the prospect for an "East Asian community" (EAC), the latest incarnation of the East Asian Economic Caucus (EAEC) first proposed by Malaysian prime minister Mahathir Mohamad in the 1990s. Mahathir had openly sought Japanese leadership, a prospect thwarted by Tokyo's deference to U.S. preferences. In January 2002, after Beijing stole a march on regional leadership, Prime Minister Koizumi called for ASEAN+3 to be used as the springboard for deepening regional cooperation. Japan's strategy was transparently designed to balance against Chinese influence.[42] Rather than try for a comprehensive framework and a set of rules, Japanese strategists proceeded functionally, building cooperation in specific policy areas such as energy, crime, the environment, and the economy. Koizumi reached out to New Zealand and Australia (but less enthusiastically to the United States), and called for an East Asian community of universal values, such as democracy and the rule of law. Taking small and very tentative steps toward a "comprehensive" (*hōkatsuteki*) arrangement, Japan called for an "open, transparent, and inclusive" regional trade bloc. A former diplomat claimed that "excluding the United States from the region is not an option for East Asia,"[43] but Tokyo has sent intermittent signals that it could accept an EAC that excludes the United States. In the run-up to the first meeting of the nascent EAC in Kuala Lumpur in December 2005, Japan's ambivalence about U.S. participation was more transparent than the economic institutions it was proposing. The best Deputy Minister of Foreign Affairs Tanaka Hitoshi could muster was that "countries with wishes and ability should join the forum from the start," hardly a ringing endorsement of U.S. membership.[44] Indeed, Japan pushed harder for New Zealand and Australian than for U.S. participation, and U.S. officials repeatedly made their concerns clear to Tokyo. According to one State Department official at the time, "America is a Pacific power, firmly rooted in this region. We are determined to play a vital role in the Asia of tomorrow that is taking shape today."[45] Although the United States was seeking "a regional architecture that allows states to build partnerships with each other, as well as partnerships with the United States,"[46] most of the evolving partnerships—especially the flagship EAC—exclude the United States.

Thus, Japan responded to the threat of Chinese regional dominance with characteristic ambiguity and a studied ambivalence about its continued dependence on the United States. This was compounded by inept diplomacy vis-à-vis China. The first EAC meeting failed when China rejected a "plus three" summit during the meeting in Kuala Lumpur. Beijing was punishing Japan for Prime Minister Koizumi's visits to Yasukuni Shrine. As Japan's leading economic daily reported after the failure of the East Asia Summit meeting in December 2005, "feuding between Asia's two largest economies—Japan and China—is blocking the strengthening of regional cooperation."[47] Sino-Japanese bilateral economic relations had never been healthier, but Japan had lost ground to China in Asia.

RESPONDING TO CHINA

If Japan's problems with China were only economic, they could be overcome. Indeed, on one analysis, their bilateral economic interaction has induced restraint from each side. The Japanese government apologized repeatedly for its wartime behavior and agreed to clean up chemical weapons dumps and stray artillery shells left in China. For its part, the PRC apologized for its submarine incursion in November 2004 and reassured Japanese officials that it would contain anti-Japanese sentiment.[48] On the economic front, cooperation is the norm. In one striking example, the two countries are cooperating on East Asian standards for "fourth generation" cellular telephony and on a Chinese-character operating system for personal computers.[49] Moreover, just one month after the failed East Asia summit, they agreed on a vice-ministerial dialogue to plan for a joint study of bilateral history.[50] After years of refusing to cooperate, and after intermittent military confrontations, Beijing and Tokyo even agreed in late 2005 to begin negotiations on joint development of East China Sea gas reserves. The two governments remained far apart and negotiations were suspended in 2006. But they were restarted in 2007 after a successful visit to Tokyo by Premier Wen Jiabao.[51] It was noteworthy that there was no resentful venting from Beijing in 2005 when Japan reoriented much of its economic development assistance toward India.[52]

But none of this negates the larger security dilemma at work in Northeast Asia.[53] Each side, claiming to be acting in its own defense, is building military capabilities to allow operations far from its littorals—thereby threatening the other. Japanese strategists have elevated their concern about China. By the early 1990s, the JDA, which had shown only a "slight concern" about China's nuclear weapons in its 1979 White Paper, was moving to enhance its capability to deal with the (still unnamed) Chinese military threat.[54] JDA White Papers began tentatively addressing China's maritime activities and force modernization. The first time a Japanese government official formally expressed concern about the Chinese military was three months after China's October 1993 nuclear tests made it impossible for Tokyo to ignore the buildup. Foreign Minister Hata Tsutomu went to Beijing to seek greater transparency. Subsequent JDA White Papers noted China's seizure of Mischief Reef in the South China Sea (1995), its weapons tests in the Taiwan Strait (1996), and PLAN activities in Japanese territorial waters (1998). In March 2006, for the first time, the foreign ministry incorporated a statement of strong concern about China's arms buildup in its *Diplomatic Blue Book*.[55]

Not everyone is convinced that the elevated rhetoric has been matched with sufficient action. One hears calls for an end to Japanese "indolence" (*ankan to shite*) and for Japan to be more "resolute" (*kakko taru*).[56] Some observers, invoking China's response when a U.S. EP-3 patrol aircraft was forced down over Hainan Island in 2001, have called on the Japanese government for similar levels of outrage and confrontation. In July 2005, a study group sponsored by the *Nippon Zaidan* issued a tough-minded set of recommendations based on its view that China is seeking regional hegemony and

Japan's response has been too conciliatory. The report called for an end to appeasement and for a policy not "driven by dependence on the Chinese market." Signatories included former JDA director general Aichi Kazuo, former GSDF commanding officer Arai Daisuke, DPJ "shadow defense minister" Nagashima Akihisa, and Tōgō Kazuhiko, a former Japanese ambassador to Russia.[57] Japan, these and many others argue, should not shrink from pointing out China's own textbook problem—its authoritarianism, its human rights violations.[58] Meanwhile, the nationalist Right has pressed the issue by building lighthouses on the disputed Senkaku Islands.[59] This did not stop seven Chinese patriots from landing there in 2004—at which point it was discovered that the SDF had no operational plan to expel them.[60] In another case, *Nippon Zaidan* sent a "survey team" to the remote and uninhabited Okinotori Islands to study ways to enlarge what the PRC refers to merely as "rocks." The Japanese government subsequently installed radar and repaired a heliport there. In August 2005, the Coast Guard announced it would build a lighthouse there "for the safety of the 440 merchant ships that pass by each year."[61]

In fact, the Japanese government did not stand idly by. Planners drew down fixed GSDF forces to enhance mobility and antisubmarine capabilities, with defense of the offshore islands and maritime resources in mind.[62] The number of tanks authorized for the GSDF was halved between the 1976 National Defense Program Outline (NDPO) and the 2004 Guidelines.[63] The four GSDF divisions eliminated in the 1995 NDPO were converted into smaller, mobile brigades, and, under the 2005–09 Midterm Defense Build-up Plan, three more such brigades were added. Expecting that China would continue on track to become the preeminent military power in the region, the SDF was repositioned from the north, where stationary troops had faced a potential Soviet attack, toward the south, for faster deployment in the event of a Chinese contingency. To support this response, F-4 squadrons were replaced by F-15s in Okinawa, providing greater range and firepower.

The 2004 Guidelines elevated the importance of mobility by seizing the opportunity to define Japanese interests more expansively than ever. Japan's latest security doctrine acknowledges the "critical [importance of] close economic ties [and] stability in the region spreading from the Middle East to East Asia." In a less visible but no less significant doctrinal change, the 2004 Guidelines replaced Japan's Basic Defense Force Concept with the Multi-Function Flexible Response Concept. The former focused on *denying* access to invaders and was not threat based. The latter authorizes *punishment* of offenders, including nonstate actors.[64] It supplemented inherited language about "defensive defense" by emphasizing new threats and calling for a central readiness command, under which more mobile forces could be dispatched. Although China still was not identified by name, the 2006 MSDF budget included funding for R & D on a next-generation sonar to detect submarines, as well as a new short-range torpedo to greet them.[65]

The JDA also began planning for three invasion scenarios in the early 2000s.[66] The first posited Chinese attacks on Japan to prevent it from aiding U.S. forces during a crisis in the Taiwan Strait. In the second scenario, China seizes the Senkaku Islands to consolidate its leadership at home. The third scenario posited Chinese moves in the East China Sea to develop gas fields near the disputed boundary. Senior politicians have supported these planning activities and have connected them to efforts to further relax legal constraints on the use of force.[67] In November 2004 the JDA completed operational plans for counteroffensive operations by a new rapid deployment force under the newly established Central Readiness Command in the event of Chinese landings on the Senkakus or other remote islands. This became more salient after September 2005, when a Chinese military vessel openly targeted an unarmed MSDF PC-3 patrol plane with its 100mm cannons near the disputed gas fields.[68] It was no surprise, then, that the ASDF leaked word in November 2005 that its fighter jets had scrambled thirty times in the previous six months—double the number of the previous period—in response to Chinese incursions.[69] Unfazed, and still publicly denying it was directed at China, in January and February 2006 the SDF participated in well-publicized joint exercises with the U.S. Marines to practice retaking islands.[70]

While ground-forces budgets were cut, naval budgets largely held their own. A new generation of P-3C antisubmarine aircraft—of indigenous design and development—was authorized in the late 1990s, and upgrades to Japan's Aegis equipment continued without interruption. The China threat was also used to justify off-budget increases in defense spending, much of which was directed toward the Coast Guard and thus did not count against the 1 percent cap. As we have seen in chapter 3, with an annual budget of 172 billion yen, the Coast Guard was already a blue-water force of considerable size when the government announced modernization plans in December 2005. Twenty-one new ships and seven new jets were to be added, and the fleet would also be reconditioned, at a cost of fifty billion yen per year between 2006 and 2012. A Coast Guard spokesman defended the budget request with explicit reference to China: "We demanded this increase...because of mounting concerns in the East China Sea area, especially near the disputed gas field."[71] Other off-budget but defense-related spending included a new intelligence office and reconnaissance satellites (the Cabinet Office), as well as the science and technology budget (Ministry of Education, Science and Technology).[72] China is modernizing its military with considerable zeal, but Japan remains far ahead, even without factoring in the U.S. Seventh Fleet.[73]

The rise of China has also propelled Japanese diplomacy toward balancing partnerships. In August 2000, former prime minister Mori Yoshirō visited India, a visit reciprocated in 2001 by Indian foreign minister George Fernandes and followed by visits at the highest level of each civil service. In May 2003, Ishiba Shigeru became the first JDA director general to visit New Delhi, where he urged that India and Japan be "vigilant" about China. The two nation's navies soon exchanged port calls and cooperated in joint exercises, while their defense ministers called on China to be more transparent.[74] By the following year, India had replaced China as Japan's largest aid recipient and the two countries were engaged in "service to service" exchanges under the aegis of a "comprehensive security dialogue."[75] India also assisted the MSDF in its Indian Ocean deployment to support U.S. forces in Afghanistan and cooperates actively with the Japan Coast Guard. One former MSDF admiral has called for a three-nation Asian maritime coalition (Ajia Kaijō Yūshi Rengō), building on naval cooperation between India and Japan, "the two largest democracies in Asia," and the United States.[76] Other initiatives have included Japanese participation in multinational exercises with the navies of Singapore, Australia, Indonesia, Thailand, the ROK, and Malaysia near Singapore in 2003–04 and in the western Pacific sponsored by Singapore and the ROK.[77] By 2004 the SDF was engaged in official security dialogues with sixteen countries, as well as NATO, and in March 2007 Japan and Australia inked a defense cooperation pact. Although most analysts understand that China's rise has propelled these developments, some mistakenly imagine Japan to be the beneficiary. As one Japanese government think tank would have it: "Wariness about China's future intentions have caused Southeast Asian countries to entertain hopes for leadership from Japan to act as a counterweight to China's growing presence."[78] Japan was active in the formation of the principal forum for security dialogue in Asia, the ASEAN Regional Forum (ARF) in 1994.[79] ARF is a fully inclusive talk shop with twenty-five members—including the U.S. and China—with rules that prohibit members from identifying one another as adversaries, thereby limiting its efficacy. Meaningful regional multilateral security cooperation is thus limited to anti-piracy initiatives and confidence-building measures.

It is impossible to rule out alternative regional security architectures, but none has emerged that seems remotely as durable or realistic as the one designed by the United States.[80] Indeed, Japanese affirmation of support for U.S. forces in the event of a Taiwan contingency is perhaps the most striking Japanese reaction to changes since the cold war. As recently as 2001, two Japan specialists, who would later join the Bush administration, could write that "there is little confidence in either Tokyo or Washington about the readiness of the alliance to deal with a Taiwan contingency."[81] Another experienced Japan hand worried aloud about "severe military consequences of base unavailability" in a Taiwan crisis.[82] By December 2004, however, repeated incursions by Chinese vessels inside Japan's EEZ (which violated no international laws) had gotten Tokyo's attention. So did intelligence that China was considering promulgating an antisecession law that would justify the use of force against Taiwan. Japan's new guidelines pulled few punches. It expressed concern about the "massive military might, including nuclear arsenals [that] continue to exist in the region" and about the "uncertainty" of cross-Strait relations. Two months later, in February 2005, Taiwan was included on the list of "common strategic objectives" shared by the United States and Japan. Japan did not commit to the use of force to defend Taiwan, but it did clarify for the first time since 1972 that peace in the Taiwan Strait is as important strategically as the Korean Peninsula and that it would "maintain the capability...to address contingencies" in the region.[83]

NORTH KOREA: FIRST CARROTS, THEN STICKS

Pyongyang was even more conspicuous: "Peaceful resolution of issues related to North Korea" was elevated above "dialogue" on Taiwan as a "common strategic objective" in the so-called 2+2 accounting in February 2005. If the cultish regime in North Korea had not existed, some Japanese strategists surely would have wished to invent it. It was easy for the Japanese public to perceive Pyongyang's militarism and persistent provocations as a threat—one much less ambiguous than China's, which was, after all, encased in considerable economic benefit. Yet, while the DPRK threat was used effectively to bring Japan out of its security shell, it was not obvious at first that Japanese strategists understood the opportunity. Japan temporized during the first North Korean nuclear crisis in 1993–94. As one former diplomat describes it, with admirable delicacy, "There was an urgent need to explore the extent to which Japan could offer support activities to U.S. forces if hostilities erupted."[84] Tokyo's support for the United States in that first crisis was so equivocal that, in the view of one analyst, it "exposed the essential emptiness of the so-called alliance and its lack of military operability."[85] Japan's ambivalence, and its willingness once again to invoke "constitutional limits" in order to resist U.S. demands, shook Tokyo and Washington alike, and alliance managers got to work. Within three years the new National Defense Program Outline had been issued and "guidelines" had been worked out widening the Japanese defense perimeter and reinforcing the alliance.

Once the alliance had been upgraded and Tokyo had assumed responsibility for defense of the "areas surrounding Japan" (*nihon no shūhen*), Japan began to use the North Korean threat to justify new weapons and doctrine. Pyongyang made it easy. After a December 2001 shootout in the East China Sea between a Japanese patrol boat and a suspected North Korean spy ship armed with antiaircraft missiles, the government beefed up the

Coast Guard.[86] What had been merely a "suspicious ship" was reclassified as a foreign government "operations boat." Once it was reclassified, the Japanese government could justify the legitimate use of deadly force—and order new military equipment. A 770–ton high-speed patrol vessel, armed with 40mm machine guns designed to fire from beyond the range of enemy vessels, was delivered in 2005. The Japanese Coast Guard, benefiting considerably from both North Korean and Chinese threats, has never been so well equipped. As reported in detail in chapter 3, by the mid-2000s it had become Japan's second navy, with responsibility for tackling armed intruders and for participating in antipiracy exercises as far away as Southeast Asia. It has patrol (*goei*) missions that are denied to the MSDF, which is limited to surveillance and cannot guard the oil rigs that will be built in the East China Sea. Some strategists argue that using the Coast Guard rather than the MSDF helps avoid militarizing a conflict too quickly, but the Coast Guard trumpets its "new military powers" and is becoming more navylike every year.[87]

Pyongyang's Taepodong launch in August 1998 was even more catalytic. Although the United States subsequently confirmed it was a failed satellite launch rather than a missile test, and although senior JDA officials insist they are not panicked by North Korea's antics, the firing of a rocket through Japanese airspace led almost immediately to legislation authorizing an indigenous Japanese intelligence satellite—a de facto abrogation of the ban on the military use of space.[88] It also led to a decision to cooperate with the United States on missile defense R & D, for which the U.S. government had been pushing since 1994. Still, according to press reports, the Japanese government made every effort to develop an *autonomous* space-based intelligence capability. As one government official remarked, "It is more effective to see with our own eyes, even if the performance is inferior."[89] The majority of concerned Japanese citizens supported other doctrinal clarifications, including the reassertion of Japan's right to use preemptive force in the face of an imminent threat. Indeed, when it was learned that the JDA had begun conducting simulations of preemptive attacks on North Korean missile bases in 1994, the news barely made the press.[90] Subsequent discussions of the need for cruise missiles or to exempt the United States from the arms export ban were likewise met with indifference. Public opinion had no difficulty appreciating the North Korean threat.[91]

Policy debate on how to respond to North Korean provocation broke out into the open in October 2006, after North Korea's nuclear test. The new Abe government worked vigorously with the United States and other UN Security Council members, including China, to pass UN Security Council Resolution 1718, which imposed sanctions on Pyongyang. Shortly thereafter, the government announced that it was considering invoking the law on "contingencies in the area surrounding Japan" so that Japan's naval vessels could assist in searches of suspicious DPRK ships mandated by the resolu-tion. The criteria for such a "contingency" are vague, and the DPJ and the LDP were each predictably split over whether they had been met in this instance, while coalition partner Kōmeitō was resolutely opposed.[92] What was abundantly clear—and quite new—however, was how fully engaged the public was. A majority was prepared to accept the legitimacy of a mili-tarized response for the first time.

The preemption issue was not new, but it did evolve considerably when the North Korean threat became apparent. In 1954 the Cabinet Legislation Bureau had identified "three conditions under which Japan can constitu-tionally exercise the right of self-defense," the first being when Japan is faced with an "imminent and illegitimate act of aggression."[93] In 1956, it issued a "unified government opinion" reinforcing this interpretation, and Prime Minister Hatoyama Ichirō reminded Japan that "the constitution is not intended to see the nation idly wait for death," a sentiment echoed al-most verbatim by JDA director general Ishiba and by a retired MSDF admi-ral in 2005.[94] Prime Minister Kishi's Cabinet Legislation Bureau clarified the legality of preemption in 1959, but there remained the question of whether Japan could even maintain weapons that could strike within enemy terri-tory. Thus the call to add Tomahawk cruise missiles to the Japanese arsenal stimulated an important clarification of the law. On the floor of the House of Representatives in January 2003 Director General Ishiba, Foreign Minis-ter Kawaguchi Yoriko, and CLB director general Akiyama Osamu affirmed that even if there were only a "high probability" that Japan were the target, Japan could legally exercise the right of preemptive self-defense. The oft-discussed acquisition of the Tomahawk system was never ruled out.[95]

In July 2006, when Pyongyang test fired a barrage of seven missiles—short-range Scuds, medium-range Nodongs, and intercontinental Taepo-dong IIs—in the Sea of Japan, preemption once again took center stage. And once again it was Japan's lack of military capacity, rather than legal authority, that caused the greatest concern.[96] Demands for acquisition of cruise mis-siles were more insistent than demands for constitutional clarification. With this and other offensive enhancements, Japan's security doctrine of "denial" would be transformed into one of "punishment"[97]—an additional "defensive enhancement" that would lock Japan and its neighbors into a textbook secu-rity dilemma.[98]

The North Korean threat was also the proximate cause of an epochal change in Japan's self-imposed ban on arms exports. As noted, the determi-nation of the ascendant antimainstream to collaborate with the United States on missile defense, which involves joint development of components, made it imperative for the government to begin dismantling the ban. Once this Ru-bicon was crossed, a great many opportunities presented themselves to the Japanese defense industry. In addition to collaboration in new multinational defense projects, the defense industry began eyeing export of nonoffensive materiel, such as surveillance systems, protective vests, and small boats for "anti-terrorist patrols."[99] JDA administrative vice minister Moriya Takemasa and former JDA director general Ohno Yoshinari have both advocated the sale of decommissioned MSDF vessels stripped of weapons, but including submarines, to Southeast Asian navies "to assist in the battle against piracy."[100] One former finance ministry defense budget officer who became a vice minister for METI after election to the Diet reported that the ministry wanted to market the JDA's new C-X transport for civilian applications "in order to assist in the development of the national aircraft industry."[101]

This was not the only reason why cooperation in ballistic missile defense (BMD) was the most consequential Japanese response to the DPRK threat. Japan is the only foreign participant in this massively complex and expensive undertaking, one that absorbed more than 2 percent of the Japanese defense budget in 2004, its first year of development.[102] The BMD architecture comprises both land- and sea-based platforms, as well as possible acquisition of preemptive capabilities that would target North Korean missiles prior to launch. Importantly, from the U.S. perspective, it also involves the provision of radar sites in Japan to detect intercontinental ballistic missile launches. Japan's ground-based platform includes plans to deploy one set of ground-based missiles per year for four years and will be operational in 2007. These PAC-3s will target incoming missiles in their terminal phase, after they have reentered the earth's atmosphere. The latter rely initially on missiles designed for antiaircraft applications (SM-2s) that are deployed on Japan's Aegis-equipped destroyers. In 2005 the MSDF committed to acquisition of an upgraded system (SM-3), designed to operate outside the earth's atmosphere, with Nodong-like medium-range missiles in mind.

In the United States, physicists have organized sustained opposition to BMD, but in Japan there has been virtually no independent analysis. Some MOD officials have glossed over questions by simply declaring that BMD will be an effective shield. Ignoring the possibility—indeed, the certainty—that this could be interpreted differently in China and Korea, the Japanese have insisted that BMD is the quintessential "defensive defense" system that threatens no neighbors and reassures the domestic population.[103] According to Nishikawa Kazumi of the MOD Defense Policy Bureau:

> Naturally, [BMD] will be able to intercept missiles headed toward Japan and prevent damage. Moreover, even if it is not used, it will have deterrent power.... Adversaries will be forced to think that having defensive missiles is useless because even if they launch them they will be intercepted.[104]

Of course, these adversaries quickly responded by working on more effective offensive weapons, to deter Japan from attacking them without fear of reprisal. Meanwhile, Japanese advocates insist that BMD will enable Japan "to stand on an equal footing with the United States," whereas others worry that close operational coordination of the sort designed into BMD systems "will entangle Japan in a [U.S.] preemptive strike."[105]

The most important political division on North Korea policy has been among revisionists within the LDP itself. As James Schoff points out, a "dialogue faction," led by Prime Minister Koizumi and his first chief cabinet secretary, Fukuda Yasuo, squared off against a "pressure faction" led by Abe Shinzō.[106] As the labels suggest, the former group believed in using carrots, the latter sticks. Abe was reportedly sidelined at first, as Koizumi proceeded with a carrot strategy in mid-2002. He did so, moreover, despite a personal visit in August from Deputy Secretary of State Richard Armitage, who warned that North Korea was operating a secret nuclear weapons program. Disregarding this unwelcome news, Koizumi arrived in Pyongyang less than one month later, where he offered grants, loans, and humanitarian assistance at the level of "several billion dollars" in exchange for positive steps toward the normalization of relations, including acknowledgement of the abductions and resolution of the nuclear issue.[107]

The Koizumi-Kim summit produced a "Pyongyang declaration" and an initial euphoria over a diplomatic victory for Japan. Kim acknowledged that the DPRK had, in fact, kidnapped Japanese nationals and promised the return to Japan of the surviving abductees. But euphoria soon turned to anguish for the abductees and their families and a growing desire for revenge. Koizumi was harshly criticized for "secret diplomacy" and for allowing Kim to drive a potential wedge into the U.S.-Japan alliance. Confirmation of the abductions and the subsequent hostage taking of their families hardened the Japanese public against North Korea. Pressure (including some violence) increased on North Korean citizens and their businesses in Japan, as the idea of engagement lost its attractions and bilateral talks became deadlocked.[108] Before long, the more hawkish group, led by Abe, found its footing—and its sticks. Abe used the abduction issue to secure an LDP electoral victory in November 2003, and in the process became a formidable political actor on the national stage. He pressed for, and won, new economic and technological sanctions. Any lingering concern in Washington that Pyongyang would drive a wedge into the U.S.-Japan relationship ended in February 2005 when the DPRK declared itself a nuclear weapons state. In July 2006, Japan and the United States engineered a unanimous UN Security Council resolution condemning Pyongyang for its missile tests. As noted above, they did so again after Pyongyang thumbed its nose at its neighbors by testing a nuclear bomb in October.

Now attention turned once again to the possibility that Japan would arm itself with nuclear weapons. As noted in chapter 2, Prime Minister Satō Eisaku announced his government's three "nonnuclear principles" in 1967, a policy that has been upheld by each subsequent administration—including Abe's in 2006. Clearly, though, the nuclear option has never been unthinkable for Japan, a country with tons of stockpiled plutonium, a sophisticated delivery capability, and a deep scientific base. As noted in chapter 3, the Cabinet Legislation Bureau ruled in 1957 at the behest of Prime Minister Kishi that possession of nuclear weapons was not unconstitutional. In chapter 4, we reviewed how the Japanese government undertook several internal studies in the 1960s and 1990s, each of which reaffirmed the strategic utility of the U.S. nuclear umbrella and the dangers of going nuclear. In 2006, Pyongyang once again raised the issue, this time in a most public way. Abe Shinzō—in office for less than three weeks at the time—immediately reinvoked the nonnuclear principles. But soon thereafter, the LDP's policy chief, Nakagawa Shōichi, suggested on national television that there ought to be a full debate of the nuclear option. Although his comments were dismissed by some as undisciplined ramblings—and while Abe immediately reaffirmed the nonnuclear principles publicly and in person at a meeting with senior Chinese officials—Nakagawa's call for debate were seconded by Foreign Minister Asō and former prime minister Nakasone, even as they insisted that a nonnuclear Japan would be the safest Japan.[109] In late December, it was reported that the Japanese government had undertaken yet another nuclear weapons feasibility study—in September, just days before the DPRK test.[110] However subtly, Japan was signaling its neighbors—and the United States—that it would keep its options open.

It is widely accepted that U.S. extended deterrence in the most significant impediment standing between Japan and the nuclear weapons option.[111] Extended deterrence requires reiterated commitment. Immediately after the nuclear option was again brought into public discourse, President Bush expressed concern about a possible Chinese response, Secretary of State Condoleezza Rice reassured the Japanese of the U.S. commitment during a visit to Tokyo, and Ambassador Thomas Schieffer insisted that "the alliance has never been stronger."[112] Washington and Tokyo were working hard to make sure that there would be no daylight between Tokyo and Washington on how to deal with Pyongyang—and most strategists in both capitals agreed that a nuclear Japan would destabilize Northeast Asia. Japan's unilateral initiatives would be limited to economic security, as in the case of Iran. It would continue to hedge on the military side by cultivating U.S. protection—for now.

JAPAN'S WILLING EMBRACE

In chapter 5 I examined how the conservatives who have ruled Japan since the end of the Pacific War have been divided over whether Japan should be more muscular and whether it could legally use force. They were never divided, however, on the importance of the Japan-U.S. alliance. Both the pragmatists and the revisionists believed strongly in the efficacy of the alliance for Japanese national security. When faced with a choice between embracing the United States and running the risk of entanglement, or distancing Japan and facing the risk of abandonment, leaders from either camp always responded first to the threat of abandonment. Chapter 4 examined the most salient recent example—Prime Minister Koizumi's dispatch of naval forces to the Indian Ocean and deployment of ground forces to Iraq a year later. This was a direct response to the threat of abandonment, though Koizumi's justification was more straightforward: Japan, he declared in testimony to the Diet, had no ally other than the United States.[113] This also explains why the 2004 Guidelines could be so explicit about the centrality of the alliance.[114] Although some saw Japan being "pulled onto the U.S. war chariot," and others saw it electing to "jointly manage the United States' continuing hegemonic presence in the region," the fact is that Japan has embraced the United States and has made the Pacific Ocean narrower and the East China Sea wider.[115]

Japan's revisionist leaders believed that aligning with the United States in this larger geostrategic context was essential if they were to make Japan more "normal." The most important feature of the global security environment after the cold war was the overwhelming military power of the United States and, since the United States was determined to reconfigure that environment, Japan needed to be aligned.[116] The first attempt to nudge Japan in this direction was Prime Minister Hashimoto Ryūtarō's statement in January 1997 that Japan had a global security role.[117] But this was too soon after he had guided Japan to accept a regional security role. Differences between the JDA and the foreign ministry prevented further change.[118] Language about Japan's global security role in alliance with the United States, rather than under UN auspices, first gained currency after the 9/11 terrorist attacks on the United States, when Japanese defense analysts adopted U.S. language about the need to enforce security along an "arc of instability" from the Far East to the Middle East. Japanese military planners were now thinking openly—with U.S. encouragement—about how unrest in the Middle East raised the need to protect the sea-lanes out to the Persian Gulf and about how the United States needed support for operations from its Japanese bases.[119] In 2002, as it prepared for war in Iraq, the DoD reportedly asked the MSDF to help protect the Seventh Fleet and to cover for part of its depleted forces in the Pacific.[120]

In conjunction with preparations for the Iraq War, the DoD declared that it would transform America's global defense posture. Japanese analysts were unsure at first what Washington had in mind, and what it would mean for U.S. forces in Japan and for the alliance more generally. Those who anticipated the impact would be greatest in Germany and Korea were correct, but Japan was hardly ignored. Washington's global review focused on the reduction of forward-deployed U.S. forces and the replacement of large, permanent bases with smaller, more flexible ones. Japan would have both. This attention regenerated the threat of entrapment—some Japanese analysts fretted that Japan's security interests might be forever subordinated to U.S. preferences. Any change to the status quo, they argued, would open a Pandora's box of domestic opposition.[121] But once again, the greater threat was abandonment. The possibility that U.S. force transformation might take place without consultation or coordination with the Japanese government was something that alliance managers were reluctant to encourage.[122]

Thus in December 2002, the United States and Japan began concerted bilateral consultations on the role of the alliance in the transformation of U.S. global forces. The two sides focused on five elements: (1) joint assessments of threats, (2) assessments of roles and missions required of each side to meet these threats, (3) evaluation of their respective force structures, (4) examination of the adequacy of basing structures, and (5) estimation of force presence issues.[123] In October 2005, these discussions bore fruit, as Secretary of State Condoleezza Rice, Secretary of Defense Donald Rumsfeld, JDA Director General Ohno Yoshinori, and Foreign Minister Machimura Nobutaka announced at their Security Consultative Committee (the 2+2) meeting that bilateral coordination would be enhanced at every level from tactical units to strategic consultations. Japan and the United States would have "close and continuous policy and operational coordination...to dissuade destabilizing military build-ups, to deter aggression, and to respond to diverse security challenges."[124] Joint force modernization would include enhanced intelligence capabilities, a coordinated network of satellites, missile interceptors, and radars, as well as increased joint training, mutual provision of aerial and maritime refueling, and even establishment of the alliance's first joint command center. In what has been described as the largest realignment in the history of the alliance, Japanese and U.S. forces would be integrated for the first time.[125]

That was easier said than done. The base issue, never fully tranquilized, reawakened with a start. Considerable political opposition greeted each of the five main components of the realignment: (1) a new command structure for the U.S. Army in Japan at Camp Zama (including colocation of the new GSDF Central Readiness Force Command), (2) a joint command center at Yokota Air Base, (3) a relocation of Futenma Air Station in Okinawa, (4) movement of seven thousand U.S. Marines to Guam, and (5) relocation of the U.S. carrier air wing in Atsugi (Kanagawa Prefecture) to Iwakuni Air Station in Yamaguchi Prefecture.[126] The emergency use of Japanese civilian facilities by U.S. forces and the colocation of command headquarters raised the specter that the SDF would become the fifth branch of the U.S.

military.[127] And the plan to move the First U.S. Army Command from the continental United States to Camp Zama further clarified the entanglement threat for many, including some within the foreign ministry, that the purpose of U.S. forces in Japan was shifting formally from the defense of Japan to the use of Japan as a forward base and command post for East Asia.[128] The relocation of Futenma became bogged down in local opposition to the new site, and the movement of the Marines was slowed by how much the Japanese government would pay and how much the Americans were demanding. In early 2006 the citizens of Iwakuni voted overwhelmingly (87.4% opposed) in a nonbinding referendum to reject the relocation of the carrier air wing.[129] Once again the LDP in Tokyo was more willing to embrace the United States than were its citizens, and the cost of this embrace

Figure 10. President Bush presents Prime Minister Koizumi the bill for relocation of a bloated U.S. military establishment. Reprinted with permission of the artist Yamada Shin and the *Asahi Shimbun*, where it originally appeared, April 28, 2006.

[179]

had become too onerous even for many of its advocates. The subsequent 2+2, held in Washington in May 2006, ended three years of talks, with the proclamation that the Futenma relocation and redeployment of eight thousand Marines to Guam would be completed by 2014 at Japanese taxpayers' expense.[130] Once again, however, a lack of public support (derived in part from incomplete consultation) and considerable resentment about the cost (and how it was calculated) blocked forward progress.

Meanwhile, constitutional issues associated with collective defense and the issue of "integration with the use of force" (*buryoku kōshi no ittaika*) were creatively ignored. But the possible contexts in which Japanese forces might be part of a unit using force, which would not be legal under existing constitutional interpretations unless acting in self-defense, were expanded. Prime Minister Koizumi and his JDA director general, Ishiba, finessed the issue in the case of the Iraq deployment by declaring that the SDF would not be in a "combat zone" and by forcing the Cabinet Legislation Bureau to look the other way. They complicated it by adding new roles and missions to the military portfolio in instances in which the SDF might encounter violence while engaged in peacekeeping with other militaries. For example, after the GSDF withdrew from Samawah in July 2006, the ASDF assumed new responsibilities for airlift in support of the U.S. mission in Baghdad, hardly a "noncombat zone."[131] Moreover, in addition to relaxing restrictions on participating in UN PKF operations and in addition to its activities in the Indian Ocean and in Iraq, the Japanese military was also approved for duty in the U.S.-led Proliferation Security Initiative (PSI) in 2003. The PSI, designed as a "global initiative with global reach," would interdict ships on the high seas suspected of transporting weapons of mass destruction.[132] France and Australia joined Japan and the United States in an exercise in Tokyo Bay in October 2004. The PSI was established outside the United Nations system, however, and does not involve the participation of China or Russia, two members of the Security Council. Since it would be invoked without UN authorization and since it is highly unlikely that the Japanese military would ignore a request by the United States to stop a suspected vessel bound to or from North Korea, the Japanese now risk crossing the line of both domestic and international law.[133] Likewise, the missile defense agreement with the United States is sufficiently ambiguous that Japanese forces might shoot down a missile aimed not at Japan but at the United States—technically another constitutional violation. There is evidence that these roles and missions are designed to break down these legal barriers. Ishiba says that Japan's inability to shoot down a missile headed toward the United States is at the very core of Japan's interpretation of collective defense, which he insists should be reinterpreted to allow Japanese action.[134] He has been joined by Abe and a raft of other politicians, analysts, and alliance managers.[135] In the meantime, until "collective security" is legalized (or the constitution revised), military officers avoid reference to jointness, sticking instead to the politically less volatile idea of "division of labor" (*yakuwari buntan*).[136]

There is evidence that Japan's embrace of the United States is more than an insurance policy. It already has been credited with delivering significant collateral benefits. Japanese trade deficits and other economic policy issues, once the source of epochal bilateral tensions, were ignored by Washington in the early 2000s. Marumo Yoshinari, an ADSF general, insists that Japanese support of the U.S. war in Iraq was rewarded by unambiguous U.S. support for Japanese territorial claims on the Senkaku Islands for the first time.[137] Likewise, a former chief cabinet secretary has even suggested that Japan's participation in the Iraq action allowed it to pursue the Azadegan oil project in Iran without fear of U.S. retribution.[138] It is clear that Tokyo's alignment with the United States is designed strategically to contribute to, rather than to impede, its pursuit of Japan's national interests, even those that are incongruent with Washington's.

It is curious that despite all the talk of "integration," of "jointness," of "interoperability," of "power sharing," and of "equality"—in short, despite Japan's willing embrace of the United States—the alliance's division of labor still remained shrouded in metaphors of "sword" and "shield." In an emergency, unless it invokes the so-called Far East clause of the Mutual Security Treaty (Article 6), Japan would become a "base of operations" (*sakugenchi*) from which the United States could project power wherever it wished.[139] Certainly, Washington is happy with this. As two U.S. alliance managers put it before assuming senior positions in the Bush administration, "Japan should still do defense and the United States should do offense."[140] But this surely was not the point for Tokyo. As we have seen, by the mid-2000s a decade of salami slicing and responding to four specific threats have left Japan with a new military, one with its own roles, missions, and popular support. Although there is still a formal insistence on "defensive defense," the Japanese military has acquired a more expeditionary profile and is poised to assume a global role.

China's economic and military modernization, Pyongyang's serial miscalculations, the fear of technoeconomic lassitude, and concern about abandonment by the United States have all combined with the strong preferences of Tokyo's revisionist leaders to enhance Japan's force posture. This enhancement, which one analyst has called "*Heisei* militarization" (a reference to the current imperial era), has proceeded at every level and in every sphere: economic and military, political and diplomatic, organizational and ideological, de jure and de facto, regional and global, and in both planning and deployment.[141] With the exception of Japan's awkward China diplomacy during the Koizumi years, Japanese security has been enhanced across the board.

An economy that had been luffing in the doldrums for more than a decade came back with a strong technonationalist tailwind. A defense industry that was facing extinction—or at least a massive consolidation and permanent subordination to U.S. systems integrators—now looks out over a vast new export horizon. No economic threat is ever gone, but the most intimidating one since the early 1950s had been overcome with considerable finesse. The remaining challenge for economic security is to find a way to regain Japanese leadership of nascent regional economic institutions without thoroughly alienating the United States.

A military that had difficulty protecting even its own coastal traffic just a generation ago is now prepared to deploy ballistic missile defense and special forces for antiguerrilla operations. It can interdict ships—with force if necessary—and can travel great distances to rescue conationals abroad. Japan's defense perimeter has expanded considerably; deployments out to the Indian Ocean and Arabian Sea have been made "semi-permanent."[142] Tokyo has significantly enhanced the administration of its military by creating a new joint-command structure and can now expect unprecedented cooperation across its service branches. The LDP reduced the bureaucratic power in both the CLB and the JDA, and it has enhanced (and centralized) its political control. The MOD, once derided as a "shopping ministry" interested only in procurements and budgets, had already become a policy ministry on a par with the Ministry of Foreign Affairs well before its formal elevation to ministry status in early 2007. The Japanese government has made its ground forces more mobile, and it can export arms in specific cases. By the early 2000s, it was preparing for amphibious assaults and for urban warfare. It had built new intelligence capabilities, both on the ground and in space, as well as a new high-tech battlefield training center. The SDF can now participate in multinational forces—within and outside the UN system—and can provide surveillance, minesweeping, and antisubmarine intelligence to allies.[143] And, as one retired admiral has boasted, the MSDF is one of a very small number of navies that can maintain an operation six thousand miles from home for four years.[144] Its Coast Guard has the surface capabilities of a small second navy, and its ASDF has some of the world's most modern equipment. In meeting a great many threats, Japan unintentionally generated a few of its own.

All this adds up to considerable change, but there is more on the horizon. Revision of Article 9—potentially the crowning achievement of the governing clique—is taking longer than its advocates had hoped. The same can be said of revision to the de jure limits to collective defense. Likewise, all the enhancements described above have been accomplished under what the 2004 Guidelines called "deteriorating fiscal conditions." Despite the increasingly strident demands of the U.S. government, the self-imposed 1 percent budget cap continues to limit the defense buildup and allows Japan to continue its cheap ride.[145] Opacity still seems to be convenient for some purposes: hence the JDA White Paper in 2004 explained that Japan's defense posture is still limited constitutionally to a "minimum necessary level," which is determined "within the context of Japan's total military strength," and weapon systems are constitutional only if they would not "cause [Japan's] total military strength to exceed the constitutional limit."[146] Still, Japan, criticized by successive U.S. administrations for its fecklessness, has repositioned itself to great potential advantage. By the early 2000s, when Tokyo had also responded effectively to the economic threats engendered by its failed fiscal policies and by the rise of China, it was better situated than ever. But how will this new capability be deployed?

Conclusion

Japan's Evolving Grand Strategy

The position of Great Britain is unique, and not free from anxiety. By herself, Great Britain is no match for the other great multi-national units and, with a population about to decline steeply, might well be on the way to become a secondary power. Were this to happen, British policy would be faced by a fearful dilemma; it would have the choice of subordinating itself to the policy either of the United States of America, or of attempting, as other secondary powers have done in the past, to play off the more powerful units against one another—with inevitably disastrous results.

E. H. Carr, 1945.

A great many historical analogies have been invoked to explain contemporary Japanese grand strategy. Some are benign: the Venetian example is used to suggest how maritime powers can safely provide both security and prosperity without becoming too aggressive, the Dutch example to show how failed empires can regain their luster through alliance with Anglo-Saxon powers.[1] Parallels have been drawn between Japan's response to the Boxer Rebellion in 1900 and the Iraq War in 2003. Both, a retired MSDF admiral has argued, were responses to requests of the international community through which Japan won the respect and trust of the great powers.[2] Soeya Yoshihide offers up modern Canada as a model for a "middle power" Japan.[3] Other analogs are more disquieting, however. Iraq has been called "America's Manchuria," for example, and by joining the United States in its intervention, Japan may once again estrange itself from the international community.[4] Then there is Japan's response to the Allies' 1918 call for intervention in Russia after the Bolshevik Revolution. Asked to contribute seven thousand soldiers to protect Czech troops in the Russian Far East, Tokyo dispatched seventy thousand and stayed until 1922—a move that raised serious doubts about the ambitions of this upstart power.

But the most compelling historical analogy concerns the impact of U.S. foreign policy on contemporary Japanese grand strategy. In chapter 1 we explored the consequences for Japanese liberalism after Woodrow Wilson—the self-anointed champion of democratic values—ignored Japan's plea for a racial equality law at Versailles. Not only did liberal internationalists lose traction within the Japanese foreign policy debate, but many switched sides, joining the Asianists and militarists who remade grand strategy. They had no answer when Yamagata Aritomo and his allies declared that the West was prosecuting a race war and Japan needed protection.[5] Today Japanese intellectuals—and not only polemicists—again perceive a gap between U.S. values and its foreign policy. Books such as *The Empire and Its Limits* and *Democracy's Empire* address contemporary U.S. unilateralism and the betrayal of American values.[6] Japanese discourse is filled with contrasts between Washington's insistence on universal values (democracy, nonproliferation, human rights) and its support for dictators, its overthrow of foreign governments, its embrace of "friendly" nuclear states, and its use of torture. When Secretary of State Condoleezza Rice criticized the idea of an East Asian community in March 2005 in Tokyo by insisting that "instead of an exclusive club of powers, we stand for a community open to all," it did not go unnoticed that the United States, Mexico, and Canada operate a closed North American free trade area back home.[7] It is clear that American universalism today, as in 1918, would be more attractive were it not so transparently self-serving. Thoughtful Japanese still have good reason to feel vulnerable.

JAPAN'S STRATEGIC CULTURE

Indeed, widespread perceptions of vulnerability and imminent decline, and the confounding constraints of alliance with the United States identified by E. H. Carr, have been ubiquitous features of Japan's security discourse for decades. A century before Washington first loomed as the deus ex machina in Japan's security drama, vulnerability had already become deeply etched in Japanese debate. The persistent sense of vulnerability is only one of the many elements of Japanese strategic culture I have documented in these pages.[8] A continental strategy or a maritime one? Strength or wealth? Asia or Europe? A great power or a lesser power? All of these questions have been fixtures of Japan's security discourse since the creation of the Meiji state. In every decade since the late nineteenth century Big Japanists have squared off against Small Japanists and autonomists have denounced internationalists. The Yoshida-Kishi debate of the 1950s echoed—and reversed

the outcome of—the Shidehara-Ishibashi debate of the 1920s. It also anticipated the Abe-Ozawa clash of the mid-2000s. Sometimes political battles
solve problems and sometimes they create new ones, but they also reinforce
values and create norms linked to national identity. The challenge for analysts of security policy is to understand how these norms and identities
matter—and when they change.[9]

We have seen how such collectively held understandings of social life and
national aspiration are not bequeathed by history but forged and reforged
in the crucible of political debate. And we have seen how political entrepreneurs have used these understandings to sell their own preferences.
The preferences of particular entrepreneurs have prevailed and became
national—at least until world order shifts, challenging the consensus and
giving way to new debate. Indeed, the most striking continuity in the history of modern Japanese security policy has been the consistency with
which discourse and consensus have alternated as new world orders have
come and gone. Values have endured sometimes as normative ends and
sometimes as political utilities, each connected to a range of policy options
in different global and regional contexts.[10] Two in particular—autonomy
and prestige—have been ubiquitous. Each one, sometimes invoked in efforts to make Japan rich and at other times in efforts to make Japan strong,
has been reinforced in multiple contexts. Sometimes they frame the essential
elements of what Japan's grand strategy ought to be. Kanehara Nobukatsu,
the political minister at the Japanese embassy in Washington, explained in
2006 that Japan must remake its strategy from one characterized by passive pacifism (*ukemi no heiwashugi*) to one of active pacifism (*nōdōteki na heiwashugi*). Japan, he insists, must transform itself from an economic superpower to a political superpower in order to gain the respect (*sonkei*) of the
rest of the world, and it must do so on its own terms and at its own pace
(*jibun de kangaete, jibun de ugoku*).[11] Others echo this position in calls for Japan
to be a "responsible nation" rather than merely a "normal" one.[12] Japan has
transformed itself from a "peace-loving" into a "peace-supporting" state,
but now it must become a "peacemaking" one if it is to realize its proper
place in world affairs.[13] Others argue that Japan should support the United
States but also "should make independent decisions and display its own
style of leadership."[14] In his inaugural policy address to the Diet in September 2006, Abe Shinzō argued that Japan must be "trusted, respected, and
loved in the world."[15] Prestige and autonomy remain the backbone of the
discourse on grand strategy.

Because these values are ubiquitous, their proponents are preaching to the
choir. Prestige—comprising strength and wealth—has long been essential to
security planners. Consider how the *loss* of prestige, measured through the
"humiliation of checkbook diplomacy," has been used to frame Japan's disappointing response to the Gulf War and to justify subsequent prodigious

efforts to enhance Japan's global peacekeeping role.[16] Likewise, as the term "sympathy budget" (*omoiyari yosan*) suggests, prestige has been invoked to justify both increases in and reduction of host nation support for U.S. forces stationed in Japan. Prestige has also been used to reinterpret restrictions on the use of force so that Japanese forces do not have to be protected by foreign troops when they are on peacekeeping missions abroad. According to Prime Minister Abe, equality will be achieved by the exercise of collective self-defense.[17] Calls for a new grand strategy "based on respect" (*sonkei ni yoru anzen hoshō*) are ubiquitous.[18]

Autonomy looms just as large and is just as uncontested. As we have seen, businessmen, politicians, and the media refer routinely to the strategic importance of "rising sun" (*hinomaru*) projects—liquid crystal display factories, jet fighters, satellite imagery, and oil exploration are all valued more highly to the extent they can reduce foreign dependence. The most compelling argument for revision of the constitution—a matter that never had as much traction as it has in the mid-2000s—is the chance for Japan to move beyond what the United States "imposed" after 1945. Former prime minister Nakasone argues that revision is finally possible because there is now "a mood favoring independence."[19] An unnamed GSDF officer expressed the concerns of many when he argued that "if we simply get onto the rails laid by the U.S. military, we will merely be their subcontractor."[20] The strategic dangers involved are explored in a 2004 report of the Japan Forum on International Relations, which concludes that "Japan should from this moment onward have its own security policy as an independent nation."[21] Its president insists that Japan needs to navigate between "declining American power and growing Chinese strength [to avoid] subservience [to either]." Indeed, the return of full sovereignty looms over all discussions of U.S. bases in Japan, even if open bilateral discussion of the need for a new status of forces agreement—and for a new, more equitable security treaty—are still avoided. The center-left *Asahi Shimbun* editorializes that Japan needs to free itself from "excessive dependence" on the United States if it is to repair relationships with the rest of Asia, and the influential center-right monthly *Bungei Shunjū* strikes exactly the same chord by insisting that "Japan needs to plan for its own defense [because] it may no longer make sense to follow the teacher's instructions."[22] Former Deputy Justice Minister Kōno Tarō expressed the more general impatience, asking, "Are we going to push back on the United States or not?" and Yamamoto Ichita, former chair of the LDP Policy Committee on Foreign Policy is emphatic: "Japan needs to stretch its wings."[23]

Whether Japan was governed by oligarchs or by democrats, its strategists weighed their options with reference to autonomy and prestige. Both continue to be legitimate values available to leaders with widely divergent preferences. As a result, analyses of Japanese security policy must incorporate agency and political debate. Values matter, but they do not determine policies. They inform policies through a political process in which majorities shift and ruling coalitions have to be reconstructed in often fickle contexts. Thus, even when Japan's leaders were at their most reckless, the process by which they deployed these values in making strategic choices was rational. Even their greatest security miscalculations were filtered through—rather than bequeathed by—the legitimating ideals of Japan's strategic culture outlined in this study, especially the ubiquitous sense of vulnerability and propensity to hedge. In short Japan's leaders, whether mainstream or antimainstream, have been *persistent* rather than "reluctant" realists.[24] Insufficient attention to agency, unwarranted assumptions about the consensual nature of Japanese politics, and the underappreciation of the political process have resulted in observers missing some continuities in strategic culture. For example, by the 1990s many analysts were impressed with the persistence of pacifism in Japan's postwar security strategy. On this account, Japanese attitudes toward the use of force shifted after the devastation of the Pacific War and became institutionalized as the norm guiding strategic choice.[25] In fact, however, pacifists assumed an important role in postwar Japan's security policy discourse, but they never dominated it. To the contrary, the pacifists were indulged. They were used by mainstream conservatives to consolidate the idea that prosperity was more important than strength. But whereas the pacifists sought to use prosperity to achieve autonomy, the calculating (and governing) mercantile realists of the Yoshida school used it to achieve prestige. This is why cheap-riding realism rather than pacifist idealism dominated Japanese grand strategy during the cold war.

The Yoshida Doctrine, Japan's postwar national security strategy, has been challenged by the confluence of fundamental shifts in world order and the emergence of a new conservative mainstream. Once again, domestic and international politics were rattling against one another. As a result, Japan finds itself in a historically familiar interregnum between broad consensuses on national strategy. We can be confident that enduring values will continue to be embedded in the political debate, just as we can be confident that a new consensus will emerge that fits Japanese strategy to the new regional and global context. We should not be surprised that this process will generate new security options for Japan—or that these options will have been strategically constructed. Let us turn to the context and the choices as we try to imagine the contours of Japan's emerging security consensus.

JAPAN'S STRATEGIC CONTEXT

As we have seen, Japan perceives new threats. Rather than the prospect of Russian-speaking foreign troops landing on the archipelago, Japan now faces Chinese submarines and stateless pirates who disrupt shipping. Global and regional competition with China for access to energy resources threatens to ignite territorial disputes and slow down economic growth. Rather than the prospect of North Korean guerrillas and kidnappers, Japan now faces the prospect of nuclear-armed North Korean missiles. Nor is the China threat as one dimensional as the Soviet one was. Some Japanese feel as threatened by the nation's growing dependence on Chinese industrial development as by the prospect of economic decline in the United States. Long accustomed to defending itself against charges of industrial espionage and technological theft, Tokyo now levels those charges at Beijing and works with its firms to protect intellectual property. Despite pressures for globalization, Japanese firms have made strategic decisions to keep their most advanced capabilities at home. Japan now is bandwagoning with the United States not to balance against Soviet expansion but to balance against Chinese coercion, which perforce requires a different security posture. Indeed, for all the continuity, there have also been a great many changes.

This is true of even the most significant element of Japan's strategic context and the greatest threat of all: its alliance with the United States. Here, too, the context has changed radically. The U.S. effort to cork the Japanese military bottle was abandoned long ago, of course. But Washington's exhortations to Tokyo to expand its security footprint have never been so strident or grandiose. The DoD promises to maintain its defense of Japan, but it now openly expects Japan to cooperate in contingencies far from the homeland. It is Washington's "clear intent" to use its Japanese bases and the alliance as instruments in its global security strategy.[26] Indeed, it expects Japan to underwrite the costs to a much greater extent than ever.[27] As a result, the raison d'être of the alliance has already been transformed. What was once a highly asymmetric arrangement, in which the United States was pledged to defend Japan but received no reciprocal commitment, is now one in which Japan has pledged lucre (but not yet blood) to support the U.S. global strategy. Japanese leaders have long referred to the archipelago as "America's unsinkable aircraft carrier," but the shared ambitions for this expeditionary platform are bolder than ever now that Japan's revisionist leaders have signed on to a global partnership.

Some have embraced this state of affairs as an opportunity. Former diplomat and defense analyst Morimoto Satoshi, for example, argues that Japan should go so far as to establish forward bases in *U.S.* territory.[28] By the early 2000s, "globalization" of the alliance had become the stock characterization of its next step. U.S. officials painted a vision for the alliance that would be "more equal, more integrated, and more normal," and Japanese leaders embraced it.[29] The tacit division of labor, in which the United States was the sword and Japan the shield, was changing, and now Japan would patrol the sea-lanes out to the Arabian Gulf and supply U.S. forces wherever they deploy in major combat operations around the world. Critics and advocates alike have suggested that the globalization of the Japan-U.S. alliance will be the core of the post-Yoshida consensus.[30]

Yet beneath the veneer of Japan's close embrace of the United States, which former prime minister Koizumi insisted is Japan's "indispensable ally," divergences have become visible. As in all alliances, Tokyo and Washington disagree. Paradoxically, however, the areas of disagreement have become more salient as the two nations' embrace has become tighter. Some seem less consequential than others. Japan compounded its inadequate response to U.S. demands in the 1991 Gulf War, for example, by taking the lead in the Cambodian peace process against the wishes of Washington. But on balance, Washington welcomed the doctrinal shift that enabled the overseas dispatch of Japanese troops. Koizumi's initiatives with North Korea proceeded in 2002 with limited prior consultation, but Tokyo contributed significantly to the six-party talks, and there was little danger that his freelance diplomacy would do any damage. Indeed, by the time North Korea test fired its missiles in July 2006, the United States and Japan were back on the same page. They grew even closer after the DPRK nuclear test in October. Still, Tokyo's overtures to Myanmar have frustrated U.S. efforts to isolate that authoritarian regime, and Japan signed international protocols that the United States had shunned; neither caused alarm for alliance managers. But Japan's plans to develop Iran's Azadegan oil field despite Tehran's open nuclear ambitions, and its willingness to build an East Asian economic community that excludes the United States, have raised eyebrows in Washington. So has open discussion in the Japanese security community that speaks hopefully of "limits [to] the U.S.-led order" and a check on U.S. unilateralism.[31] These more fundamental divergences combine with Tokyo's preferences for autonomy and prestige in ways that may threaten the currently close relationship.

Given the steady drumbeat of insistence on the globalization of the alliance, we have to remind ourselves that abandonment has never disappeared as an option for either side. Indeed, some argue that the United States has reasons to care less about Japan today than ever. Although Washington welcomes Japanese contributions to U.S. policing along the "arc of instability" from East Asia to the Middle East, and although advocates insist that Japanese bases are the "heart," the "key," the "cornerstone," the "anchor," and the "foundation" of the relationship, some in the Pentagon are unconvinced that large forward bases remain the most effective means to win the "war on terror" or to police stability along trade routes.[32] For one thing, technological change has made offshore balancing more attractive. U.S. Navy doctrine now calls for a "sea strike" to project power, a "sea shield" to extend defense far from U.S. shores, and "sea basing" to project U.S. sovereignty deep into international waters. Former Chief of Naval Operations Vernon

Clark explains: "The independence of naval vessels operating on the high seas allows us to conduct combat operations anywhere, anytime, without having to first ask for permission."[33] This doctrine, and the capabilities on which it is based, degrade the relative value of large U.S. bases in Japan. Indeed, the Pentagon has recognized that such high-value targets are highly vulnerable.[34] So although U.S. bases in Japan have been identified as strategic "hubs" rather than tactical "lily pads," it is not at all clear that this logic will prevail. As the bases become less significant, the United States is likely to ask Japan to add value in different ways—ways in which it may be loathe to contribute. Once this split becomes clear, the United States will begin to recalculate its guarantee of Japan's defense, which will force Japan to reconsider whether to pursue a security policy premised on U.S. protection.[35] It ought to concern Japanese strategists that less than half the U.S. elites surveyed by the Japanese Ministry of Foreign Affairs in 2005 named Japan as America's most important partner in Asia.[36] Nor should they ignore the 2004 survey in which 40 percent of U.S. elites expressed opposition to the long-term stationing of U.S. forces in Japan.[37]

Some in the Pentagon also seem to be responding to the suggestion that alliances, too, may have seen their day. Flexible "coalitions of the willing"— loosely integrated networks of overlapping partnerships—may yet prove more effective than top-heavy and diplomatically expensive formal alliances. This sort of open security architecture, in which webs replace hubs and spokes, threatens to raise the costs Japan bears for the provision of its own security. Limited abandonment also promises to reduce the chance of entanglement for both sides. For the United States, it reduces (albeit slightly) the risk that it might be dragged into a dispute between Japan and China over territory or seabed resources. For Japan, it increases the legitimacy of opting out of U.S. missions that it deems are not in its national interest. The United States and Japan may remain tied diplomatically, economically, ideologically, as well as by many common strategic interests, but the formal alliance could become less constricting. Setting aside the jingoism and hype, all we can say with certainty about the future of the alliance is that it will be more fluid over the next two decades than at any time in its existence, and that its future will continue to be guided by strategic choices made in Tokyo as well as in Washington.

JAPAN'S STRATEGIC CHOICES

Given these changes in the strategic context and the challenge they represent for Japan, what should we expect Japan to do? Japan has four nominal choices consistent with its enduring values. It can achieve prestige by increasing national strength. This, of course, is the path Japan is already embarked on. It is the first choice of Japan's *normal nation-alists*, especially of the revisionists among them who would bulk up what is already the most modern indigenous military in the Far East. They openly seek to equalize the alliance in order to build an even better military shield. This raises the danger of entrapment for Japan, but is a risk these revisionists have already accepted. If their preferences prevail, Japan's post–Yoshida Doctrine consensus would be forged out of the "globalization of the alliance," a path first articulated by Prime Minister Koizumi when he visited President Bush at Crawford, Texas, in May 2003 and reaffirmed in the 2004 Araki Commission Report and National Defense Program Guidelines.[38] Prime Minister Koizumi made this position even more vigorously on the floor of the Diet by invoking the once taboo term for "alliance" and proclaiming it already global (*sekai no naka no nichibei dōmei*).[39] Over time, the "unsinkable aircraft carrier" will be configured to launch Japanese war fighters alongside U.S. ones. Joint military operations far afield, formal commitments to policing sea-lanes out to the Arabian Sea, collective self-defense, and the joint use of force would each be fully legitimate. Japan would acquire even more modern military capabilities, many of them interoperable with U.S. systems. As a JDA think tank report explains, Japanese planners are considering "how Japan's defense forces should be put to use, not only in the protection of Japan's peace and independence, but also in the sphere of global security," adding that "it is in this context that the Japan-U.S. alliance must be reviewed."[40] In October 2006, after Abe had become prime minister, JDA director general Kyūma Fumio argued in the Diet that it was difficult to distinguish "collective" from "individual" self-defense, and that the Japanese military could use force to repel an attack on U.S. vessels while they were being refueled by Japanese tankers at sea.[41] Japan would cease pretending to follow the Yoshida script.

A second possibility is to achieve autonomy by increasing national strength, the preferred path of Japan's *neoautonomists*. They, too, would build a better military shield, but theirs would be nuclear and operationally independent of the United States. In addition to a credible, independent nuclear deterrent, Japan would acquire a full-spectrum military configured not merely to support U.S. forces or to defend against terrorists and missile attacks but to "reach out and touch" adversaries. Armed with an improved shield and a sharpened sword, Japan would seek to maintain a military advantage over peer competitors. The neoautonomists would shift Japanese doctrine from a tethered, defensive realism to an untethered, offensive realism, in which strategists would be ever alert to exploit opportunities to expand Japan's power.[42] Japan, which has been *ab*normal, would then truly be "normal." It would join the other great powers in a permanent struggle to maximize national strength and influence, and it would not be averse to revising the status quo in the process. Such a program will certainly generate pressure for the elimination of U.S. bases in Japan and will enhance the prospect of abandonment by Washington. It will also accelerate the security dilemma already under way in Northeast Asia.

A third choice, the one preferred by the *middle power internationalists*, is to achieve prestige by increasing prosperity and reducing Japan's exposure in world politics. This requires turning back the clock and reversing some of the more audacious assaults on the Yoshida Doctrine. Japan would once again eschew the military shield in favor of the mercantile sword. It would bulk up Japan's considerable soft power in a concerted effort to knit East Asia together without generating new threats or becoming vulnerable. The Asianists in this group would aggressively embrace regional economic institutions to reduce Japan's reliance on the U.S. market. They would not abrogate the military alliance, but they would resist U.S. exhortations for Japan to expand its roles and missions. The mercantile realists in this group would support the establishment of more open regional economic institutions as a means to reduce the likelihood of abandonment by the United States, and they would seek to maintain America's protective embrace as cheaply and for as long as possible.

The final, least likely, choice is to achieve autonomy through prosperity. This is the choice of the *pacifists*, many of whom today are active in civil society through NGOs that are not affiliated with traditional political parties. Like the mercantile realists, they would reduce Japan's military posture—possibly even eliminate it. But unlike the mercantile realists, they reject the alliance as dangerously entangling. They would eschew hard power for soft power and campaign to establish Northeast Asia as a nuclear-free zone, expand the "defensive defense" concept to the region as a whole, negotiate a regionwide missile control regime, and rely on the ASEAN Regional Forum for security.[43] Their manifest problem is that the Japanese public is unmoved by these prescriptions. Antiwar rallies no longer attract large numbers and political parties that oppose a robust defense no longer attract many voters. Pacifist ideas about prosperity and autonomy seem relics of an earlier, more idealistic time when Japan could not imagine, much less openly plan for, military contingencies.

JAPAN'S STRATEGIC CONSTRAINTS

Each of these four different choices is consistent with Japan's national values and strategic culture as they have developed during the past century and a half. It is possible that one will prevail, but none alone seems fully plausible as the basis for a post-Yoshida consensus. One reason is that the Yoshida Doctrine has been institutionalized in ways that make sharp discontinuity less likely than continued, incremental change.

Budgeting may be the best example. As we have seen, Japan's postwar defense posture was determined by a fiscal logic as well as by a strategic one. Yoshida's cheap-riding realism required low military budgets and sustained resistance to the demands of both the United States and an ambitious domestic defense industry. Despite decades of salami slicing that expanded roles and missions, cheap-riding realism remains a stubborn fact of life. After 1976, when the first NDPO was issued—and even after 1995, when the alliance was reaffirmed in the second NDPO and Japan committed to a greater role—the numbers of Japanese ground troops, surface ships, and fighters were all reduced.[44] In 2004, defense spending was 6 percent of the general account budget, lower than the 8.2 percent level of 1965.[45] MOF budget officers refused JDA requests for manpower increases and required each service branch to submit a list of "cold war–oriented" equipment to be eliminated.[46] Likewise, the 2004 National Defense Program Guidelines (NDPG) calls for a 12 percent reduction in MSDF ships and planes, even though the MSDF is now patrolling six thousand nautical miles out and the government has committed to missile defense and antipiracy roles.[47] The decision to bulk up and further militarize Japan's off-budget coast guard only partly reconciles the mismatch between the government's stated goals and its willingness to pay for their realization. Nor will a separate budget to subsidize the realignment with U.S. forces, as preferred by the MOD, bring Japanese defense spending up to "normal" levels, especially if, as expected, Japan continues to reduce host nation support.[48] "Deteriorating fiscal conditions" are repeatedly mentioned in the 2004 NDPG, which insists that Japan can build a "state of the art" military "without expanding its size," and that it has to do so "with the limited resources that are available."[49] Future salami slices may push Japan over the edge of its tacit 1 percent of GDP cap—which was, after all, supposed to be temporary and which has once been exceeded—but changes to date have not done so. To the contrary, defense budgets have not gone up or down by more than 0.5 percent since 1997, and they have been effectively flat since 1994, actually declining in nominal and real terms. Defense buildups that might otherwise have proceeded without restriction, and that seemed to have the approval of the Cabinet Office, have been effectively contained. In 2007, the defense budget was reduced for the fifth year in a row.[50] Barring a dramatic and unforeseen shift in the world order, Japan will continue to enjoy its cheap ride, something even the revisionists have not seemed eager to change.

While these normal nation-alists have been consolidating their power, there are several additional reasons why we should not expect the preferences of any single group to prevail for long. First, Japan is a robust democracy, and democracies tend to self-correct for policy excesses. Although much maligned by analysts and participants alike, the Japanese political process has never been more transparent and has never engaged the public more fully than it does today. In particular, there are two important criticisms of the democratic process that no longer seem apt. The first is that politicians have ceded civilian control of the military to bureaucrats with a resulting lack of democratic accountability. Although Prime Minister Yoshida designed the JDA to be dominated by bureaucrats from other ministries, politicians never ceded their authority. Councillors (*sanjikan*) seconded from other parts of Japan's elite civil service were always influential but never fully autonomous. Well before it became a full-fledged ministry in 2007, the MOD was a policy agency, having grown its own elite civil servants under the control of the LDP. Likewise, when politicians needed a congenial ruling from the Cabinet Legislation Bureau, they got one. When politicians needed to circumvent CLB interpretations, they did so. As former JDA director general Ishiba points out in his memoirs, civilian control works only when politicians understand military issues.[51] Today, elected representatives understand strategic issues better than at any time since the 1950s. Japanese voters, through their elected representatives, may not be more engaged in the minutiae of policy than, say, U.S. voters, but they certainly are no less so. They are not likely to reward their leaders for excessive tilts in one direction or another for long. And, as we have repeatedly seen, their leaders—even the revisionists in power today—have always been remarkably pragmatic.

The second criticism of Japanese democracy is that there has been no alternation in power and that therefore the security policy process has failed to express the preferences of large numbers of Japanese voters. We have seen that this, too, is a mistaken view of Japan's highly contested democratic polity. The internal dynamics of the LDP—pitting mainstream pragmatists against revisionist conservatives since the early 1950s—never abated. Instead, the former group reached out to find common cause with the pacifists in the 1950s and 1960s, and pragmatists and revisionists competed for (and alternated in) power along the way. After 2000, when Koizumi Junichirō became prime minister—and after he was succeeded in 2006 by Abe Shinzō—it seemed that the revisionists had finally consolidated power. And the transformations in Japanese security policy that they prosecuted were accompanied by shifts in popular opinion on such issues as the legitimacy of the SDF, its overseas deployment, and revision of the constitution itself. Even at that point, however, the LDP secretary general, Abe's handpicked aide—Nakagawa Hidenao—declared his intent to erase the strong conservative image of the Abe administration and be "more considerate to those on the left."[52] The LDP leadership knows as well as anyone that no group has a lock on the Japanese electorate. Democracy is functioning well in Japan.

Indeed, this suggests a further reason why we should not expect the security preferences of any single faction to prevail for long. Specifically, the normal nation-alists and the middle power internationalists—the two groups that have shared and alternated power for the past sixty years—are each divided. Among the normal nation-alists are globalists, such as Ozawa Ichirō, who believe that Japanese forces should be placed under UN auspices, as well as revisionists, such as Abe Shinzō, and realists, such as Watanabe Tsuneo, who would continue to embrace the United States as tightly as possible. Some are more likely to find common cause with middle power internationalists than with neoautonomists. Likewise, among the middle power internationalists, there are those like Koga Makoto and Tanigaki Sadakazu who would be inclined to reposition Japan closer to Asia than some of their mercantile realist brethren.[53] As if to make the point that these positions are fluid, the "pro-China dove" Tanigaki has shown flexibility on the security issue by supporting collective self-defense.[54] If, as we have seen over more than a century and a half, pragmatism remains a force for moderation in Japanese strategic thinking, then it is reasonable to expect Japanese policy to moderate itself and to adopt a less entangled posture. Even Prime Minister Abe seemed prepared to moderate his hard line by visiting Beijing and Seoul before visiting Washington, by endorsing official government apologies for wartime aggression, and even by acknowledging the war responsibility of his grandfather, Kishi Nobusuke, soon after taking office.[55] These moves had the immediate effect of unfreezing PRC-Japan defense consultations, launching a long-stalled bilateral history commission, and making it possible for the China-Japan-Korea "plus 3" group to meet for the first time in two years.[56]

Of course, any formation of a post-Yoshida consensus will depend on strategists' perceptions of the regional and world order. In this regard, three related developments will be prominent. The first is the relative decline of the United States. Although the United States will undoubtedly remain the world's preeminent military power for decades more—and possibly longer—Tokyo sees its diplomatic vigor, moral authority, and economic allure as already waning, particularly in Asia.[57] It has not gone unnoticed that by the mid-2000s, Washington had ceded leadership of the six-party talks to Beijing. Nor did Japanese analysts fail to observe that Washington needed (but could not coerce) cooperation from China and Russia to pressure Iran to abandon its nuclear program. It was further a matter of discussion that the United States was unable to conclude even a regional free trade agreement with Latin America, and that it had exhausted its moral authority in its ill-conceived intervention in Iraq. A more widespread Japanese perception that the comprehensive power of the United States is in decline will likely engender reconsideration of the risks of entanglement. The second is the rise of a China with considerable soft power resources and economic opportunities that may come to rival those the United States can offer. Beijing's attractiveness could blunt the hard edge of military realism. The extent to which China displaces the United States as a target for investment and a market for goods and services will be reflected in the extent to which the China threat gives way to a China opportunity. Although the majority of those surveyed by the *Yomiuri Shimbun* in December 2003 thought the United States was Japan's most important political partner, an equal number (53%) believed that China was Japan's most important economic partner.[58]

Finally, any overt sign of Japanese ambitions for great power status and a full security autonomy is bound to stimulate balancing behavior by Japan's neighbors and, undoubtedly, opposition from the United States as well. Japan suffers from what Ohtomo Takafumi has aptly identified as the "sheep in wolf's clothing" problem. As he notes, it takes a very long time of good behavior to overcome the distrust of other states, and Japan has not gone nearly far enough to merit the trust of its neighbors. It still has a bad reputation in East Asia.[59] Although the Chinese and the Koreans have reached agreement on the language of history textbooks, Japan and its neighbors have found it impossible to agree on a common narrative about the Pacific War. Japan's unwillingness or inability to confront its history is undoubtedly the largest single constraint on its soft power.

These several elements in Japan's strategic context—institutional inertia, the dynamics of democratic competition, pragmatism, concern about the future of U.S. power, and shifting regional balances of power—converge to make Japan's strategic adjustment seem overdetermined. If not a straight path toward Japanese muscularity, then what? The evidence here suggests a "Goldilocks consensus"—one that positions Japan not too close and not too far from the hegemon-protector, that makes it stronger but not threatening, and that provides new and comprehensive security options.

JAPAN'S "STRATEGIC CONVERGENCE"

Hedging is a fundamental principle of any realist grand strategy, especially for midsized powers. As Ronald Reagan's famous dictum "trust but verify" indicates, ensuring against risk is hardly unique to Japan. Given the country's geopolitical location and late development, it is no surprise that hedging has long been an arrow in Tokyo's strategic quiver. Few prewar planners were prepared to pursue either cooperation with the West or autarky to the exclusion of the other.[60] In the postwar period, Japan's first order of business was to consolidate its alliance with the United States, and its second was to make that relationship as unprovocative as possible to the Soviet Union.[61] Despite explicit requirements to do so, for example, Tokyo invoked its ban on collective self-defense and refused to share information about Soviet practice bombing runs on U.S. bases in Japan during the cold war.[62] Since 1957, when the Ministry of Foreign Affairs issued its first postwar diplomatic blue book, every formal statement of Japanese grand strategy has articulated mutually inconsistent goals. The first blue book insisted that Japan's diplomacy would be UN-centered, regionally oriented, and based on its "membership in the free world"—all at the same time. Immediately after the 2000 Prime Minister's Commission on Japan's Goals opened with a call for Japan "to overcome the constraints of the postwar period and address security issues itself...[because] making the effort to deal with one's own security [is] the natural thing to do," it then defended the utility of the U.S. alliance and the importance of the United Nations. Without any hint of irony, it concluded that Japan "should not concentrate on one level to the exclusion of the others, but rather take a balanced approach."[63] The most recent doctrinal elaboration of this position, the Araki Commission Report of 2004, similarly stipulated that Japan should pursue self-help, alliance cooperation, and international citizenship, simultaneously.[64] Every formal security document is filled with rocks and hard places, and none fails to genuflect in each of several consistently inconsistent directions.

The United States has been both the largest rock and the hardest place. Fears of entrapment and of abandonment have propelled Japan into a perpetual "hedging cycle" vis-à-vis its alliance partner. Tokyo's fear of entrapment has occasionally led it to take steps in effect to balance against the United States, a move that invariably increased its fears of abandonment and which, in turn, led it to bandwagon with U.S. power.[65] The only way to stop this cycle has been to hedge. As Natsume Haruo, a former JDA Defense Policy Bureau chief, explained, Japan's defense plans "are formed on the assumption and premise of U.S. support and assistance, but it would have been unrealistic to rely completely on the fact that the United States would come to Japan's aid."[66] Kawashima Yutaka, a former diplomat, wonders aloud if it was ever a truly safe assumption that the United States would forever see its military presence in Asia as a vital national interest, and he notes that Japan was always ready to review its options in the event of U.S. abandonment.[67] It is no secret, then, that Japan has retained some degree of "strategic independence." Hedging has been unavoidable.[68]

Ironically, the Japanese language has no indigenous word that captures the concept of hedging, despite its centrality to Japan's strategic discourse. Apart from the borrowed term *hejju*, the closest approximation is found in the testimony to the Diet by one of Japan's leading security policy intellectuals, Tokyo University professor Tanaka Akihiko. Japan, he says, needs "a strategy to prevent the worst (*saiaku*) while trying to construct the best (*saizen*)." As Tanaka explains it, "preventing the worst" requires a strong alliance with the United States and a Japan that plays a more active role in international security affairs. Meanwhile, an East Asian community that resembles the stable, prosperous, economically integrated Western Europe—and built on Japanese commitment to the values of democracy and freedom—would, in his view, go a long way toward "constructing the best."[69]

To demonstrate that these need not be mutually inconsistent, Tanaka offers the U.S. relationship to NATO (in) and to the EU (out) as a model for a possible East Asian future.[70] He knows that this will require considerable diplomatic skill and a level of institution building that has thus far exceeded the region's grasp—and he realizes that the analogy is imperfect—but he and others urge Japan to use this model to both sharpen its mercantile sword and polish its military shield.

This particular framing of the balance between security hedge and economic optimization strikes at a defining characteristic of Japan's grand strategy—the analytic separation of military and mercantile components—under the aegis of "comprehensive security."[71] Japan not only hedges against U.S. abandonment by courting entrapment, it simultaneously hedges against predation by courting protectionism. There have been many manifestations of this dual hedge, including the formal recommendation by the 2000 Prime Minister's Commission on Japan's Goals that Japan "build creative relationships with Asia while continuing to use the Japan-U.S. relationship as an invaluable asset."[72] But the most ambitious concrete proposal is suggested by the analog of the U.S. relationship with western Europe. Scholars such as Professor Tanaka (and Soeya Yoshihide, whose "middle power" theory we explored earlier) who believe that a U.S.-led security community can co-exist with an Asian-led economic community are clear about the advantages for Japanese security that would accrue from such a parallel construction in Asia. Japan could balance against U.S. and European economic power while simultaneously balancing against Chinese military power.

This suggests two ways for Japan to escape the "hedging cycle." The first is to indulge the Americans by building a bigger military shield. As we have seen, this is the preference of the normal nation-alists who look to transform the alliance to reempower Japan. They would continue with their salami slicing as opportunities present themselves, and they would likely do so in ways consistent with the two enduring values of autonomy and prestige. There remains more to be done before the Yoshida Doctrine is entirely abandoned. To maximize autonomy, for example, Japan would acquire more offensive weapons, allow its defense firms to participate in international development of weapons systems, lift the cap on defense spending, enlarge Japan's defense perimeter to include patrols of the Persian Gulf, and abandon the doctrine of defensive defense by formally embracing collective self-defense. To enhance national prestige, Tokyo could change the name of the Self-Defense Forces (now called *jieitai*) to the Self-Defense Military (*jiei-gun*) and establish battlefield legitimacy by placing troops in harm's way. The second is to alleviate the concerns of its neighbors by honing a sharper mercantile sword and playing a more active regional role in environmental protection, antipiracy initiatives, disease control, and cultural diplomacy. This is consistent with the preference of the middle power internationalists, who place as much faith in regional economic development as in military deterrence. Japan could use regional and bilateral preferential trade agreements to hedge against U.S. and European predation, as well as to hedge against the possibility of Chinese economic dominance and to enhance its smooth integration.

Elements of this dual hedge were central features of the Yoshida Doctrine from the very beginning. Japanese-Chinese trade never disappeared during the Korean War, when U.S. forces were fighting Chinese troops on the peninsula and stimulating the Japanese economy with procurements. Tokyo and Beijing even signed a "private" trade agreement in 1952, immediately after the armistice. As Akira Iriye notes: "China was an important market and [Japanese leaders] had no intention of giving it up just because they placed their country in the U.S. camp in the Cold War."[73] Japan indulged China throughout the cold war, seeking to integrate it as smoothly as possible into the world trading system without alienating the United States. Tokyo provided considerable development assistance, even though its own rules prohibited aid to states that produce weapons of mass destruction.[74] In fact, Japan was faster than any other county to repair relations with China after the Tiananmen incident in 1989. Within little more than three months, a group from Keidanren was in Beijing exploring ways to enhance economic ties. By 2003, it has been reported, the economic dimension of the China threat was no longer a struggle between China and Japan for leadership of Asia, but one between the United States and Europe on the one hand and Japan on the other over who gets access to the China market.[75] Even Abe Shinzō calls for a "separation of politics and economics" (*seikei bunri no gensoku*) to stabilize Sino-Japanese relations.[76]

A fully institutionalized East Asian community combined with a globalized U.S.-Japan alliance—what the MOD's National Institute for Defense Studies has called "strategic convergence"[77]—would constitute a considerably more robust security arrangement for Japan than the Yoshida Doctrine could provide. Japan could help create prosperity in China while relying on the United States to help check the Chinese military. It could build prosperity without undermining security. It could have its pacifist cake and eat it too. But why would the United States continue to guarantee Japanese security if it is kept at arm's length from the economic dynamism of the region? The challenge for Japanese diplomats and strategists is to make "strategic convergence" acceptable to the United States and attractive to China. There are no guarantees, and hedging is always fraught with danger. But the hope is that the United States will respond positively as long as the new economic architecture is built on a liberal vision. Universal principles of human rights and democracy will have to be showcased, "Asian values" suppressed. The regional identity that such an arrangement would generate will have to be flexible and accessible rather than rigid or exclusive.

[201]

Such are the dreams of some strategic thinkers in Tokyo. But before such a "strategic convergence" can even be tested, Japanese strategists have to repair their relationships with Korea and China. Revisionists have stumbled on the history and textbook issues, exacerbating mistrust and undermining prospects for an effective East Asian community in the near term. This mistrust has been evident in military confrontations. South Korean president Roh Moo-hyun dispatched warships to the disputed Takeshima/Tokdo Islands in April 2006 to chase away Japan Coast Guard vessels sent to undertake geological surveys in the neighboring waters, an act Roh proclaimed was "an attempt to justify Japan's history of aggression."[78] Japan will have to rebalance its recently acquired hard power resources with renewed attention to its soft power attractions in the region. The newly established Office of Public Diplomacy in the foreign ministry has been hard at work to craft Japan's attractions, in part by appealing to neighbors as a non-Western success story.[79] Ambassador Kitaoka Shinichi, Japan's former deputy permanent representative to the United Nations, recently described Japan's attraction to the rest of Asia as being a bridge between East and West. In his view—and it is an influential one—the core of Japan's identity and attraction derives from its independence. Japan sits *outside* Western civilization and has never been overwhelmed by Western culture. This, he says, is "the most important message Japan can send to other cultures."[80]

Long before any of Japan's neighbors will be inclined to respond positively to this message, Japan's dual hedge has an even more urgent test. In Iran two of Japan's most vital national interests, energy security and nonproliferation, collide. The Japanese government had been determined to avoid a decision one way or another, either for Iranian oil (and against proliferation concerns) or for western Europe and the United States (and against the source of 15% of Japan's oil imports). Even the most senior officials of the Japanese government seemed ambivalent. As Senior Vice Minister for Foreign Affairs Shiozaki Yasuhisa has insisted: "We are trying to do both. We will stick to our own way to impose sanctions *if we have to,* and we will stick to our national interest, energy security."[81] This position seemed undermined by Foreign Minister Asō's declaration in August 2006 that Japan would join the international community and sanction Iran, even if the Azadegan deal were taken "hostage."[82] But failure to find a solution consistent with its long-term national interests threatens Tokyo with the loss of *both* prestige *and* autonomy, and undermines the prospects for any "strategic convergence."

It is more likely, though, that each corner of the Japanese security discourse will be represented in the new consensus. Representatives of each group have crossed into other's domains in order to consolidate power. Within the LDP, normal nation-alists and middle power internationalists have coexisted for decades.[83] This is the most likely crossover, but there are others.

During Diet interpellations in January 2006, for example, Prime Minister Koizumi affirmed pacifism as "the basic philosophy of our constitution [that] we must firmly maintain in the future as well."[84] Meanwhile, when he was deputy chief cabinet Secretary in 2003, Abe Shinzō insisted that "while it is vital to maintain a relationship of trust with the United States, maintaining trust and being at its beck and call are two different things." If the alliance were more equal, Japan would be better positioned to "speak out" more vigorously to the United States.[85] In fact, in early 2007 Prime Minister Abe visited the major nations of the European community "to add a new diplomatic axis" and to shift from [Japan's] U.S.-centered policies."[86] Here we have Japan's leading revisionist genuflecting toward pacifist values and his successor genuflecting toward autonomy, evidence that the final shape of Japan's new security consensus is still up for grabs.

Meanwhile, even some of the most enthusiastic supporters of the alliance insist that Japan must leave room for independent action on matters of vital national interest, such as access to Middle Eastern oil.[87] Not surprisingly, the Japanese government has retained "opt out" clauses in its tilt toward globalizing the alliance. Missions have been authorized through temporary "special measures" laws with sunset clauses, its forces were dispatched to noncombat zones, and, as Christopher Hughes insists, "if Japan does not deem there to be a sufficient situational need in a regional contingency, then it can define this as outside the scope of the [alliance] guidelines and exercise the option not to support the United States."[88] Its willingness to jointly develop and deploy missile defense and to move toward an integrated command-and-control structure with U.S. forces make it clear that Japan has lost some of its fear of entrapment. But it has not abandoned pragmatism altogether. Its close hug of the United States is not debilitating but, rather, is generating options for national security that may render Japan stronger and more independent. Just as the end of the cold war and the subsequent reconfiguration of the U.S. alliance created space for a realignment of Japanese domestic politics, so they also have created new possibilities for security strategy.[89] The former chair of the LDP's Policy Committee on Foreign Affairs, Yamamoto Ichita, acknowledges:

> We are always worried about entanglement and hedge the risk…. Having U.S. bases on Japanese territory is necessary. But if we can amend the alliance, we can accept the U.S. presence as a policy, not as an obligation. The alliance should be our policy decision, so that if we decide not to have bases, we can just ask the United States to leave…. Shifting from obligation to policy is a way to create options for Japan later on.[90]

These new options normally are couched in terms of the additional muscle Japan must provide for the United States. But there are many other ways to think about the future. If Tokyo is diplomatically competent, its newly acquired strength and confidence could make it more attractive to other potential security partners in the region, such as India and the ASEAN states.[91] Ishiba Shigeru has made this point by deftly shifting the conventional argument for collective self-defense. In addition to making Japan a more attractive partner for the United States, he insists, collective self-defense will also enable Japan to assist ASEAN states if they are threatened by China.[92] In his view—and in the view of other realists—a stronger Japan will create new possibilities for regional security.[93] Retired admiral Yamazaki Makoto concurs, arguing that "it will be necessary for Japan to build a defense capability that can provide regional stability as well as protect the national interest against the various threats along the 'arc of instability'" if Japan is to become a "responsible nation."[94] First, of course, Tokyo will need to reassure its neighbors and avoid isolation, which is why a continued tether to the United States makes sense. Some have even suggested that by enhancing its role in the alliance, Japan could become the cork in the *American* bottle.[95]

These shifts await a skilled consensus builder, someone who will see new possibilities for Japanese security and can soften the harder edges of the contemporary discourse by recombining values and options. Such leaders reside in each corner of Japan's strategic discourse. On becoming head of the Democratic Party of Japan in early 2006, Ozawa Ichirō, the godfather of normal nation-alism, lost no time in criticizing Prime Minister Koizumi for visiting Yasukuni Shrine and for tilting too far in favor of the United States. Sounding like Goldilocks herself trying to get things just right, Ozawa insisted that Japan needs to mend its relationships with Asia and that it must distance itself from the "hegemonic tendencies" of both China and the United States.[96] Abe, for his part, could begin to deemphasize Japan's military power and stress Japan's soft power advantages over China, including its democratic political system and its protection of human rights and political liberty.[97] And, indeed, in the same week he visited Europe to stake out his independence from the United States, he joined Chinese Premier Wen Jiabao and ROK president Roh Moo-Hyun for the first trilateral "Plus-3" summit in two years. Even neoautonomists such as Nakanishi Terumasa have voiced limited support for the U.S.-Japan alliance, and Terashima Jitsurō has written about "how to be pro-American and part of Asia at the same time."[98] Mercantile realists who already argue for improved ties with China would have to accede to the idea that a stronger Japan is here to stay. But, if the 2001 conversion of their mentor, Miyazawa Kiichi, is any indication, this journey should not be too far to travel. Moreover, once-confirmed pacifists such as Kan Naoto have already migrated to a more central position.

Although we cannot identify with certainty the Japanese leaders with whom the new security consensus will be identified, we can expect them to be conservative and to be committed democrats with independent, full-throated voices on security issues. They will not lead Japan too far toward great power status and abandonment nor allow it to remain so dependent on the United States as to risk further entanglement. They will abandon cheap-riding realism and consolidate the military gains of the revisionists' tight embrace of the United States, but they will not allow that embrace to drag Japan into undesirable territory. In short, they will appreciate that the costs of remaining a U.S. ally—still Japan's most attractive option—are escalating but will not allow them to become too great to bear. Rather than expect Japan's continued migration from the status quo as a junior partner or "poodle" toward greater symmetry (including joint war fighting and "joint management of American hegemony"), we should instead expect the new security discourse to resolve itself in the form of a fuller maturation of Japan's dual hedge.[99]

IMPLICATIONS FOR U.S. POLICY

Washington understands that Tokyo will work hard to reconcile its Asian diplomacy and economic interests with its global diplomacy and military interests. It knows that its friends in Japan's military establishment are doing rhetorical battle with those in the economic establishment who are less convinced of the value of the "globalized" alliance. Thus, recent agreements on "alliance transformation" notwithstanding, it is by no means a foregone conclusion that either Japan or the United States will continue to see an enhanced, militarized alliance as its best choice. Having examined Japanese strategic options, then, it is useful to glance at those of the United States as well.

Ever since Alfred Thayer Mahan elaborated his maritime strategy for the United States, U.S. strategists have sought to establish Pacific outposts to secure American commerce and to balance against a rising hegemon in the region.[100] In so doing, the United States found itself in successive Pacific wars—the first with Japan in the 1940s, then with China on the Korean Peninsula in the 1950s, and finally with Vietnam in the 1960s and 1970s. Since then, though, only after construction of a series of "hub and spoke" alliances through which the United States could ensure that its relationship with each of the region's powers was more robust than any of the relationships among them, the regional balance has been stable. Indeed, the region has prospered, the United States along with it. Now, however, China is poised to become a peer, and its rise would ensure a relative decline of U.S. power that could destabilize the region.[101] It is of vital importance to the United States that China become a great power without alarming Japan and its other neighbors.

Not everyone appreciates this necessity, however. Some in Washington believe that an alarmed Japan is an allied Japan. They have used the yearnings of Japan's revisionists to divide East Asia and to position Japan in balancing against China's rise. They warn that China will try to drive a wedge between Japan and the United States.[102] When Japan suggested that China be included in the Proliferation Security Initiative, the U.S. vetoed the idea.[103] The Bush administration refused to intervene in the controversies over Japanese historical revisionism or prime ministerial visits to the Yasukuni Shrine, insisting that Beijing not be allowed to see any "daylight" between Washington and Tokyo.[104] Even as they assemble ad hoc "coalitions of the willing," U.S. officials insist that bilateral alliances must remain the backbone of security in the region, and point to the success of the 2+2 realignment process and the bilateral embrace of "common strategic interests" (described in chapter 6) as evidence that Japan agrees.[105]

But many in Japan do not. Some see this as divide and conquer, and urge the government not to collude with a suboptimal strategy. A Sino-Japanese rapprochement may be Washington's nightmare, they say, but it would be of incalculable benefit to both sides, to the region as a whole, and even to the United States.[106] Many Americans also believe this. Some welcome stable Sino-Japanese relations for their own sake, as a means toward the deep reconciliation that has eluded the region since the Pacific War. Others, worried that Sino-Japanese tensions could reverse the possibility of entrapment, urge Tokyo and Beijing to reduce the temperature in their overheating relationship.[107] In this view, the United States needs to avoid getting entangled in Japan's conflicts (Senkaku Islands, Yasukuni, textbooks) just as much as Japan needs to avoid being entrapped in American ones. If Japan strays from a pragmatic path, it risks losing the support of the United States.

Indeed, as I have suggested in some detail earlier in this book, the United States may decide—independent of Japanese hedging and despite its geostrategic attractions—that the formal alliance is too great a burden for too limited a gain. Should it replace the alliance with a less constraining alignment, Japan and other regional actors will have to increase their level of self-help.[108] Such an outcome would place Japan in dangerous new territory, requiring greater diplomatic skills than it has displayed to date. A journalist who later became a spokesman for the Ministry of Foreign Affairs, musing openly about the possibility that U.S. security guarantees may expire, framed this in the language of Japan's hedging policy:

Tokyo has been able since the end of World War II to purchase its marine insurance policy solely from the United States. It has continued to pay the premium by hosting U.S. forces.... However, in the event that Taiwan falls to

China, Japan and Korea will find themselves buying insurance policies from Beijing."[109]

But it seems far more likely that Japan will choose to self-insure.

When it does, and even before it does, the construction of a new multi-lateral security regime may prove to be the most effective option for the United States. One template for this new architecture, acknowledged by former deputy secretary of state Robert Zoellick, would be to use the six-party talks on the future of the Korean Peninsula as a "springboard" for a Northeast Asia security talk shop that might mirror the Asian Regional Forum in Southeast Asia.[110] The advantages of multilateralism in the con-text of Chinese-Japanese competition for leadership are manifold. First, it would provide a broader and more stable infrastructure than the patron-client hierarchies that characterize the current hubs and spokes. The possi-bilities for transparency—a requirement for averting a debilitating regional security dilemma—would be multiplied, albeit not guaranteed. Second, as in Europe, where multilateralism has had a longer and more stable run, it would give Japan and the other states in the region a larger stake in the con-struction of their own future, a development that surely would enhance the standing of the United States in the region as well. Third, it would reduce the considerable costs to Washington of supplying the regional public good of security. Should Washington elect to become the engaged, albeit distant, balancer on the European model, it would be more likely to enjoy the bene-fits of regional economic prosperity while avoiding excessive entanglement at a time when its power is in relative decline.[111]

We have seen how more than a century of changes in international politics have affected domestic political discourse. The mainstream shifted repeatedly, as strategies came and went. Over the course of the past century, two consensuses about national security, the first militarist and the second pacifist, were established. Each was built by shaving the sharp edges of ideological division to accommodate a coherent national strategy. In the process, the mainstream shifted course; once-marginal views were embraced, and broadly shared values splintered. Japanese grand strategy was buffeted by shifts in the domestic civil-military relationship from political leadership to military leadership in the 1930s, from military leadership to bureaucratic leadership in the 1950s, and from bureaucratic to political leadership today. The current discourse is often termed *mosaku* (groping or fumbling), for it is not the first time that a national consensus has been undone without a clear guide to the next stable solution. Deep divisions within the Japanese body politic of the past were reconciled temporarily, first under the banner of Prince Konoye's Greater East Asia Co-Prosperity Sphere, with disastrous consequences, and later under the banner of Prime Minister Yoshida Shigeru's Yoshida Doctrine. Today we are witness to an active debate about the value of the strategic doctrine that contributed so much to postwar Japanese prosperity and stability. The Yoshida Doctrine has not yet been replaced, but by making Japan more muscular and by incrementally eliminating many of the constraints on the use of force, revisionists have made sure that its contours are definitively changed.

Japan's junior partnership with the United States may be slipping into history. If so, the question is how a more muscular Japan will position itself. Will it be a fully entangled global partner, or a fully hedged independent power? The answer depends on too many factors to allow confident prediction. We can be confident, though, that it will depend on national identity, on whether Japan comes to see itself as a great or a middle power, and whether it will define its role in regional or in global terms. And it will depend on shifting balances of power, particularly between China and the United States. But above all, it will depend on the way Tokyo opts to balance its need to hedge against risk against its chance to optimize for gain.

As I have argued, much remains to be done before Japan can claim to have revamped its cold war posture on defense. The largest obstacle remains the self-imposed budget cap that limits defense spending to 1 percent of GDP. It has been compounded by Japan's fiscal difficulty, which has led to absolute *decreases* in defense budgets since the beginning of the "transformation." Moreover, collective self-defense is still not yet part of legal practice, even if it has become a de facto arrow in Japan's security quiver. Still, much more has changed than most analysts imagined possible even five years ago, including the elevation of the JDA to ministry status and legislation enabling the SDF to use force to protect itself and, perhaps, its peacekeeping partners. In the somewhat longer term, there will be the renaming of the SDF to include the term "military," and either formal reinterpretation or outright revision of the constitution to enable collective self-defense. The change in Japanese security policymaking has been auspicious for the U.S.-Japan alliance, for the development of a more muscular and autonomous Japan, and for regional and global security. Japan may never again be as *central* to world affairs as it was in the 1930s nor as *marginal* to world affairs as it was during the cold war. Once revisionism has run its course, however, and once accommodations are made in its economic diplomacy, Japan will have cleared for itself a policy space in which it can be selectively *pivotal* in world affairs. It will have created security options for itself.

The twin rewards of autonomy and prestige are within Japan's grasp for the first time in living memory. To reduce associated risks, Japan will be cautious. It will be normal. It will hedge. The security strategy and institutions abetting this hedge will be neither too hard nor too soft. Japan will be neither too close to China nor too far from the United States. A "Goldilocks consensus" will replace the Yoshida one. Kenneth Pyle argues that "Japan's future foreign policy will be very different from the grand strategy that Yoshida Shigeru pioneered. Its Cold War role as a merchant nation and the core domestic institutions associated with that role will then seem part of a distant past."[112] LDP representative Gotōda Masazumi insisted that this "elastic band" had been "stretched to the breaking point" in 2001.[113] But this may be too dismissive of the continuities we have identified on these pages. Perhaps, as Mike Mochizuki argues, we are seeing a "recalibration of policy within an existing strategy" rather than the adoption of a new one.[114] Soeya Yoshihide concurs, arguing that Japan is not replacing its pacifist national identity with a great power one and that the Yoshida consensus is being reformulated rather than abandoned. He predicts that a new consensus will "steadily come into focus over time."[115] The "strategic convergence" predicted here is more than a robust version of the Yoshida Doctrine and less than its wholesale replacement.

This debate will continue, as it should. The evidence I have advanced suggests that if the norms of the Yoshida Doctrine have not been violated, they certainly have been challenged, perhaps fatally. Japan has actively—albeit cautiously—created new options for itself. Whether one sees the Yoshida Doctrine as still robust or in tatters, a rubber band or an inflatable tube, it is clear that Japanese strategists have responded to profound changes in their strategic environment since the end of the cold war. It is even clearer that there is more change waiting in the wings. We await the appearance of Japan's Goldilocks, the pragmatic leader who will get it "just right."

Notes

Introduction: Understanding Japan's Grand Strategy

1. Ogata 1988, 99.
2. Okazaki 1986, 75–76, 129.
3. Ienaga 1978, chap. 3.
4. Kitaoka 1995a, 11–12.
5. Hosoya 1971, 92.
6. Watanabe 1996.
7. Tanaka 1997; Morimoto 2005, 80; Takahara 2004, 171.
8. Iriye (1997, 67) points out that this is much like what happened to the August 1936 "Fundamentals of National Policy." This policy statement failed to set priorities among diverse strategies, e.g., development of Manchuria, increased defense spending, removal of the Soviet threat in the north, preparation for war with the United States, etc. The result was an incompatible set of objectives and a cataclysmic misadventure. Rozman (2002) analyzes this dynamic in a contemporary context.
9. Okazaki 1986.
10. Honda et al. 2005, 156.
11. Prime Minister's Commission on Japan's Goals 2000, chap. 6, p. 4.
12. Jain and Inoguchi 1996, xv.
13. *Asahi Shimbun*, 23 April 2006.
14. *People's Daily*, 13 June 2006, and *Xinhua News*, 19 November 2004, represent the Chinese position. Similar concerns were echoed repeatedly in interviews in Seoul in December 2005. Park (2005) makes this point but does not share this view.
15. Calder (1988) calls Japan a "reactive state." Potter and Sudo (2003) disagree. Green (2001) draws a portrait of "reluctant realism." Mochizuki is an exception. He credits Japan with long having exercised strategic pragmatism (Mochizuki 1983–84, 2004). Also see Iklé and Nakanishi 1990 for a realist analysis of Japan's security policy choices.
16. Kōsaka 1996; Soeya 2005.
17. This strategy was propounded by Defense Agency official Kubo Takuya. See Michishita 2005a, 218–20, Sadō 2003, and Tokuchi 2001, 68.
18. See C. Hughes (2004b) for analysis of the 1975 National Defense Program Outline (NDPO).
19. Weinstein 1971, 128.
20. Hook 2001, 376.
21. Katahara 1996.
22. Heginbotham and Samuels 1998.
23. Despite considerable evidence that Japan was thinking strategically about its choices, Japanese planners are instructed not to attach the term "national security strategy" to their national strategy documents. One author of the 2004 National Defense

Program Guidelines explained that the term "strategy" was vetoed by political leadership. Interview, Cabinet Office official, 9 September 2005.

24. Fukuzawa quoted in Craig 1968, 129–30.

25. It was also invoked when Yamagata and his allies believed these relationships were no longer serving Japanese interests and should be abrogated. Iokibe 2000 and Iriye 1997. Foreign Minister Komura Jutarō was explicit about the advantages of alliance with Britain over Russia in 1902: Russia was aggressive, Britain status quo. There were trade advantages with the latter that did not match those with the former. Japan still needed support from the Europeans to push Russia out of Korea, and Japan's interests in China were expected to further expand. See Okazaki 1986, 47–48.

26. Samuels 2003. Joseph Nye makes this point eloquently in his work on soft power. See Nye 2004.

27. Goldstein 2005.

28. Katzenstein 1996, 204; emphasis added.

29. Pyle 2007, chap. 1.

30. Riddell 2003.

31. Jervis 1978; Christensen 1999.

32. See Lim (2003) for a geostrategic analysis of Japanese security policy. Mochizuki (2004) explores how Japan's strategic calculus evolved.

33. Pyle 2007, chap. 3.

34. Yoshida 1963, 203–4.

35. See his testimony before the 63rd Diet House of Representatives Budget Committee in February 1970: *Shūgiin Kaigiroku Jōhō*, 24 February 1970.

36. Kissinger 1973, 19. Another classic of modern history filled with analysis of hedging behavior is Carr 1945. Art (2004) characterizes post–cold war Europe as a complex hedging game.

37. Conybeare (1992a) applies finance theory of diversification to hedging and alliance behavior. For a general review of the history of risk, see Moss 2002, esp. chap. 2. Weitsman (2004) sees hedging as the strategy of choice when threats are relatively low. As threats increase, states find it more difficult to split their bets and are more likely to overtly balance or bandwagon. Prospect theory is another literature that utilizes risk as an organizing concept. See Levy 1997 and Levy 2000.

38. This is a brief sketch of the differences between "defensive" and "offensive" realists. For an example of the former, see Levy 1997. Twomey (2000) applies defensive realism to the case of Japan. Mearsheimer (2001) is a widely cited example of offensive realism.

39. Moravcsik (1997) is an effort to examine these issues from a liberal perspective.

40. Crawford (2003, 203) cites Morrow (2000) on this point.

41. See Pyle 1992.

42. Menon 2007, chap. 4.

43. National Institute for Defense Studies 2003, 23, and National Institute for Defense Studies 2005, 221–22. Abe 2006, 135.

1. Japan's Grand Strategies: Connecting the Ideological Dots

1. Pyle 2007 explores how Japan has adjusted to successive new world orders. Wakamiya (2006) connects many of these ideological dots across the Pacific war.

2. "Trying debut" is the apt formulation of Dickinson 1999, 7.

3. Iriye (1997) agrees that Japanese grand strategy was essentially realist. So does Taka-hashi (2004, 70), who argues that the Imperial Navy was operating with a sophisticated geopolitical perspective as early as 1897.

4. Kitaoka 2005.

5. Iriye 1997, 4–5.

6. Yamagata presented this strategic doctrine to the first Meiji Diet. Iokibe 2000, 4; Kitaoka 2005, 21; Iriye 1997, 11.

7. Fujiwara 1973, 189; Dickinson 1999, 27.

8. Iriye 1997, 26. Tanaka, who became prime minister in 1927, had been the staff officer responsible for operational planning during the Russo-Japanese War and had drafted Yamagata's Basic Plan in 1907. See Dickinson 1999.

9. Dickinson 1999, 117.

10. Dickinson 1999, 25.

11. Liberals were split on the Twenty-One Demands. Ishibashi Tanzan was openly crit-ical, but Ōkuma Shigenobu endorsed them. See Nolte 1987 and Kerr 1998.

12. Morley 1957, 310. Hosoya (1971, 84) reports that Diet politicians severely criticized this intervention and demanded to know why the soldiers did not return to Japan at the end of their mission.

13. This was a concern both of Tanaka Giichi and of Alfred Thayer Mahan. See Dick-inson (1999) on the former and Mahan (1900) on the latter. Also see E. Miller (1991) for how the U.S. Department of the Navy began developing its War Plan Orange in 1906, the first such plan in which Japan was the hypothetical enemy.

14. The Diet had the temerity to cap defense budgets in 1908, and when the politicians relented to allow increased defense spending in 1911, it was the navy they privileged. Dickinson (1999, 27) and Pyle (2007, chap. 3).

15. Itō 1973.

16. For more on Kita, see Samuels 2003. Peattie (1975) is an excellent study of Ishiwara. Lebra 1975, Miwa 1990, Koschmann 1997, Radtke 1998, and Saaler 2002 and 2004, and Shōji 2005 are good sources on prewar Asianism.

17. An analogous nativism gripped some nineteenth-century social Darwinists in the United States. Rev. Josiah Strong was representative. He called Americans "a race of unequaled energy (and) representative…[of] the highest civilization…destined to dis-possess many weaker races, assimilate others, and mold the remainder until…it has Anglo-Saxonized mankind." See MacDougall 1997.

18. Miyazaki 1982, xxi, and Miwa 1990, 134.

19. Lebra 1975, chap. 5. Asianism actually originated in Western ideas about an "other" in what was an otherwise very heterogeneous Far East.

20. Koschmann 1997, 83. Duus (2001) and Saaler (2002) also sketch out the constructiv-ist basis of Japanese Asianism. Koschmann (1997, 87) reminds us that there were both esoteric and exoteric forms of Asianism. The former was closest to nativism, while the latter emphasized harmony and a commitment to family that was said to be region-wide.

21. Lebra (1975) outlines the various forms of Asianist groups in the 1930s. See Mi-yazaki 1982, Saaler 2004, and Miwa 1990 for more on leftist Asianism.

22. Itō 1973, 492.

23. Titus 1994, xxxvii.

24. Asada 1973.

25. Yamagata quoted by Dickinson 1999, 43–44.

26. Lebra 1975; Miwa 1990, 136.

27. Peattie 1975, 166.

28. From *Daitōa Kensetsu Shingikai*, cited in Kim 2005, 68.
29. Iriye 1997, 18, 45.
30. Peattie 1975, 165–66.
31. Ishiwara cited in Nish 1993, 25. "First step…" is from Peattie 1975, 167.
32. Iriye 1971, 114.
33. This is based on the vivid account of this deliberation in Macmillan 2002, 306–21.
34. Burkman 2003 and Akami 2002.
35. Elite support for Japan as a trading state predates the formation of Japan's great industrial zaibatsu. Iokibe (2000) suggests that Sakamoto Ryōma was an early advocate of Japan as a merchant nation. Kitaoka (2005) places Fukuzawa Yukichi in the same category.
36. Matsuo (1995) reprints the full series. Miura opposed the Pacific War but also argued that Japan would be saved by defeat. He lived to see the Japan of his dreams and remained active until his death in 1972.
37. There is a rich literature on Ishibashi's extraordinary career as policy intellectual and, later, as politician. See Nolte 1987; Masuda 1990; Nish 1993; Radtke 1998; Kerr 1998; Doak 2003; and Jiang 2003.
38. Nolte 1987, 163.
39. Kerr 1998, 57; Kitaoka (2005, 26) compares Ishibashi to Fukuzawa on this point.
40. Nolte (1987, 36) tells of how Ishibashi once published verbatim a warning he received from the army about his criticism of the Siberian Intervention in order to expose the pomposity and menace of the military.
41. This account of interwar economic diplomacy is from Bamba 1972; Ogata 1973; Hosoya 1971; Nish 1993; Iriye 1997; Radtke 1998; Iokibe 2000; Akami 2002; and Pyle 2007. Note that Ienaga (1978) sees little difference among these liberals, except vis-à-vis the implementation of foreign policy.
42. This is a description of Nitobe Inazō, but it aptly captures the profile of most Big Japanists. Burkman 2003, 90.
43. After Japan's defeat, Shidehara became a caretaker prime minister for seven months (October 1945–May 1946) and is credited by many with authorship of Article 9 of the postwar Japanese constitution. He had long since become disenchanted with imperialism. See Nish 1993, 242.
44. "Stabilize the status quo" is from Pyle 2007, chap. 6. "Contain through cooperation" is from Iokibe 2000, 4. As we shall see, this was not the last time the United States defended the status quo by containing Japanese power.
45. Bamba 1972, 164.
46. So did Kaneko Kentarō, president of the America-Japan Society. Ogata 1973, 468. Doak (2003, 28) reminds us that while Nitobe was concerned with Japanese immigrants in the United States, he celebrated colonialism and held firmly to the racial hierarchies of social Darwinism. On this point also see Dudden 2005.
47. The best account of the institute is Akami 2002.
48. See Horiuchi 1950, Shidehara 1998, and Bamba 1972 for more on Shidehara's strategy in these negotiations.
49. Shidehara quoted in Iriye 1997, 57.
50. G. Berger 1974, 472.
51. Maruyama 1960, xix.
52. Maxon 1957, 89. This fait accompli was legitimated by *gekokujō*, the norm by which senior officers delegate decisions to their staff and accept responsibility for the outcome. In this case, however, responsibility was passed all the way up the line—as far as the imperial palace. See also Fujiwara 1973.
53. Byas 1942.

54. Metzler 2006, 247.

55. Maxon 1957, 29. War Minister Araki Sadao reportedly told Prince Konoye that it no longer mattered who led the next cabinet, so long as he followed army orders. Maxon 1957, 92.

56. Akami 2002, 190; Ogata 1973, 471.

57. Nolte 1987, 270. Nolte makes every effort to demonstrate that Ishibashi remained stridently antimilitary, and that his survival during the war was because he was "savvy" (241). Nitobe and Ishibashi were only two of many whose views had shifted. Others included Rōyama Masamichi, an influential academic who supported the army's actions in Manchuria as "active" and "concrete." See Rōyama 1941, 10, 68–69; Kobayashi 2003; Han 2005; and Fletcher 1979.

58. On this point, see Akami 2002, Fletcher 1979, Ogata 1973, and Nish 1993.

59. Fletcher 1979, 51. See also Han 2005.

60. For more on Konoye, see G. Berger 1974; Akami 2002; Iokibe 2000; Saaler 2002; and Iriye 1997. The greatest irony of all was that Prince Konoye sent his son to the Lawrenceville prep school in Princeton, New Jersey, for his secondary education. See also his exchange with Colonel House in the 14 October and 7 December 1935 issues of *Liberty Magazine*.

61. Konoye quoted in Akami 2002, 62–63.

62. Kitaoka (1995a, 11) argues that because Konoye had an emotional and idealized view of Japan's destiny, he was not a realist.

63. Han 2005, 482. This is a detailed examination of Rōyama's ideas and "conversion" (*tenkō*).

64. Miwa 1990, 138; Koschmann 1997, 91; Shōji 2005, 34.

65. Samuels 2003.

66. The Imperial Navy preferred instead to emphasize its role as a "stabilizing power in East Asia." Both are quoted in Lebra 1975, 61.

67. The navy's preferred national strategy was "defending the north and advancing to the south" (*hokushu nanshin*). See Peattie 1975, 189–90.

68. Iriye 1971, 125. Kitaoka (2005, 29) points out that there were strategists within the navy who believed that autarky was a fool's errand and that alliance with Italy and Germany was a terrible mistake. In particular, he mentions Inoue Shigeyoshi, who critiqued the navy's plans in 1941, arguing that the resources it was seeking could better be acquired through trade.

69. Iriye 1971, 137.

70. "Wishful thinking" is from Iriye 1971, 115. "Vigorous defense..." is from G. Berger 1974, 458.

71. Hosoya (1971, 88) reports that Nimiya Takeo, a "progressive" ideologue in the Ministry of Foreign Affairs, produced a 152-page pamphlet in 1936 called the "Guiding Principles Characterizing Japanese Diplomacy" (Nihon Koyū no Gaikō Shidō Genri Kōryō), which became the "ideological basis" for Japanese expansion.

72. One famous exception was the 1940 criticism of Japan's China policy by Diet member Saitō Takao, who was forced immediately to resign.

73. Konoye cited in Bamba 1972, 376.

74. Konoye quoted in Hosoya 1971, 91. See also Shōji 2005.

75. "Nucleus" is the term used by General Tōjō, quoted in Lebra 1975, 79. Miwa 1990, 142.

76. Shiraishi (1990, 172) calls this a "phantom vision conjured up in a moment of desperation."

77. "Invisible hand" is Soeya's (2005, 98) apt metaphor. This discussion of the three main groups in postwar Japan's security debate is derived in part from Boyd and Samuels 2005. For excellent analysis of the evolution of early postwar Japanese security policy, see Tanaka 1997; Soeya 2005; and Sadō 2003.

78. Guillain (1952), Kinoshita (1953), and Morris (1960) are excellent accounts.

79. Samuels (2003, chap. 5) explores Sasakawa's relationship with Kishi Nobusuke, his Sugamo cellmate and a founder of the Liberal Democratic Party.

80. Kinoshita 1953, 246. The Hattori Organization was led by Hattori Takushirō, the former chief of operations for the Imperial Army's General Staff, who had won the confidence of General Willoughby, the chief counterintelligence officer of the Supreme Commander of the Allied Powers (SCAP), and who plotted a coup d'etat in 1952.

81. Morris 1960, 188.

82. Morris 1960, 116.

83. This is examined in Samuels (1994) and in Sadō (2003).

84. Sadō 2003, 16.

85. Kishi quoted in Sadō 2003, 17. According to documents released by the U.S. State Department in July 2006, this was the moment at which the Central Intelligence Agency began disbursing cash to win over Kishi and the LDP. See U.S. Department of State 2006.

86. Bamba (1972, 197) reminds us that antimilitarism was not new to postwar Japan. In the 1920s, having witnessed the brutality of World War I, intellectuals, businessmen, and politicians—particularly in the Kenseikai—all criticized the militarists.

87. Maruyama 1960 and Hook 1996, 26–41.

88. See Dower 1979, 318–20, and Ōtake 1984, 59–69.

89. Kitaoka (2005, 27–29) notes that Yoshida came around to the view of Japan as a trading state—and to "Shidehara diplomacy"—rather late in his career. Until the Manchurian Incident, and possibly longer, he supported the idea of Japanese sovereignty on the continent.

90. Weinstein 1971, 130.

91. Amaya (1980) summarized this position with exceptional clarity.

92. By the 1960s, the leading theoretician of this view was Kyoto University professor Kōsaka Masataka. He saw this as nothing less than a "civilizational choice." See Kōsaka 1964. For an excellent analysis of the formation of the Yoshida Doctrine, see Tanaka 1997, 100–129.

93. Yoshida was explicit about the economic reasons for not remilitarizing quickly. The military would be a "financial burden." See Yoshida 1961, 97, 146. Also see Pyle 1996, 23–28.

94. Soeya 2005, 64–80.

95. This, despite a chapter in Yoshida's memoirs entitled "Bōei wa shūdan no chikara ni yoru hoka nashi" (There Is No Defense Other Than through Collective Power). Yoshida 1963, 133–34.

96. For a fuller examination of these debates, see Boyd and Samuels 2005.

97. Samuels 1994.

98. Ōtake 1983, 14.

99. "Defense production" (*bōei seisan*) was the euphemism adopted to make the idea of arms manufacture more palatable to the general public. Industry first organized to promote arms manufacture as part of a visit to Japan by John Foster Dulles in January 1951. The same group later organized the Defense Production Committee of Keidanren, the most important lobby for the arms industry.

100. *Nihon Keizai Shimbun*, 2 August 1953; *Asahi Shimbun*, 18 June 1953.

101. Details are in Sadō 2003, 68–70, and Samuels 1994.

102. Sadō 2003, 44–45.

103. When it was apparent Japan would lose the war, Ishibashi and Yoshida participated in a group that began planning for the postwar period. Ishibashi even served as Yoshida's first finance minister. Masuda 1990, 298. But he soon concluded that Japan and the United States would not remain close and, after having been purged by SCAP, Ishibashi tilted toward Hatoyama and Kishi, his old nemesis. See Nolte 1987 and Radtke

2003. He died under mysterious circumstances soon after becoming prime minister in December 1956.

104. Soeya 2005, 16–17.

105. Sadō 2003, 15–19.

106. Soeya 2005, 5, 81, 97.

107. Kōsaka (cited in Soeya 2005, 97) described the revisionists as having been "drawn in" (*hikiyoserareta*) to the Yoshida line. See also Mochizuki 1995, 2–4.

108. This is Nagai Yōnosuke's characterization of 1970s Japan. See Soeya 2005, 94–97.

109. Sadō 2003, 224, for example. Soeya (2005) reevaluates Nakasone.

110. Soeya (2005, 94–95) and Kitaoka (2005) identify this with Kōsaka's influential January 1963 essay in *Chūō Kōron*: "Genjitsushugisha no Heiwaron" (A Realist's Argument for Peace).

111. Shiraishi 2004, 176.

112. Kishi quoted in Shiraishi 2004, 112–15.

113. This is also the view of Pyle (2007) and Iriye (1997).

114. Kerr 1998, 51. Masuda 1990, 100.

115. Katō quoted by Iriye 1997, 52.

116. Pyle acknowledges this as "the product of a carefully constructed and brilliantly implemented foreign policy," adding that "Not since the Meiji Period had Japan possessed such a coherent, integrated and purposeful set of policies designed to secure its long-term interests." Pyle 2007, 13, 241.

2. BAKING THE PACIFIST LOAF

1. Temerson 1991, 3. Temerson attributes the dual containment idea to Secretary of State Dean Acheson (58).

2. Quoted in Temerson 1991, 56. "Plans for an entangling alliance" is from p. 58.

3. Shiraishi 2004, 110.

4. Tanaka (1997) is the most authoritative history of the U.S.-Japan alliance. See also Sakamoto 2000. In English, see Schaller 1997.

5. Iokibe 2000, 8. Now that Tanaka Hitoshi, one of Japan's most distinguished senior diplomats, has retired, he can be equally blunt: "It is perfectly apparent to everyone that the United States and Japan do not have an equal partnership, despite the catchphrase concocted for summit meetings." Tanaka 2005, 83.

6. Interview, Yamamoto Ichita, chair of the LDP Policy Committee on Foreign Policy, 9 June 2006.

7. Yoshida 1963, 165. U.S. documents from that same period concur. See, for example, National Security Council 1960. Olson and Zeckhauser (1966) were the first to identify the reasons why weaker alliance partners gain relatively more from alliances than do stronger powers.

8. Kitaoka 2005, 30; Soeya 2005, 16; Deming and Lawless 1986, 8.

9. Kennan 1972, 40, 52.

10. Sakamoto 2000, 16–17, 107.

11. Sadō 2004, 5, on "hand-me-down" guns.

12. C. Hughes 2004a, 22–24.

13. Sadō 2003, 30, 63.

14. Deming and Lawless 1986, 5.

15. Defense Agency 1976, 129.

16. Bōei Tsūshinsha 2005, 332. National Security Council (1960, 30) has details on the U.S. drawdown.

17. Office of the Secretary of Defense 1998, no page number.

18. Iguchi 2001, 75.
19. Ishiba 2005a, 87.
20. Ōta 2005, 159.
21. This observation, and the notion of "asymmetric reciprocity," is from the memoirs of Nishimura Kumao, former senior diplomat with responsibility for the U.S.-Japan Mutual Security Treaty. His analysis is cited in Sakamoto 2000, i–ii.
22. Shiraishi 2004, 111.
23. Morris 1960, 128–31.
24. Quoted in Morris 1960, 128.
25. Sadō 2003, 17.
26. Sadō 2003, 229–30.
27. Sadō 2003, 66–67.
28. "Tō no Seikō: Dokuritsu Taisei no Seibi" (Party Platform: Establishing an Independent Structure), 15 November 1955.
29. By 1970, JDA director general Nakasone was referring to the alliance as a "semipermanent necessity." See his testimony to the House of Representatives Budget Committee, *Shūgiin Kaigiroku Jōhō*, 24 February 1970.
30. The "more" was in the form of cash payments from the Central Intelligence Agency. See U.S. Department of State 2006.
31. National Security Council 1960, 12.
32. National Security Council 1960, 21. The NSC also noted that the Department of Defense and the Joint Chiefs of Staff vigorously pressed for a U.S. policy that would encourage Japan to "discreetly" extend its defense mission beyond the immediate area.
33. National Security Council 1960, 1.
34. The MOF was only too happy to limit Japanese spending as well. Sadō 2003, 92.
35. Nakayama quoted in Sadō 2003, 161. See chap. 6 for an account of how efforts by JDA officials to increase budgets and increase autonomy were defeated by Yoshida-ites in the early 1960s.
36. For more on the continuity of these pragmatists within Japanese factional politics, see Kitaoka 1995b, Hara 1988, and Kōchikai 1983.
37. Sakamoto (2000) and Soeya (2005) are particularly interesting accounts of these dynamics. The term Satō used was *jiritsu no bōeiryoku* rather than *jishu bōei*, the term preferred by revisionists. See the account by Sadō 2003, 214.
38. This, after having just studied the efficacy of nuclear deterrence for Japan and issuing reassurances that nuclear arms were not unconstitutional. See Higuchi and Ōsuka 1994, 89. This has been reaffirmed repeatedly since—by his CLB director, General Takatsuji, in 1969, and by the governments of Prime Minister Fukuda in 1978 and of Prime Minister Koizumi in 2002.
39. Tanaka 1997, 215–30, and Soeya 2005, 90–91. Ota (2000, 4) makes the argument that Satō had sought U.S. approval to acquire nuclear arms earlier in the 1960s and that he told U.S. Ambassador U. Alexis Johnson that the three principles were "nonsense" in January 1969.
40. Ōtake 1983, 147–58.
41. See Tanaka and Murata (1996a) for background on the experience of Prime Minister Miki Takeo at the Rambouillet summit in 1975. "National Guard" is the view of former JDA vice minister Nishihiro Seiki. See his interview in Tanaka and Murata 1995, 5.
42. JDA director general Sakata Michio in the foreword of the 1976 JDA White Paper, p. 8, and interview with Tanaka Akihiko in *Securitarian*, April 2004, 21.
43. Katahara (2001, 79–80) reports on the secret military consultations and Sakata's reaction.

44. Giarra 2001, 66.

45. Soeya 2005, 108–9. Deming and Lawless (1986, 1) report that the Soviets needed similar reassurance that Japan would not become a "loose cannon." "Resetting the chessboard" is the apt phrase of Wampler (n.d., 8).

46. Armitage quoted in Deming and Lawless 1986, 21.

47. In 1990, U.S. Marine General Henry Stackpole was relieved of duty after referring to the alliance as a "cork in the Japanese bottle."

48. Yoshida 1963, 161.

49. Postwar France, Brazil, Italy, Germany all wrote constitutions renouncing war as an instrument of the state. Japan, however, was different. First, unlike these other states, Japan did not write its own postwar constitution. Second, the one "imposed" on it by the United States goes beyond outlawing wars of aggression to formally repudiating the maintenance of military forces for that purpose. For comparisons, see Kodaira (1967) and Nonaka and Urabe (1989).

50. Schlichtmann 1995, 51–53, and Maki 1964, 305, 298–365. This section is derived from Boyd and Samuels 2005.

51. Examples include the 1952 Suzuki case, in which the supreme court refused to consider a legislator's claim that the National Police Reserves violated Article 9, on the grounds that the court could not interpret law outside the bounds of a concrete case, and the 1959 Sunakawa case, in which the court argued it could not determine the constitutionality of the U.S.-Japan Security Treaty due to its "highly political nature" (*kōdo no seijisei*).

52. Quoted in Beer and Itoh 1996, 91. See also Nonaka and Urabe (1989) for analysis of the failed legal challenges to the SDF.

53. Nakamura 2001, 99.

54. Yoshida, speaking during Diet interpellations on 26 June 1946, is quoted in Nakamura 2001, 62–63.

55. Nakamura 2001, 147.

56. *Mainichi Shimbun*, 8 January 2007.

57. Kishi quoted in Higuchi and Ōsuka 1994, 79–80. According to the CLB in 1969, "When it comes to nuclear weapons, there are those that can be maintained and those that may not." CLB quoted in Boyd 2003, 58.

58. MOFA report quoted in L. Hughes 2007. See Iinuma (2006) for the status of Japan's nuclear weapon debate after North Korea's provocative test in 2006.

59. *Voice*, December 2001. Akiyama 2002, 178. The constitutionality of the use of preemptive force has often been reasserted.

60. This concise definition is from Michishita 2005a, 232. Soeya (2005, 144–45) describes the origin of the term.

61. For references to this distinction, see *Yomiuri Shimbun*, 3 May 1997; Nakamura 2001, 255–57; and Asagumo Shimbunsha 2005, 557–62, 571.

62. National Institute for Defense Studies 2002, 315.

63. Jameson speech to the Defense Research Institute, Tokyo, 21 August 2004.

64. Frühstück and Ben Ari 2002, 2.

65. Hikotani 2004. Feaver et al. (2005) place this in comparative perspective. See Hanami (1996) for "ubiquitous pacifist culture," T. Berger (1998) for "anti-militarist ethos," and Katzenstein (1996) for analysis of Japanese security policy based on this presumed norm.

66. Okazaki 1986, chap. 7.

67. This is the solution described by Nishihara 1985, 135.

68. Hirose 1989, 43.

69. This discussion of the CLB is from Samuels 2004a.

70. Nishihara 1985, 135. The term "in-house lawyer" was used by *Asahi Shimbun* editorial writers on 6 November 2001. The term "check point" is from Nishikawa 2000, 37. Nishikawa (242) also uses the metaphors of "brake," "wall," "bastion," and "watchdog."

71. Interview, senior METI official, June 2001.

72. The first female "legal professional" was appointed to the CLB in July 1997. See *Yomiuri Shimbun*, 28 July 1997.

73. *Yomiuri Shimbun*, 27 July 1997.

74. Nishikawa 1997, 190–91.

75. Nishikawa 2000, 74.

76. For career data on these officials—and the so-called royal road within the CLB—see Nishikawa 2000, 84.

77. *Amakudari* literally means "descent from heaven" and refers to the postretirement positions of Japan's most elite civil servants.

78. Discussion with METI official, November 2002. Nishikawa (1997, 186) reports that bureaucrats refer to these as visits to the "devil's gate" (*kimon*).

79. Nishikawa 1997, 219.

80. In addition to four laws, there was one cabinet order. See Nakamura 2001, 29–31.

81. CLB director general Ōmori Masasuke quoted in *Yomiuri Shimbun*, 12 October 1997.

82. *Yomiuri Shimbun*, 9 August, 1997. The official quoted here also may be Ōmori.

83. Naikaku Hōseikyoku Hyakunenshi Henshū Iinkai 1985, 38, 41. See *Jyurisuto*, 1 February 1953, for Takatsuji's explanation of self-defense and the constitution.

84. Sadō 2003, 82.

85. Nakamura 2001, 142–43.

86. Sadō 2003, 46. For more on Hattori, who had won the confidence of the Occupation counterintelligence officials, see Samuels 1987. This issue was never fully settled. In May 1965 and again in December 1973, the director general of the CLB had to issue rulings on who, exactly, was a civilian. See Higuchi and Osuka 1994, 90–91.

87. Hirose 1989, 82, 97.

88. Sadō 2003, 77–78. See Hirose (1989, table 1) for a list of the bureaucratic origins of the JDA's top officials.

89. Nishihara 1985, 137.

90. *Bōeichō* 1970, section 2.2.

91. The simulators made a particularly egregious error in using the 1930s term for "national mobilization" (*kokka sōdōin taisei*). See the accounts in Nishioka (1988) and Beer and Itoh (1996).

92. *Shūkan Posuto*, 22 July 1978.

93. Nishioka 1988, 283–84; T. Berger 1998, 138; Ōtake 1983, chap. 14.

94. Nishioka 1988. Abe Shinzō recalls the Kurisu affair and its consequences in Abe 2006, 62.

95. National Institute for Defense Studies 2003, 29.

96. Hirose 1989, 57.

97. Hirose 1989, 56–57; Hikotani and Kamiya 2004, 9.

98. Samuels 1994 and chapters 6 and 7 of this book.

99. Ishiba 2005a, 101.

100. Sadō 2003, 178–80.

101. Sadō (2003, 153–63) describes these efforts of the early 1960s.

102. Sadō 2003, 315–16.

103. Tanaka 1997, 265–80, and Soeya 2005, 153–56.

104. Deming and Lawless 1986, 10. Interview with Tanaka Akihiko, *Securitarian*, April 2004, 21.

105. The view that security derives from prosperity contrasts sharply with U.S. understandings, which insist that prosperity follows security. See, for example, the White House Fact Sheet, 23 March 2005.

106. The canonical work on "bureaucratic dominance" is Johnson (1982), but virtually all textbooks and case studies acknowledge the role of these unelected mandarins in the policy process.

107. For example, see Nishioka 1988; Watanabe 1996; and Hirose 1989. For a dissenting view, see Kitaoka 2005. Hirose (1989, 44) notes that there were not even standing committees in the Diet dedicated to defense and security issues as late as 1989.

108. Hikotani 2004b, 32. Editorial writers at the *Asahi Shimbun* fretted openly about the threat to civilian control posed by the elevation of the JDA to MOD. See *Asahi Shimbun*, 4 January 2007.

109. Nonaka and Urabe 1989, 122.

110. Soeya 2005.

111. For another expression of these views, see Takemura (1994) and nearly any public interview with Miyazawa Kiichi during the past fifty years. Miyazawa, another former MOF official in the Yoshida line to become prime minister, consistently opposed military spending. Miyazawa and Kōsaka (1984) is representative.

112. Yoshida 1967, 106.

3. The Change to Change

1. Lim 2003, 11.

2. Park 2007, 196. It was at this time that Morita Akio and Ishihara Shintarō published their provocative dialogue: *The Japan That Can Say "No"*.

3. This evaluation was offered by a retired MSDF vice admiral. Interview, 11 January 2006.

4. National Institute for Defense Studies 2003, 45.

5. See Tanaka (1997, chap. 5) and Sadō (2003) for details on the formation of the Basic Defense Law and the SDF.

6. Murata 1996. Mochizuki (1983–84) reminds us that Soviet belligerency in the late 1970s to early 1980s did stimulate Japanese planners to think seriously about threats from the north.

7. Michishita 2005a, 222–23.

8. Taoka 1997; Honda et al. 2005, 115.

9. In the account of Ishiba Shigeru, then a second-term Diet member, the LDP leadership was especially confused. He recalls being "shocked" at first that no one in the LDP leadership had even heard of a peacekeeping operation, himself included. Ishiba 2005a, 80.

10. Nishikawa 1997, 226–34.

11. See *Yomiuri Shimbun*, 15 August 1997, for details of this exchange. Also see Tanaka 1997, 180–85. Kōsaka Masataka was the most prominent Kōchikai brain-truster to criticize the CLB, arguing that Article 9 had become a crutch, a device enabling Japan to avoid thinking about security. His influential critique is Kōsaka 1993.

12. Nishikawa 1997, 235–26.

13. Ishiba (2005a, 87) acknowledges that not being thanked for its $13 billion contribution to the Gulf War was a "transformative event" for Japan. Soeya (2005, 183–86) calls it Japan's "greatest trial" after the end of the cold war. Terashima (2005b, 1) calls it a "trauma." Abe Shinzō reflects on this in Abe 2006, 136.

14. Honda et al. 2005, 135.

15. Declassified cable from Ambassador Michael Armacost posted by the National Security Archives on 14 December 2005 at http://www.gwu.edu/~nsarchiv/NSAEBB/NSAEBB175/index.htm.

16. Okamoto 2002a, 63.

17. Okamoto 2002a, 62.

18. Soeya 2005, 189–90.

19. So, his interlocutor reported, did China. See Daniels 2004, 13.

20. Declassified cable from Ambassador Armacost posted by the National Security Archives on 14 December 2005 at http://www.gwu.edu/~nsarchiv/NSAEBB/NSAEBB175/index.htm.

21. The best accounts of the 1994 NDPO are Tokuchi 2001; C. Hughes 2004b; Michishita 2005a; and National Institute for Defense Studies 2003.

22. C. Hughes 2004b, 178. This new responsibility first became an object of serious debate after the North Korean nuclear test in October 2006. See chapter 7 of this book.

23. For one example, see Yokochi 2005. The author is a former GSDF general who insists that China intends "to destroy Japan." See also Hiramatsu 2002.

24. This includes Hong Kong. U.S.-Japan trade was close to $200 billion in 2005. See http://www.jetro.go.jp/jpn/stats/data/pdf/trade2005.pdf.

25. Nanto and Chanlett-Avery 2005, 6.

26. Taniguchi 2005, 445–46; *Nihon Keizai Shimbun*, 28 July 2005.

27. Briefing by C. H. Kwan, Nomura Institute of Capital Markets Research, Tokyo, 24 October 2005. Also, Prime Minister Koizumi has often spoken of the complementarity of the two economies.

28. Yokochi 2005.

29. Interview, Umeda Kunio, deputy director general of the Asia-Oceana Bureau, Ministry of Foreign Affairs, Tokyo, 26 October 2005; Interview, former JDA director general Ishiba Shigeru, Tokyo, 26 October 2005.

30. Taniguchi 2005, 456; Yamazaki 2005, 14. Japan first sought control of Taiwan in the early seventeenth century when the Dutch were using it to enforce control of their treaty ports in the region. Later, the Japanese used Taiwan as its own platform to project power to the west and south.

31. See Keidanren (2001, 1) on complementarity and Lim (2003, 1) on the unprecedented coexistence of great powers in East Asia.

32. Nanto and Chanlett-Avery 2005, 17.

33. See, for example, Testimony Of Admiral Thomas B. Fargo, United States Navy Commander, U.S. Pacific Command, before the House Armed Services Committee, United States House Of Representatives, Regarding U.S. Pacific Command Posture, 31 March 2004.

34. *Nihon Keizai Shimbun*, 1 August 2005.

35. "Unipolar moment" is from Krauthammer 1990–91.

36. This analysis is derived from a lecture by Michishita Narushige: "Senryaku kara mita Nihon no Bōei" (Japan's Defense Viewed Strategically), Sophia University, 26 September 2005.

37. Deputy Assistant Secretary John Hill in speech to the American Enterprise Institute Conference called "Transforming the U.S.-Japan Alliance," Tokyo, 25 October 2005.

38. Japan was ranked seventy-fourth of seventy-four countries surveyed by the World Value Survey. China was ranked fourth, the United States thirty-sixth. Reported in Tadokoro 2005a, 8. See Frühstück (2007) on attitudes toward violence within the SDF.

39. Morris 1960, 207; Auer 1973, 183.

40. Kataoka and Myers 1989.

41. Honda et al. 2005, 433.

42. Kawano 2002, 280–81. There have been suicides among returnees from Iraq, however. See *Asahi Shimbun*, 10 March 2006. Concern for the mental health of SDF personnel led to the establishment of counseling offices and the Defense Agency Headquarters to Prevent Suicide in July 2003. See *Defense of Japan* 2004, 344.
43. Frühstück and Ben-Ari (2002) is an excellent summary of the efforts that have been made to soften their image, and Frühstück 2007 offers an intimate look at the concerted JDA effort to "normalize" and "familiarize" the military in civilian society by focusing on "youth," "friendship," and "peace" rather than on "other concepts the Japanese state once had exploited for the purposes of militarization and war." Frühstück 2007, 233.
44. Morris 1960, 256; Frühstück and Ben-Ari 2002, 6.
45. Colonel quoted in Frühstück 2007.
46. The syllabi of the Defense Academy focus on liberal education, and cadets cannot major in defense studies. They must major in either humanities and social science or engineering, and are required to study political thought, international relations, public opinion, and comparative politics. See Bōei Daigakkō 2005a and 2005b. See also Honda et al. 2005.
47. See Naikaku Seifu Kōhō Shitsu 2006.
48. See Japan Defense Agency (2004, 370) and Tokuchi (2001, 73) for more on demographic constraints.
49. Kawakatsu 2006, chap. 6, 387.
50. This group debated introducing legislation to allow the Coast Guard to protect survey ships and platforms in the East China Sea, for example. Interview, DPJ Diet representative and member of the Wakate Giin no Kai, 20 October 2005.
51. Ishiba, who became Koizumi's defense minister, has written his memoirs. See Ishiba 2005a. Schoff (2006) reminds us that this new generation was not always on the same page on security policy, particularly with regard to North Korea. Differences on China also came to the fore in 2006, as jockeying began to succeed Koizumi as prime minister.
52. Shinoda (2004) is an excellent study of the rise of the Kantei.
53. Headquarters for the Administrative Reform of the Central Government, "Establishing a System with More Effective Political Leadership," January 2001, 5.
54. Shinoda 2004, 28.
55. Schoff 2004, 82–90.
56. Shinoda 2004.
57. Shinoda 2004, 105. *Japan Times*, 18 November 2004. Koizumi created a similar cabinet task force in 2002 to work on the North Korean abduction problem. See Schoff 2006, 12.
58. Interview, Yamamoto Ichita, 9 June 2006.
59. Schoff 2006, 28. See also Morimoto (2005, 221) on this point.
60. Data supplied by director, Secretarial Division, JDA, 22 November 2005.
61. *Nihon Keizai Shimbun*, 25 April 2006, and interview, Yamamoto Ichita, chair of the LDP Policy Committee on Foreign Affairs, 9 June 2006.
62. *New York Times*, 27 September 2006.
63. The revisionists conveniently ignored the fact that when they were in power, the CLB did their bidding. The best examples were in 1957, when Prime Minister Kishi required a CLB interpretation that nuclear weapons were not unconstitutional and in 1985 when Prime Minister Nakasone forced the CLB to change the guidelines on visits to Yasukuni Shrine. For details, see Mikuriya 1996 and Samuels 2004a.
64. Nishikawa (1997) is the best case study of the CLB's role in this epochal policy debate.
65. *Yomiuri Shimbun*, 25 August 1999.

66. The influential *Yomiuri Shimbun* editorial chief, Watanabe Tsuneo, was one who had argued for the outright elimination of the CLB. In May 2003, Tasso Takuya, a young Liberal Party legislator who formerly had been an official in the Ministry of Foreign Affairs, introduced a bill in the Diet that would eliminate the CLB altogether. Since the Liberals were by then in the opposition, the LDP ignored the measure.

67. Statement to the Diet by CLB director general Ōmori Masasuke. *Yomiuri Shimbun*, 10 August 1997.

68. Katahara 2001, 80; Sadō 2003.

69. Interview, Ishiba Shigeru, 26 October 2005.

70. Interview, JDA cabinet official, 28 September 2005, and interview, JDA official, 26 December 2005. See also Honda et al. 2005, 215. Ishiba's own account is at Ishiba 2005a, 181–83.

71. See, for example the editorials of the *Asahi Shimbun* and the *Mainichi Shimbun* in June 2003, when the Iraq bill was introduced. On 8 June the *Asahi* editorialized that "present conditions regarding civilian control are by no means free from worry," and the 16 June *Mainichi* insisted that "the Diet should impose tighter civilian control over the Self-Defense Forces." These concerns were reprised in January 2007 when the JDA became the MOD. See the *Asahi Shimbun* editorial of 4 January 2007.

72. Honda et al. 2005.

73. Taoka 1997, 4. Note, however, that *Asahi Shimbun* and *Mainichi Shimbun* editorials continued to express concern over the extent of civilian control. See the *Asahi* editorial of 8 June 2003 and the *Mainichi* editorial of 16 June 2003, both written while the emergency legislation was under consideration in the Diet.

74. Honda et al. 2005, chap. 7.

75. Interview, Arai Shougo, former director general of the Japan Coast Guard, 31 May 2006.

76. There are reliable reports that the DPRK ship was sunk by direct fire from the JCG. Interview, former government official, 25 April 2006.

77. Leheny 2006, 165.

78. Interview, Arai Shougo, former director general of the Japan Coast Guard, 31 May 2006. Councillor Arai also notes that the modernization was accelerated after the JCG's widely reported failure in March 1999 to pursue intruders off the Noto Peninsula.

79. Interview, Arai Shougo, former director general of the Japan Coast Guard, 31 May 2006.

80. *Kaijō Hoanchō* 2006, 1, 9 (exclamation point in the original).

81. The text of the joint statement is at http://www.mofa.go.jp/region/asia-paci/india/partner0504.html#eight.

82. Interview, senior JDA official, 26 May 2006.

83. Interview, senior intelligence officer, 17 May 2006.

84. Interview, senior JDA official, 26 May 2006.

85. Interview, Yamamoto Ichita, 9 June 2006.

86. I am grateful to Eric Heginbotham for this comparison.

87. AFX News, 2 December 2005, and *Sankei Shimbun*, 2 December 2005.

88. Kaijō Hoanchō 2006, 9. For direct comparisons online, see http://www.globalsecurity.org/military/world/japan/hatsuyuki.htm. Former JCG director general Arai Shougo insists that the JCG's two-thousand-ton ships have "thin skins" and were much more cheaply constructed than naval destroyers. He also insists that the 20mm and 40mm guns are "just for decoration." Interview, 31 May 2006.

89. Kaijō Hoanchō 2006, 18. See pages 24–27 for bilateral arrangements with each neighbor and pages 34–35 for details on the territorial disputes.

90. Kaijō Hoanchō 2006, 8. *Tokyo Shimbun,* 24 May 2006. See the *Asahi Shimbun,* 29 May 2006, for more on JCG's antipiracy activities.

91. Interview, Arai Shougo, former director general of the Japan Coast Guard, 31 May 2006.

92. Kaijō Hoanchō 2006, 29.

93. *Tokyo Shimbun,* 2 June 2006; *Sankei Shimbun,* 14 June 2006; *Nihon Keizai Shimbun,* 14 August 2006.

94. Kaijō Hoanchō 2006, 29; interview, senior JDA official, 26 May 2006; interview, Arai Shougo, former director general of the Japan Coast Guard, 31 May 2006.

95. Kitaoka (1999) is an example of this generational shift.

96. Yoshida 1961, 146.

97. *Jieitai/Bōei ni kan suru Yoron Chōsa, 2003.* Tokyo: Naikakufu.

98. *Jieitai/Bōei ni kan suru Yoron Chōsa, 2003.* Tokyo: Naikakufu.

99. Asahi Shimbun, ed., *Kenpō Chōsa,* April 2004 and April 2005, and Yomiuri Shimbun, ed., *Yomiuri Yoron Zenkoku Yoron Chōsa Mensetsu Chōsahyō,* March 2005.

100. C. Hughes 2004a, 97–98.

101. This view was embedded in the so-called Nye Initiative undertaken by Joseph Nye, then the DoD assistant secretary for international security affairs.

102. Honda et al. 2005, 427.

103. National Institute for Defense Studies 2003, 15.

104. Ishiba 2005a, 100.

105. Honda et al. 2005, 214.

106. Maeda 2005, 173. Nakanishi (2005, 80) is one who remained convinced that abandonment remains the great danger.

107. See the debate in the December 2004 issue of *Sekai:* "Anzen Hoshō Seisaku no Dai Tenkan ga Hajimatta" (The Great Change in the National Defense Policy Has Started), 77–92.

108. *Tokyo Shimbun,* 19 July 2006.

109. C. Hughes 2004a, 147. Ōta (2005, 173) specifically addresses "the risk of spilling blood."

110. This is the term used by DoD Deputy Undersecretary Richard Lawless at an American Enterprise Institute conference, "Transforming the U.S.-Japan Alliance," Tokyo, 25 October 2005. At the same conference, GSDF general Yamaguchi Noboru worried that "the SDF may not be able to keep up with the U.S. revolution in military affairs."

111. These entreaties were sounded at the American Enterprise Institute conference "Transforming the U.S.-Japan Alliance," Tokyo, 25 October 2005, by Deputy Undersecretary Richard Lawless and by White House adviser Aaron Friedberg. They echoed earlier pleas by the DoD regional director for Asia, John D. Hill, and Mutual Security Assistance Officer Lt. Cdr. Mark Staples at the Center for Global Partnership conference on "Non-Traditional Security," also in Tokyo (19 July 2005).

112. Cossa 2005, 66.

113. *Gaikō Fōramu* 2006.

114. *Japan Times,* 24 July 2005, and *Yomiuri Shimbun,* 15 December 2005.

115. Interview, 26 January 2006.

116. *Yomiuri Shimbun,* 23 August 2006.

117. "Judiciously utilize" is from National Institute for Defense Studies 2003, 23, and "jointly manage" is from Taniguchi 2005, 455.

118. Interview, senior DPJ Diet member, 20 October 2005.

119. C. Hughes 2004a, 24.

120. Tokuchi quoted in *Securitarian,* March 2005, 13–14.

121. This agreement will be examined more fully in chapter 7 of this book. The full text of the February 2005 "Joint Statement of the U.S.-Japan Security Consultative Committee" can be found at http://japan.usembassy.gov/e/p/tp-20050219–77.html. Soeya (2005, 93) reminds us that Prime Minister Satō and President Nixon made a similar declaration about both Korea and Taiwan in their November 1969 joint statement. See also Przystup (2005) for the significance of this February 2005 meeting of U.S. and Japanese foreign and defense ministers (the so-called 2+2 meeting).

122. Ishiba 2005a, chap. 9 and p. 215.

123. Yamazaki 2005, 3.

124. Daniels 2004, 7, 28 (emphasis in original).

125. Prime Minister's Commission on Japan's Goals 2000, chap. 6, p. 5.

126. Eleven commissions studied Japan's security options between 1990 and 2004 alone and issued the following reports:
(1) Council on Defense-Strategic Studies. 2001. "Report on Defense and Strategic Studies 1999–2000." Tokyo: National Institute for Defense Studies. http://www.nids.go.jp. (2) Council on Defense-Strategic Studies. 2003. "Report on Defense and Strategic Studies 1999–2000." Tokyo: National Institute for Defense Studies. http://www.nids.go.jp. (3) Itō Kenichi et al. 1998–2000. "Maritime Nation Seminar, Parts 1–3." Tokyo: Japan Forum on International Relations. (4) Itō Kenichi et al. 2004. "Policy Recommendations on New World Order of No-War Community and Future of Japan-US Alliance." Tokyo: Japan Forum on International Relations. (5) Japan Business Federation. 2001. "Japan-China Relations in the 21st Century." http://www.keidanren.or.jp/english/policy/2001/006.html. (6) Kokusai Heiwa Kyōryoku Kondankai [International Peace Cooperation Council]. 2002. "Hōkokusho." http://www.kantei.go.jp/jp/singi/kokusai/kettei/021218houkoku_s.html. (7) Ministry of Foreign Affairs. 1999. "Challenge 2001—Japan's Foreign Policy toward the 21st Century." http://www.mofa.go.jp/policy/other/challenge21.html. (8) Ozawa Committee (Special Study Group on Japan's Role in the International Community, LDP). 1992. "Japan's Role in the International Community—Draft Report." *Japan Echo* 19, no. 2 (Summer): 49–58. (9) Prime Minister's Advisory Group on Defense Issues. 1994. "The Modality of the Security and Defense Capability of Japan" [Nihon no Anzen Hoshō to Bōeiryoku no Arikata] (Higuchi Report). http://www.ioc.u-tokyo.ac.jp/~worldjpn/documents/texts/JPSC/19940812.O1J.html. (10) Prime Minister's Commission on Japan's Goals in the 21st Century. 2000. "The Frontier Within: Individual Empowerment and Better Governance in the New Millennium." http://www.kantei.go.jp/jp/21century/report/pdfs/index.html. (11) Taigaikankei Tasuku Fōsu. 2002. "21 Seiki Nihon Gaikō no Kihon Senryaku" [A Basic Strategy for Twenty-first-Century Japanese Diplomacy]. http://www.kantei.go.jp/jp/kakugikettei/2002/1128tf.html.

4. Whither the Yoshida Doctrine?

1. Park 2005, 5. Bōeichō 2003.

2. "Rudimentary phase" was the expression used by a senior JDA official from the Cabinet Office. Interview, 23 November 2005. Prime Minister Obuchi is quoted in Hikotani and Kamiya 2004, 6.

3. Csaki 2003, 4, 12. I am grateful to Leonard Schoppa for alerting me to the salami slice metaphor and to Hans Maull for informing me of its origin. The Japanese analogue is *kodashi ni suru*, referring to incremental change.

4. Daniels (2004, 2–7) also offers 1990s German salami slicing as a model for Japan.

5. "*Sarete iru* not *shite iru*," he insisted. Interview, 21 December 2005.

6. Interview, Cabinet Office JDA official, 26 December 2005.

7. Interview, senior JDA official, 11 January 2006. The official also reports that Hatakeyama was following the ideas of his predecessor, Nishihiro Seiki, suggesting that this list had been gestating for quite some time.

8. Interview, 26 May 2006.

9. Text provided by senior JDA official, 8 June 2006.

10. The most famous—and most extensive—report was the one on weapons of mass destruction in the second round, which concluded that Japan should not acquire nuclear weapons. See L. Hughes 2007.

11. National Institute for Defense Studies 2003, 17–18.

12. Leheny 2006, chap. 6.

13. Hook 1996, 98. By the 2000s, "international cooperation" was supplanted by "national interest."

14. Kataoka and Myers 1989; Sadō 2003.

15. Honda et al. 2005, 374.

16. Kataoka and Myers 1989, 83.

17. These are not purely commercial agreements. "Formal" means that Japanese firms have cooperated with the JDA to make their technology available to U.S. firms, through the good offices of the U.S. DoD. Memo from the Keidanren Defense Production Committee, based on data from Asagumo Shimbunsha (2005) and the JDA homepage, 9 September 2005, http://www.mod.go.jp/.

18. Interview, deputy director, JDA Finance and Equipment Bureau, R & D Planning Division, 12 October 2005. See Samuels (1994) and chapter 7 of this book for fuller analysis of the Japanese defense industry.

19. The official Japanese account is online at http://www.mofa.go.jp/policy/other/bluebook/1985/1985-3-3.htm.

20. Cronin, Giarra, and Green 1999, 172.

21. "Greatest trial" is from Soeya 2005, 183–86. It is difficult to judge the extent to which this humiliation was inflated in order to gather domestic support for expansion of SDF roles and missions.

22. C. Hughes (2005b) offers the framework of "cycles of military modernization." His three cycles are: (1) the period after the end of the cold war and the 1994 *taikō*, (2) the period after the 1994 *taikō* and the 2004 *taikō*, and (3) the period after the 2004 *taikō*.

23. See National Institute for Defense Studies 2003, 17–18.

24. Purrington 1992, 171. Even the scholar Kōsaka Masataka joined the fray. Singling out the issue of collective self-defense, he declared the CLB interpretations matters of "technical sophistry" (*kiben ni chikai hōkaishaku no gijutsu*) that had to be overturned. See Kōsaka 1993, 132.

25. Honda et al. 2005, 138.

26. Interview, former JDA vice minister, 25 November 2005. The JDA's English language explanation for freezing of Japan's PKF capabilities is at http://www.jda.go.jp/e/pab/ojdp02/english.htm.

27. Nishimoto 2001, 10–11.

28. Cossa (2005, 65) refers to "Japan-bashing."

29. Daniels 2004, 14. See also *Asahi Shimbun*, 19 December 2004.

30. This is suggested by Gen. Banshō Kōichirō who, when still a colonel, commanded Japanese forces in Iraq. See Honda et al. 2005, 428.

31. There was other legislation as well, including the Ship Inspection Law in 2000. See Michishita 2002, 94.

32. Sadō 2003; Murata 1996.

33. Defense of Japan 2004, 502.

34. Speech by General Timothy Larsen, commander, U.S. Forces Japan, at American Enterprise Institute conference on "Transforming the U.S.-Japan Alliance," Tokyo, 25 October 2005.

35. Kanehara 2005, 5.

36. Kyodo, 21 April 2001, and *Asahi Shimbun*, 6 November 2001. In late August 2003, during a political campaign, Koizumi reversed himself and instructed his deputy, Yamazaki Taku, to draft the text of a revised Article 9.

37. *Nihon Keizai Shimbun*, 3 January 2003.

38. Schoppa 1997 is a good example.

39. Honda et al. 2005, 36–37.

40. Interview with Admiral Kaji Masakazu, in Honda et al. 2005, 24, 32. Confirmed by former White House official in interview, 24 February 2006.

41. It is widely reported that the MSDF was more avid about deployment than the GSDF, the latter believing that assistance to refugees on the ground in Afghanistan would be too dangerous and that loss of troops would undermine public support. The politicians agreed. Bungei Shunjū 2005, 180; Honda et al. 2005, 38–39.

42. Michishita (2003) is an excellent summary of the law's provisions. See also *Gendai*, 2 January 2002.

43. *Yomiuri Shimbun*, 26 October 2001.

44. *Asahi Shimbun*, 6 November 2001; *Sankei Shimbun*, 29 December 2001.

45. Quoted in Honda et al. 2005, 157.

46. Michishita 2003, 47.

47. *Nihon Keizai Shimbun*, 2 January 2003.

48. Kyodo, 30 January 2003; Jiji Press, 30 January 2003.

49. *Asahi Shimbun*, 16 April 2003.

50. The formal name of the legislation is Iraku ni okeru Jindō Fukkō Shien Katsudō oyobi Anzen Kakuho no Jisshi ni kansuru Tokubetsu Setchi Hōan [Humanitarian Relief and Iraqi Reconstruction Special Measures Law].

51. *Asahi Shimbun*, 25 June 2003.

52. Prime Minister Koizumi's testimony to the Foreign Affairs and Defense Committee of the upper house, 16 December 2003, can be found at http://kokkai.ndl.go.jp/.

53. Okamoto, Ōshika, and Hamada 2003 and Japan Defense Agency 2005. Former JDA director general Ishiba lists access to Middle Eastern oil as the first reason for Japanese support of the war. See his very pragmatic explanation at Ishiba 2005a, 32, 43–45.

54. Honda et al. 2005, 80–81.

55. *Yomiuri Shimbun*, 7 June 2003.

56. This was the only exchange on collective security identified by Professor Nishikawa Shinichi's electronic search of the Diet website: http://kokkai.ndl.go.jp. Correspondence, July 2003.

57. *Yomiuri Shimbun*, 10 June 2003.

58. *Yomiuri Shimbun*, 4 May 2003.

59. *Tokyo Shimbun*, 22 May 2003. The Koizumi government's call for revision of the constitution was renewed immediately after the November 2003 election.

60. Yoshida 1963, 159.

61. *Asahi Shimbun* editorial, 8 June 2003.

62. Sadō (2003, 33–41) reviews the early debates. T. Berger (1998) reviews those in the 1970s and 1980s. Kōketsu (2002) and Jiyū Hōsōdan (2002) review the legislation from an opposition perspective.

63. *Yomiuri Shimbun*, 16 May 2003, lists the provisions of each law. Within four months of becoming prime minister, Abe Shinzō assigned the National Security Council long-

range strategic planning responsibility. See *Mainichi Shimbun*, 11 January 2007 and *Asahi Shimbun*, 13 January 2007.

64. Remarks of Tanaka Akihiko at the conference on "The Future of Article Nine" at the Center for Strategic and International Studies, Washington, D.C., 10 June 2005. Ishiba 2005a, 103.

65. Armitage et al. 2000.

66. C. Hughes 2004a, 73–76.

67. According to former JDA director general Nishihiro Seiki. Quoted in Tanaka and Murata 1995, 2.

68. Hirose 1989, 72.

69. Katahara 2001, 82, and Feaver, Hikotani, and Narine 2005, 246. It has even been reported that Prime Minister Kaifu instructed uniformed officers to be kept away from the Cabinet Office during the debate over the PKO dispatch in 1990–91. Kaifu also refused to see off the MSDF minesweepers and complained about martial music. He would meet uniformed officers only at hotels and never at his official residence. Funabashi 1999, 119–20.

70. Ishiba 2005a, 102, and *Asahi Shimbun*, 4 August 2005. The uniformed chair of the Joint Staff Council would be the equivalent of the JDA administrative vice minister.

71. C. Hughes 2004a, 62. Interview, JDA councillor who opposed the reform, 23 November 2005.

72. National Institute for Defense Studies 2003, 18. Honda et al. 2005, 92.

73. Okamoto 2002a, 66, and Michishita 2002.

74. Japan Defense Agency 2004, 319.

75. Bungei Shunjū 2005, 181, and *Asahi Shimbun*, 23 July 2005.

76. *Sankei Shimbun*, 4 February 2006.

77. Hook 1996, chap. 4.

78. Honda et al. 2005, 196.

79. Michishita 2002, 95.

80. Honda et al. 2005, 200–202.

81. *Tokyo Shimbun*, 10 July 2005. In February 2006 it was announced that creation of this unit was delayed until 2007 due to budget constraints. *Tokyo Shimbun*, 26 February 2006.

82. See reports in *Asahi Shimbun*, 26 September 2005; *Nihon Keizai Shimbun*, 31 December 2005; and *Asagumo*, 3 March 2005, on the budget for defense of 160 inhabited and uninhabited islands in Japan's "southwest." See *Japan Times*, 30 December 2006, which reported the U.S. aircraft carrier Kitty Hawk took part in the 2006 exercise.

83. Japan Defense Agency 2004, 124.

84. Honda et al. 2005, 365.

85. Interview, 19 December 2005, with LDP Diet member who attended the meeting.

86. *Nihon Keizai Shimbun*, 27 January 2006; *Asagumo*, 10 March 2005, offers the graphic comparison.

87. *Asahi Shimbun*, 29 March 2006; *Asahi Shimbun*, 10 September 2006.

88. For background on this so-called BADGE system, see Samuels 1987.

89. Honda et al. 2005, 274–75.

90. Katayama 2005, 161.

91. *Yomiuri Shimbun*, 15 December 2005, and *Japan Times*, 1 September 2005. Later, when development was extended to ten years, the costs mounted commensurately. *Yomiuri Shimbun*, 25 September 2005.

92. Ishiba 2005a, 147. See also Honda et al. 2005, 238–39.

93. This is remarked on in Honda et al. 2005, 243.

94. Quoted in Honda et al. 2005, 242–43.

95. See the reports in *Asahi Shimbun*, 17 July 2005; *Sankei Shimbun*, 20 July 2005; and chapter 7 of this book. In his memoirs, Director General Ishiba acknowledged that the early equipment (Block 04) will be entirely "made in America," but suggests that Japanese technology is being used for development of the next block. See Ishiba 2005a, 138–39.

96. See the review of early efforts in Ōtake 1983, 318–22. Samuels (1987) updates Ōtake. More recent efforts include three reports by the Defense Production Committee of Keidanren. The first was issued in May 1995: *Shinjidai ni Taiōshita Bōeiryoku Seibi Keikaku no Sakutei o Nozomu* (Seeking a Policy for Defense Equipment Planning to Respond to the New Age). The second was issued in September 2000: *Jikibōeiryoku Seibi Keikaku ni tsuite no Teigen* (A Proposal Related to the Next Midterm Defense Build-up Plan). The third was issued in July 2004: *Kongo no Bōeiryoku seibi no Arikata ni Tsuite* (Concerning the Future Shape of Defense Equipment). They are summarized in Nippon Keizai Dantai Rengōkai 2005, 17.

97. The Araki Commission was the report on which the 2004 National Defense Program Guidelines was based. Report quoted in Tsutsui 2005, 20.

98. Statement of the chief cabinet secretary, 10 December 2004.

99. Honda et al. 2005, 264.

100. Nippon Keizai Dantai Rengōkai 2005, 15, 17.

101. Daniels 2004, 15.

102. Speech by deputy chief of mission, U.S. Embassy Tokyo, Joseph Donovan, at American Enterprise Institute conference "Transforming the U.S.-Japan Alliance," Tokyo, 25 October 2005.

103. Kato 2005, 17.

104. Michishita 2002, 91–93.

105. Green and Sakoda (2001, 1–2) refer to a "maturing alliance," Daniels (2004, 11) speaks of "erosion," and Schoff (2005, 44) refers to "tinkering."

106. National Institute for Defense Studies 2003, 17.

107. See Mochizuki 2006b.

5. The Discourse

1. Morris 1960. See also the *Yomiuri Shimbun*, 1 December 2005, for a comparison of "progressive" bureaucrats during Konoye's ascendance in the 1930s to the reformism (*kaikaku*) of Prime Minister Koizumi seventy years later.

2. Koschmann 1997, 109.

3. Kitaoka 2002.

4. Samuels 1994.

5. Koschmann (1997) and Saaler (2005) explore these connections and transformations. See also Duus 2001.

6. Shiraishi (2006) is an incisive analysis of these differences. See also Bungei Shunjū 2005, 197, and *Sankei Shimbun*, 22 August 2005.

7. This point was driven home by a senior JDA bureaucrat who clearly identified himself as sympathetic with Kobayashi Yoshinori and other nationalists "who are reluctant to identify with the West." Interview, 23 November 2005.

8. *Sentaku*, August 2005.

9. Morris-Suzuki 2005.

10. *Nihon no Ronten 2005* (Bungei Shunjū 2005), an annual review of Japanese politics, economy, and society, devotes a large section to the contemporary debate on these issues.

11. Hosaka 2005.

12. Miura (2005) is a sympathetic book about the Yasukuni Shrine. Abe Shinzō devoted considerable space to the Yasukuni issue in his campaign manifesto. See Abe 2006, 66–74.

13. Yasukuni's English language website is at http://www.yasukuni.or.jp/english/index.html.

14. *Ronza*, February 2006, 31; *Asahi Shimbun* 20 March 2007.

15. See Miura (2005, 36) and Bungei Shunjū (2005) for the list of all postwar visits by Japanese prime ministers.

16. *Asahi Shimbun* and Chinese Academy of Social Sciences 2005. For a book critical of the Yasukuni Shrine, see Takahashi 2005. See Togo (2006) for an insider's compelling analysis.

17. He 2004.

18. Bungei Shunjū 2005, 260–61.

19. *Wall Street Journal*, 16 August 2005.

20. *Tokyo Shimbun*, 26 August 2005.

21. Smith (2006) is the most comprehensive treatment of contemporary base issues. See also Hashimoto et al. 2005 and Japan Defense Agency 2004, 373.

22. *Mainichi Shimbun*, 7 September 2005; Shimaguchi 2005.

23. *Japan Times*, 24 October 2005.

24. Interview, 26 January 2006.

25. The full text of the treaty is at http://www.mofa.go.jp/region/n-america/us/q&a/ref/1.html. Shimaguchi (2005, 16) argues vigorously that Article 6 is the source of continued extraterritorial privilege for U.S. forces. (Shimaguchi is the former director general of the Defense Facilities Administration.)

26. The National Police Agency reported 157 criminal investigations of U.S. military personnel in 2004, only slightly fewer than the 174 in 1995. See its statistics online at http://www.npa.go.jp/toukei/keiji30/18.1–8(hp).pdf.

27. See, for example, the headlines that followed a hit-and-run accident in which a U.S. sailor hurt three Japanese schoolboys but was released by authorities: *Tokyo Shimbun*, 29 December 2005 ("SOFA Used as Shield"; "Special Treatment Unforgivable") and *Mainichi Shimbun*, 29 December 2005 ("Accountability at Issue").

28. Umebayashi 2005, 117.

29. A list of suits is provided in the JDA White Paper each year. See, for example, Defense of Japan 2004, 374.

30. *Tokyo Shimbun*, 9 February 2006.

31. Such accidents are uncommon but have a long history. In 1964, two U.S. planes crashed near Tokyo, injuring forty-three people. After another crashed in Yokohama in 1977, the U.S. military refused to reveal the results of its investigation and left compensation payments up to the Japanese side.

32. Smith 2006, 45.

33. Ina 2005, 42.

34. For more on this Special Action Committee on Okinawa (SACO) agreement, see Defense of Japan 2004; Hashimoto et al. 2005; and Smith 2006.

35. The 1950s was already a time of pitched antibase furor. Sadō (2003) reviews the most politicized cases, beginning with Ishikawa in 1953 and Sunagawa in 1955.

36. Mochizuki 1983–84, 164, and Nagai 1983, chap. 3.

37. Ishiba 2005a, 28.

38. Soeya 2005, 174.

39. Japan Defense Agency 2004, 390, and Tokuchi 2001, 72–73.

40. Honda et al. 2005, 156.

41. Soeya 2005, 20.
42. http://www.komei.or.jp/manifest/policy/manifest2005/08.html.
43. For examples, see statements on Article 9 and the U.S.-led war in Iraq by Yo-komichi Takahiro and Hironaka Wakako at http://www.yokomichi.com/monthly_message/2000.11.01.htm (1 November 2000) and http://www.hirowaka.com/eng_dietact/plenary_20030321_e.html (21 March 2003).
44. Curtis 1999, 239.
45. http://www.jcp.or.jp/jcp/Koryo/index.html.
46. Participation data on the peace movement can be found in the *Nihon Rōdō Nenkan*, published annually.
47. "Chronic nationalism" is Morris's apt term. Morris 1960, 393.
48. For analysis of the changing salience of "autonomous defense" (*jishu bōei*), see Sadō 2003 and Soeya 2005. The latter, in particular, relocates Nakasone Yasuhiro in the history of Japan's postwar security discourse. Nish (1993, 15) reminds us that the term "autonomous diplomacy" was used by conservative politicians such as Matsuoka Yūsuke and Konoye Fumimaro, who opposed "Shidehara diplomacy" in the 1920s and 1930s.
49. "Gaullists" were first identified by Mochizuki 1983–84 and by Nagai 1983. See also Sadō 2003.
50. Interview, Professor Fujiwara Kiichi, Tokyo University, 8 August 2005.
51. Samuels (2003, chap. 12) reviews Ishihara's political development. See also Park 2005.
52. Ishihara 2005.
53. Interview, 15 July 2005.
54. He had earlier been joined by the late Shimizu Ikutarō, who famously declared that "Japan is alone!" See Shimizu 1980, 930.
55. Morris 1960, 423.
56. Nishibe 1988.
57. Nishibe 2004.
58. Nishibe 2004.
59. Nishibe 2003a.
60. Takubo and Nishibe 2004, 50–51.
61. *Ronza* 2005, 31.
62. Nishibe 2003b and Takubo and Nishibe 2004.
63. Takubo and Nishibe 2004, 52.
64. There is an "unofficial fan site" for Nakanishi at http://blog.livedoor.jp/strategy001/.
65. Nakanishi 2003a, 25–26; Nakanishi 2000.
66. Nakanishi 2004b.
67. Nakanishi 1990; Nakanishi 2003a, 25–26.
68. Nakanishi rejects appeals from Korea and China for stronger relations with Japan as a "malignant virus" (*akusei no uirusu*). Nakanishi 2003a, 27–28.
69. Nakanishi 2003a, 28.
70. Quoted by Berkofsky 2004 and in Agence France-Presse, 27 January 2004.
71. *Sankei Shimbun*, 17 February 2003.
72. Nakanishi 2003a, 35.
73. Nakanishi 2003a, 36–37. See also his "Nuclear Declaration for Japan" in *Voice*, February 2003. Writing with U.S. strategist Fred Iklé immediately after the fall of the Berlin Wall, Nakanishi disavowed the need for Japan to build its own nuclear arsenal. See Iklé and Nakanishi 1990, 82.
74. Nakanishi 2003a, 36. The nuclear debate in Japan was full-throated in late 2006 after a senior LDP official close to Prime Minister Abe called for a review of government

policy. See Iinuma 2006. Nakanishi was joined by another Kyoto University professor, Saeki Keishi, who argued in the midst of this debate that "it is a mistake to entrust Japan's security to an emotionally unstable American democracy. Japan must not postpone forever its decision on whether or not to possess nuclear weapons." *Sankei Shimbun*, 15 November 2006.

75. Saaler (2002) places the textbook debate in historical context. *People's Daily*, 17 May 2001, is one example of China's reaction to Japanese revisionism.

76. In the January 2003 issue of *Shokun!* he singles out Okazaki Hisahiko.

77. Kobayashi and Nishibe 2003. *Shūkan Tōyō Keizai*, 20 March 2004.

78. "Okinawa no kichi no kikensei o yamato (hondo) ni uttaetai." *Okinawa Taimusu*, 15 August 2005.

79. Interview with upper house LDP Diet representative, 21 December 2005, and with senior JDA official, 11 January 2006.

80. *Oriental Economist*, July 2006, 7. Abe bemoans the inability of the SDF to protect Japanese citizens in his campaign manifesto. See Abe 2006, 140–42.

81. Samuels (2003, chap. 12) reviews Ozawa's political development.

82. *Mainichi Shimbun*, 11 April 2006. Nakanishi Terumasa also uses the term "normal nation" but chastizes Ozawa and other conservatives for positing the "immature" idea that the United Nations might provide Japan security. Nakanishi 2003a.

83. Ishiba reports that he left the Shinshintō for the LDP over this issue. Ishiba 2005, 85 and 203. See Kitaoka (2004) for more on the differences among conservatives vis-à-vis the role of the United Nations.

84. Watanabe in *Yomiuri Shimbun*, 25 November 2005. He also reports that he tried to talk Koizumi out of visiting Yasukuni. See *Ronza*, February 2006. Kōno interview: 21 December 2005.

85. *Gaikō Fōramu*, January 2006.

86. *Tokyo Shimbun*, 6 December 2005.

87. Watanabe in *Ronza*, February 2006, 33.

88. See the dialogue between *Asahi Shimbun* editorial chief Wakamiya Yoshibumi and Watanabe in *Ronza*, February 2006.

89. Watanabe in *Ronza*, February 2006, 37. For analysis of Nakasone's realism, see Park 2005 and Soeya 2005. Maehara Seiji, former head of the DPJ, is also a realist but was reluctant to tilt too vigorously in the direction of the United States. See *Tokyo Shimbun*, 24 November 2005, and *Yomiuri Shimbun*, 10 December 2005.

90. See Mochizuki (1983–84) for an analysis of this position during the cold war.

91. Ishihara 2005, 151; Park 2005.

92. Nakasone feels a special responsibility on this issue, as he was the first to visit Yasukuni on 15 August 1985 (the fortieth anniversary of the end of the war), an act that transformed a domestic issue into an international one. His tilt away from Yasukuni in deference to Chinese and Korean sensibilities incensed many on the right.

93. Ishiba 2005a, 151.

94. The term "new conservative mainstream" was suggested by Professor Son Kissup. Interview, Seoul, 30 November 2005.

95. *Nihon Keizai Shimbun*, 28 July 2005. In February 2006, Chinese foreign minister Li Zhaoxing compared Prime Minister Koizumi's visits to Yasukuni Shrine to visits to the graves of Nazi leaders and called them "foolish" and "immoral." Chief Cabinet Secretary Abe formally protested, and declared that China's top leaders "lacked respect." *Asahi Shimbun*, 9 March 2006. His views are elaborated in Abe 2006.

96. *Yomiuri Shimbun*, 25 November 2005.

97. Asō was also of the opinion that Koreans "voluntarily" adopted Japanese names during the colonial period. *Tokyo Shimbun*, 2 February 2006. In July 2006 it was learned

that the Shōwa emperor stopped visiting Yasukuni because he did not wish to be associated with the war criminals enshrined there. See *Asahi Shimbun*, 19 July 2006.

98. Kitaoka (2004) lists the realists' criteria.

99. *Sankei Shimbun*, 3 August 2005. If the realists' views are best reflected in the pages of the *Yomiuri Shimbun*, the revisionists' position is found in the smaller, but still influential, daily, the *Sankei Shimbun*.

100. Interview, 21 December 2005, LDP member, House of Councillors.

101. Ina 2005, 42.

102. Kawakatsu (2006, chap. 6) reviews the "China threat" arguments in Japan.

103. Iriye (1997) examines the LDP-PRC relationship in the 1950s. See Taniguchi (2005) for more on the pro-China (Keiseikai) faction within the LDP.

104. Soeya 2005, 22. One former senior diplomat suggests that "any notion that Japan had of itself as a great power was pitiably smashed (*mijime ni uchikudaku*)" in the 1990s. Tanaka 2005, 83.

105. Kōsaka 1996, 121.

106. Kōsaka 1996, 118–24. He said little of the Dutch colonies in South America and Southeast Asia.

107. Soeya 2005.

108. Kitaoka (1995a, 32–37) reviews this position. See also Takemura (1994) and the discussion between Miyazawa Kiichi and Kōsaka Masataka in Miyazawa and Kōsaka 1984. Kōsaka was a mercantile realist who never failed to argue for security policy in the national interest. See Kōsaka 1996.

109. Kōsaka (1996) coined the term "civilian great power" (*bunminteki taikoku*). Funabashi (1998) modifies it to "global civilian power."

110. *Asahi Shimbun*, 28 August 2005.

111. Speaking of Prime Minister Koizumi, Kōno suggested that "policymakers feel good when they see nationalism on the rise. However, Japan will be isolated in the international community and could suffer great damage." Quoted in *Tokyo Shimbun*, 11 August 2005. In March 2006, forty-one lawmakers from the three former Kōchikai factions met to hammer out a common Asia policy. See the account in the *Asahi Shimbun*, 16 March 2006.

112. This distinction was made by Keio University professor Tadokoro Masayuki, interview, 6 July 2005. See also S. Morimoto 2005, 162.

113. Duus (2001) is a useful review. See also Mochizuki 2004.

114. *Tokyo Shimbun*, 7 July 2005.

115. *Asahi Shimbun*, 10 May 2006; *Nihon Keizai Shimbun*, 1 May and 11 May 2006.

116. Duus 2001, 250; Koschmann 1997; Ogoura 2005b.

117. Ogoura 1993.

118. Yamakage 1997, 300–301; Koschmann 1997, 109; Tanaka 2005.

119. *Mainichi Shimbun*, 17 August 2005.

120. *Asahi Shimbun*, 7 April 2006.

121. Terashima 2005b and *Zaikai*, 24 May 2005.

122. *Gendai*, 1 February 2005, 70; *Nihon Keizai Shimbun*, 5 June 2006.

123. Terashima 2002, 262, and *Gendai*, 1 February 2005, 67. Terashima (2002, chap. 3) explores the lives of such twentieth-century Asian intellectuals as Okakura Tenshin, who first argued for "self respect" in a Western-dominated world order.

124. Terashima 2005a.

125. *Ronza* 2005. 45.

126. Terashima 1996.

127. Shiraishi 2004.

128. He is referring to such things as Japanese manga, Korean television dramas, and Hong Kong films. Shiraishi 2004, 162–65, 182.

129. Shiraishi 2004, 13, 132.
130. Shiraishi 2004, 133.
131. Shiraishi 2004, 218–19.
132. Shiraishi 2004, 186–88.
133. Soeya 2005, 223.
134. *Asahi Shimbun*, 8 December 2003.
135. Soeya 2005, 217.
136. Testimony by Tanaka Akihiko to lower house Budget Committee. Yosan Iinkai 2005, 19.

6. The New Threat Environment

1. See Moravcsik 1997.
2. National Institute for Defense Studies (2005) reviews maritime security issues, including piracy. Admiral Yamazaki Makoto (ret.) says that the Malacca Strait is "the Achilles heel of the global economy." See Yamazaki 2005, 11.
3. One former JDA administrative vice minister warns of the threat of a "giant China" (*kaibutsu chūgoku*), and Kyoto University professor Nakanishi Terumasa argues that China is the same threat to Japan today that the Soviet Union was during the cold war. Interview, 15 July 2005, and Nakanishi 2005, 79.
4. This complementarity was acknowledged by Prime Minister Koizumi at the April 2002 Boao Forum. Cited in National Institute for Defense Studies 2005, 52. For a similar view from Keidanren, see Keidanren 2001, 1.
5. Richard Katz in *Oriental Economist*, April 2006.
6. By 2005, China had effectively assuaged the concerns of its southeast neighbors who had felt most threatened by its rise. See Glosny 2006.
7. Taniguchi 2005, 446.
8. *Nihon Keizai Shimbun*, 28 July 2005.
9. Kwan 2004, 1.
10. Soeya 2005, 219–22.
11. Przystup 2004.
12. Mochizuki 2004, 122–23.
13. Kokubun 2005, 12–13.
14. Takahara 2004.
15. Kokubun 2005, 15.
16. See Ogoura 2005b and Kokubun 2005 for two examples.
17. Swaine and Pei (2005) is an excellent snapshot of the bilateral relationship.
18. Lim 2003, 1.
19. Meeting with former Chinese ambassador, Tokyo, 24 August 2005.
20. China has settled the vast majority of its territorial disputes. Japan has settled none. See Fravel 2005.
21. Kokubun 2005, 14.
22. Okamoto Yukio in *Chūō Kōron*, June 2005. Shu (2005, 266) denies that Chinese textbooks are any more state-controlled than Japanese ones.
23. Ogoura 2005b, 48. *Chūō Kōron*, June 2005.
24. A former JDA administrative vice minister called anti-Japanism a "path for their survival" (*ikinokori no michi*). Interview, 15 July 2005.
25. Yokochi 2005, 4.
26. Kokubun 2005, 5.
27. Kawakatsu 2006, chap. 6, 10–11, 14.

28. Tabata (2004, 76) cites statements by Tokyo governor Ishihara and Kyoto University professor Nakanishi Terumasa.

29. Yokochi 2005, 7.

30. *Gaikō ni kansuru Yoronchōsa,* http://www8.cao.go.jp/survey/h16/h16–gaikou/images/h05.csv.

31. Sakaba and Yasuda 2005.

32. Tabata 2004, 75.

33. Hung 2005 and *New York Times,* 19 November 2005.

34. Polling data from the 2004 Beijing Area Study provided by Alastair Iain Johnston.

35. *Zong Huaying Cai Wang,* 2005.

36. *Asahi Shimbun* and Chinese Academy of Social Sciences 2005.

37. *People's Daily,* 15 August 2005.

38. *Sankei Shimbun,* 15 August 2005.

39. For evaluations of China's military capabilities, see Shambaugh 2005; Crane et al. 2005; and Segal et al. 2003. One U.S. DoD analysis is posted at www.defenselink.mil/news/Jul2005/d20050719china.pdf.

40. *Yomiuri Shimbun,* 14 August 2005.

41. For an authoritative Japanese evaluation that comes to the conclusion that the PLA is not presently a threat to Japan, see Ishiba 2006. He calls the PLA a "paper tiger" (139) and derides its inability to command the sea and air around Taiwan and the age of its equipment.

42. Ōta 2005, 142.

43. Hiramatsu 2002. It is unclear how such sensors might transmit data secretly.

44. Hiramatsu 2002, 219.

45. Ōta 2005, 144; Yokochi 2005; Michishita 1999.

46. Taniguchi 2005, 456; Yamazaki 2005, 14.

47. Interview, Nippon Zaidan research fellow, 9 August 2005.

48. Lim 2003, 5.

49. The Coast Guard sighted fifteen Chinese research ships in the Japanese EEZ in 1995 and twice that many in 1999. It also reported sighting PLAN war ships on a regular basis. Kawakatsu 2006, chap. 6.

50. Associated Press, 9 November 2005.

51. See Schoenbaum (2005) for a useful brief review of the claims.

52. As the March 2001 EP-3 incident involving a U.S. Navy electronic surveillance plane illustrated, the Convention on the Law of the Sea did not alter the freedom of states to sail or fly outside of their (or others') territorial waters.

53. Kokubun 2005, 25–26.

54. Yokochi 2005, 6. Negotiations were resumed in April 2007 after a conciliatory summit meeting in Tokyo.

55. Yokochi 2005, 11.

56. Interview, 28 September 2005.

57. Kawakatsu (2006, chap. 6) reports that by 1996 the China threat had shifted from military to economic.

58. See Nakamura and Shibuya (1995) for an official analysis.

59. *Shūkan Daiyamondo,* 7 June 1997.

60. *Yomiuri Shimbun,* 14 October 2001; *Asahi Shimbun,* 27 September 2002.

61. In 2004, Japanese FDI to China (including Hong Kong and Taiwan) increased by 54 percent and reached $5.7 billion. That same year, Japanese FDI to the United States declined by 56 percent to $4.7 billion. Data from the Ministry of Finance at http://www.mof.go.jp/english/e1c008.htm.

62. Kagaku Gijutsuchō 1997.

63. *Nihon Keizai Shimbun,* 4 September 1997.

64. *Nihon Sangyō Shimbun,* 5 June 1997.

65. Nakamura 2002, 1.

66. One of the leading proponents of Japanese leadership—and the promoter of an ASEAN "look East" policy—was Malaysian prime minister Mahathir Mohamad, who had been courted by Japanese business and government for years.

67. Nanto and Chanlett-Avery 2005, 1–3.

68. See the editorial in the *Nihon Keizai Shimbun,* 1 August 2005.

69. Soeya 2005, 220; Pempel 2005b.

70. Takahara 2004, 158.

71. *Mainichi Shimbun,* 14 December 2005.

72. *Sankei Shimbun,* 4 February 2005.

73. Pempel 2005b, 5.

74. For example, see Bōei Seibi Shutoku 2005.

75. See American Chamber of Commerce 2006 and *Nihon Keizai Shimbun,* 2 February 2006.

76. In *"Rich Nation, Strong Army"* I trace this "three note chord of Japanese techno-nationalism" back to Meiji-era industrial policy. Suzuki (2006) calls for a "new techno-nationalism to reinvigorate the defense industry."

77. This is from the last section of the 2004 National Defense Program Guidelines.

78. Japan Defense Agency 2005, 532.

79. "Sense of crisis" according to the JDA director general for R & D, Sasaki Tatsurō. Interview, 8 November 2005. "Weakening of base" from Bōei Seibi Shutoku 2005, 1. "Gathering anxiety," ibid., 3.

80. The Technology Research and Development Institute (TRDI), Japan's DARPA (Defense Advanced Research Projects Agency), has only twelve hundred employees, compared to 145,000 in the U.S. military defense technology establishment. Defense R & D as a percent of total defense budget is roughly 60 percent of German levels and barely 20 percent of U.S. levels. Data supplied by the office of the JDA director general for R & D.

81. Nippon Keizai Dantai (2005, 4) and Japan Defense Agency 2005, 354.

82. Nippon Keizai Dantai 2005, 4.

83. Data supplied by Keidanren staff, 26 September 2005.

84. Honda et al. 2005, 272.

85. Portions of this section are derived from Samuels 2004b. For a concise history of the North Korea–Japan relationship, see Green (2001, chap. 4) and Manyin 2003.

86. MOFA Blue Book 2003, chap. 1, sec. 1, at http://www.mofa.go.jp/mofaj/gaiko/bluebook/2003/gaikou/html/honpen/index.html.

87. Bōeichō 2003, 44–45.

88. Ishiba 2005a, 14.

89. Ishiba 2005a, 30, for example. Schoff (2006) unbundles Japanese strategic thinking about the DPRK, and finds considerable variation.

90. Teuben 2004, 38.

91. Teuben 2004, 42.

92. Michishita 2004b.

93. Green 2001, 117.

94. Kyodo, 10 November 2003. See also *Sankei Shimbun,* 11 November 2003.

95. See Akaha 2002.

96. Giarra 2001, 70. Michael Green (2001, 277–78) disagrees.

97. Menon 2007, chap. 4.

98. C. Hughes 2004a and 2004b. Christensen and Snyder (1990) and Christensen (1997) frame this common alliance predicament. See Sadō (2003, 203) for analysis of the

"entanglement thesis" (*makikomare ron*). An ASDF general, Marumo Yoshinari, insists that the greatest threat to Japan is "isolation" (*koritsuka*). See Honda et al. 2005, 410. Schoff (2006, 20–21) addresses Japan's "abandonment fear," which he says is more often expressed in private than in public by Japanese strategists.

99. Przystup (2005, 2) speaks of "an ongoing convergence of a common strategic vision." An earlier version of this list was in Samuels and Twomey 1999. In February 2005, the U.S.-Japan Consultative Committee issued a similar list.

100. Takahashi 2004, 20.

101. National Institute for Defense Studies 2003, 60.

102. In 2006, U.S. ambassador Thomas Schieffer expressed concerns that "it seems [Japan's] intention is to exclude the United States from Asia." *Nihon Keizai Shimbun*, 20 April 2006.

103. Pekkanen 2005, 2, 8.

104. Soeya 2005, 221.

105. Kawashima 2003, 31; Morimoto 2005, 141; *Sankei Shimbun*, 1 March 2006, 5.

106. *Mainichi Shimbun*, 19 February 2006.

107. One Japanese estimate holds that production from the Azadegan field could eventually account for between 4 percent and 6 percent of Japan's total crude imports of around five million barrels a day. *Financial Times*, 19 February 2004. Morimoto 2005, 139–40.

108. *Oil and Gas Journal*, 19 April 2004.

109. *Mainichi Daily News*, July 2, 2003.

110. Kyodo News, February 19, 2004.

111. *Sankei Shimbun*, August 12, 2004, 9.

112. *Tokyo Shimbun*, 31 July 2005. Some specialists believe that the Azadegan project is a bad deal for Japan. They are eager for U.S. pressure on METI to prevail. Interview, trading company oil expert, 8 June 2006.

113. Japanese vice minister for economy, trade and industry press conference, 22 September 2004.

114. This according to Vice Minister for Foreign Affairs Takeuchi Yukio, 23 August 2004.

115. *Nihon Keizai Shimbun*, 2 June 2005.

116. Agence France-Presse, 14 November 2003.

117. Agence France-Presse, 14 November 2003.

118. MOFA press release, August 2005.

119. *Sankei Shimbun*, 16 March 2006. By this time, the U.S. Congress had passed a law requiring the imposition of sanctions on foreign firms that invest more than $20 million in Iran. See the Congressional Research Service Report for Congress on "The Iran-Libya Sanctions Act," 3 April 2006, at http://fpc.state.gov/documents/organization/64937.pdf.

120. *Nihon Keizai Shimbun*, 16 September 2006.

121. *Asahi Shimbun*, 29 December 2005; *Sankei Shimbun*, 23 March 2006.

122. *Yomiuri Shimbun*, 28 August 2006.

123. *Yomiuri Shimbun*, 14 September 2006.

124. Agence France-Presse, 29 September 2006.

125. Nakamoto Ryōichi of the Japan Petroleum Development Association, quoted in *Yomiuri Weekly*, 26 March 2006.

126. Kyodo, 23 March 2006.

127. *Yomiuri Shimbun*, 14 September 2006.

128. Agence France-Presse, 29 September 2006.

129. For three prominent examples, see Morimoto 2005; Ōta 2005; and Okamoto Yukio in *Yomiuri Shimbun*, 3 January 2005.

130. *Oriental Economist*, January 2006, 15. Shiozaki became chief cabinet secretary in September 2006.

131. Tanaka 2006, 20.
132. *Asahi Shimbun,* 2 August 2006; *Tokyo Shimbun,* 2 August 2006.
133. *International Business Times,* 6 October 2006.
134. *Asahi Shimbun,* 11 January 2007.
135. Green (2001, 277) suggests that divergences between U.S. and Japanese interests are "primarily tactical" and marginal to the shared core interests. He adds that even though Japan has forged coalitions to constrain the United States, Japan simply has too few reasonable alternatives to the alliance for this divergence to amount to much.
136. Kokubun (2005, 4) offers a reminder of this important fact.
137. Pekkanen 2005, 17. (Emphasis in original.)
138. Crawford 2003, 196.
139. *Daily Yomiuri,* 28 February 2005.
140. Japan-China Seminar, November 2005. Comments by Michael Schiffer. See also Schoff 2006, 20–21. The divergence in U.S. and Japanese interests vis-à-vis China is developed further in Pyle 2007.
141. Daniels (2004, 7) says that "the potential for divergence between Japan and the United States is real—a dangerous proposition for both countries."
142. Weinstein 1971, 66.
143. *Mainichi Shimbun,* 1 January 2006; Park 2007.

7. Meeting (and Making) Threats

1. *Nihon Keizai Shimbun,* 19 August 2004, and *Businessweek,* 11 October 2004.
2. Nanto and Chanlett-Avery 2005.
3. *Sankei Shimbun,* 23 February 2004; *Nihon Keizai Shimbun,* 19 August 2004; *Mainichi Shimbun,* 8 February 2004.
4. Data supplied by the office of the parliamentary vice minister of the Ministry of Economy, Trade and Industry, 21 December 2005.
5. See, for example, Ando and Kimura 2004; Fukao, Ishido, and Itō 2003; Ng and Yeats 2003; S. Berger 2005.
6. This analysis is first made explicit in the 2003–2004 METI White Paper.
7. Jiji Press, 3 June 2004. Vogel (2006) examines this economic adjustment.
8. The first paragraph establishes that manufacturing is Japan's most "basic industry."
9. Intellectual Property Strategy Council, "Plan for the Creation, Defense, and Utilization of Intellectual Property," Prime Minister's Office, 3 July 2002.
10. Nippon Keizai Dantai Rengōkai 2003.
11. Keizai Sangyōshō (2003) is one example.
12. *Nihon Keizai Shimbun,* 17 May 2004.
13. *International Herald Tribune,* 3 January 2006.
14. Nakamura quoted in *Keizai Kōhō,* November 2004, 3.
15. *Keizai Kōhō,* January 2006, 2–3.
16. *Nihon Keizai Shimbun,* 22 October 2005. In its survey of Japanese manufacturers, two-thirds reported plans to increase domestic production in the next three years.
17. *Keizai Kōhō,* January 2005, 3–4.
18. Morimoto 2004.
19. Nakamura and Shibuya 1995 and Nakamura 2002.
20. Remarks by Aoki Terumaki, senior adviser to the Sony Corporation, a pioneer of this approach, are in Boyd 2006. A senior research manager at the Fujitsu Research Institute tied this to the Chinese challenge, insisting that "today, all important R & D is done at home in Japan. It will never go to China." Interview, 24 October 2005.
21. This is examined in detail in Samuels 1994 and Green 1995.

22. Honda et al. 2005.
23. Interview, Cabinet Office JDA official, 9 September 2005.
24. Honda et al. 2005, 272.
25. Council on Security and Defense Capabilities 2004, 21–22. Note that the report also added that Japan should retain "state of the art production capabilities in core weapons systems."
26. Nippon Keizai Dantai 2004.
27. Bōei Seibi Shutoku 2005, 5.
28. Nippon Keizai Dantai 2005a, 6.
29. Some hope for more. Interview, deputy director, JDA Finance and Equipment Bureau, Research and Development, Planning Division, 12 October 2005.
30. *National Defense Program Guideline, FY 2005*, December 10, 2004, at http://www.kantei.go.jp/foreign/policy/2004/1210taikou_e.html.
31. In March 2006, U.S. ambassador J. Thomas Schieffer reportedly urged Japan to lift the self-imposed constraint. *Mainichi Shimbun*, 18 March 2006. But the FY 2007 budget plan, announced in July, called for further cuts—for the fifth straight year. *Mainichi Shimbun*, 20 July 2006. *Nihon Keizai Shimbun*, 19 December 2006.
32. Interview, Nagamatsu Keiichi, executive director, Keidanren Defense Production Committee, 30 August 2005. A senior JDA official responsible for research and development denied that the JDA is moving R & D off budget, but he acknowledged that the JDA "does benefit from civilian R & D done in the development of dual-use technologies." Interview, 8 November 2005.
33. Honda et al. 2005, 261. Note, too, that the JDA abandoned plans for a domestic unmanned aerial vehicle in 2005. *International Herald Tribune*, 9 June 2005.
34. Nippon Keizai Dantai 2005b, 16. See also Nippon Keizai Dantai 2004.
35. *Yomiuri Shimbun*, 8 August 2004, and interview, senior official of the JDA Technical Research and Development Institute, 26 May 2006, who pointed to the Boeing contract as evidence that "*kokusanka* worked." In 2006, MHI began marketing its "MJ" (Mitsubishi Jet), a follow-on to the YS-11. See Samuels 1994.
36. *Sankei Shimbun*, 24 December 2004. See also Suzuki 2006.
37. *Defense News*, 17 July 2006; interview, senior JDA official, 26 May 2006; interview, Arai Shougo, former director general, Japan Coast Guard, 31 May 2006.
38. Shiraishi (2004) provides a good account.
39. Shiraishi 2004, 184, and *Nihon Keizai Shimbun*, 1 August 2005. Pekkanen 2005.
40. Tanaka 2005, 84. Pekkanen (2005) is the source on "FTA frenzy" and reports that both METI and MOFA added Economic Partnership divisions in 2004 with responsibility for designing and negotiating them. METI alone put eighty-five officials to the task.
41. Soeya 2005, 221.
42. Soeya 2005, 223; *Nihon Keizai Shimbun*, 25 August 2006.
43. Yamada 2005, 33.
44. Tanaka quoted in *Nihon Keizai Shimbun*, 12 April 2005.
45. Remarks by Mitchell B. Reiss, director of policy planning, U.S. Department of State, delivered to the Japan Institute of International Affairs, Tokyo, 30 November 2004, 9.
46. Ibid., 5.
47. *Nihon Keizai Shimbun*, 15 December 2005.
48. Nanto and Chanlett-Avery 2005, 20–23.
49. *Nikkei Telecom*, 23 August 2005.
50. When this path was taken by Tokyo and Seoul in 2003–04, it ended in embarrassing disagreement about the most fundamental facts associated with the Japanese annexation of Korea in 1910. *Nihon Keizai Shimbun*, 25 January 2006.

51. *Yomiuri Shimbun,* 2 March 2006.

52. *Sankei Shimbun,* 17 April 2006. Both sides agreed Japan would formally end its yen loans to China in 2008. See *Yomiuri Shimbun,* 7 June 2006.

53. Jervis 1978.

54. Kawakatsu 2006, chap. 6.

55. *Asahi Shimbun,* 23 March 2006.

56. Yokochi 2005.

57. Taichū Gaikō Seisaku Kenkyū Gurūpu 2005.

58. Nishihara 2005, 2; Yokochi 2005, 10; interview, Akiyama Masahiro, former JDA administrative vice minister, 15 July 2005.

59. See the description of the actions of the nationalist Nippon Seinensha on its website: www.seinensya.org.

60. Honda et al. 2005, 178.

61. *International Herald Tribune,* 11 July 2005; *Sankei Shimbun,* 24 August 2005.

62. Honda et al. 2005, 172.

63. Bōeichō 2005. The Japanese term *taikō* was used for each of these national security strategy documents (1976, 1995, and 2004), but its English translation was changed from "outline" to "guidelines" in 2004.

64. For lucid accounts of the change, see Michishita 2005a; *Securitarian,* March 2005; Council on Security and Defense Capabilities 2004; *Asagumo,* 3 March 2005; and National Institute for Defense Studies 2005.

65. *Nihon Keizai Shimbun,* 31 December 2005, and *Sankei Shimbun,* 29 November 2005.

66. Reported by Kyodo News, 8 November 2004.

67. *Sankei Shimbun,* 1 October 2005. In his memoirs, Ishiba Shigeru is even more explicit: "If you read Article 9 very carefully, in theory the use of force is possible. The problem of whether or not it will be used is a policy decision." Ishiba 2005a, 204. Also see the October 2004 report that an unidentified LDP member of the party's Committee on Ocean Interests declared that "we need to stand firm, including the use of force." *Asahi Shimbun,* 5 October 2004.

68. The P3-C followed its rules of engagement and flew away after photographing the guns pointed in its direction. Kyodo News, 1 October 2005.

69. Associated Press, 9 November 2005.

70. *Los Angeles Times,* 13 January 2006; *Asahi Shimbun,* 26 February 2006; *Sankei Shimbun,* 27 January 2006.

71. AFX News, 2 December 2005. I am grateful to Eric Heginbotham for his analysis of the Japanese Coast Guard in private correspondence.

72. Interview, director, Secretarial Division, Japan Defense Agency, 22 November 2005. Interview, Nagamatsu Keiichi, executive director, Keidanren Defense Production Committee, 30 August 2005.

73. Japan's military advantage over China is acknowledged in Ishiba 2005a and Ishiba 2006. For a detailed analysis of PLA vs. SDF weapons systems, see *Jieitai vs. Chūgokugun: Jieitai wa Kaku tatakaeri,* 1 September 2005.

74. Interview, Ishiba Shigeru, 26 October 2005; interview, former JDA vice minister, 21 November 2005; Yamazaki 2005, 10–11. *Hindustan Times,* 30 January 2005. *Tokyo Shimbun,* 26 May 2006.

75. Details of this "dialogue" are available at http://www.kantei.go.jp/foreign/koizumi speech/2005/04/29seimei_e.html.

76. Yamazaki 2005, 8–11. One government adviser explained that a formal coalition might be too provocative, but increasing military-to-military contacts "is not a bad idea and is prudent to do in a multilateral context." Interview, 6 October 2005. Abe Shinzō concurs. See Abe 2006, 158–61. India, Japan and the U.S. held a joint naval drill in April 2007.

77. Data supplied by the Bōeichō Chōkan Kanbō Hōdōshitsu, December 2005. In August 2003, the MSDF even participated in a joint exercise with the Russian navy in Nakhodka Bay. See Mochizuki 2004, 125.
78. National Institute for Defense Studies 2005, 48.
79. Soeya (2005, 181) credits diplomat Satō Yukio.
80. Tokuchi 2001. See Menon (2007) for a different view.
81. Green and Sakoda 2001, 3.
82. Giarra 2001, 67.
83. The February 2005 2+2 joint statement is available at http://www.mod.go.jp/e/pab/joint/20050219.htm.
84. Kawashima 2003, 37.
85. C. Hughes 2004a, 43.
86. Kyodo News, 11 April 2005. Leheny 2006, chap. 6.
87. Interview, JDA Cabinet Office official, 28 September 2005. Kaijō Hoanchō 2006, 9.
88. *Asagumo*, 23 July 2005, reported that the ASDF was conducting missile-defense tests at the Japan Aerospace Exploration Agency's Uchinoura Space Center in Kagoshima, formally a civilian site. One senior JDA official avers that Tokyo has little to worry about from Pyongyang: "Kim Jong-Il is more rational than we expected." Interview, 26 May 2006.
89. *Asahi Shimbun*, 10 September 2006.
90. Agence France-Presse, 8 November 2005.
91. See *Japan Times*, 25 January 2005; *Tokyo Shimbun*, 27 March 2003; Daniels 2004, 12; Jiji Press, 24 January 2003; and *Hindustan Times*, 30 January 2005. Also, interview, Ishiba Shigeru, 26 October 2005.
92. *Yomiuri Shimbun*, 18 October 2006; *Nihon Keizai Shimbun*, 18 October 2006; *Sankei Shimbun*, 10 October 2006.
93. Satō Tatuo, statement to the lower house Committee on the Cabinet, 6 April 1954.
94. Ishiba 2005a, 26, and Yamazaki 2005, 17.
95. Kyodo News, 24 January 2003. See Suematsu 2003 and Akiyama 2002, 176–77. C. Hughes (2005b, 121) reports that the MSDF has openly sought acquisition of cruise missiles for preemption.
96. Associated Press, 10 July 2006. *Mainichi Shimbun*, 11 July 2006.
97. Michishita 2005a, 243.
98. Jervis 1978.
99. Interview, JDA cabinet official, 25 September 2005. This official added that the export of arms is the "next step," one that would already be in place had the LDP's coalition partner, the Kōmeitō, not stood in the way.
100. Honda et al. 2005, 276. Kyodo News, 22 December 2004; and Jijiweb, 25 March 2005.
101. Interview, 19 December 2005.
102. Michishita 2004c. See also *Asagumo*, 3 March 2005.
103. Interview, Sasaki Tatsurō, JDA director general for research and development, 8 November 2005.
104. Nishikawa 2005, 18.
105. *Tokyo Shimbun*, 6 April 2006.
106. Schoff (2006) deftly unbundles this debate.
107. Japan Institute for International Affairs 2005.
108. Teuben 2004.
109. Reuters, 18 October 2006; *Tokyo Shimbun*, 17 October 2006; *Asahi Shimbun*, 13 October 2006.

110. The study reportedly concluded it would take Japan three years to develop a prototype nuclear weapon, far longer than is conventionally assumed. *Sankei Shimbun*, 25 December 2006.

111. L. Hughes (2007) reviews a full range of disincentives for Japan to go nuclear.

112. *Los Angeles Times*, 18 October 2006.

113. Prime Minister Koizumi's testimony to the Foreign Affairs and Defense Committee of the upper house on 16 December 2003. A foreign policy task force came to a similar conclusion: "Only the United States will defend Japan in the event of attack." See Gaikō Kankei Tasukufōsu 2002, 13.

114. In describing the new *taikō*, which he helped draft, Tokuchi Hideshi explains that the alliance is indispensable for Japanese security, that the U.S. military is indispensable for peace and security in East Asia, and that Japan and the United States have to work together to deal with new threats. See his interview in *Securitarian*, March 2005, 13.

115. Taniguchi (2005, 445) invokes this metaphor. See Yan (2005) for the "chariot" and Taniguchi (2005, 457) on "joint hegemony."

116. Posen 2003.

117. Fred Iklé and Terumasa Nakanishi anticipated the geographic expansion of Japan's defense policy and of the U.S.-Japan security alliance seven years earlier. The time had come, they argued in 1990, "for Japan to shift its strategic emphasis from self defense...to one of coresponsibility for the defense of the global security system." Iklé and Nakanishi 1990, 92.

118. Akiyama 2002, 25.

119. See the review of these issues by Admiral (ret.) Yamazaki Makoto in Yamazaki 2005. Also see Shikata 2005 and Daniels 2004.

120. Honda et al. 2005, 71.

121. Apparently, this was the view of the Ministry of Foreign Affairs. See Shimaguchi 2005, 21.

122. Morimoto 2005, 186. Deputy Undersecretary Richard Lawless warned that there was too much uncertainty about how Japan's force posture would change. If overestimated, he said, the United States might leave Japan underprotected, and if underestimated, the United States would end up with too many troops in Japan and exacerbate frictions. Speech at the American Enterprise Institute conference "Transforming the U.S.-Japan Alliance," Tokyo, 25 October 2005.

123. This review process was described in a speech by Deputy Undersecretary Richard Lawless at the American Enterprise Institute conference "Transforming the U.S.-Japan Alliance," Tokyo, 25 October 2005.

124. Rice et al. 2005, 5.

125. Smith 2005 and *Nihon Keizai Shimbun*, 26 September 2005.

126. Foreign Press Center of Japan 2005. Difficulty implementing these operational changes was nothing new. Paul Giarra, a veteran alliance manager has observed that "the political costs of Japanese cooperation expand exponentially the closer the request comes to the time of the requirement, and the quality and extent of that cooperation decrease in the inverse proportion." Giarra 2001, 64–65.

127. *Tokyo Shimbun*, 19 July 2005.

128. *Sankei Shimbun*, 9 October 2004. C. Hughes 2005b, 116.

129. Agence France-Presse, 12 March 2006; *Asahi Shimbun*, 6 November 2005, 8 February 2006, 13 March 2006, and 16 March 2006; *Yomiuri Shimbun*, 3 November 2005 and 16 March 2006; *Mainichi Shimbun*, 2 November 2005 and 24 March 2006.

130. *Nihon Keizai Shimbun*, 2 May 2006.

131. *Tokyo Shimbun*, 19 July 2006; Associated Press, 24 July 2006.

132. Cossa 2005, 70.
133. Marc Valencia, "Japan in a Corner over Interdictions at Sea," *International Herald Tribune*, 22 October 2005.
134. Ishiba 2005a, 142.
135. For example, see Akiyama 2002; Morimoto 2005; Institute for National Strategic Studies 2000; and Okamoto 2002a. DPJ leader Maehara Seiji concurs (*Tokyo Shimbun*, 19 December 2005). One U.S. DoD official, Japan Desk Officer John D. Hill, called debates on whether the right to collective self-defense is permissible "ridiculous." *Asahi Shimbun*, 20 July 2005.
136. Honda et al. 2005, 430.
137. Honda et al. 2005, 409–10.
138. *Asahi Shimbun*, 4 April 2004.
139. Shikata 2005, 168.
140. Green and Sakoda 2001, 5. C. Hughes (2004a) and Shikata (2005) also invoke the metaphors. This, of course, ignores the fact (and mixes the metaphor) that Japan's largest shield of all is the nuclear umbrella provided by the United States.
141. "*Heisei* militarization" is the term used by Tanter 2004.
142. Taniguchi 2005. A JDA official seconded to the Cabinet Office explained that this provision will be included in a revision of the SDF Basic Law, which would replace the need for temporary laws, like the one that authorized the Indian Ocean dispatch in 2001. Interview, 23 November 2005.
143. Michishita (2004d) is a lucid analysis of contemporary SDF roles and missions. See also *Asagumo*, 30 June 2005 and 7 July 2005.
144. Yamazaki 2005, 5.
145. In March 2006, U.S. ambassador J. Thomas Schieffer reportedly criticized the cap as "something the American people find hard to understand." *Mainichi Shimbun*, 18 March 2006.
146. Defense of Japan 2004, 105.

Conclusion: Japan's Evolving Grand Strategy

1. Johnson (1984) reviews ideas about the Japan-Venice comparison. Okazaki (1991) invokes the Dutch case. In addition, Kōsaka (1964) and Iokibe (2000) compare Japan to the United Kingdom, a commercial nation that could enjoy the entire world as its trading partner.
2. Kaneda 2004.
3. Soeya 2005.
4. Kang and Katō 2004.
5. Macmillan 2002, 312.
6. Shiraishi 2004; Fujiwara 2002.
7. *International Herald Tribune*, 16 December 2005.
8. For a sophisticated examination of how to assess the norms, values, beliefs, and ideologies that "strategic culture" comprises, see Johnston 1995.
9. Boyd (forthcoming) explores this.
10. Pyle (2007) is a brilliant account of values, discourse, and Japanese responses to new world orders.
11. *Asahi Shimbun*, 24 April 2006. The term "active pacifism" was earlier invoked by the Japan Forum on International Relations 2004, 13–14.
12. Yamazaki 2005, for example.
13. Interview, former JDA director general Ohno Yoshinari, 26 January 2006.

14. Japan Forum on International Relations 2004, 13–14.
15. Kyodo, 30 September 2006.
16. Japan lags far behind China in this regard. Beijing provides more peacekeepers for UN operations than any other member of the United Nations Security Council. In September 2006, when China pledged one thousand more soldiers to support UN peacekeeping in Lebanon, Japan was still silent. BBC News, 18 September 2006.
17. Comments by Abe Shinzō at the Tokyo Forum called "The Next U.S. Administration and Japan—Outlooks for Security and Economy," 17 November 2004. For Abe's view on the humiliation of checkbook diplomacy, see Abe 2006, 136.
18. ASDF general Marumo Yoshinari's call for "respect" is in Honda et al. 2005, 410.
19. *Tokyo Shimbun*, 30 March 2005.
20. *Asahi Shimbun*, 19 February 2006. Itō 2000, 1.
21. Japan Forum on International Relations 2004, 20; Itō 2000, 1.
22. *Asahi Shimbun*, 1 January 2006, and Bungei Shunjū 2005, 175.
23. Kōno interview, 21 December 2005; Yamamoto interview, 9 June 2006.
24. Green 2001.
25. See, for example, T. Berger 1998; Katzenstein 1996; and Hook 1996.
26. C. Hughes 2005b, 124.
27. In late April 2006, Deputy Undersecretary of Defense Richard Lawless announced that Japan would pay $26 billion to support U.S. force realignment in Japan, a sum that shocked even Abe Shinzō, the chief cabinet secretary. *Sankei Shimbun*, 27 April 2006. Several weeks later, JDA director general Nukaga Fukujirō denied having agreed to that amount. *Nihon Keizai Shimbun*, 15 May 2006.
28. Morimoto 2006.
29. Remarks by Aaron Friedberg, former deputy assistant for national security affairs and director of policy planning in the Office of the Vice President in a speech to the American Enterprise Institute conference "Transforming the U.S.-Japan Alliance," Tokyo, 25 October 2005.
30. National Institute for Defense Studies 2003, 20, 34. Honda et al. 2005, 71. Interview, senior JDA official, 14 November 2005.
31. Japan Forum on International Relations 2004, 11. This report was signed by former JDA vice minister Aichi Kazuo and other senior strategists, including Imai Ryūkichi, Arima Tatsuo, Kakizawa Kōji, and Watanabe Akio.
32. "Key" and "heart" are from Gregson and Sakoda 1999. "Cornerstone" and "foundation" are from Cossa 2005. "Anchor" is from Rice et al. 2005. "Keystone" is from Przystup 2005.
33. Clark quoted in Daniels 2004, 62.
34. Lim (2003, 157) anticipated this. See also Daniels 2004 and Giarra 2001.
35. Menon 2007, chap. 4.
36. *Nihon Keizai Shimbun*, 26 August 2005. More disconcerting than the absolute level (48%) was the fact that the number of respondents who identified Japan dropped 17 points in the same year that the number who identified China rose by 14 points to 38%.
37. *Asahi Shimbun*, 30 September 2004.
38. Honda et al. 2005, 76.
39. *Mainichi Shimbun*, 20 October 2005.
40. National Institute for Defense Studies 2003, 17. Akiyama (2002, 24) explains that the JDA has been a vigorous proponent of this global posture, a reconfigured doctrine that the foreign ministry has tried unsuccessfully to block.
41. *Asahi Shimbun*, 18 October 2006.
42. Mearsheimer 2001; Twomey 2000.

43. These plans are laid out by one such group, Peace Depot, at http://www.peacedepot. org/e-news/frame.html.
44. Bōeichō 2005, 105.
45. Defense of Japan 2004, 488.
46. For a revealing firsthand account by a former MOF Budget Bureau official in charge of defense budgets, see Katayama 2005. *Nihon Keizai Shimbun*, 2 November 2004; *Yomiuri Shimbun*, 1 November 2004.
47. Yamazaki 2005, 20.
48. Nominal host nation support increased between 1990–2001, but relative to the defense budget, it declined. In 1991, host nation support was 9.6% of the JDA budget. In 2005, it was 8.7%. Data provided by Defense Facilities Administration Agency official, 11 January 2006. Former JDA director general Nukaga and administrative vice minister Moriya Takemasa have each insisted that the MOF create a separate budget to pay for the realignment. See *Sankei Shimbun*, 8 November 2005, and *Asahi Shimbun*, 1 May 2006. Note also that Japan's cost sharing has long been higher than that of any other U.S. ally. Office of the Secretary of Defense 1998.
49. National Defense Program Guidelines (provisional translation) 2004, 5–6. See http://www.jda.go.jp/e/policy/f_work/taikou05/fy20050101.pdf#search=%22national%20defense%20program%20guidelines%202004%22.
50. *Mainichi Shimbun*, 20 July 2006.
51. Ishiba 2005a, 15–16.
52. *Sankei Shimbun*, 9 November 2006.
53. Koga and Tanigaki sought to field a single "anti-Abe" candidate in the 2006 LDP presidential election, insisting that Japan needed to improve relations with China. See *Asahi Shimbun*, 7 June 2006.
54. *Asahi Shimbun*, 2 August 2006.
55. Kyodo World Service, 5 October 2006; *Nihon Keizai Shimbun*, 6 October 2006.
56. Xinhua News Agency, 29 November 2006; *Sankei Shimbun*, 17 November 2006; Agence France Presses, 14 January 2007.
57. In addition to the pronouncement of the neoautonomists reviewed in chapter 5, see also Itō 2000 and the Japan Forum on International Relations 2004.
58. Cited in Przystup 2004.
59. Ohtomo 2003, 46–50.
60. Morley 1957, 311. See Goldstein 2005 and Przystup and Saunders 2006 on U.S. hedging vis-à-vis China.
61. Weinstein 1971, 2.
62. Daniels 2004, 16.
63. Prime Minister's Commission on Japan's Goals 2000, 2.
64. Council on Security 2004, 5.
65. This dynamic was first suggested by Katō Yōichi of the *Asahi Shimbun*, 10 November 2005. See also C. Hughes (2004a) and Daniels (2004) for analyses that identify hedging as a central element in Japanese grand strategy. Green (2001, 24) dismisses Japanese hedging as "marginal," insisting that the Japanese know they have "no place else to go."
66. Tanaka and Murata 1996b, 11.
67. Kawashima 2003, 45.
68. This was confirmed in numerous interviews with policy intellectuals, as well as by senior MOFA and JDA officials, one of whom insisted that "'hedge and engage' is our basic national policy." 24 October 2005. "Strategic independence" is from C. Hughes 2004b, 181.
69. Testimony by Professor Tanaka Akihiko to the House of Representatives Budget Committee, 23 February 2005. See Yosan Iinkai 2005, 18.

70. *Mainichi Shimbun,* 23 July 2005.
71. The concept of a "dual hedge" was introduced in Heginbotham and Samuels (2002) and was examined in detail in chap. 6 of this book. See also C. Hughes 2005b.
72. Prime Minister's Commission 2000, chap. 6, p. 1.
73. Iriye 1997, 117.
74. Takahara 2004, 159.
75. Kawakatsu 2006 and *Shūkan Daiyamondo,* "Chūgoku wa Shusenjō" (China Is the Main Battlefield), 24 April 2004.
76. Abe 2006, 152–53.
77. National Institute for Defense Studies 2005, 8, 35–36.
78. *Yomiuri Shimbun,* 19 April 2006.
79. The foreign ministry reorganized its Cultural Affairs Department into the Public Diplomacy Department in August 2004. The department's director general, Kondō Sei-ichi, wrote an article entitled "Iraku ni Ikizuku Karatedō ga Shimesu Nihon Gaikō no Mirai" (Karate in Iraq Signals the Future of Japanese Foreign Policy) in the September 2004 issue of *Seiron* magazine in which he argued that Japanese assistance in such areas as culture and sports is particularly well received because "they incorporate spiritual value systems not found in the West."
80. Kitaoka Shinichi, "Japan's Identity and What It Means," Japan Forum on International Relations 2000.
81. Interview, 25 April 2006; emphasis added. Others reluctantly acknowledge that Japan will ultimately tilt toward the alliance. Asked what Japan would do if forced to choose, Yamamoto Ichita, former chair of the LDP Policy Committee on Foreign Policy, opined that "unfortunately, we would have to side with the United States." Interview, 9 June 2006.
82. *Asahi Shimbun,* 2 August 2006.
83. In the early 1980s, Japan's Gaullists and military realists—what today are the neo-autonomists and normal nation-alists—found common ground because "in concrete policy terms, there is little difference between those who support a defense buildup to meet American requests and to strengthen the alliance, and those who want an au-tonomous defense capability to put Japan on an equal footing with the United States." Mochizuki 1983–84, 174.
84. *Mainichi Shimbun,* 25 January 2006.
85. *Shūkan Posuto,* 25 April 2003, 44.
86. *Mainichi Shimbun,* 3 January 2007, and *Asahi Shimbun,* 11 January 2007.
87. See Ōta (2005, 174) for a particularly clear example.
88. C. Hughes 2004b, 181. Although he insists that Japan has erected strategic "fire-walls...[to] limit on a case by case basis the extent of support that it provides the United States," Hughes suggests elsewhere that Japan has become "inescapably dependent" on the United States. See Hughes (2004a, 131, 143) and Hughes (2006, 12).
89. Mochizuki (2004, 104) concurs. For the impact of the end of the cold war on do-mestic Japanese politics, see Samuels 2003. The creation of new options was stressed in several interviews with senior JDA officials during 2005–06.
90. Interview, Yamamoto Ichita, 9 June 2006.
91. C. Hughes (2005b) explores this point. Daniels (2004) also concludes that Japan is creating new options for itself.
92. Ishiba 2006, 141.
93. For the weighing of Japanese strategic options from the perspective of a former GSDF general, see Yokochi 2005.
94. Yamazaki 2005, 21.
95. Okamoto 2002a, 61.

96. *Asahi Shimbun*, 11 April 2006; *Mainichi Shimbun*, 15 April 2006; *Nihon Keizai Shimbun*, 5 June 2006; *Mainichi Shimbun*, 13 July 2006.

97. He began doing so in his 2006 *tour d'horizon*. See Abe 2006, 68–69.

98. Terashima 1996.

99. "Poodle" was the metaphor used by an official of the National Institute for Defense Studies, 22 August 2005. "Joint management of U.S. hegemony" is from Taniguchi 2005, 454.

100. Mahan 1890 and Mahan 1900. Lim (2003, 2) reminds us that the "essential" U.S. interest is not in *who* is strong or weak in Asia, but that there is a balance within the quadrilateral among Japan, Russia, China, and itself.

101. Mearsheimer 2001.

102. See, for example, the remarks by Aaron Friedberg, former deputy assistant for national security affairs and director of policy planning in the Office of the Vice President, and by Torkel Patterson, former senior director for Asian affairs at the National Security Council, in their speeches to the American Enterprise Institute conference "Transforming the U.S.-Japan Alliance," Tokyo, 25 October 2005.

103. C. Hughes 2004a, 135.

104. Conversation, U.S. official, 4 June 2006.

105. Speech by John D. Hill, regional director for Northeast Asia, at the Center for Global Partnership conference "Non-Traditional Security," 19 July 2005, Tokyo.

106. *Ronza*, March 2005, 30–31.

107. Daniels 2004, 71.

108. Menon 2007, chap. 4.

109. Taniguchi 2005, 456.

110. *Washington Post*, 7 September 2005.

111. This argument is also made by Mochizuki (2004, 130–31) and Mochizuki (2005, 35).

112. Pyle 2007, 1.

113. C. Hughes 2006, 15. Original quotation in *Asahi Shimbun* (evening edition), 5 October 2001.

114. Mochizuki 2004, 127.

115. Soeya 2005, 179 and 207.

References

Abe, Shinzō. 2006. *Utsukushii Kuni E* [Toward a Beautiful Country]. Tokyo: Bungei Shunjū.

Agawa, Naoyuki, and James Auer. 1996. "Pacific Friendship." *Proceedings of the U.S. Naval Institute*. http://www.vanderbilt.edu/VIPPS/VIPPSUSJ/publications/friendship/htm.

Akaha, Tsuneo. 2002. "Japan's Policy toward North Korea: Interests and Options." In *The Future of North Korea*, edited by Tsuneo Akaha, chap. 5. London: Routledge.

Akami, Tomoko. 2002. *Internationalizing the Pacific: The United States, Japan, and the Institute of Pacific Relations in War and Peace, 1915–45*. London: Routledge.

Akiyama, Masahiro. 2002. *Nichibei no Senryaku Taiwa ga Hajimatta* [The Japan-U.S. Strategic Dialogue Has Begun]. Tokyo: Akishobō.

Amaya, Naohiro. 1980. "Nihon Chōnin Kokkaron" [A Theory of Japan as a Merchant State]. *Bungei Shunjū*, March. Reprinted in *Sengo Nihon Gaikō Ronshū* [Collected Essays on Postwar Japanese Diplomacy], edited by Kitaoka Shinichi, 365–95. Tokyo: Chūō Kōronsha, 1995.

American Chamber of Commerce in Japan, ed. 2006. "Business White Paper on JDA Procurement Reform." Tokyo, November.

Ando, Mitsuyo, and Kimura Fukunari. 2004. "The Formation of International Production and Distribution Networks in East Asia." Conference paper at the 14th NBER Annual East Asia Seminar on Economics, Taipei.

Arasaki, Moriteru. 2001. "The Struggle against Military Bases in Okinawa: Its History and Current Situation." *Inter-Asia Cultural Studies* 2, no. 1.

Arase, David. 1995. *Buying Power: The Political Economy of Japan's Foreign Aid*. Boulder: Lynne Rienner.

Armacost, Michael H. 1996. *Friends or Rivals? The Insider's Account of U.S.-Japan Relations*. New York: Columbia University Press.

Armitage, Richard, et al. 2000. *The United States and Japan: Advancing toward a Mature Partnership*. Washington, D.C.: Institute for National Strategic Studies, National Defense University.

Art, Robert J. 2004. "Europe Hedges Its Security Bets." In *Balance of Power: Theory and Practice in the 21st Century*, edited by T. V. Paul, James J. Wirtz, and Michel Fortmann, 179–214. Stanford: Stanford University Press.

Asada, Sadao. 1973. "The Japanese Navy and the United States." In *Pearl Harbor as History: Japanese-American Relations, 1931–1941,* edited by Dorothy Borg and Shumpei Okamoto. New York: Columbia University Press.

Asagumo Shimbunsha. 2005. *Bōei Handobukku, 2005* [Defense Handbook, 2005] Tokyo: Asagumo Shimbunsha.

Asahi Shimbun and Chinese Academy of Social Sciences. 2005. *Japan-Korea-China Three Country Opinion Survey.*

Auer, James E. 1973. *The Postwar Rearmament of Japanese Maritime Forces: 1945–1971.* New York: Praeger.

Avant, Deborah D. 1994. *Political Institutions and Military Change: Lessons from Peripheral Wars.* Ithaca: Cornell University Press.

Bamba, Nobuya. 1972. *Japanese Diplomacy in a Dilemma: New Light on Japan's China Policy, 1924–1929.* Vancouver: University of British Columbia Press.

Beer, Lawrence, and H. Itoh. 1996. *The Constitutional Case Law of Japan, 1970 through 1990.* Seattle: University of Washington Press.

Berger, Gordon M. 1974. "Japan's Young Prince: Konoe Fumimaro's Early Political Career, 1916–1931." *Monumenta Nipponica* 29, no. 4: 451–75.

Berger, Suzanne. 2005. *How We Compete.* New York: Random House.

Berger, Thomas U. 1993. "From Sword to Chrysanthemum: Japan's Culture of Anti-Militarism." *International Security* 17, no. 4: 119–50.

——. 1998. *Cultures of Antimilitarism: National Security in Germany and Japan.* Baltimore: Johns Hopkins University Press.

Berkofsky, Axel. 2004. "Feckless Opposition Can't Halt Troop Dispatch." *Asia Times* Online, 5 February.

Berner, Steven. "Japan's Space Program: A Fork in the Road?" Technical report. Santa Monica, Calif.: RAND Corporation, National Security Research Division.

Bōeichō, ed. 1970. *Nihon no Bōei* [Japan's Defense]. October.

——. 2003. *Heisei 15 Nenban Nippon no Bōei Hakusho* [The Defense of Japan 2003: Defense White Paper]. Tokyo: Gyōsei.

Bōeicho. 2005. *Nihon no Bōei* [Japan's Defense]. Tokyo: Bōeichō.

Bōei Chōtatsu Kiban Seibi Kyōkai, ed. 2003. *Hantō o Meguru Heiki Gijutsu Iten no Shomondai* [Problems Associated with the Transfer of Military Technology to the Peninsula]. Tokyo: March.

Bōei Daigakkō. 2005a. *Bōeigaku Shirabasu Heisei 17 Nendo* [2005 Defense Studies Syllabus]. Yokosuka: Bōei Daigakkō.

——. 2005b. *Rishū Yōran* [Outline of the Course of Study]. Yokosuka: Bōei Daigakkō.

Bōei Seibi Shutoku Senryaku Kondankai, ed. 2005. *Arata na Jidai no Seibi Shutoku o Mezashite: Makoto ni Hitsuyō na Bōei Seisan Gijutsu Kiban no Kakuritsu ni Mukete* [Aiming for a New Era in Equipment Acquisition: Toward Establishing a Truly Necessary Defense Industrial and Technology Base]. Unpublished report. June. Tokyo.

Bōei Seisan Iinkai Jimukyoku, ed. 2005. "Bōei Seisan ni Taisuru Gaishi Kisei ni Tsuite" [Concerning Foreign Investment in the Defense Industry]. Unpublished memorandum. Tokyo.

Bōei Tsūshinsha. 2005. *Bōei Chōtatsu Yōran Heisei 17 Nendo Ban* [Defense Procurement Handbook: 2005 Edition]. Tokyo: Bōei Tsūshinsha.

Boyd, J. Patrick. 2003. "Nine Lives: Pragmatism, Pacifism, and Japan's Article Nine." Master's thesis, Massachusetts Institute of Technology.

——. 2006. "Globalization and the Future of the National Economy: Keizai Koho Center and MIT Japan Program Symposium Report." MIT Japan Program Working Paper 06–01. Cambridge, Mass.

——. Forthcoming. *Nationalism in Normal Times: Identity and Change in Post–Cold War Japan*. Ph.D. diss. Cambridge: Massachusetts Institute of Technology.

Boyd, J. Patrick, and Richard J. Samuels. 2005. "Nine Lives? The Politics of Constitutional Reform in Japan." *Policy Studies* 19. Washington, D.C.: East West Center.

Breer, William. 2001. "Japan's Contribution to the Campaign against Terror." *Japan Watch*. Washington, D.C.: Center for Strategic and International Studies.

Bungei Shunjū. 2005. *Nihon no Ronten 2006* [Issues for Japan: 2006]. Tokyo: Bungei Shunjū.

Burkman, Thomas W. 2003. "Nationalist Actors in the Internationalist Theater: Nitobe Inazō and Ishii Kikujirō and the League of Nations." In *Nationalism and Internationalism in Imperial Japan: Autonomy, Asian Brotherhood, or World Citizenship*, edited by D. Stegewerns, chap. 5. London: Routledge.

Burstein, Daniel. 1988. *Yen! Japan's New Financial Empire and Its Threat to America*. New York: Simon and Schuster.

Byas, Hugh. 1942. *Government by Assassination*. New York: Alfred A. Knopf.

Calder, Kent. 1988. "Japanese Foreign Economic Policy Formulation." *World Politics* 40: 517–41.

Carr, Edward Hallett. 1945. *Nationalism and After*. New York: Macmillan.

Christensen, Thomas J. 1997. "Perceptions and Alliances in Europe, 1865–1940." *International Organization* 51, no. 1: 65–97.

——. 1999. "China, the U.S.-Japanese Alliance, and the Security Dilemma in East Asia." *International Security* 23, no. 4 (Spring): 49–80.

Christensen, Thomas J., and Jack Snyder. 1990. "Chain Gangs and Passed Bucks: Predicting Alliance Patterns." *International Organization* 44: 137–68.

Conybeare, John A. C. 1992. "A Portfolio Diversification Model of Alliances: The Triple Alliance and Triple Entente, 1879–1914." *Journal of Conflict Resolution* 36, no. 1 (March): 53–85.

Cossa, Ralph A. 2005. "U.S. Security Strategy in East Asia and the Prospects for an Asian Regional Security Regime." *Asia-Pacific Review* 12, no. 1: 64–86.

Council on Security and Defense Capabilities. 2004. "The Council on Security and Defense Capabilities Report: Japan's Vision for Future Security and Defense Capabilities" (Araki Commission). Tokyo: October.

Craig, Albert M. 1968. "Fukuzawa Yukichi: The Philosophical Foundations of Meiji Nationalism." In *Political Development in Modern Japan*, edited by R. E. Ward, 99–148. Princeton: Princeton University Press.

Crane, Keith, et al. 2005. *Modernizing China's Military: Opportunities and Constraints*. Santa Monica, Calif.: RAND Corporation.

Crawford, Timothy. 2003. *Pivotal Deterrence: Third Party Statecraft and the Pursuit of Peace*. Ithaca: Cornell University Press.

Cronin, Patrick H., Paul S. Giarra, and Michael J. Green. 1999. "The Alliance Implications of Theater Missile Defense." In *The U.S.-Japan Alliance: Past, Present, and Future*, edited by Michael Green and Patrick M. Cronin, 170–85. New York: Council on Foreign Relations.

Crowley, James B. 1971. "Intellectuals as Visionaries of the New Asian Order." In *Dilemmas of Growth in Prewar Japan*, edited by J. W. Morley, 319–73. Princeton: Princeton University Press.

Csaki, Sebastian M. 2003. "Civilian Power Germany? Civilian Elites and the Development of ESDI/ESDP." Paper presented to the panel on "Comparative National Approaches to National Security," European Consortium for Political Research, Marburg, 18–21 September.

Curtis, Gerald L. 1999. *The Logic of Japanese Politics: Leaders, Institutions, and the Limits of Change*. New York: Columbia University Press.

Daniels, Paul R. 2004. "Beyond 'Better Than Ever': Japanese Independence and the Future of the U.S.-Japan Relationship." IIPS Policy Paper 308E. Tokyo: Institute for International Policy Studies, July.

Defense Agency. 1976. *Defense of Japan*. Tokyo: Japan Defense Agency.

Deming, Rust M., and Bernard J. Lawless. 1986. "Japan's Defense Policy." Washington, D.C.: National Defense University, Strategic Studies Project.

Diamond, Larry, and M. F. Plattner. 1996. Introduction to *Civil-Military Relations and Democracy*. Baltimore: Johns Hopkins University Press.

Dickinson, Frederick R. 1999. *War and National Reinvention: Japan in the Great War, 1914–1919*. Cambridge: Harvard University, Asia Center.

Doak, Kevin M. 2003. "Liberal Nationalism in Imperial Japan: The Dilemma of Nationalism and Internationalism." In *Nationalism and Internationalism in Imperial Japan: Autonomy, Asian Brotherhood, or World Citizenship*, edited by D. Stegewerns, chap. 2. London: Routledge.

Dore, Ronald. 1973. *British Factory, Japanese Factory: The Origins of National Diversity in Industrial Production*. Berkeley: University of California Press.

———. 1997. *Japan, Internationalism, and the UN*. London: Routledge.

Dower, John W. 1979. *Empire and Aftermath: Yoshida Shigeru and the Japanese Experience, 1878–1954*. Cambridge: Harvard University Press.

Dudden, Alexis. 1999. "Japan's Engagement with International Terms." In *Tokens of Exchange: The Problem of Translation in Global Circulations*, edited by Lydia H. Liu. Durham, N.C.: Duke University Press.

———. 2005. *Japan's Colonization of Korea: Discourse and Power*. Honolulu: University of Hawaii Press.

Dujarric, Robert. 2005. "U.S. Military Presence and Northeast Asian Regional Stability: Comparative Perspective between U.S.-Japan Alliance and U.S.-Korea Alliance and the Future of the Alliances." *Korean Observer* 36, no. 3 (Autumn): 445–63.

Duus, Peter. 2001. "The New Asianism." *Can Japan Globalize? Studies on Japan's Changing Political Economy and the Process of Globalization in Honour of Sung-Jo Park*, edited by Arne Holzhausen, 245–56. Heidelberg: Physica-Verlag.

Eckert, Carter J., Ki-baik Lee, Young Ick Lew, Michael Robinson, and Edward W. Wagner. 1990. *Korea: Old and New: A History*. Cambridge: Korea Institute and Harvard University Press.

Edmonds, Martin. 1985. *Central Organizations of Defense*. Boulder: Westview.

Esenbel, Selçuk. 2004. "Japan's Global Claim to Asia and the World of Islam: Transnational Nationalism and World Power, 1900–1945." *American Historical Review* 109, no. 4: 1140–70.

Fallows, James. 1989. "Containing Japan." *Atlantic* (May): 40–54.

Feaver, Peter, D. T. Hikotani, and S. Narine. 2005. "Civilian Control and Civil-Military Gaps in the United States, Japan, and China." *Asian Perspective* 29, no. 1: 233–71.

Finer, Samuel E. 1988. *The Man on Horseback: The Role of the Military in Politics*. Boulder: Westview.

Fletcher, Miles. 1979. "Intellectuals and Fascism in Early Shōwa Japan." *Journal of Asian Studies* 39, no. 1 (November): 39–63.

Foreign Press Center of Japan. 2005. "Interim Report Issued on US Military Realignment in Japan: Integration of American and Japanese Forces to Advance." 4 November.

Fravel, M. Taylor. 2005. "Regime Insecurity and International Cooperation: Explaining China's Compromises in Territorial Disputes." *International Security* 30, no. 2 (Fall): 46–83.

Friedman, George, and Meredith LeBard. 1991. *The Coming War with Japan*. New York: St. Martin's Press.

Frühstück, Sabina. 2007. *Uneasy Warriors: Gender, Memory, and Popular Culture in the Japanese Army*. Berkeley: University of California Press.

Frühstück, Sabina, and Eyal Ben-Ari. 2002. "'Now We Show It All!': Normalization and the Management of Violence in Japan's Armed Forces." *Journal of Japanese Studies* 28, no. 1: 1–40.

Fujiwara, Akira. 1973. "The Role of the Japanese Army." In *Pearl Harbor as History: Japanese-American Relations, 1931–1941*, edited by Dorothy Borg and Shumpei Okamoto. New York: Columbia University Press.

Fujiwara, Kiichi. 2002. *Demokurashii no Teikoku: Amerika, Sensō, Gendai Sekai* [The Empire of Democracy: The United States, War, and the Modern World]. Tokyo: Iwanami Shoten.

Fukao, Kyoji, Ishido Hikari, and Itō Keiko. 2003. "Vertical Intra-Industry Trade and Foreign Direct Investment in East Asia." *Journal of Japanese and International Economics* 17: 468–506.

Fuller, Graham E. 2005. "The Decline of American Power." *La Vanguardia* 7 (December).

Funabashi, Yoichi. 1998. "Tokyo's Depression Diplomacy." *Foreign Affairs* (November–December): 26–36.

——. 1999. *Alliance Adrift*. New York: Council on Foreign Relations.

Gabe, Masaaki. 2000. "Futenma Air Station: The Okinawa Problem in Japan-U.S. Relations." *Japan Echo* 27, no. 3 (June): 19–24.

Gaikō Fōramu, ed. 2006. "Kuraimake o Shinai Gaikō O: 2006 Nen ni Chokumen Suru Gaikō Mondai" [Toward a Diplomacy Not Unworthy of Our Status: Squarely Facing the Diplomatic Issues of 2006]. Discussion among Nishihara Masashi, Tadokoro Masayuki, and Ina Hisashi. January, 24–33.

Gaikō Kankei Tasukufōsu, ed., 2002. *21 Seiki Nihon Gaikō no Kihon Senryaku: Arata na Jidai, Arata na Bijyon, Arata na Gaikō* [A Basic Diplomatic Strategy for Japan in the 21st Century: A New Age, a New Vision, a New Diplomacy]. Tokyo: Shushō Kantei.

Giarra, Paul. 2001. "American Bases in Japan: Strategic Importance, Local Treatment." In *United States–Japan Strategic Dialogue: Beyond the Defense Guidelines*, 60–74. Honolulu: Pacific Forum CSIS.

Glosny, Michael A. 2006. "Heading toward a Win-Win Future? Recent Developments in China's Policy toward Southeast Asia." *Asian Security* 2, no. 1: 24–57.

Goldstein, Avery. 2005. *Rising to the Challenge: China's Grand Strategy and International Security*. Stanford: Stanford University Press.

Goto-Shibata, Harumi. 1995. *Japan and Britain in Shanghai, 1925–1931*. New York: St. Martin's Press.

Green, Michael J. 1995. *Arming Japan: Defense Production, Alliance Politics, and the Postwar Search for Autonomy*. New York: Columbia University Press.

——. 2001. *Japan's Reluctant Realism*. New York: Palgrave.

Green, Michael J., and P. M. Cronin. 1999. *The U.S.-Japan Alliance: Past, Present, and Future*. New York: Council on Foreign Relations.

Green, Michael J., and Robin Sakoda. 2001. "Agenda for the U.S.-Japan Alliance: Rethinking Roles and Missions." In *United States–Japan Strategic Dialogue: Beyond the Defense Guidelines*, 1–7. Honolulu: Pacific Forum CSIS.

Gregson, Walter C., and Robin Sakoda. 1999. "Overseas Presence: Maintaining the Tip of the Spear." *Marine Corps Gazette* 83, no. 4 (April).

Guillain, Robert. 1952. "The Reemergence of Military Elements in Japan." *Pacific Affairs* 25, no. 3: 211–45.

[253]

Han, Jung-Sun. 2005. "Rationalizing the Orient: The 'East Asia Cooperative Community' in Prewar Japan." *Monumenta Nipponica* 60, no. 4 (Winter): 481–507.

Hanami, Andrew K. 1996. "Japan." In *The Political Role of the Military*, edited by C. Danopoulos and C. Watson. Westport, Conn.: Greenwood Press.

Hara, Yoshihisa. 1988. *Sengo Nihon to Kokusai Seiji: Ampo Kaitei no Seijirikigaku* [Postwar Japan and International Politics: The Political Dynamics of the Security Treaty Revision]. Tokyo: Chūōkōronsha.

Harries, Meirion, and Susie Harries. 1987. *Sheathing the Sword: The Demilitarization of Japan*. London: Hamish Hamilton.

Hashimoto, Akikaku, Mike Mochizuki, and Kurayoshi Takara, eds. 2005. *The Okinawa Question and the U.S.-Japan Alliance*. Washington, D.C.: Sigur Center for Asian Studies.

Hatch, Walter, and K. Yamamura. 1996. *Asia in Japan's Embrace: Building a Regional Production Alliance*. New York: Cambridge University Press.

He, Yinan. 2004. "Overcoming Shadows of the Past: Post-Conflict Interstate Reconciliation in East Asia and Europe." PhD diss., Massachusetts Institute of Technology.

Heginbotham, Eric, and Richard J. Samuels. 1998. "Mercantile Realism and Japanese Foreign Policy." *International Security* 22, no. 4: 170–202.

———. 2002. "Japan's Dual Hedge." *Foreign Affairs* 81, no. 5 (September–October): 110–21.

Higuchi, Yōichi, and Osuka Akira, eds. 1994. *Kenpō no Kokkairongi: Nihonkoku Kenpō Shiryōshū Kenpō Rongi Hen* [The Constitution and Diet Debate: Collected Japanese Constitutional Data and Debates]. Tokyo: Sanseidō.

Hikotani, Takako. 2004a. "Reisengo Nihon no Seigun Kankei" [Civil-Military Relations in Post—Cold War Japan]. In *Nihon no Higashi Ajia Kōsō* [Japan's Conception of East Asia], edited by Yoshihide Soeya and Tadokoro Masayuki, chap. 11. Tokyo: Keiō Daigaku Shuppankai.

———. 2004b. "Rearming Japan: Consequences and Lessons Learned." Paper presented to the Annual Meeting of the American Political Science Association, Chicago.

Hikotani, Takako, and Kamiya Matake. 2004. " 'Hataraku Jieitai' no Jidai no Shibirian Kontorōru o Kakuritsu Seyo" [We Must Establish Civilian Control for the Age of a 'Working Self-Defense Force']. *Nihonjin no Chikara* 10 (July): 6–9.

Hiramatsu, Shigeo. 2002. *Chūgoku no Senryakuteki Kaiyō Shinshutsu* [China's Strategic Ocean Advance]. Tokyo: Keisō Shobō.

Hirose, Katsuya. 1989. "Kanryō to Gunjin: Bunmin Tōsei no Genkai" [Bureaucrats and Civilians: The Limits on Civilian Control]. Tokyo: Iwanami.

Honda Masaru, et al., eds., 2005. *Jieitai: Shirarezaru Henyō* [Self-Defense Forces: The Unknown Changes]. Tokyo: Asahi Shimbunsha.

Hook, Glenn D. 1996. *Militarization and Demilitarization in Contemporary Japan*. London: Routledge.

Hook, Glenn D., Julie Gilson, Christopher W. Hughes, and Hugo Dobson. 2001. *Japan's International Relations*. London: Routledge.

Horiuchi, Tateki. 1950. *Chūgoku no Arashi no Naka de: Nikka Gaikō Sanjūnen Yawa* [In the Middle of the Chinese Storm: Thirty Years of Sino-Japanese Diplomacy]. Tokyo: Kangensha.

Hosaka, Masayasu. 2005. " 'Ano Sensō' o Shinryaku de mo Naku, Seisen de mo Naku, Rekishi to Shite Kataritsugu Toki ga Kita" [The Time Has Come to Transmit to the Next Generation a History of 'That War' Which Was Neither an Aggressive War nor a Holy War]. In *Nihon no Ronten 2006* [Issues for Japan: 2006], 214–17. Tokyo: Bungei Shunjū.

Hoshino, Eiichi. 2000. "Economic Sanctions against Myanmar." In *The Japan-U.S. Alliance: New Challenges for the 21st Century*, edited by Masashi Nishihara, 123–59. Tokyo: Japan Center for International Exchange.

Hosoya, Chihiro. 1971. "Retrogression in Japan's Foreign Policy Decision-Making Process." In *Dilemmas of Growth in Prewar Japan*, edited by J. W. Morley, 81–105. Princeton: Princeton University Press.

Hughes, Christopher W. 2004a. *Japan's Reemergence as a "Normal" Military Power*. Adelphi Paper 368–9. London: Institute for International Strategic Studies.

——. 2004b. *Japan's Security Agenda: Military, Economic, and Environmental Dimensions*. Boulder: Lynne Rienner.

——. 2005a. "Japan–North Korean Relations and the Political Economy of Remittances." Unpublished paper, Warwick University, January.

——. 2005b. "Japanese Military Modernization: In Search of a 'Normal' Security Role." In *Strategic Asia 2005–2006: Military Modernization in an Era of Uncertainty*, edited by Ashley J. Tellis and Michael Wills, 105–34. Seattle: National Bureau of Asian Research.

——. 2006. "Japanese Constitutional Revision and Security Policy: What Might Happen and What Might It Mean?" Paper presented to conference on "Constitutional Change and Foreign Policy in East Asia," Foreign Policy Research Institute, University of Pennsylvania, March.

Hughes, Llewelyn. 2007. "Why Japan Will Not Go Nuclear (Yet): International and Domestic Constraints on the Nuclearization of Japan." *International Security* 31, no. 4 (Spring): 67–96.

Hung, Joe. 2005. "Manga: A Repetition of History?" *China Post* (online edition), 12 December.

Huntington, Samuel P. 1957. *The Soldier and the State: The Theory and Politics of Civil-Military Relations*. New York: Vintage Books.

——. 1968. *Political Order in Changing Societies*. New Haven: Yale University Press.

——. 1996. "Reforming Civil-Military Relations." In *Civil-Military Relations and Democracy*, edited by L. Diamond and M. F. Plattner, 3–11. Baltimore: Johns Hopkins University Press.

Ienaga, Saburō. 1978. *The Pacific War, 1931–1945: A Critical Perspective on Japan's Role in World War II*. New York: Pantheon.

Iguchi, Haruo. 2001. "Complication: American Military Presence in Okinawa and Enhancing the U.S.-Japan Alliance." In *United States–Japan Strategic Dialogue: Beyond the Defense Guidelines*, 75–89. Honolulu: Pacific Forum CSIS.

Iinuma, Yoshisuke. 2006. "Nuclear Fallout." *The Oriental Economist* (December): 8–9.

Iklé, Fred Charles, and Terumasa Nakanishi. 1990. "Japan's Grand Strategy." *Foreign Affairs* 69, no. 3 (Summer): 81–95.

Ilari, V. 1985. "The Italian Central Organization of Defense." In *Central Organizations of Defense*, edited by M. Edmonds, 108–31. Boulder: Westview.

Ina, Hisayoshi. 2005. "Implementing the SACO and Revising the SOFA." In *The Okinawa Question and the U.S.-Japan Alliance*, edited by Hashimoto Akikaku, Mike Mochizuki, and Kurayoshi Takara, 41–40. Washington, D.C.: Sigur Center for Asian Studies.

Inamine, Keiichi. 2000. "Okinawa as Pacific Crossroads." *Japan Quarterly* 47, no. 3 (July–September): 10–16.

Inoguchi, Takashi, et al. 1999. "Challenge 2001: Japan's Foreign Policy toward the 21st Century." Report to Foreign Minister Kōmura Masahiko, 4 January.

Institute for National Strategic Studies. 2000. "The United States and Japan: Advancing toward a Mature Partnership." Institute for National Strategic Studies Special

Report (Armitage-Nye Report). Washington, D.C.: National Defense University Press, October.

Iokibe, Makoto. 2000. "The Japan-US Alliance as a Maritime Alliance." In *Japan's Grand Strategy for the 21st Century: From an Insular Nation to a Maritime Nation*, edited by K. Itō et al. Tokyo: Japan Forum on International Relations.

Iriye, Akira. 1974. "The Failure of Economic Expansionism, 1918–1931." In *Japan in Crisis: Essays on Taishō Democracy*, edited by Bernard S. Silberman and H. D. Harootunian, 237–69. Princeton: Princeton University Press.

——. 1971. "The Failure of Military Expansionism." In *Dilemmas of Growth in Prewar Japan*, edited by J. W. Morley, 107–38. Princeton: Princeton University Press.

——. 1990. "Japan against the ABCD Powers." In *American, Chinese, and Japanese Perspectives on Wartime Asia, 1931–1949*, edited by A. Iriye and W. Cohen, 223–42. Wilmington, Del.: Scholarly Resources.

——. 1997. *Japan and the Wider World: From the Mid-Nineteenth Century to the Present.* London: Longman.

Ishiba, Shigeru. 2005a. *Kokubō* [National Defense]. Tokyo: Shinchōsha.

——. 2005b. "Bunmei Tōsei to wa Kanryō Shihai no Koto de wa Nai. Gunji o Katareru Seijika Koso Hitsuyō" [Civilian Control Is Not a Matter of Bureaucratic Management. It Especially Requires Politicians Who Can Discuss Military Affairs]. In *Nihon no Ronten 2006* [Issues for Japan: 2006], 176–79. Tokyo: Bungei Shunjū.

——. 2006. "Nitchū Arasowaba Katsu no wa Dotchi Da" [If Japan and China Were to Fight, Which One Would Win?]. *Bungei Shunjū* 1 (May): 138–42.

Ishida, Ken. 2004. "Haisen to Kenpō: Nichi-Doku-I Sankoku ni okeru Kenpō Settei no Hikaku" [The Constitution and Loss of War: A Comparison of the Process of Establishing the Constitutions in Japan, Germany, and Italy]. *Chiba Daigaku Hōgaku Ronshū* 19, no. 2 (September).

Ishihara, Shintarō. 2005. "Amerika wa Katemai" [America Cannot Win]. *Sankei Shimbun*, 5 December.

Ishikawa, Michi, and Shima Haruko. 2004. "Jieitai ni yoru Kokusai Katsudō ni Kansuru Kōsaku" [Considerations about the International Activities of the SDF]. *Kokusai Anzen Hoshō* 32, no. 1 (June): 67–93.

Ishimaru, Tōta. 1936. *Japan Must Fight Britain*. New York: Telegraph Press.

Itō, Kenichi. 2000. Introduction to *Japan's Identity: Neither East nor West*, edited by Kenichi Itō et al. Tokyo: Japan Forum on International Relations.

Itō, Takashi. 1973. "The Role of Right-Wing Organizations in Japan." In *Pearl Harbor as History: Japanese-American Relations, 1931–1941*, edited by Dorothy Borg and Shumpei Okamoto. New York: Columbia University Press.

——. 2005. "Zentaishugi o Mezashita Ugoki" [A Movement Aimed at Totalitarianism]. *Yomiuri Shimbun*, 1 December.

Jain, Purendra, and Takashi Inoguchi. 1996. *Japanese Politics Today*. London: St. Martin's.

Jameson, Sam. 1996. "Can Japan Emerge from a Half Century of One-Nation Pacifism? Japan's Security Problems and Challenges to the US-Japan Security Treaty." Speech presented to the Defense Research Institute, Tokyo.

Janowitz, Morris. 1971. *The Professional Soldier: A Social and Political Portrait*. New York: Free Press.

Japan Defense Agency. 2004. *Defense of Japan*. Tokyo: Japan Times.

——. 2005. *Overview of Japan's Defense Policy*. May. Tokyo: Defense Agency of Japan.

Japan Forum on International Relations. 2004. "New World Order of No-War Community and Future of Japan-US Alliance." Tokyo: Japan Forum on International Relations.

Japan Institute for International Affairs, ed. 2005. "Resolving the North Korean Nuclear Problem: A Regional Approach and the Role of Japan." Paper prepared for the Project for Northeast Asian Security. Tokyo, July.

Jervis, Robert. 1978. "Cooperation under the Security Dilemma." *World Politics* 30, no. 2 (January): 167–214.

Jiang, Keshi. 2003. *Ishibashi Tanzan no Sengo: Hikitsugareyuku Shōnihonshugi* [Ishibashi Tanzan's Postwar: The Handover of "Small Japanism"]. Tokyo: Toyo Keizai Shimpōsha.

Jiyū Hōsōdan. 2002. *Yūji Hōsei no Subete: Sensō Kokka e no Michi* [All about the National Emergency System: The Road to the Warring Nation]. Tokyo: Shinnihon Shuppansha.

Jiyū Minshutō, ed. 1955. *Tō no Seikō* [Party Platform]. Tokyo.

Johnson, Chalmers, 1982. *MITI and the Japanese Miracle: The Growth of Industrial Policy, 1925–1975*. Stanford: Stanford University Press.

——. 1984. "La Serenissima of the East." *Asian and African Studies* 18, no. 1 (March).

Johnston, Alastair Iain. 1995. "Thinking about Strategic Culture." *International Security* 19, no. 4: 33–64.

Kagaku Gijutsuchō, ed. *Nitchū no Gijutsu Iten ni kansuru Chōsa Kenkyū* [A Survey of Sino-Japanese Technology Transfer]. November 1997.

Kaijō Hoanchō, ed. 2006. *Kaijō Hoan Repōto 2006* [Maritime Safety Report, 2006]. Kokuritsu Insatsu Kyoku.

Kaneda, Hideaki. 2004. "Significance of the Humanitarian and Restoration Aid to Iraq." *US-Japan Navy Friendship Association Bulletin* no. 26 (August).

Kanehara, Nobukatsu. 2005. "Japan's Grand Strategy." Speech to the Asia Society, Washington, D.C., 27 January.

Kaneko, Kumao. 1997. *Nippon no Kaku–Ajia no Kaku: Nipponjin no Kakuonchi o Tsuku* [Japanese Nukes, Asian Nukes: Confronting the Tone-Deaf Japanese]. Tokyo: Asahi Shimbunsha.

Kang, Sangjung, and Katō Shūichi. 2004. "Rekishi no Bunkiten ni Tatte" [Standing at an Historical Juncture]. *Ronza* (April): 10–23.

Kase, Yuri. 2001. "The Cost and Benefits of Japan's Nuclearization: An Insight into the 1968–70 Internal Report." *Nonproliferation Review* (Summer): 55–68.

Katahara, Eichi. 1996. "Japan's Concept of Comprehensive Security in the Post–Cold War World." In *Power and Prosperity: Economics and Security Linkages in Asia-Pacific*, edited by Susan L. Shirk and Christopher P. Twomey. New Brunswick, N.J.: Transaction Publishers.

——. 2001. "Japan: From Containment to Normalization." In *Coercion and Governance: The Declining Political Role of the Military in Asia*, edited by Muthiah Alagappa, 69–91. Stanford: Stanford University Press.

Kataoka, Tetsuya, and Ramon H. Myers. 1989. *Defending an Economic Superpower: Reassessing the U.S.-Japan Security Alliance*. Boulder: Westview.

Katayama, Satsuki. 2005. "Jieitai ni mo Kōzō Kaikaku ga Hitsuyō Da" [Structural Reform of the SDF Is Also Necessary]. *Chūō Kōron* 1 (January): 156–63.

Kato, Yoichi. 2005. "Japan's Security Strategy after 9/11." In *The Okinawa Question and the U.S.-Japan Alliance*, edited by Akikazu Hashimoto, Mike M. Mochizuki, and Kurayoshi Takara, 17–22. Washington, D.C.: Sigur Center for Asian Studies.

Katzenstein, Peter J. 1996. *Cultural Norms and National Security: Police and Military in Postwar Japan*. Ithaca: Cornell University Press.

Kawakatsu, Chikako. 2006. "The Rise of the 'China Threat' Arguments." PhD diss., Massachusetts Institute of Technology.

Kawano, Hitoshi. 2002. "The Positive Impact of Peacekeeping on the Japan Self-Defense Forces." In *Armed Forces and the International Diversities*, edited by Leena Parmar, 244–83. Jaipur: Pointer.

Kawashima, Yutaka. 2003. *Japanese Foreign Policy at the Crossroads: Challenges and Options for the Twenty-first Century*. Washington, D.C.: Brookings Institution.

Kebschull, Harvey G. 1994. "'Operation Just Missed': Lessons from Failed Coup Attempts." *Armed Forces and Society* (Summer): 565–79.

Keidanren. 2001. "Japan-China Relations in the 21st Century: Recommendations for Building a Relationship of Trust and Expanding Economic Exchanges between Japan and China." 20 February. Tokyo: Keidanren.

Keizai Sangyōshō, ed. 2003. "Gijutsu Ryūshutsu Bōshi Shishin" [Pointers for the Prevention of Technology Leakage]. 14 March. Tokyo.

Kennan, George F. 1972. *Memoirs: 1950–1963*. Vol. 2. Boston: Little, Brown.

Kerr, Ian J. 1998. "Ishibashi Tanzan's Theory of 'Small-Japanism.'" Master's thesis, Monash University, Victoria, Australia.

Kim, Keong-il. 2005. "Nationalism and Colonialism in Japan's 'Greater East Asia Co-Prosperity Sphere' in World War II." *Review of Korean Studies* 8, no. 2: 65–90.

Kinoshita, Hanji. 1953. "Echoes of Militarism in Japan." *Pacific Affairs* 26, no. 3 (September): 244–51.

Kissinger, Henry A. 1973. *A World Restored: Metternich, Castlereagh, and the Problems of Peace, 1812–1822*. Boston: Houghton Mifflin.

Kitaoka, Shinichi. 1995a. "Sengo Nihon no Gaikō Shisō" [The Concept of Postwar Japanese Diplomacy]. In *Sengo Nihon Gaikō Ronshū* [Collected Essays on Postwar Japanese Diplomacy], edited by Kitaoka Shinichi, 5–42. Tokyo: Chūō Kōronsha.

——. 1995b. *Jimintō: 39-Nen no Chōki Seiken* [LDP: 39 Long Years of Power]. Tokyo: Yomiuri Shimbunsha.

——. 1999. "Kenpō Kyūjō no Jubaku Kara Nukedasu Toki" [Time to Break the Spell of Article 9]. *This Is Yomiuri* (March): 126–35.

——. 2002. *Dokuritsu Jison: Fukuzawa Yukichi no Chōsen* [Independence and Self-Respect: The Challenge of Fukuzawa Yukichi]. Tokyo: Kōdansha.

——. 2004. *Nihon no Jiritsu: Taibei Kyōchō to Ajia Gaikō* [Japanese Independence: Emphasis on the United States and Asian Diplomacy]. Tokyo: Chūō Kōronsha.

——. 2005. "Kaiyō Kokka Nihon no Senryaku: Fukuzawa Yukichi kara Yoshida Shigeru Made" [Japan's Strategy as a Maritime State: From Fukuzawa Yukichi to Yoshida Shigeru]. In *Nichibei Senryaku Shisōshi* [History of U.S.-Japan Strategic Thinking], edited by Ishizu Tomoyuki and Murray Williamson, 17–32. Tokyo: Sairyūsha.

Kobayashi Hiroharu. 2003. "Rōyama Masamichi's Perception of International Order from the 1920s to 1930s and the Concept of the East Asian Community." In *Nationalism and Internationalism in Imperial Japan: Autonomy, Asian Brotherhood, or World Citizenship*, edited by D. Stegewerns, chap. 7. London: Routledge.

Kobayashi, Yoshinori, and Susumu Nishibe. 2003. *Ahō Koshinuke Byōki no Shinbei Hoshu* [Pro-American Conservatives Who Suffer as Crippled Fools]. Tokyo: Asuka Shinsha.

Kōchikai, ed. 1983. *21-Seiki e no Dōhyō: Sengo Nihon to Kōchikai no 25-Nen* [Milestone to the 21st Century: The Kōchikai's 25 Years and Postwar Japan]. Tokyo: Seikōsha.

Kodaira, Osamu. 1967. "Kenpō Daikyūjō to Nihon Kenpō Ishiki [Article Nine and Japan's Constitutional Consciousness]." *Jieitai to Kenpō no Kaishaku* [The Self-Defense Forces and Constitutional Interpretations]. Shūzō Hayashi and Kikuo Nakamura. Tokyo, Yūshidō Sōsho.

Kōketsu, Atsushi. 2002. "Sengo Yūji Hōsei Rongi no Kiseki" [On the Track of the Postwar National Emergency System Debate]. *Sekai* (May): 126–33.

Kokubun, Ryōsei. 2005. "Nitchū Kankei wa Kongo Dō Arubeki ka" [What Should the Japan-China Relationship Be from Now On?]. Sentaa Pokketo Edishon Shirizu, no. 59. Tokyo: Keizai Kōhō Sentaa.

Kokusai Heiwa Kyōryoku Kondankai, ed. 2002. "Kokusai Heiwa Kyōryoku Kondankai: Hōkokusho" [Report of the International Peace Cooperation Study Group]. Tokyo: Shushō Kantei, 18 December [available at http://www.kantei.go.jp/jp/sing/kokusai/kettei/021218houkoku.html].

Kōsaka, Masataka. 1964. "Kaiyō Kokka Nihon no Kōsō" [The Concept of Japan as a Maritime State]. *Chūō Kōron* (September): 48–80.

——. 1975. "Tsūshō Kokka Nippon no Unmei" [The Fate of Japan as a Trading State]. *Chūō Kōron* (November): 116–40.

——. 1993. "Genjitsu ga Gensokuteki na Nayami to Kenmei na Handan o Yōkyū Suru Kagiri Kenpō Kaisei wa Sakerarenai" [To the Extent There Is a Demand for Wise Choices and for Reality over Theoretical Problems, There Is No Avoiding Constitutional Revision]. In *Nihon no Ronten 1993* [Issues for Japan: 1993]. Tokyo: Bungei Shunjū.

——. 1996. *Kōsaka Masataka Gaikō Hyōronshū: Nihon no Shinro to Rekishi no Kyōkun* [The Collected Essays on Diplomacy of Kōsaka Masataka: Japan's Course and the Precepts of History]. Tokyo: Chūō Kōron.

Koschmann, J. Victor. 1997. "Asianism's Ambivalent Legacy." In *Network Power: Japan and Asia*, edited by Peter J. Katzenstein and Takashi Shiraishi, 83–110. Ithaca: Cornell University Press.

Krauthammer, Charles. 1990–91. "The Unipolar Moment." *Foreign Affairs* 70, no. 1: 23–33.

Kwan, Chi Hung. 2004. "Why Japan Should Pursue an FTA with China: The Need to Prevent a Hollowing-Out of Domestic Industry." RIETI online column at http://www.rieti.go.jp/en/columns/a01_0122.html.

Larson, Arthur D. 1974. "Professionalism and Civil Control of Volunteer Forces." *Journal of Political and Military Sociology* 2 (Spring).

Lasswell, Harold D. 1937. "Sino-Japanese Crisis: The Garrison versus the Civilian State." *China Quarterly*: 643–49.

LDP Special Study Group, ed. 1992. "Japan's Role in the International Community." *Japan Echo* 19, no. 2 (Summer): 49–58.

Lebra, Joyce C., ed. 1975. *Japan's Greater East Asia Co-Prosperity Sphere in World War II: Selected Readings and Documents*. Kuala Lumpur: Oxford University Press.

Leheny, David. 2006. *Think Global, Fear Local*. Ithaca: Cornell University Press.

Levy, Jack S. 1997. "Prospect Theory, Rational Choice, and International Relations." *International Studies Quarterly* 41, no. 1 (March): 87–112.

——. 2000. "Loss Aversion, Framing Effects, and International Conflict: Perspectives from Framing Theory." In *Handbook of War Studies II*, edited by M. I. Midlarsky, 193–221. Ann Arbor: University of Michigan Press.

Lim, Robyn. 2003. *The Geopolitics of East Asia: The Search for Equilibrium*. London: Routledge.

——. 2005. "Remarks." Paper presented to the American Enterprise Institute conference on "U.S.-Japanese Security Cooperation," Tokyo, October.

Lind, Jennifer. 2004. "Pacifism or Passing the Buck?" *International Security* (Summer): 92–121.

Little, D. R. 2002. *Peacekeeping: Japanese Style*. Chicago: Midwest Political Science Association.

Lowry, Rich. "Time for the Sun to Rise." *National Review*, 4 July, 29–31.

MacDougall, Walter A. 1997. *Promised Land, Crusader State: The American Encounter with the World since 1776*. New York: Houghton Mifflin.

Macmillan, Margaret. 2002. *Paris 1919: Six Months That Changed the World*. New York: Random House.

Maeda, Tetsuo. 2005. "Beigun Saihen de Jieitai wa Beigun no Ichiin ni Naru. Kiken na Shūdan Jieiken no Kōshi wa Hisshi" [With U.S. Force Transformation, the SDF Will Become Part of the American Military. The Dangers of Collective Self-Defense Are Inevitable]. In *Nihon no Ronten 2006* [Issues for Japan: 2006], 170–73. Tokyo: Bungei Shunjū.

Mahan, Alfred Thayer. 1890. *The Influence of Sea Power upon History: 1660–1783*. Boston: Little, Brown.

——. 1900. *The Problem of Asia and Its Effect upon International Policies*. Boston: Little, Brown.

Maki, John. 1964. *Court and Constitution in Japan*. Seattle: University of Washington Press.

Maniruzzman, Talukder. 1987. *Military Withdrawal from Politics: A Comparative Study*. Cambridge, Mass.: Ballinger.

Manning, Robert A. 2000. *The Asian Energy Factor: Myths and Dilemmas of Energy, Security, and the Pacific Future*. New York: Palgrave.

Manyin, Mark E. 2003. "Japan–North Korean Relations: Selected Issues." Congressional Research Service Report for Congress, 26 November.

Maruyama, Masao. 1960. Introduction to *Nationalism and the Right Wing in Japan: A Study of Postwar Trends*, edited by I. I. Morris. London: Oxford University Press.

Masuda, Hiroshi. 1990. *Shōnihonshugi: Ishibashi Tanzan Gaikō Ronshū* [Small Japanism: The Collected Diplomatic Writings of Ishibashi Tanzan]. Tokyo: Sōshisha.

Matsuo, Takayoshi. 1995. *Dainihonshugika Shōnihonshugika: Miura Tetsutarō Ronsetsusho* [Big Japanism or Small Japanism: The Collected Works of Miura Tetsutarō]. Tokyo: Tōyō Keizai Shinpōsha.

Matsuoka, Yosuke. 1937. *Building Up Manchuria*. Tokyo: Herald of Asia.

Maxon, Yale Candee. 1957. *Control of Japanese Foreign Policy: A Study of Civil-Military Rivalry, 1930–1945*. Berkeley: University of California Press.

McCormack, Gavan. 1996. *The Emptiness of Japanese Affluence*. Armonk, N.Y.: M. E. Sharpe.

Mead, Walter Russell. 2002. *Special Providence: American Foreign Policy and How It Changed the World*. New York: Routledge.

Mearsheimer, John J. 2001. *The Tragedy of Great Power Politics*. New York: W. W. Norton.

Menon, Rajan. 2007. *The End of Alliances*. New York: Oxford University Press.

Metzler, Mark. 2006. *Lever of Empire: The International Gold Standard and the Crisis of Liberalism in Prewar Japan*. Berkeley: University of California Press.

Michishita, Narushige. 1999. "Alliance after Peace in Korea." *Survival* 41, no. 3 (Autumn): 68–83.

——. 2002. "The Changing Faces of Defense Policy: Past and Future." *Global Economic Review* 32, no. 4: 91–100.

——. 2003. "Japan's Response to 9-11." In *Coping with 9-11: Asian Perspectives on Global and Regional Order*, edited by Han Sung-Joo, 40–55. Tokyo: Japan Center for International Exchange.

——. 2004a. "Calculated Adventurism: North Korea's Military-Diplomatic Campaigns." *Korean Journal of Defense Analysis* 16, no. 2 (Fall): 181–226.

——. 2004b. "North Korea's 'Second Nuclear Diplomacy': Rising Risks and Expectations." In *East Asian Strategic Review, 2004*, 10–79. Tokyo: National Institute for Defense Studies.

——. 2004c. "Nodong no Kyōi to Misairu Bōei" [Missile Defense and the Nodong Threat]. *Sekai Shuhō* 17–24 (August): 14–17.

——. 2004d. "Kawariyuku senryaku Kanryō to Nihon no Bōei seisaku" [The Changing Security Environment and Japan's Defense Policy]. In *Sensō no Honshitsu to Gunjiryoku no Shosō* [Various Aspects of the Realities of War and Military Power], edited by Ishizu Tomoyuki, 288–308. Tokyo: Sairyūsha.

——. 2005a. "Senryaku Shisō to shite no 'Kibanteki Bōeiryoku Kōsō'" [The Basic Defense Capabilities Doctrine as a Strategic Concept]. In *Nichibei Senryaku Shisōshi* [History of U.S.-Japan Strategic Thinking], edited by Ishizu Tomoyuki and Murray Williamson, 217–45. Tokyo: Sairyūsha.

——. 2005b. "Anzen Hoshō to Nihon no Shōrai" [National Security and Japan's Future]. Lecture at Sophia University, Spring.

Midford, Paul. 2006. "Globalization and National Security: Is Japan *Still* an Island?" In *Globalization and National Security*, edited by Jonathan Kirschner, 259–92. New York: Routledge.

Mikuriya, Takashi. 1996. "Jishasa 'Kettei Sakiokuri' no Kōzō" [The Structure of LDP-SDPJ-Sakigake Decision Postponement]. *Chūō Kōron* (March): 62–71.

Miller, Edward S. 1991. *War Plan Orange: The U.S. Strategy to Defeat Japan, 1897–1945*. Annapolis, Md.: Naval Institute Press.

Miller, John. 2002. "Japan Crosses the Rubicon?" *Asian-Pacific Security Studies* 1, no. 1: 1–4.

Misawa, Shigeo, and Ninomiya Saburō. 1973. "The Role of the Diet and Political Parties." In *Pearl Harbor as History: Japanese-American Relations, 1931–1941*, edited by Dorothy Borg and Shumpei Okamoto. New York: Columbia University Press.

Miura, Shumon. 2005. *Yasukuni Jinja: Tadashiku Rikai Suru Tame Ni* [The Yasukuni Shrine: Toward a Correct Understanding] Tokyo: Kairyūsha.

Miwa, Kimitada. 1990. "Japanese Policies and Concepts for a Regional Order in Asia, 1938–1940." In *The Ambivalence of Nationalism: Modern Japan between East and West*, edited by J. W. White, M. Umegaki, and T. R. H. Havens, 133–56. Lanham, Md.: University Press of America.

Miyazaki, Tōten. 1982. *My Thirty Years' Dream: The Autobiography of Miyazaki Tōten*. Princeton: Princeton University Press.

Miyazawa, Kiichi, and Kōsaka Masataka. 1984. *Utsukushii Nihon e no Chōsen* [Challenges for a Beautiful Japan]. Tokyo: Bungei Shunjū.

Miyazawa, Sakuta. 1997. *Ima Shinsei Kanbojia wa PKO no Chi to Ase wa Ikiru Ka?* [Is the New Cambodia Alive Thanks to the Blood and Sweat of the PKO?]. Tokyo: Nippon Goyū Renmei.

Mochizuki, Mike M. 1983–84. "Japan's Search for Strategy." *International Security* 8, no. 3: 152–79.

——. 1992. *Japan and the Persian Gulf Crisis: The Lessons Learned*. Los Alamos, N.M.: Los Alamos National Laboratory, Center for National Security Studies.

——. 1995. *Japan: Domestic Change and Foreign Policy*. Santa Monica, Calif.: RAND Corporation.

——. 2004. "Japan: Between Alliance and Autonomy." In *Confronting Terrorism in the Pursuit of Power: Strategic Asia, 2004–2005*, edited by A. Tellis and M. Wills, 103–39. Seattle: National Bureau of Asian Research.

——. 2005. "U.S. Strategy in the Asia-Pacific: Alliances and Coalitions, Wheels and Webs." In *The Okinawa Question and the U.S.-Japan Alliance*, edited by Akikazu Hashimoto, Mike Mochizuki, and Kurayoshi Takara, 17–22. Washington, D.C.: Elliot School of International Affairs.

[261]

Mochizuki, Mike M. 2006a. "Paradigms Lost: Japan's National Drift." *American Interest* 2, no. 1 (September–October), online at http://www.the-american-interest.com/ai2/contents.cfm?MId=5.

——. 2006b. "Japan's Changing International Role." In *Japan in International Politics: The Foreign Policy of an Adaptive State*, edited by Thomas U. Berger, Mike Mochizuki, and Jitsuo Tsuchiyama. Boulder: Lynne Rienner.

Moravcsik, Andrew. 1997. "Taking Preferences Seriously: A Liberal Theory of International Politics." *International Organization* 51, no. 4 (Autumn): 514–53.

Morimoto, Mitsuhiko. 2004. "Appliance Firms Returning Home." *Daily Yomiuri*, 9 September.

Morimoto, Satoshi. 2005. *Morimoto Satoshi no Me: Nihon no Bōei to Anzen Hoshō Seisaku* [The Insight of Morimoto Satoshi: Japan's Defense and National Security Policy]. Tokyo: Gurafusha.

——. 2006. "Guamu no Nihon mo Zenshin Kichi Kensetsu o." *Sankei Shimbun*, 31 March, 11.

Morley, James William. 1957. *Japan's Thrust into Siberia*. New York: Columbia University Press.

Morris, I. I. 1960. *Nationalism and the Right Wing in Japan: A Study of Post-war Trends*. London: Oxford University Press.

Morris-Suzuki, Tessa. 2005. "Free Speech–Silenced Voices: The Japanese Media and the NHK Affair." *Asia Rights*, no. 4. http://rspas.anu.edu.au/asiarightsjournal/Morris-Suzuki.pdf.

Morrow, James D. 1991. "Alliances and Asymmetry: An Alternative to the Capability Aggregation Model of Alliances." *American Journal of Political Science* 35: 904–33.

——. 2000. "Alliances: Why Write Them Down?" *Annual Review of Political Science*, no. 3: 63–83.

Moss, David. 2002. *When All Else Fails: Government as the Ultimate Risk Manager*. Cambridge: Harvard University Press.

Murata, Koji. 1996. "Naotoshi Sakonjo Oral Interview." 16 November. http://www.gwu.edu/~nsarchiv/japan/sakonjoohinterview.htm.

Myers, Ramon H., and Mark R. Peattie, eds. 1984. *The Japanese Colonial Empire: 1895–1945*. Princeton: Princeton University Press.

Nagai, Yōnosuke. 1983. *Gendai to Senryaku* [Modernity and Strategy]. Tokyo: Bungei Shunjū.

Naikaku Hōsei Kyoku Shi Henshū Iinkai, ed. 1974. *Naikaku Hōsei Kyoku Shi* [The History of the Cabinet Legislation Bureau]. Tokyo: Ōkurashō Insatsu Kyoku.

Naikaku Hōsei Kyoku Hyakunenshi Henshū Iinkai, ed. 1985. *Shōgen: Kindai Hōsei no Kiseki* [Testimony: The Path of Modern Legislation]. Tokyo: Gyōsei.

Naikaku Seifu Kōhō Shitsu, ed. 2006. *Jieitai/Bōei Mondai ni Kansuru Yoron Chōsa* [Public Opinion Survey Issues]. Tokyo.

Najita, Tetsuo. 1971. "Nagano Seigō and the Spirit of the Meiji Restoration in Twentieth-Century Japan." In *Dilemmas of Growth in Prewar Japan*, edited by J. W. Morley, 375–421. Princeton: Princeton University Press.

Nakamura, Akira. 2001. *Sengo Seiji ni Yureta Kenpō Kyūjō* [Article 9 That Shook Postwar Politics]. Tokyo: Chūō Keizaisha.

Nakamura, Hideichirō. 1973. "The Activities of the Japan Economic Federation." In *Pearl Harbor as History: Japanese-American Relations, 1931–1941*, edited by Dorothy Borg and Shumpei Okamoto. New York: Columbia University Press.

Nakamura, Yoshiaki. 2002. "What Are the Issues Surrounding Hollowing Out of Industry?" RIETI online column at http://www.rieti.go.jp/en/columns/a01_0028.html.

References

Nakamura, Yoshiaki, and Shibuya Minoru. 1995. "The Hollowing Out Phenomenon in Japanese Industry." Tokyo: Research Institute of International Trade and Industry.

Nakanishi, Terumasa. 1990. "Saying 'Yes' to the U.S.-Japan Partnership." *Japan Echo* 17, no. 1 (Spring): 36–42.

——. 2000. "Goals for Japan in Its Second Postwar Period." *Media Resources: Views from Japan.* February. Tokyo: Foreign Press Center of Japan.

——. 2003a. "Nihonkoku Kakubusō e no Ketsudan" [Japan's Decision to Go Nuclear]. *Shokun!* (August): 22–37. Available in an abridged English version: "Nuclear Weapons for Japan." *Japan Echo* 30, no. 5 (October): 48–54.

——. 2003b. "'Pushing Back to Conservatism' Is Necessary to Overcome Current Crisis in Japan." *Sankei Shimbun* (online version): 4 April 2003.

——. 2004a. "Chūgoku ga Minshuka Suru made wa Nichibei Dōmei no Kyōka igai ni Nihon no Sentakushi wa Nai" [Until China Democratizes, Japan Has No Choice but to Strengthen the US-Japan Alliance]. In *Nihon no Ronten 2005* [Issues for Japan: 2005]. Tokyo: Bungei Shunjū.

——. 2004b. "Kōen: Jimintō Rittō 50-nen Purojekuto Kihon Rinen Iinkai Sōkai" [Address to the Basic Principles Committee for the Liberal Democratic Party Fiftieth Anniversary Project]. 30 March. http://www.jimin.jp/jimin/project/index6.html.

——. 2005. "Bōchō Suru Chūgoku no Kyōi: Nichibei Dōmei no Jūyōsei wa Katsutenaku Takamatte Iru" [The Threat of an Engorged China: The Japan-U.S. Alliance Is More Important Than Ever]. In *Nihon no Ronten 2006* [Issues for Japan: 2006], 78–81. Tokyo: Bungei Shunjū.

Nakasone, Yasuhiro. 2004. "21 Seiki no Kokubō Seisaku" [A National Defense Strategy for the 21st Century]. *Voice*, 1 April, 50–57.

Nanto, Dick K., and Emma Chanlett-Avery. 2005. "The Rise of China and Its Effect on Taiwan, Japan, and South Korea: U.S. Policy Choices." Congressional Research Service Report for Congress. Washington, D.C.: Library of Congress, 12 April.

National Institute for Defense Studies. 2002. *East Asia Strategic Review, 2002.* Tokyo: National Institute for Defense Studies.

——. 2003. *2001–2002 Report on Defense and Strategic Studies: Council of Defense-Strategic Studies.* Tokyo: National Institute for Defense Studies.

——, ed. 2005. *East Asia Strategic Review, 2005.* Tokyo: Japan Times.

National Security Council, ed. 1960. "U.S. Policy toward Japan." NSC 6008/1, 20 May.

Ng, Francis, and Alexander Yeats. 2003. "Major Trade Trends in East Asia: What Are Their Implications for Regional Cooperation and Growth?" World Bank Policy Research Working Paper 3084. Washington, D.C.

Nippon Keizai Dantai Rengōkai, ed. 2003. *Katsuryoku to Miryoku Afureru Nihon o Mezashite* [Aiming for a Vigorous and Attractive Japan]. January.

——. 2004. "Kongo no Bōeiryoku Seibi no Arikata ni Tsuite: Bōei Seisan, Gijutsu Kiban no Kyōka ni Mukete" [Concerning the Condition of Defense Equipment in the Future: Facing the Strengthening of the Defense Production and Technology Base]. Tokyo: 20 July policy paper.

——. 2005. "Waga Kuni no Kihon Mondai o Kangaeru: Kore kara no Nihon o Tenbō Shite" [Thinking about Japan's Basic Problems: The Prospects for Japan's Future]. Tokyo: 18 January policy paper.

Nippon Keizai Dantai Rengōkai Bōei Seisan Iinkai, ed. 2005. "Bōei Seisan Gijutsu Kiban ni Tsuite: Kokunai Kiban no Jūjitsu to Kokusai Kyōryoku" [Concerning the Defense Production and Technology Base: Consolidating the Domestic Base and International Cooperation], slide presentation to the fifth meeting of the Bōei Sōbi Shutoku Senryaku Kondankai, Tokyo, 9 June.

Nish, Ian, 1993. *Japan's Struggle with Internationalism: Japan, China and the League of Nations, 1931–33.* London: Kegan Paul International.

Nishibe, Susumu. 1988. *Hagasareta Kamen: Tōdai Komaba Sōdōki* [Villains Unmasked: A Turbulent Period at the Komaba Campus of Tokyo University]. Tokyo: Bungei Shunjū.

———. 2000. "Amerika no Mane o Shinakute wa Naranai to Yū 'Shinwa' no Uso ni Sekai ga Kigatsuite Yokatta" [Luckily the World Now Realizes the Falsehood of the 'Myth' That We Must Imitate the United States]. *Ekonomisuto* 28 (November): 46–47.

———. 2003a. "Kakubusōron ga Jishu Bōei e no Michi o Kirihiraku" [The Debate over Nuclear Armament Will Pave the Way for Autonomous Defense]. *Seiron* (September): 86–98.

———. 2003b. "Amerika Senryaku ni Haramareru Kyōki" [The Madness Inherent in American Strategy]. *Seiron* (April): 64–77.

———. 2004. "Rachi wa Kokken Shingai to no Ninshiki Wasureru Na" [We Must Not Forget to Recognize Abduction as an Infringement of Sovereignty]. *Sankei Shimbun*, 25 May.

Nishihara, Masashi. 1985. "The Japanese Central Organization of Defense." In *Central Organizations of Defense*, edited by M. Edmonds, 132–44. Boulder: Westview.

———. 2005a. "Atarashii Bōei no Katachi: Dandō Misairu Bōei Shisutemu" [The Shape of the New Defense: The Guided Missile Defense System]. *Securitarian* (March): 18–19.

———. 2005b. "Gaikō no Tachiōjō o Dakai Suru" [Breaking the Deadlock in Diplomacy]. *Nihonjin no Chikara* 25 (October): 2–3.

Nishikawa, Shinichi. 1997. "Naikaku Hōsei Kyoku: Sono Seidoteki Kenryoku e no Sekkin" [The Cabinet Legislation Bureau: An Approach to Its Systemic Authority]. *Meiji Daigaku Seikei Ronsō* 65, nos. 5–6: 185–251.

———. 2000. *Shirarezaru Kanchō: Naikaku Hōsei Kyoku* [The Unknown Agency: The Cabinet Legislation Bureau]. Tokyo: Gogatsu Shobō.

Nishimoto, Tetsuya. 2001. "Roles and Missions of the United States and Japan in the Japan-U.S. Alliance." In *United States–Japan Strategic Dialogue: Beyond the Defense Guidelines*, 8–28. Honolulu: Pacific Forum CSIS.

Nishimura, Shigeki. 2004. "Shinsenryaku no Sanbon Bashira: Chitsujo Keisei, Risuku Hejji, Yokushi Taisho" [The Three Pillars of the New Strategy: Order Setting, Risk Hedging, and Deterrence]. In *Gendai no Anzen Hoshō Kōza*, 4–14. Tokyo: Zenkoku Bōei Kyōkai Rengōkai.

Nishioka, Akira. 1988. *Gendai no Shibirian Kontorōru* [Modern Civilian Control]. Tokyo: Chishikisha.

Noguchi, Yukio. 1995. *1940 Nen Taisei: Saraba "Senji Keizai"* [The 1940 System: In That Case, "Wartime Economy"]. Tokyo: Tōyō Keizai Shimpōsha.

Nolte, Sharon H. 1987. *Liberalism in Modern Japan: Ishibashi Tanzan and His Teachers, 1905–1960.* Berkeley: University of California Press.

Nonaka, Toshihiko, and Urabe Noriho. 1989. *Kenpō no Kaishaku* [Interpretations of the Constitution, vol. 1]. Tokyo: Sanseidō.

Nordlinger, Eric. 1977. *Soldiers and Politics.* Englewood Cliffs, N.J.: Prentice Hall.

Nye, Joseph. 1996. Epilogue to *Civil-Military Relations and Democracy*, edited by L. Diamond and M. F. Plattner. Baltimore: Johns Hopkins University Press.

———. 2004. *Soft Power: The Means to Success in World Politics.* New York: Public Affairs.

Oberdorfer, Donald. 1997. *The Two Koreas.* Indianapolis: Basic Books.

Office of the Secretary of Defense. 1998. "Report on Allied Contributions to the Common Defense." Report to the United States Congress, Washington, D.C., March.

Ogata, Sadako. 1973. "The Role of Liberal Non-Governmental Organizations in Japan." In *Pearl Harbor as History: Japan-American Relations, 1931–1941*, edited by D. Borg and S. Okamoto, 459–86. New York: Columbia University Press.

——. 1988. *Normalization with China: A Comparative Study of the U.S. and Japanese Processes.* Berkeley: University of California, Institute of East Asian Studies.

Ogawa, Shinichi, and Michael Schiffer. 2005. "Japan's Plutonium Reprocessing Dilemma." *Arms Control Today* 35, no. 8 (October): 20–24.

Ogoura, Kazuo. 1993. "Ajia no Fukken no Tame Ni" [Toward the Revival of Asia]. *Chūō Kōron* (July): 60–71.

——. 2005a. *Jōshiki ni Hisomu Muttsu no Ayamari* [Six Errors Hidden in Conventional Wisdom]. *Ronza* (March): 47–51.

——. 2005b. "Tōajia de Ōshūryū no Tōgō wa Fukanō Da ga Keizai Bunka no Kyōdō Hochō wa Imi ga Aru" [European-Style Integration Is Impossible in East Asia, but a Paced Cooperation Based on Economic Culture Makes Sense]. In *Nihon no Ronten 2006* [Issues for Japan: 2006], 132–35. Tokyo: Bungei Shunjū.

Ohashi, Hideo. 2004. "The Impact of China's Rise on Sino-Japanese Economic Relations." In *The Rise of China and a Changing East Asian Order*, edited by Kokubun Ryosei and Wang Jisi, 175–93. Tokyo: Japan Center for International Exchange.

Ohtomo, Takafumi. 2003. "Bandwagoning to Dampen Suspicion: NATO and the US-Japan Alliance after the Cold War." *International Relations of the Asia-Pacific* 3: 29–55.

Okamoto, Susumu, Ōshika Yasuaki, and Hamada Keiko. 2003. "Beikoku no Tsuijū: Nihon no Sontoku" [The Costs and Benefits of Following the United States]. *Aera*, 15 December, 12–14.

Okamoto, Yukio. 2002a. "Japan and the United States: The Essential Alliance." *Washington Quarterly* 25, no. 2 (Spring): 59–72.

——. 2002b. "Paradaimu wa Kawatta no Ka? 'Jiyū' kara 'Anzen' no Jidai Ni" [Paradigm Shift? From the Age of "Free" to the Age of "Secure"]. *Gaikō Fōramu* (January): 28–37.

Okazaki, Hisahiko. 1986. *A Japanese Grand Strategy for Japanese Defense.* Lanham, Md.: University Press of America.

——. 1991. *Hanei to Suitai to Orandashi ni Nihon ga Mieru* [Prosperity and Decline: Japan as Seen through Dutch History]. Tokyo: Bungei Shunjū.

Olson, Mancur J., and R. Zeckhauser. 1966. "An Economic Theory of Alliances." *Review of Economics and Statistics* 48, no. 3: 266–79.

Orr, Robert M. J. 1990. *The Emergence of Japan's Foreign Aid Power.* New York: Columbia University Press.

Ōta, Fumio. 2005. *"Jōhō" to Kokka Senryaku* ["Intelligence" and National Strategy]. Tokyo: Fuyōshobō.

Ota, Masakatsu. 2000. "Will Japan Keep Renouncing Nuclear Weapons in the Coming Century?" Issue Brief No. 2. College Park, Md.: University of Maryland, Program on Global Security Disarmament.

Ōtake Hideo. 1980. "Nihon no 'Gunsan Fukugotai' to Zaisei Kiki" [Japan's Military Industrial Complex and the Fiscal Crisis]. Part 1. *Asahi Jaanaru*, 25 July, 31.

——. 1983. *Nihon no Bōei to Kokunai Seiji* [Japan's Defense and Domestic Politics]. Tokyo: Sanichi Shobō.

——. 1984. "Nihon ni Okeru 'Gunsankan Fukugotai' Keisei no Zasetsu" [The Frustrated State of the "Military-Industrial-Bureaucratic Complex" in Japan]. In *Nihon Seiji no Sōten* [The Japanese Political Debate], edited by Ōtake Hideo. Tokyo: Sanichi Shobō.

Ozawa, Ichirō. 1993. *Nihon Kaizō Keikaku.* Tokyo: Kōdansha.

Pacific Forum CSIS. 2001. *United States–Japan Strategic Dialogue: Beyond the Defense Guidelines.* Honolulu: Pacific Forum CSIS.

Park, Cheol Hee. 2005. "Japanese Conservatives' Conception of Japan as a Normal Country: Comparing Ozawa, Nakasone, and Ishihara." Unpublished paper for project on "Japan as a Normal Country." Tokyo: Shibusawa Foundation.

Park, Cheol Hee. 2007. "Japanese Strategic Thinking toward Korea." In *Japanese Strategic Thought toward Asia*, edited by Gilbert Rozman. New York: Palgrave.

Peattie, Mark R. 1975. *Ishiwara Kanji and Japan's Confrontation with the West*. Princeton: Princeton University Press.

Pei, Minxin, and Michael Swaine. 2005. "Simmering Fire in Asia: Averting Sino-Japanese Strategic Conflict." Policy Brief no. 44. Washington, D.C.: Carnegie Endowment for International Peace, November.

Pekkanen, Saadia. 2005. "Japan's FTA Frenzy." Unpublished manuscript. Seattle: University of Washington, Jackson School of International Studies.

Pempel, T. J. 2005a. "Firebreak: East Asia Institutionalizes Its Finances." Paper prepared for the conference on "Institutionalizing Northeast Asia: Making the Impossible Possible?" United Nations University and Aoyama Gakuin University, 20–22 September.

——. 2005b. "Japanese Strategy under Koizumi." Paper prepared for the conference on "Strategic Thought in Japan," Princeton University, 6–7 May.

Perlmutter, Amos. 1977. *The Military and Politics in Modern Times*. New Haven: Yale University Press.

Posen, Barry. 1984. *The Sources of Military Doctrine: France, Britain, and Germany between the World Wars*. Ithaca: Cornell University Press.

——. 2003. "Command of the Commons: The Military Foundation of U.S. Hegemony." *International Security* 28, no. 1 (Summer): 5–46.

Potter, David, and Sudo Sueo. 2003. "Japanese Foreign Policy: No Longer Reactive?" *Political Studies Review* 1: 317–32.

Prestowitz, Clyde. 1988. *Trading Places: How We Allowed Japan to Take the Lead*. New York: Basic Books.

Prime Minister's Commission on Japan's Goals in the 21st Century, ed. 2000. "The Frontier Within: Individual Empowerment and Better Governance in the New Millennium." Tokyo: Office of the Prime Minister's Commission on Japan's Goals in the 21st Century, Cabinet Secretariat, January.

Przystup, James J. 2004. "Dialogue of the Almost Deaf." *Comparative Connections* 6, no. 1 (first quarter): 103–15.

——. 2005. "U.S.-Japan Relations: Progress toward a Mature Partnership." Occasional Paper no. 2. Washington, D.C.: Institute for National Strategic Studies, June.

Przystup, James J., and Phillip C. Saunders. 2006. "Visions of Order: Japan and China in U.S. Strategy." *Strategic Forum*, no. 220 (June): 1–6.

Purrington, Courtney. 1992. "Tokyo's Policy Responses during the Gulf War and the Impact of the 'Iraqi Shock' on Japan." *Pacific Affairs* 65, no. 2: 161–81.

Pyle, Kenneth B. 1989. "The Burden of Japanese History and the Politics of Burden Sharing." In *Sharing World Leadership? A New Era for America and Japan*, edited by John H. Makin and Donald C. Hellmann, 41–80. Washington, D.C.: American Enterprise Institute.

——. 1992. *The Japanese Question: Power and Purpose in a New Era*. Washington, D.C.: American Enterprise Institute.

——. 1996. *The Making of Modern Japan*. New York: Houghton Mifflin.

——. 2007. *Japan Rising: The Resurgence of Japanese Power and Purpose*. New York: Public Affairs Books.

Pyle, Kenneth B., and E. Heginbotham. 2001. "Japan." In *Strategic Asia: Power and Purpose 2001–02*, edited by R. Ellings and A. Friedberg. Seattle: National Bureau of Asian Research.

Radtke, Kurt W. 1998. "The Japanese Context of Ishibashi Tanzan's Liberalism: Economic Rationalism versus Morality." Unpublished paper, Institute of Asia Pacific Studies, Waseda University.

——. 2003. "Nationalism and Internationalism in Japan's Economic Liberalism: The Case of Ishibashi Tanzan." In *Nationalism and Internationalism in Imperial Japan: Autonomy, Asian Brotherhood, or World Citizenship*, edited by D. Stegewerns, chap. 8. London: Routledge.

Radtke, Kurt W., and Raymond Feddema, eds. 2000. *Comprehensive Security in Asia: Views from Asia and the West on a Changing Security Environment*. Leiden: Brill.

Rice, Condoleezza, Donald Rumsfeld, Nobutaka Machimura, and Yoshinori Ohno. 2005. "U.S.-Japan Alliance: Transformation and Realignment for the Future." Security Consultative Committee document, 29 October. http://www.defenselink.mil/news/Oct2005/d20051029document.pdf.

Riddell, Peter. 2003. *Hug Them Close: Blair, Clinton, Bush, and the "Special Relationship."* London: Politico's.

Ronza. 2005. "Ajia o Butai ni 21 Seiki no Geemu ga Hajimatte Iru" [The 21st Century Game Has Begun on the Asian Stage]. *Ronza* (March): 28–45.

Rōyama, Masamichi. 1941. *Foreign Policy of Japan: 1914–1939*. Tokyo: Japan Council, Institute of Pacific Relations.

Rozman, Gilbert. 2002. "Japan's Relations with the U.S. and Its North Korean Option." *E-Notes*. Foreign Policy Research Institute, 3 December.

Saaler, Sven. 2002. "Pan-Asianism in Meiji and Taishō Japan: A Preliminary Framework." Working paper 02/4. Tokyo: Philipp Franz von Siebold Stiftung Deutsches Institut für Japanstudien.

——. 2004. "Takeuchi Yoshimi, Asianism, and International Relations: What Can Philosophers Tell Us about Politics?" Paper presented at the conference on "Takeuchi Yoshimi—Thinker of a Different Modernity in East Asia." Tokyo: Deutches Institut für Japanstudien, September.

——. 2005. *Politics, Memory, and Public Opinion: The History Textbook Controversy and Japanese Society*. Tokyo: Monographien aus dem Deutschen Institut für Japanstudien.

Sadō, Akihiro. 2003. *Sengo Nihon no Bōei to Seiji* [Postwar Japanese Defense and Politics]. Tokyo: Yoshikawa Kōbunkan.

——. 2004. "Shinjidai no Jieitai e no Tenkan to sono Kadai" [Problems for the SDF and Its Transformation in a New Era]. *Kokusai Anzen Hoshō* 32, no. 1 (June): 1–19.

Sakaba, Noboru, and Tamami Yasuda. 2005. "Chūgoku no Nihon Kigyō Imeeji: Chōsa Repōto" [The Image of Japanese Firms in China: A Research Report]. Unpublished report, CRC-CASS Research Center, Beijing. July.

Sakamoto, Kazuya. 2000. *Nichibei Dōmei no Kizuna: Ampo Jōyaku to Sōgosei no Mosaku* [The Yoke of the Japan-U.S. Alliance: Groping for Reciprocity and the Security Treaty]. Tokyo: Yūhikaku.

Samuels, Richard J. 1983. *The Politics of Regional Policy in Japan: Localities Incorporated?* Princeton: Princeton University Press.

——. 1987. *The Business of the Japanese State: Energy Markets in Comparative and Historical Perspective*. Ithaca: Cornell University Press.

——. 1994. *"Rich Nation, Strong Army": National Security and the Technological Transformation of Japan*. Ithaca: Cornell University Press.

——. 2003. *Machiavelli's Children: Leaders and Their Legacies in Italy and Japan*. Ithaca: Cornell University Press.

——. 2004a. "Politics, Security Policy, and Japan's Cabinet Legislation Bureau: Who Elected These Guys, Anyway?" Japan Policy Research Institute Working Paper No. 99, March.

——. 2004b. "Payback Time: Japan–North Korean Economic Relations." Paper prepared for the American Enterprise Institute conference on "Peaceful Resolution with North Korea: Towards a New International Engagement Framework," 12–13 February.

Samuels, Richard J., and Christopher P. Twomey. 1999. "The Eagle Eyes the Pacific: American Foreign Policy Options in East Asia after the Cold War." In *The U.S.-Japan Alliance: Past, Present, and Future,* edited by M. Green and P. Cronin. New York: Council on Foreign Relations.

Satō, Ken. 2005. "Ippan Hō no Sōki Seitei ga Kyūmu" [The Early Enactment of a General Law Is Urgently Needed]. *Yomiuri Shimbun,* 24 October.

Schad-Seifert, Annette. 2003. "Constructing National Identities: Asia, Japan, and Europe in Fukuzawa Yukichi's Theory of Civilization." In *Nationalism and Internationalism in Imperial Japan: Autonomy, Asian Brotherhood, or World Citizenship?* edited by D. Stegewerns, chap. 3. London: Routledge.

Schaller, Michael. 1997. *Altered States: The United States and Japan since the Occupation.* New York: Oxford University Press.

Schlictmann, Klaus. 1995. "The Ethics of Peace: Shidehara Kikujirō and Article 9 of the Japanese Constitution." *Japan Forum* 7, no. 1: 33–67.

Schoenbaum, Thomas J. 2005. "Resolving the China-Japan Dispute over the Senkaku Islands." ZNet, http://www.zmag.org/content/showarticle.cfm?SectionID=17&ItemID=7256.

Schoff, James L. 2005. *Tools for Trilateralism: Improving U.S.-Japan-Korea Cooperation to Manage Complex Contingencies.* Dulles, Va.: Potomac Books.

——. 2006. *Political Fences and Bad Neighbors: North Korean Policymaking in Japan and Implications for the United States.* (Early Web edition). Cambridge, Mass.: Institute for Foreign Policy Analysis.

Schoff, James L., ed. 2004. *Crisis Management in Japan and the United States.* Washington, D.C.: Institute of Foreign Policy Analysis.

Schoppa, Leonard J. 1997. *Bargaining with Japan: What American Pressure Can and Cannot Do.* New York: Columbia University Press.

Sebata, Takao. 1997. "Creation of the National Defense Program Outline in 1976 and Japan's Military Expansion in the 1990s." Occasional Paper No. 2. Palmerston North, New Zealand: International Pacific College.

Securitarian. 2005. "Atarashii Taikō o Kaibō Suru" [Analyzing the New National Defense Program Guidelines]. *Securitarian* (March): 11–20.

Segal, Adam, et al. 2003. *Chinese Military Power.* New York: Council on Foreign Relations.

Shambaugh, David. 2005. "China's Military Modernization: Making Steady and Surprising Progress." In *Strategic Asia 2005–06: Military Modernization in an Era of Uncertainty,* edited by Ashley J. Tellis and Michael Wills, chap. 3. Seattle: National Bureau of Asian Research.

Shidehara, Kijūrō. 1998 [1951]. *Gaikō Gojūnen* [Fifty Years of Diplomacy]. Tokyo: Nihon Tosho Sentaa.

Shikata, Toshiyuki. 2005. "Nihon Bōei no Taishō wa Nihon Shūhen Nomi ni Arazu. Sekai Kibo no Beigun Saihen to Kyōdō Se Yo" [The Object Of Japanese National Defense Is Not Only the Area Surrounding Japan. We Must Join Forces with the U.S. Military on a Global Scale]. In *Nihon no Ronten 2006* [Issues for Japan: 2006], 166–69. Tokyo: Bungei Shunjū.

Shimaguchi, Takehiko. 2005. "Zainichi Beigun Kichi o Meguru Shomondai" [Problems Related to U.S. Bases in Japan]. *Bōeigaku Kenkyū* 32 (February): 15–41.

Shimizu, Ikutarō. 1980. *Nippon Yo Kokka Tare: Kaku no Sentaku* [Japan! Be a True State: The Nuclear Option]. Tokyo: Bungei Shunjūsha.

Shinoda, Tomohito. 2004. *Kantei Gaikō Seiji Riidaashippu no Yukue* [Cabinet Diplomacy: Toward Political Leadership]. Tokyo: Asahi Shimbunsha.

——. 2005. *Japan's Policy Process to Dispatch the SDF to Iraq.* Asia-Pacific Policy Paper Series. Edwin O. Reischauer Center for East Asian Studies, January.

Shiraishi, Takashi. 1990. "Japan and Southeast Asia." In *Network Power: Japan and Asia*, edited by Peter J. Katzenstein and Takashi Shiraishi, 168–94. Ithaca: Cornell University Press.

——. 2004. *Teikoku to Sono Genkai* [Empire and Its Limits]. Tokyo: NTT.

——. 2006. "Higashi Ajia Kyōdōtai no Kōchiku wa Kanō Ka?" [Is It Possible to Create an East Asian Community?] *Chūō Kōron* (January): 118–27.

Shōji, Junichirō. 2005. "Shinchitsujo no Mosaku to Kokusai Seigi-Ajiashugi: Konoye Fumimaro o Chūshin to Shite" [The Groping of the New Order and International Justice and Asianism Centered on Konoye Fumimaro]. In *Nichibei Senryaku Shisōshi* [History of U.S.-Japan Strategic Thinking], edited by Tomoyuki Ishizu and Murray Williamson, 33–53. Tokyo: Sairyūsha.

Shotwell, James T. 1928. *War as an Instrument of National Policy*. New York: Harcourt, Brace.

Shu, Kenei. 2005. "Han Nichi Demo wa 'Aikoku Kyōiku' No Sei ni Arazu. Nihonjin wa Chūgoku no Henka o Shiranai" [The Anti-Japanese Demonstrations Were Not Due to "Patriotic Education." The Japanese Are Ignorant of the Changes in China]. In *Nihon no Ronten 2006* [Issues for Japan: 2006], 266–67. Tokyo: Bungei Shunjū.

Sigal, Leon. 1999. *Disarming Strangers: Nuclear Diplomacy with North Korea*. Princeton: Princeton University Press.

Singer, James David. 1958. "Threat Perception and the Armament Tension Dilemma." *Journal of Conflict Resolution* 2, no. 1: 90–105.

Singh, Bhubhindar. Forthcoming. PhD diss., University of Sheffield, Sheffield, U.K.

Smith, Sheila A. 2000. "Challenging National Authority: Okinawa Prefecture and the U.S. Military Bases." In *Local Voices, National Issues*, edited by Smith, 75–114. Ann Arbor: University of Michigan, Center for Japanese Studies.

——. 2001. "A Place Apart: Okinawa and Japan's Postwar Peace." In *Partnership: The United States and Japan, 1951–2000*, edited by Akira Iriye and Robert A. Wampler, 179–98. Tokyo: Kodansha International.

——. 2005. "Japan-U.S. Expand Defense Alliance." *East-West Wire*, 1 November. http://www.eastwestcenter.org/events-en-detail.asp?news_ID=301.

——. 2006. "Shifting Terrain: The Domestic Politics of the U.S. Military Presence in Asia." Special Reports No. 8. Honolulu: East-West Center, March.

Soderberg, Marie. 1987. *Japan's Military Export Policy*. Stockholm: University of Stockholm.

Soeya, Yoshihide. 2005. *Nihon no "Midoru Pawaa" Gaikō: Sengo Nihon no Sentaku to Kōsō* [Japan's "Middle Power" Diplomacy: Postwar Japan's Choices and Conceptions]. Tokyo: Chikuma Shinsho.

Suematsu, Yoshinori. 2003. "Kimujoniru no Madan ni Sonae wa Aruka—Ishiba Bōeichō Chōkan ni Tadasu" [Is There a Way to Prepare for Kim Jong Il's Magic Bullet? Questioning JDA director general Ishiba]. *Shokun!* 35, no. 4 (April): 70–77.

Suzuki, Michihiko. 2006. "Atarashii Gijutsu e no Michi: Bōei Sangyō no Shiten Kara" [The Road to New Technology from the Perspective of the Defense Industry]. *Anzen Hoshō o Kangaeru*, no. 612, 1 May. Tokyo: Anzen Hoshō Kondankai.

Swaine, Michael, and Minxin Pei. 2005. "Simmering Fire in Asia: Averting Sino-Japanese Strategic Conflict." Policy Brief No. 44. Washington, D.C.: Carnegie Endowment for International Peace, November.

Tabata, Mitsunaga. 2004. "Zasshi ga Aoru Hanchūgoku Mūdo: *Bungei Shunjū, Shokun!, Seiron, Voice, Sapio*, o Bunseki Suru" [Magazines Incite an Anti-China Mood: Analyzing *Bungei Shunjū, Shokun!, Seiron, Voice*, and *Sapio*]. 1 October, 72–81.

Tadokoro, Masayuki. 2005a. "After Ten Years: Japan Then and Now." Paper prepared for the Shibusawa Seminar, June, Toronto.

Tadokoro, Masayuki. 2005b. "Sengo Nihon no Kenpō Taisei no Henyō to Tenbō" [The Prospects for and Changes in Postwar Japan's Constitutional System]. *Asuteion* 62: 12–33.

Taichū Gaikō Seisaku Gurūpu, ed. 2005. "Taichū Gaikō: Kinkyū Seisaku Teigen" [Urgent Policy Recommendations for Japan's China Diplomacy]. Unpublished position paper, 5 July.

Takahara, Akio. 2004. "Japan's Political Response to the Rise of China." In *The Rise of China and a Changing East Asian Order*, edited by Ryosei Kokubun and Jisi Wang, 157–74. Tokyo: Japan Center for International Exchange.

Takahashi, Fumio. 2004. "The First War Plan Orange and the First Imperial Japanese Defense Policy: An Interpretation from the Geopolitical Strategic Perspective." *NIDS Security Reports*, no. 5 (March): 68–103.

Takahashi, Hideo. 2004. "The Reliability of the U.S.-Japan Alliance after 9/11." USJP Occasional Paper 04–13. Cambridge: Harvard University, Program on U.S.-Japan Relations.

Takahashi, Tetsuya. 2005. *Yasukuni Mondai* [The Yasukuni Problem]. Tokyo: Chikuma Shinsho.

Takemura, Masayoshi. 1994. *Chiisaku to mo Kirari to Hikaru Kuni Nihon* [A Small and Shining Japan]. Tokyo: Kōbunsha.

Takubo, Tadae, and Susumu Nishibe. 2004. "Shinbei Hoshu vs. Hanbei Hoshu: Iraku Kessen" [Pro-American Conservatives vs. Anti-American Conservatives: A Fight to the Finish over Iraq]. *Shokun!* (January): 38–53.

Tanaka, Akihito. 1997. *Anzen Hoshō: Sengo 50 Nen no Mosaku* [National Security: Fifty Postwar Years of Groping]. Tokyo: Yomiuri Shimbunsha.

———. 2004. "Higashi Ajia ni okeru Jieitai oyobi Zainichi Chūryū Beigun no Yakuwari" [The SDF in East Asia and the Role of the U.S. Forces Stationed in Japan]. *Securitarian* (April): 20–24.

Tanaka, Akihiko, and Koji Murata. 1995. "Seiki Nishihiro Oral Interview." 16 November. http://www.gwu.edu/~nsarchiv/japan/nishihiroohinterview.htm.

———. 1996a. "Takashi Maruyama Oral Interview." 16 November. http://www.gwu.edu/~nsarchiv/japan/maruyamaohinterview.htm.

———. 1996b. "Natsume Haruo Oral Interview." 16 November. http://www.gwu.edu/~nsarchiv/japan/natsumeohinterview.htm.

———. 1996c. "Yukoh Kurihara Oral Interview." 16 November. http://www.gwu.edu/~nsarchiv/japan/kuriharaohinterview.htm.

Tanaka, Hitoshi. 2005. "Higashi Ajia Kyōdōtai o Shiya ni Nichibei Dōmei o Katsuyō Shi, Baransu aru Nōdōteki Gaikō o" [Activating the Japan-U.S. Alliance in the Context of an East Asian Community: Toward a Balanced and Lively Diplomacy]. In *Nihon no Ronten 2006* [Issues for Japan: 2006], 82–85. Tokyo: Bungei Shunjū.

Tanaka, Kōichirō. 2006. "Dameeji Kontorōru ni Keichū subeki Nihon Gaikō [A Japanese Diplomacy That Must Be Devoted to Damage Control]. *Gaikō Fōramu* (October): 18–20.

Taniguchi, Tomohiko. 2005. "A Cold Peace: The Changing Security Equation in Northeast Asia." *Orbis* 49, no. 3 (Summer): 445–57.

Tanter, Richard. 2004. "With Eyes Wide Shut: Japan, Heisei Militarization, and the Bush Doctrine." In *Confronting the Bush Doctrine: Critical Views from the Asia-Pacific*, edited by Peter Van Ness and Melvin Gurtov. New York: Routledge.

Taoka, Shunji. 1997. "The Way to Save the US-Japan Alliance." *NIRA Review* (Summer): 3–8.

Taylor, Brian D. 1998. *The Russian Military in Politics: Civilian Supremacy in Comparative and Historical Perspective*. Cambridge: Massachusetts Institute of Technology, Department of Political Science.

Temerson, Timothy D. 1991. "Double Containment and the Origins of the U.S.-Japan Security Alliance." Working Paper 91–14. Cambridge: MIT-Japan Program.

Terashima, Jitsurō. 1996. "Shinbei Nyūa no Sōgō Senryaku o Motomete" [Seeking an Integrated Strategy for Being Both "Pro-American" and "Part of Asia"]. *Chūō Kōron* (March): 20–38.

———. 2002. *Rekishi o Fukaku Suikomi, Mirai o Omou: 1900 Nen no Tabi, America no Seiki, Ajia no Jison* [Deeply Inhaling History and Thinking of the Future: A Trip to 1900, the American Century, and Asian Self-Respect]. Tokyo: Shinchōsha.

———. 2005a. "Seiki o Koeta Nihon no Kodoku" [The Isolation of Japan across the Century]. Tokyo: Mitsui Bussan Senryaku Kenkyūjo, June.

———. 2005b. "Koizumi Gaikō no Banshō: Seijiteki Genjitsushugi no Genkai" [The Evening Bells of Koizumi's Diplomacy: The Limits of Political Realism]. Tokyo: Mitsui Bussan Senryaku Kenkyūjo, August.

Teuben, M. H. I. 2004. "Japan and North Korea: How the Abduction Issue Has Frozen Bilateral Relations." Master's thesis, Faculteit der Maatschappij- en Gegragswetenschappen, Universiteit van Amsterdam, September.

Themis. 2002. "Ima ya Gokenha no Mamorigami 'Naikaku Hōsei Kyoku' no Uchimaku" [The True Character of the Cabinet Legislation Bureau, Even Now the Defending God of the "Constitutional Safeguard Faction"]. *Themis* 11, no. 3 (March): 23–25.

Tilly, Charles. 1975. "Reflections on the History of European State-Making." In *The Formation of National States in Western Europe,* edited by Tilly, 3–83. Princeton: Princeton University Press.

Titus, David. 1994. Introduction to *The Final Confrontation: Japan's Negotiations with the United States, 1941,* edited by J. W. Morley, xix–xxxviii. New York: Columbia University Press.

Togo, Kazuhiko. 2006. "A Moratorium on Yasukuni Visits." *Far Eastern Economic Review* (July–August).

Tokuchi, Hideshi. 2001. "Reisengo no Nihon no Bōei Seisaku ni Tsuite" [Regarding Japanese Security Policy after the Cold War]. *Kokusai Anzen Hoshō* 29, no. 3: 66–79.

Tsurumi, Shunsuke. 1967. "Tenkō no Kyōdō Kenkyū ni Tsuite" [Regarding Cooperative Research on Apostasy]. In *Tenkō* [Apostasy], edited by Shisō no Kagaku Kenkyūkai. Tokyo: Heibonsha.

Tsutsui, Kazuto. 2005. "Bōei Yushutsu Sangensoku to Dandō Misairu Bōei Shisutemu" [The Three Non-Export Principles and the Guided Missile Defense System]. *Securitarian* (March): 20.

Twomey, Christopher P. 2000. "Japan: A 'Circumscribed Balancer'; Building on Defensive Realism to Make Predictions about East Asian Security." *Security Studies* 9, no. 4: 167–205.

Umebayashi, Hiromichi. 2005. "Kore wa Mohaya 'Zai Nichi Beigun' de wa Nai" [These Are No Longer U.S. Forces in Japan]. *Sekai* (December): 112–22.

Union of Concerned Scientists, ed. 2004. *Technical Realities: An Analysis of the 2004 Deployment of a U.S. National Missile Defense System.* Cambridge, Mass., May.

U.S. Department of State, ed. 2006. *Foreign Relations of the United States.* Vol. 29, pt. 2. Washington, D.C.: U.S. Government Printing Office.

Usui, Katsumi. 1990. "Japanese Approaches to China in the 1930s: Two Alternatives." In *American, Chinese, and Japanese Perspectives on Wartime Asia, 1931–1949,* edited by A. Iriye and W. Cohen, 93–115. Wilmington, Del.: Scholarly Resources.

Valenzuela, Samuel J. 1992. "Democratic Consolidation in Post-Transitional Settings: Nation, Process, and Facilitating Conditions." In *Issues in Democratic Consolidation: The New South American Democracies in Comparative Perspective,* edited by Scott Mainwaring. South Bend: University of Notre Dame Press.

Van Doorn, Jacques. 1975a. "The Decline of the Mass Armed Force." *Armed Forces and Society* 1, no. 2: 147–58.

———. 1975b. *The Soldier and Social Change*. Beverly Hills, Calif.: Sage.

Vogel, Steven K. 2006. *Japan Remodeled: How Government and Industry Are Reforming Japanese Capitalism*. Ithaca: Cornell University Press.

Wakamiya, Yoshibumi. 2006. *Wakai to Nashyonarizumu* [Reconciliation and Nationalism]. Tokyo: Asahi Shimbunsha.

Walt, Stephen. 1978. *Origin of Alliances*. Ithaca: Cornell University Press.

Wampler, Robert. N.d. "Japan and the United States: Diplomatic, Security, and Economic Relations, 1960–1976." Digital National Security Archive. http//nsarchive.chadwyck.com/jap_essay.htm.

Watanabe, Tsuneo. 1996. "The Bankruptcy of Civil-Military Relations in Japan." *NIRA Review* (Summer).

Weiner, Myron, and Richard J. Samuels, eds. 1992. *The Political Culture of Foreign Area and International Studies: Essays in Honor of Lucian W. Pye*. Washington, D.C.: Brassey's.

Weinstein, Martin. 1971. *Japan's Postwar Defense Policy, 1947–1968*. New York: Columbia University Press.

Weitsman, Patricia A. 2004. *Dangerous Alliances: Proponents of Peace, Weapons of War*. Stanford: Stanford University Press.

White, James W. 1990. Introduction to *The Ambivalence of Nationalism: Modern Japan between East and West*, edited by J. W. White, M. Umegaki, and T. R. H. Havens, 1–37. Lanham, Md.: University Press of America.

Yakanuki, Nobuhito, Nobuo Saiki, and Naoya Tamura. 2004. *Zukai Zatsugaku Jieitai* [Learning Widely about the Self-Defense Forces through Pictures]. Tokyo: Natsumesha.

Yamada, Takio. 2005. "Toward a Principled Integration of East Asia: Concept for an East Asian Community." *Gaiko Forum* (Fall): 24–35.

Yamakage, Susumu. 1997. "Japan's National Security and Asia-Pacific's Regional Institutions in the Post–Cold War Era." In *Network Power: Japan and Asia*, edited by Peter J. Katzenstein and Takashi Shiraishi, 275–305. Ithaca: Cornell University Press.

Yamamura, Katsurō. 1973. "The Role of the Finance Ministry." In *Pearl Harbor as History: Japanese-American Relations, 1931–1941*, edited by Dorothy Borg and Shumpei Okamoto. New York: Columbia University Press.

Yamazaki, Makoto. 2005. "Wagakuni Kaijō Bōei Senryaku no Yotei" [A Plan for Our Nation's Maritime Defense Strategy]. *Anzen Hoshō o Kangaeru* no. 603 (August). Tokyo: Anzen Hoshō Konwakai.

Yan, Jin. 2005. "A Strategic Dislocation Emerges in the U.S.-Japanese Alliance." 25 November. http://www.people.com.cn/GB/paper68.

Yokochi, Hiroaki. 2005. "Chūgoku no Tainichi Senryaku no Akumu: Nihon wa Chūgoku to Dō Mukaiaubeki Ka" [The Nightmare of China's Japan Strategy: How Should Japan Confront China?]. *Anzen Hoshō o Kangaeru* no. 604 (September). Tokyo: Anzen Hoshō Konwakai.

Yosan, Iinkai, ed. 2005. "Yosan Iinkai Kōchōkai Giroku: Dai Ichi Gō" [Budget Committee Public Hearings: Number One]. 23 February. Testimony by Tanaka Akihiko.

Yoshida, Shigeru. 1961. *The Yoshida Memoirs: The Story of Japan in Crisis*. London: Heinemann.

———. 1963. *Sekai to Nihon* [The World and Japan]. Tokyo: Banchō Shobō.

———. 1967. *Japan's Decisive Century: 1867–1967*. New York: Frederick Praeger.

Young, Louise. 1998. *Japan's Total Empire: Manchuria and the Culture of Wartime Imperialism*. Berkeley: University of California Press.

Zhang, Yun. 2005. "Sino-Japan Relations and the Future of East Asia." *Lianhe Zaobao*, 24 April.

Index

Abe, Shinzō, 74, 80, 83, 197
  as a normal nation-alist, 5, 74
Airforce of Japan. *See* Air Self Defense
    Force; Self Defense Forces
Air Self Defense Force, 83, 98
Akamatsu, Kaname, 22
Anglo-Japanese alliance (1902), 16, 18,
    212n25
Antiterror Special Measures Law, 95–96
Araki Commission, 162, 193
Armitage, Richard, 44, 95, 175
Arms exports, 80, 90, 106, 173
Arms Manufacturing Law (1953), 33–34
Army of Japan. *See* Ground Self
    Defense Force; Imperial Army;
    Self Defense Forces
Article Nine, 33, 40, 45–49, 188
  collective security, 48, 66, 180
  collective self defense, 48, 66, 76, 83, 94,
    96–100, 180
  interpretations, 46–48, 51–52, 54, 95–100,
    219n51, 241n67
  and overseas deployment, 91, 94, 97
  and revision in the 1950s, 30–32
  revision in the 2000s, 80–82
  use of force, 46–47, 66, 97, 180
  and war potential, 46–47, 76, 78
ASEAN, 146, 165, 170, 204
Asianism, 18, 20–21, 213n20
  See also Neoasianism
Autonomous defense, 7, 35, 120, 232n48
Azadegan oil field, 153–55

Ballistic missile defense, 91, 104–6, 174–75
Basic Defense Force Concept, 2, 68, 92, 168
Big Japanism, 18, 23

Boxer Rebellion, 16
Bureaucratic reform, 74–78, 182

Cabinet Legislation Bureau, 46–51, 75, 99, 173
Checkbook diplomacy, 67
China
  anti-Japanese feelings, 139
  and détente, 44
  economic relations with Japan, 136–37,
    144–48, 156, 159–61, 165–71, 190
  and history, 113–14
  and Japan's neo-Asianism, 129–31
  May 30th Movement, 24
  military, 68–71, 138, 140–41
  military relations with Japan, 103, 167
  nationalism, 17, 24–25, 138
  open door policy, 24
  pro-China faction in Japan, 126–27
  relations with Japan, 23, 69, 136–48,
    165–71, 201
  Shandong Province. *See* Imperialism
    in Japan
Civil-military relations, 51–52, 53–54,
    76–77, 101–2, 196
Cold War, 40, 44, 55–56
  end of, 64–65, 87
Common defense, 40, 82–84
Comprehensive security, 3, 35, 56–57, 200
Constitution of Japan. *See* Article Nine

Dan, Takuma, 26
Defense budget of Japan, 40–41, 43, 55–56,
    63, 79, 105, 168, 195, 218n35, 246n48
  and the Japan Coast Guard, 79
Defense industry, 33, 55, 57, 105–6, 146–48,
    161–64, 174, 182